For

my mother, Mary Alexander,
and in loving memory of my father,
George Alexander (1921–98)

Name me a word

Great, simple, vast as the sky

A word that has, like the intimate hand

Of the woman I have loved forever,

Washed the dirty innards of history.

—JIBANANANDA DAS,

"Name Me a Word" ("Amake ekti katha dao")

Name Me a Word

Name Me a Word

Indian Writers Reflect on Writing

Edited by MEENA ALEXANDER

Yale
UNIVERSITY PRESS
New Haven and London

Published with assistance from the foundation established in memory of Philip Hamilton McMillan of the Class of 1894, Yale College.

Copyright © 2018 by Meena Alexander.

All rights reserved.
This book may not be reproduced, in whole or in part, including illustrations, in any form (beyond that copying permitted by Sections 107 and 108 of the U.S. Copyright Law and except by reviewers for the public press), without written permission from the publishers.

Yale University Press books may be purchased in quantity for educational, business, or promotional use. For information, please e-mail sales.press@yale.edu (U.S. office) or sales@yaleup.co.uk (U.K. office).

Designed by Sonia Shannon.
Set in Fournier type by Integrated Publishing Solutions.
Printed in the United States of America.

Library of Congress Control Number: 2017958267
ISBN 978-0-300-22258-6 (pbk. : alk. paper)

A catalogue record for this book is available from the British Library.
This paper meets the requirements of ANSI/NISO Z39.48-1992 (Permanence of Paper).

10 9 8 7 6 5 4 3 2 1

Contents

Preface xiii

RABINDRANATH TAGORE	1
Letter	3
From *Boyhood Days*	3
From *Final Poems*	
"Sickbed 21"	6
"Recovery 4"	6
SAROJINI NAIDU	9
To Arthur Symons	10
From a Letter to Edmund Gosse	13
To Rabindranath Tagore (1912)	15
To Rabindranath Tagore (undated)	16
PREMCHAND (DHANPAT RAI)	17
"Two Autobiographical Sketches"	18
NIRAD C. CHAUDHURI	25
From *The Autobiography of an Unknown Indian*	
From "My Birthplace"	26
From "The English Scene"	34
From "The Englishman in the Flesh"	39
JIBANANANDA DAS	42
"The Professor"	43
"Name Me a Word"	43

"Poetry"	44
"The Windy Night"	45
R. K. NARAYAN	47
From *My Days: A Memoir*	48
VAIKOM MUHAMMAD BASHEER	56
From "Pattumma's Goat"	57
RAJA RAO	66
"Entering the Literary World"	67
LALITHAMBIKA ANTHERJANAM	73
"Childhood Memories"	74
AGYEYA (SACHCHIDANANDA VATSAYAN)	82
"The Signs"	83
"Words and Truths"	85
"Three Words to Make a Poem"	86
"The Revolving Rock XVI"	86
"The Revolving Rock XXV"	87
UMASHANKAR JOSHI	88
"My Four-Sided Field"	89
From "The World of Birds"	90
Acceptance Speech for the 1968 Bharatiya Jnanpith Award	93
SAADAT HASAN MANTO	97
"First Letter to Uncle Sam"	98
ISMAT CHUGTAI	104
"We People"	105
AMRITA PRITAM	114
"To Waris Shah"	115

From *The Revenue Stamp*
    My Sixteenth Year   117
    A Shadow   119

NISSIM EZEKIEL   122
"Background, Casually"   123
"Poet, Lover, Birdwatcher"   125

MAHASWETA DEVI   127
"So Many Words, So Many Sounds"   129

NAYANTARA SAHGAL   143
"Rejecting Extinction"   144

QURRATULAIN HYDER   152
"Beyond the Stars"   153

JAYANTA MAHAPATRA   163
From an Autobiographical Essay   164
"Grandfather"   166
"The Abandoned British Cemetery at Balasore"   167
"Hunger"   169

A. K. RAMANUJAN   170
"Elements of Composition"   171
"Saturdays"   173
From "Is There an Indian Way of Thinking?
    An Informal Essay"   175

NIRMAL VERMA   179
"Returning to One's Country"   180

K. AYYAPPA PANIKER   186
"Why Write?"   187
"Upon My Walls"   189
"Epitaph"   190
From "Passage to America"   190

ARUN KOLATKAR	193
"From an Undated Sheet"	194
From "Making Love to a Poem"	195
U. R. ANANTHAMURTHY	203
From "Five Decades of My Writing"	204
KAMALA DAS	209
From *My Story*	
"The Bougainvillea"	210
From "The P.E.N. Poetry Prize"	212
"The Old Playhouse"	213
From "An Introduction"	214
KEKI DARUWALLA	216
"The Decolonised Muse (A Personal Statement)"	217
ANITA DESAI	222
"On Being an Indian Writer Today"	223
GIRISH KARNAD	227
From Author's Introduction to *Three Plays*	228
NABANEETA DEV SEN	238
"In Poetry"	239
"Alphabets"	239
"Combustion"	240
"The Year's First Poem"	240
"Broken Home"	241
From *My Life, My Work*	241
ADIL JUSSAWALLA	248
"Being There: Aspects of an Indian Crisis"	249
AMBAI (C. S. LAKSHMI)	259
From "Squirrel"	260

PAUL ZACHARIA 268
From "Sinning in Mysore" 269

K. SATCHIDANANDAN 278
"Gandhi and Poetry" 279
"Stammer" 280
"Burnt Poems" 281
"About Poetry, About Life" 282

ARVIND KRISHNA MEHROTRA 291
"Engraving of a Bison on Stone" 292
"Distance in Statute Miles" 292
"Where Will the Next One Come From" 293
"Inscription" 294

SALMAN RUSHDIE 295
"Imaginary Homelands" 296

AGHA SHAHID ALI 307
From "In Search of Evanescence" 308

NAMDEO DHASAL 314
"Approaching the Organized Harem
    of the Octopus" 315
"Mandakini Patil: A Young Prostitute,
    My Intended Collage" 316
"The Day She Was Gone" 318

MEENA ALEXANDER 319
From "Illiterate Heart" 320
"Crossroad" 324

GITHA HARIHARAN 327
"A Note on Writing *When Dreams Travel*" 328

VIJAY SESHADRI 332
"My First Fairy Tale" 333

AMITAV GHOSH	338
From "The Testimony of My Grandfather's Bookcase"	339
RAGHAVAN ATHOLI	350
"The Poet with a Forest Fire Inside"	351
JEET THAYIL	357
"The Heroin Sestina"	358
"Malayalam's Ghazal"	359
"Spiritus Mundi"	360
ARUNDHATI ROY	362
From "Like Sculpting Smoke: Arundhati Roy on Fame, Writing and India"	363
AMIT CHAUDHURI	374
From "Interlude"	375
SUDEEP SEN	386
"Photons, Graphite, Blood"	387
"Postcards"	389
ARUNDHATHI SUBRAMANIAM	392
"To the Welsh Critic Who Doesn't Find Me Identifiably Indian"	393
"First Draft"	395
S. SUKIRTHARANI	396
"Night Beast"	397
"Gigantic Trees"	398
"Untitled Poem—2"	399
"Pariah God"	400

Acknowledgments 401
Credits 405

Preface

I

Hyderabad, monsoon season. I remember a table on a verandah, two wicker chairs, the scent of damp jasmine. I was a young writer trying to find her way in the sometimes bewildering world of Indian letters. Beside me sat Raja Rao with his white hair and elegant bearing. I had just taken him on a tour of the campus. He was particularly interested in the old stone walls and overgrown vegetation, and now he was talking to me about an invented English he used, a way of negotiating the multiple languages and worlds into which, in our separate ways, we were plunged. It was much later that I realized that before working the polished and yet jagged English he had perfected, Raja Rao had turned to his mother tongue, a necessity for him, writing a few stories quickly in Kannada. And so in France, where he was living at the time, he composed the fable-like novel *Kanthapura* set in an imagined Indian village. This is what he wrote in a 1938 preface to the novel: "English is not really an alien language to us. It is the language of our intellectual make-up—like Sanskrit or Persian was before—but not of our emotional make-up. [. . .] We cannot write like the English. We should not. We cannot write only as Indians. We have grown to look at the large world as a part of us." He went on to argue that "time alone" would justify the English that Indians used, just as it had done for the Irish and Americans.

Surely that time has come. A wave of Indian writing in English, both from the subcontinent and the diaspora, has swept over us. A little over four decades after Raja Rao's preface, Salman Rushdie burst onto the world stage with *Midnight's Children*. And it was clear that for Indians, "the large world" that Raja Rao evoked was indeed, "part of us." The English language Rushdie created through multiple, cacophonous voices broke open a whole new landscape for post-independence writing, creating yet another layer to what was already a palimpsest—Indian regional languages and the English that sprouted from them, and through them, revealing the mixed and vibrant world of the subcontinent. Indeed, the porous slipping borders of multiple languages that Indian writers inherit is often in evidence, if not overtly in the work, whatever the language of composition, then in its dream life, the undertow that takes hold of the reader and tugs her in.

II

In his poem "Name Me a Word," the Bengali poet Jibanananda Das searches for a word that even as it evokes the vastness of the sky, possesses the delicate power of touch that only love can bring—a woman's hand capable of cleansing "the dirty innards of history." The poem that dwells on what it means to name ends with the evocation of a supernal thirst that birds possess—and by extension the maker of words and all who seek the mortal power of language. His poem seems the perfect invocation of this gathering of voices, reflections by Indian writers over the course of a century and more, writing in multiple languages. Poems, fictions, essays, and notes are all gathered here, a veritable river of words into which many languages flow.

I have put this anthology together in the hope of clarifying a multifoliate pattern in twentieth-century Indian writing. Each of the writers reveals something of the intricate emotion and thought involved in the process of writing, either through a direct reflection on the act or in more allusive fashion. And there are powerful impulses behind the choice of materials for an anthology that begins with the early twentieth century and reaches into the early twenty-first. Whether it is the writing by Rabindranath Tagore in his native Bengali, his own life straddling the border between the nineteenth and twentieth centuries, or poems by the Dalit poet S. Sukirtharani in the early twenty-first century (Dalit being a term for those formerly known as Untouchable), we as readers face the knotty issues of embodiment and self-creation, dislocation and belonging. Through the flow of the selections, I hope to reveal various kinds of literary cross-pollination—how the writers speak to each other, and oftentimes with the ghosts of others; how issues and themes ripple and flow with fine variations across temporal and linguistic borders.

There are recurring themes of identity and embodiment, language and community and the tensions involved in the public act of becoming an author. And there are sharp contrasts in self-apprehension—how the writer reveals her or his sense of self—for example, between Sarojini Naidu in the earlier part of the twentieth century caught within the overarching presence of British imperialism, expressing herself in English, and Sukirtharani in the early twenty-first, a Dalit woman searching to carve out her own identity in the Tamil language, in a republic that would cast her out.

The works are arranged chronologically so that lines of access and influence emerge. In the earliest material we sense the colonial presence of the British and the struggle for national visibility. Indeed, questions of selfhood and nation, of language and authorship become highlighted in the era of anticolonial struggle, and many of the earlier writers, even if they are not directly followers of Gandhi, are in some measure touched and molded by Gandhian nationalism. But there are others, particularly some Dalit writers in the second half of the twentieth century, for whom the nonviolent ideals of Indian nationalism ring hollow. In their view, the community of those formerly known as Untouchable, relegated to Outcaste status, need to forge a radically different vision of language and belonging.

The writing by women highlights the struggles for gender rights and access to language. Time and again tensions emerge between the intimate self, often bound within patriarchal restraints, and a woman's claim to public authorship. Events in shared history inevitably mark the psyche. The Partition of the country in 1947 brought in its wake a whole consort of voices, men and women haunted by violence and dislocation. The Indian diaspora in turn shapes writers who need to imagine and name their migrant selves. Indeed, transnational mobility can bring in its wake difficult racial reckonings and the painful, if sometimes exhilarating, reinvention of identity. But these are not necessarily new themes. Both Tagore and Naidu were world travelers, and there are others like Vaikom Muhammad Basheer and Arun Kolatkar who may not have traveled outside the borders of the subcontinent but were nevertheless deeply influenced by cosmopolitan ideals. In an era of globalization, as indeed well before, the writer needs both the privacy of a deeply personal process and a shared community or network to create and disseminate the work.

I should add, though, that even as fresh ways emerge, in an era of globalization, of creating cultural memory and fashioning a house of words, there are often powerful bonds between writers based abroad and writers in India. And in the last few years, writers such as U. R. Ananthamurthy and Nayantara Sahgal, K. Satchidanandan and Githa Hariharan have been in the forefront of the struggle against a creeping fascism and the overt repression of writers in India, and several India diaspora writers based abroad have been active supporters of this effort.

III

Each of the writers here, whether writing in Malayalam or Tamil, Kannada or Marathi, Hindi or Urdu, Bengali or Gujarati or English, voices questions about home and belonging, landscape and language, body and soul, and states of mind that become in turn aspects of a shared, evolving world, vital, unstable. Clearly there could have been one such volume for each of the Indian languages, and I think with regret of the fine writers, some celebrated, others lesser known, who for a host of reasons we were not able to include.

For any writer, there is a point at which one comes to an awareness, however fleeting, that language, the very medium in which one lives and moves, cannot be taken for granted. Perhaps this awareness becomes more acute for Indian writers who willy-nilly find themselves in a realm of multiple languages and shifting cultural borders. There are twenty-two languages currently recognized by the Constitution of India and many more unofficial ones, together with hundreds of variants: there are ancient poetic traditions, both oral and written, and there is ongoing traffic between the regional languages and Sanskrit, the great classical language whose roots branch into varieties of literary and philosophical texts. And in the north and the Deccan there was the flowering of what was once the courtly language of Urdu, the language in which the poet Mirza Ghalib (1797–1869) crafted his exquisite ghazals—a poetic form in couplets stemming from Arabic and Persian and central to Urdu poetry. English came to the subcontinent with British colonialism. Who can forget Lord Thomas Macaulay's infamous 1835 report on Indian education? After suggesting that no one could deny that "a single shelf of a good European library was worth the whole native literature of India and Arabia," he went on to argue that the task at hand was to "form a class who may be interpreters between us and the millions who we govern—a class of persons Indian in blood and color, but English in tastes, in opinions, in morals and in intellect."

English has its uses. Chandra Ban Prasad, the Dalit activist, decided it was necessary to create a goddess of English. So he fashioned a bronze figurine looking much like Lady Liberty but complete with a cowboy hat to signal her freedom from the usual dress codes. He established festivities for her timed to take place on Macaulay's birthday. In her right hand, the new deity holds a pen—she is entirely literate and a writer—in her left hand a book, the Constitution of the Republic of India, which guarantees equal rights to all citizens irrespective of caste or religion. English seemed to Prasad the only language that could give his people a way out of the centuries-old caste system that had systematically oppressed them. Access to a world language would allow them into the sunlight of the twenty-first century. Raghavan Atholi, a Dalit poet and sculptor writing in Malayalam, feels that the making of poems permits him to cut through the borders of nations and even languages. He claims his own poetry is a universal poetry, a black poetry. The music of the gospel singer Mahalia Jackson moves him as much as anything he can think of. There has been a flowering of Dalit writing in India, and those represented here use regional, or *bhasha*, languages; like so many others in this anthology, they are represented in translated form.

IV

India now has two national languages, Hindi and English. The latter, not merely the language of the elite, has become in many instances the language of ordinary life and commerce, and almost because, rather than in spite, of this, a supple instrument in which poems and prose can be fashioned, a language of the marketplace and of the public, well able to express the rough and tumble, the subtleties and inner longings of the writer. Yet there is no doubt that English is mostly available in the urban centers of the country and in the upper-class schools that cater to the aspiring middle classes. And while in the past there has been a certain amount of tension between writers in English and *bhasha* writers—writers in Hindi and the regional languages—with some of the former claiming a world audience and some of the latter claiming a superior connection to subcontinental soil and region, there are many others who have embraced the multiplicity and rich heritage of Indian languages, as well as the urban, globalized audience that English makes available. There is no question that the wealth of writing in the Indian languages needs to be made more readily available in translation—to what would surely be a receptive world audience. And rather than thinking of the regional languages as rooted to place and English as a nowhere language, we would do well to think of the hybrid nature of India itself, a syncretic culture where over centuries languages and literatures have met and mingled. Inevitably there are frictions that emerge, fractious versions of the tense present, even as there are rich intercuttings and graftings of linguistic and sensorial knowledge, subterranean flows.

Viewed in this fashion, writing from the Indian diaspora becomes both part of an ever evolving Indian literature and an intrinsic portion of other literatures with their complex traditions. Indeed, the rich humanism of a cosmopolitan existence deeply rooted in place but reaching out to the larger world was embraced by Tagore and others. We could argue that such a humanism provided a stay on the one hand against the violence of colonialism and on the other against a stringent nationalism and its vision of cultural purity. How can one forget that in the many centuries before European colonialism, there was peaceful trade across the Indian Ocean, with Persia, Rome, Arabia, China? And surely these ancient voyages have left their traces. The fiction of Amitav Ghosh dealing with the opium trade and the passage of migrant labor from the subcontinent points us in this direction.

Might the whole earth be one's home? The poet Arun Kolatkar, who lived most of his life in the bustling, teeming city of Bombay, wrote both in Marathi and in English. In his notebook entries "Making Love to a Poem," he writes of how he felt he was "a double agent, stealing the secrets of one language and selling them to the other." He quotes the Russian poet Marina Tsvetayeva, who in a letter to Rainer Maria Rilke suggested that the poet belonged to no nation: "To create a poem means to translate from the mother tongue into another language. [. . .] No language is the mother tongue. A poet can write in French but he cannot be a French poet. [. . .] Orpheus exploded and broke up the nationalities."

While this is certainly one powerful view, there are other ways of thinking about the reach of literature. Consider the Kannada writer U. R. Ananthamurthy, born in 1932, a year after Kolatkar. One of the foremost writers of India, Ananthamurthy found his residence, both spiritual and material, in his mother tongue, Kannada—a language that came to him from the voices of women, from his earliest childhood, and sustained him in the years he spent as a student abroad; a language that opened him up to the sensuous qualities of the natural world as well as the social injustices of a communal life. And from this mother tongue he turned outward to the reaches of world literature often encountered in translation. And perhaps it is no accident that he emerged as one of the most powerful defenders of the rights of free expression in India, in a time of creeping repression.

As writers, we dwell in language. And it could be that as soon as we enter language we become translated beings, with all the turmoil of the flesh and spirit pressed into cords of alphabets that even as they soar and sing, threaten to fray and snap, under the burden.

V

Rabindranath Tagore, the earliest writer included here, was born in 1861, wrote in Bengali, and achieved world renown. Tagore's letters reveal how conflicted he was by the extravagant praise accorded him by those who could not read his poems in the original. It was all the more painful because he felt the poems in his volume *Gitanjali* were truly intimate—"revelations of my true self to me." Tagore continued in this letter to Edward Rothenstein on December 30, 1912: "The literary man was a mere amanuensis—very often knowing nothing of the true meaning of what he was writing." Yet these intimate revelations had to depend on the dark mirror of translation. W. B. Yeats's 1912 passionate introduction to Tagore's poems forever marked them for a generation of readers: "I have carried the manuscript of these translations about with me for days, reading it in railway trains or on the tops of omnibuses and in restaurants, and I have often had to close it lest some stranger would see how much it moved me. These lyrics [. . .] display in their thought a world I have dreamed of all my life

preface

long. The work of a supreme culture, they yet appear as the grass and the rushes."

It is possible that Tagore experienced this as a double estrangement—his access to his own quicksilver consciousness as mirrored in the work, blocked by a stranger's inordinate praise, and poems, so dear to the poet, transmogrified into a strange tongue—and this was what the world at large, the non-Bengali-speaking world knew of him. "You have alluded to the English translation of *Gitanjali*," he wrote to his niece Indira Devi on May 6, 1913: "I have not been able to imagine to this day how people came to like it so much. [. . .] That I have written in English seems to be the delusion." Four years later, in a letter of January 28, 1917, it was Yeats who felt compelled to complain to his publisher about Tagore's English, and how hard he had to work at revising the poet's translation of his own Bengali poems: "Tagore's English was a foreigner's English and as he wrote to me 'he could never tell the words that had lost their souls or the words that had not yet got their souls from the rest.'" William Radice, in his fresh translation of *Gitanjali* (going back both to the Bengali original and a variant manuscript of Tagore's translation stored with the Rothenstein Papers at Harvard), points out that phrases Yeats used to complain about his Indian friend might well have come from a letter that Tagore wrote on January 5, 1913, to Ezra Pound: "I do not know the exact value of your English words. Some of them may have their souls worn out by constant use and some others may not have acquired their souls yet."

VI

What does it mean for a writer to seek out the souls that might inhabit his or her words? Nabaneeta Dev Sen, who was named by Tagore and who knew him in childhood, speaks of how her mother, the writer Radharani, had suggested that in order to gain a broader audience she should choose English over Bengali. It was a choice the daughter rejected: In her essay "The Wind Beneath My Wings," Dev Sen writes, "I continued to write in my mother tongue and it continued to inhabit my speech standing over me like my own mother." For Kamala Das, born four years earlier in 1934, there was a different choice to be made. Her mother, Balamaniamma, had achieved renown as a poet in Malayalam, but for the daughter, the home language was reserved for her wealth of writings in prose. Poetry made for a different compulsion. English, by drawing Das further away from familial constraints, at the same time liberated her, revealing in this way an intimate self that might otherwise have been buried. In her poem "An Introduction," she writes,

> I am Indian, very brown, born in
> Malabar, I speak three languages, write in
> Two, dream in one. Don't write in English, they said.
> English is not your mother-tongue. Why not leave
> Me alone, critics, friends, visiting cousins,
> Every one of you? Why not let me speak in
> Any language I like? The language I speak
> Becomes mine, its distortions, its queernesses
> All mine, mine alone. . . .
> . . .
> It is as human as I am human, don't
> You see?
> ("AN INTRODUCTION")

For many of the women writers included in this anthology, there is a great deal at stake in coming to words, in taking on the public role of author. Lalithambika Antherjanam, who was born into an upper-caste Namboodiri Brahmin family in the first decade of the twentieth century, speaks of how as a young girl she was able to read and write; make her own ink with hibiscus petals, nuts, and copper sulfate; and craft her own writing instrument with an ostrich feather. At puberty, in accordance with social custom, she was forced into seclusion in the *antahpuram*, the women's quarters of the great house. All her reading and writing stopped, a bitter moral education. It was marriage to an understanding husband that allowed her to save her writing soul.

VII

The shadow of Partition falls on twentieth-century Indian writing. Several of the writers included in this anthology have firsthand knowledge of the violence that came in its wake. Some of these writers were adults, others children. Still others, like Salman Rushdie, were born in 1947, the very year of Partition, and inherited the painful realities of migration and forced dislocation. At the time of the fracturing of the subcontinent and the bloody creation of two new nations, India and Pakistan, an estimated 12 million people migrated in both directions across the newly created borders. Some traveled in railway cars heaped with dead bodies, or in long *kafilas,* human caravans that passed from town to town. The terror of those days remained in memory together with the experience of ethnic killings, random slaughters, and violent rapes of women. Documented in the oral histories are tales of women forced by families to save themselves from possible rape and mutilation by taking their own lives; some jumped into wells or swallowed poison. Still others, to save them from real or imagined dishonor, were slaughtered by men in their own families. The fiercest, most brilliant chronicler of the insane violence of Partition was the Urdu short story writer Saadat Hasan Manto. At the time of Partition, Manto, who had been living and working in Bombay for the film industry, left that city and moved to Lahore in Pakistan. There he continued writing his gemlike stories that revealed the darkness of the human psyche and the utter frailty of existence in a world gone mad. It was in the courthouse in Lahore, some years earlier, in what was then undivided India, that Manto and his good friend Ismat Chugtai were made to stand trial on obscenity charges. In Manto's case, the charges had to do with his vivid sexual descriptions, often in the context of unbearable violence. In the case of Chugtai, the charges were based on her explicit depiction of lesbian eroticism between a lonely, high-born lady and her maid in the short story "The Quilt."

One of the few others to write from both sides of the post-Partition border was Qurratulain Hyder, the exact contemporary of Chugtai. Born in India in 1928, Hyder left for Pakistan but after a few years traveled to Britain, returning finally to India. In her novel *Sita Haran,* she created a modern, self-reliant woman who searches for love, a midcentury heroine scarred by the memories of violence, roaming through a partitioned land she has lost and needs to find afresh.

VIII

Some of the writers in this anthology belong to the Indian diaspora. Questions arise: What does it mean to create a world where memories of an earlier life take hold within the fluid borders of the present? What kind of self is at stake? Can literature claim for itself the task of creating a new cultural memory? In extreme situations the past might indeed implode in the present. One thinks of what is now known as the "Rushdie affair," the invocation of blasphemy, the *fatwah*, the murder of innocent civilians in a world driven by the wild waves of virtual reality, unrest in one place igniting violent response in another. And Rushdie's *Satanic Verses* was banned in India, though given the nature of Indian entrepreneurship, pirated copies were freely available on urban sidewalks.

Or one thinks of the poet and translator A. K. Ramanujan, who spent most of his adult life in Chicago where he composed finely chiseled stanzas evoking the burden of an ancestry that was always with him. A decade and a half after his untimely death, Ramanujan's essay "Three Hundred Ramayanas" came under attack by right-wing Hindu forces. Under political pressure the essay was pulled from the syllabus of Delhi University. What was so shocking in the piece? It was Ramanujan's vision of cultural pluralism, of the rich and variant oral traditions that animate the many-voiced life of the ancient epic. In one version of the Ramayana story sung by an Untouchable bard, the royal heroine Sita pops out of Rama's nostril when he sneezes. Elsewhere in the essay Ramanujan speaks of the multiple tellings of this great epic: "Each author if one may hazard a metaphor dips into this [common pool] and brings out a unique crystallization, a new text with a unique texture and a fresh context. [...] The story has no closure though it may be enclosed in a text."

In this spirit one might dream of as many Sitas as there are epics of exile and dislocation, and imagine a twenty-first-century poem where Sita wanders through the streets and subways of present-day Manhattan.

Name Me a Word

RABINDRANATH TAGORE

1861–1941

(Bengali)

Rabindranath Tagore was born in Calcutta, in what is now West Bengal, to a wealthy, landowning family. His father was a businessman who took to spiritual pursuits and became part of a reformist group called the Brahmo Samaj. Tagore's astonishing creativity was well known in his lifetime. It led to an outpouring of poems, songs, essays, plays, short stories, novels, and, toward the end of his life, a whole body of drawings and paintings. As a child, Rabindranath was raised in a large joint family, in Jorasanko, a mansion in Calcutta. He grew up learning to play music and sing. The family performed plays at home, a tradition that the poet continued later in his life.

The progressive thinking of his father, together with the great debates animating Bengal at the time—freedom from the British and the emancipation of women—profoundly marked Tagore. The poet composed thousands of songs, some of which are still sung in India today, and his plays, including the gemlike Dhak Ghar *(Post Office, 1911),* Chitrangada *(1891), and* Raktakorabi *(Red Oleanders, 1926), are among his most important achievements. He wrote* Post Office *after a series of tragedies: the deaths of his wife, youngest son, and daughter. At the heart of the play is Amal, a dying child who keeps waiting for a letter from the king.*

The play had a powerful afterlife. It was broadcast on French radio during World War II when France was under Nazi occupation. In contravention of the ban by Nazi censors, it was performed in the Warsaw Ghetto, in an orphanage.

For Dr. Korczak, the heroic director of the orphanage, the play was a mood, an emotion so close to life, and the actors were not merely actors, they were children. Through a note in Janusz Korczak's Ghetto Diary—*the manuscript was preserved by his friend and helper Igor Newerley—we learn how Dr. Korczak is said to have responded when asked why he had chosen Tagore's play: "We must all learn to face the angel of death." Three weeks later, together with the children of the orphanage who he refused to leave, Korczak was taken to Treblinka death camp.*

Tagore's world travels began after several tragic deaths in his family. In 1912, he sailed to Britain. The translations he had made of his own poem cycle Gitanjali *so entranced W. B. Yeats that the Irish poet took upon himself to retranslate Tagore's work, selecting and rearranging the poems, then arranging for publication. In 1915, Tagore was knighted by the British, but in horror at the massacre of unarmed protestors in Jalianawalabagh, he returned his knighthood. On May 31, 1919, he wrote to Lord Chelmsford, the British viceroy in India: "The accounts of insults and sufferings undergone by our brothers in the Punjab have trickled through the gagged silence, reaching every corner of India, and the universal agony of indignation roused in the hearts of our people has been ignored by our rulers—possibly congratulating themselves for what they imagine as salutary lessons."*

Tagore's friendship with Mahatma Gandhi and his support of the noncooperation movement persisted in spite of deep temperamental differences between the two men. But the writer as a public man still believed deeply in the powers of privacy, in the silence out of which poetry springs. The human need for love in the midst of loneliness runs like a red thread through all his work. In 1924, on a journey to Argentina, Tagore met Victoria Ocampo, a writer and publisher. He remained as a guest in her home for several months. Their intimacy inspired new writing and also the haunting drawings and paintings that had their genesis in doodles he made as he revised the manuscript of Purabi *(1925). This book of poetry is dedicated to "Vijaya," which was what he called her—a literal translation of Victoria. The poet's creativity persisted till the very end. We have as testament his poems of the end, their language pared down, luminous. At times too weak to write, he kept dictating his poems until at the very brink of death.*

Letter

SHILAIDAHA
8 May 1893

Poetry is my long-time sweetheart—indeed, we probably got engaged when I was Rathi's age. From then on, the base of the banyan tree near our pond, the garden inside the house, the undiscovered rooms in the ground floor of the house, the whole outside world, and the rhymes and the fairy-tales I heard from the female servants created a world of enchantment inside me. It is very difficult to express the feelings of my singular shadowy mind, but this much I can say—I had, by then, already exchanged garlands with Poetic Fancy. But I have to admit that the lady is hardly auspicious; if anything, she never brings good luck. I can't say she doesn't give happiness, but when it comes to comfort, she has nothing to do with it. Whoever she embraces, she gives intense pleasure for a while, but then the embrace becomes so tight that she seems to suck all the blood out of his heart. The person she selects—the luckless one—finds it impossible to pitch himself in the middle of domestic life as a householder and stay placid and relaxed. But I have pawned my real life to her. Whether I write for *Sadhana* or look after my estate, whenever I begin to write a poem, I enter into what is my eternal, true self—I quite realize that this is where I belong. It is possible to indulge in many falsities in life, either knowingly or unknowingly, but I never lie in my poems—it is the only sanctuary of all the profound truths of my life.

From *Boyhood Days*

The old indigo factory still remained. The river Padma was far away. The courthouse was on the ground floor, and on the upper storey, our lodgings. In front was a huge terrace, and beyond it, some enormous *jhau*, tamarisk trees, that had flourished in tandem with the white indigo-planter's trade, once upon a time. Today, in place of the rampant power of the indigo-trading sahib, utter stillness reigns. Where has he gone, the *dewan* from the indigo factory who was like a messenger from hell? Where is the band of soldiers with belted waists and staves on their shoulders? Where has it gone, the hall with the long banquet table, where the sahibs would enter, riding up from the front door, turning night into day with all their feasting and the whirl of ballroom dancing, their blood bubbling with the intoxication of champagne? The piteous cries of the hapless *ryots* would not reach the ears of their masters, whose power extended all the way to the distant jail. Today, none of this holds true; the only surviving facts from the past are the graves of two sahibs. The tall tamarisks sway in the breeze, and the grandchildren of those old-time peasants sometimes glimpse the sahibs' ghosts wandering in the abandoned garden of the indigo factory in the dead of night.

There I remained, in a solitary frame of mind. I stayed in a small room in the corner, my hours of leisure stretching to fill the vast expanse of the open terrace. This vacation in a different, unfamiliar place was like the dark water of an ancient pond, its depth impossible to plumb. I hear the ceaseless call of the *bou-kotha-kau,* the Indian nightingale, and a succession of stray thoughts drifted through my mind. Meanwhile, the pages of my notebook had begun to fill with poems. Like the early mango blossom, ready to scatter before the first crop in the month of Magh, those poems have fallen away.

Those days, if a young boy—or especially a girl—set a couple of lines to metre and rhyme, the wise men of the nation would hail it as an unprecedented event, a wonder never to be repeated. I know the names of those maiden poets; their works have appeared in print, as well. Then, as the fashion for expressing nice thoughts in carefully measured fourteen-syllable awkwardly rhymed lines declined, their names were erased and at once replaced by row upon row of names, belonging to the girls of today.

Boys are far more timid than girls, and much shyer. I don't remember any young male writer who composed poems, then, save me. One day, a nephew older than me pointed out that words, if cast in a fourteen-syllable mould, assume the shape of a poem. I witnessed this magic myself. In my hands, the fourteen-syllable frame blossomed like a lotus; it even attracted the amorous bee. I had crossed the gulf that separated me from the poets, and I have continued to bridge that gap, ever since.

I remember, when I was studying in the class junior to the year for scholarships, the superintendent, Mr. Gobinda, heard it rumoured that I wrote poetry. Imagining that I would bring glory to the name of Normal School, he ordered me to compose verse. I had to write, and recite, for my classmates. I had to hear them remark that the poem was surely plagiarized. The fault-finders did not guess the truth, but later, with maturity, I became an expert at stealing ideas. But then, such stolen goods are precious things.

I remember combining the *payar* and *tripadi* metres to compose a poem, expressing the grief I felt when, as I swam to pluck a lotus blossom, the movement of my arms made waves that constantly pushed the lotus away, beyond my reach. Akshay Babu took me to his relatives' home and made them listen to this poem. The boy has a flair for poetry, the relatives declared.

Bouthakrun's behavior was entirely contrary. She would never acknowledge that I might become a writer, some day. I could never write like Bihari Chakrabarti, she would always say, just to taunt me. Had I but deserved even a much lower rank, I would dejectedly think, she would have demurred at dismissing your young *deor*'s distaste for women's fascination with clothes.

There remains an entertaining anecdote to be told. In Shilaidaha, the gardener would pluck flowers and arrange them in vases. It occurred to me that I could inscribe my verse in the coloured sap of flowers. The fluid I managed to squeeze out with much effort would hardly rise to the nib of the pen. I began to think of creating a machine. A perforated wooden bowl and above it, a rotating pestle, were all that one required. It could be operated with a rope-bound wheel. I informed Jyotidada of my needs. He may have been secretly amused, but outwardly, it was impossible to tell. At his bidding, along came the carpenter with his bits of wood. The machine was constructed. Much as I churned the flower-filled wooden bowl with the rope-bound pestle, the blossoms were crushed to a muddy past, but no juice flowed from them. Jyotidada realized that flower sap would not rhyme with machine-applied pressure. But still, he did not mock me openly.

In my whole life, this was my only venture at engineering. They say in the scriptures that there is a deity always waiting to humiliate the one who presumes to become what he is not. On this occasion, the same divinity had looked askance at my engineering project. I have stopped handling machinery ever since, avoiding even the stringing of instruments like the *sitar* and the *esraaj*.

From *Final Poems*

"SICKBED 21"

Waking in the morning,
I saw a rose in my vase,
and wondered—
in the cycle of ages,
what force brought it to this peak of beauty,
side-stepping pits of imperfection?
Was it blind, forgetful, like the ones who renounce the world,
not distinguishing beauty from ugliness?
Was it strictly logical? Material?
Nothing of the spirit?
Some argue that in the congress of creation
beauty and ugliness sit equally.
Neither is kept out.
I am a poet—I won't take sides.
I see the world whole, the billions of planets and stars in the sky
balancing vast beauty.
Their rhythms are not tripped, their songs are not choked.
Distortions cause no lapses.
In the sky I see layer upon layer, petals spreading
a luminous, vast rose.

24 November 1940 (morning)

"RECOVERY 4"

A bell rings in the distance
and the city's cloud-scraping self-announcing
chatter vanishes from the mind.
In sun-warmed winter light, for no reason, images emerge
neglected at the edges of life's travels.

A field-path threading villages wanders far off
by the riverbanks.
Under an ancient fig tree

people are waiting for the ferry
beside their market wares.
In a tin-roofed village hut—
jaggery jars lined in rows,
neighborhood dogs' greedy tongues,
flies crowding.
A cart on the road
heavy-loaded with jute.
Sacks dragged, one by one, weighed, voices shrill
behind the warehouse.
Untied oxen
return from munching grass by the path,
tail-whips lashing their backs.
Piles of mustard
wait for the storehouse.
A fishing boat docks,
fisherwomen gather, baskets in the crooks of their arms—
a hawk flies overhead.
Side by side, merchant boats tied on the steep bank.
In the sun, on rooftops, oarsmen mend nets.
Hugging the necks of their buffalo, farmers float across
to the rice fields on the other side.
In the distance, above the forest-line, a temple crest
shimmers in the morning sun.
At invisible edges of fields—a train
stretches dim, dimmer
sound-lines across the breast of the wind,
smoke trailing
a long flag vanquishing distance.

I remember—nothing much—long ago
in deepest night,
a boat tied to the banks of the Ganges.
Polished water at dusk,
shadow-shapes thickening hushed forest edges,
lamp flames through cracks in the woods.
Suddenly I wake.

rabindranath tagore

In the wordless night sky
a song lifts from a young voice.
A slim boat rushes on the ebbing current,
disappears.
On both banks by the forest, a shiver keeps vigil—
sculpted stillness of a moon-crowned night,
silence on my mat of broken sleep.

The west bank of the Ganges—a house at the edge of town.
The shallows stretch into distance,
emptiness under a blank sky.
A few cows graze in a harvested millet field.
Farmer boys, with their sticks, fend goats
from melon tendrils.
Somewhere, from a village, a woman by herself,
a basket in her arm, walks off to find spinach.
And always, down by the line of the river
in a row, bent-backed, slow-pulling oarsmen.
In the water, on land, all day, no other signs of life.
Nearby in the garden, neglected, a flowering tree
beside a grand old neem tree, a bench embedded in its trunk,
its dense aristocratic shadow
at night a shelter for egrets.
Well water
gurgles all day through the canal
to feed the corn crop.
Someone is singing, grinding wheat,
jingling bracelets of brass.
The noon is enfolded by one melody repeating.

These path-meetings while walking,
little moments, wake
at the edges of consciousness.
All these neglected images,
life's last dividing pains,
arrive with the far tolling of the bell.

                                            31 January 1941 (evening)

SAROJINI NAIDU

1879–1949

(English)

Sarojini Naidu was born into a Bengali family in the princely state of Hyderabad. Her father, Agorenath Chattopadhya, a chemist, was the founder of what was to become the Nizam College, and her mother, Barada Sundari Devi, wrote poems in Bengali. Sarojini was a precocious child who spoke Urdu, the language of Islamic culture in her city. She refused to learn English. In a letter quoted by Arthur Symons in his introduction to her first volume of poetry, The Golden Threshold *(1905), we learn of how when she was a young girl, her father locked her up in a room as punishment, and the child "came out of it a full-blown linguist." The young Sarojini was sent off to England at the age of seventeen, to get her away from what was felt to be an unsuitable love affair with Dr. Govindarajulu Naidu, a young medical doctor. But her three years in England only served to stoke a passionate sensibility, and in letters home she writes of her loneliness and longing for the man who would later become her husband.*

English was the language into which she poured her feelings, crafting delicate, artful poems, influenced by the fin-de-siècle poetry of the Decadents, one of whom, Arthur Symons, in his fulsome introduction, praised the poems for their "bird-like quality of song," remarking on their "Eastern magic." For many of those who encountered her in this foreign country she cut an exotic figure, something she herself seemed to have played on, in spite of herself. In the same introduction we read of her tiny figure, her straight black hair, and how she dressed in "clinging dresses of Eastern silk." The volume appeared with a soulful pen-and-ink portrait of the young poet by the artist J. B. Yeats, father of the poet W. B. Yeats. Naidu in her November 16, 1912, letter to Tagore describes the poet as "my old friend Yeats the most subtle and delicate poet of modern Britain."

Later in her life, deeply influenced by meeting with Gandhi, Naidu became an important figure in the Indian National movement. Like Gandhi she suffered imprisonment at the hands of the British. As her political life flowered, she stopped writing poetry, and her eloquence flowed into anticolonial speeches, also delivered in English. In 1925, she became the first Indian woman president of the National Congress. One of the early figures of Indian poetry in English, Naidu published volumes of poetry including The Bird of Time *(1912) and* The Broken Wing: Songs of Love, Death and the Spring *(1917).*

To Arthur Symons

RYEDALE HOUSE, HARTLEPOOL
31 July 1896

Dear "Singer of Scents":

Your previous letter greeted me this morning and upset all my solemn theories with regard to yourself. You are frivolous—and you are enjoying yourself in that wild west of Ireland. What you tell me is most fascinating —but I hope the priest and the bishop will do you good. You do need it you know! Tell me of your adventurous visit to the Isle of Aran, and did you see visions there? Do the gods speak unto the children of men in that sacred spot, and do beautiful demons lure mad poets to their destruction in that magical haunt? And there are quite a hundred things I want to tell you about, and I am quite sure are not prepared to hear one quarter! You must tell me if I bore you—I am not a "crushable quantity" as I told you.

You see I am not yet in Switzerland, but in a far different place— Hartlepool. I came up on Wednesday (I was quite alone in my glory all the way from London, and devoted myself, loudly, in the empty compartment to studying the wonderful cadences and rhymes of *Silhouettes* and I benefitted by so charming a study).

It is the quaintest little town I've ever seen; just nice for a week. An unlovely but rather interesting village, with a poverty-stricken air and shoals of barefoot children and untidy-looking women about: who beholding one so wildly strange and foreign to them say: "here is one on whom the sun has looked, and whose garments have borrowed the colours of the sun; let us stare," and they stare! There are about a dozen families or so, and half a dozen shy, young men whom one might even know: a little café where everyone goes, a bare-looking tennis court where for want of anything better the landlady plays tennis; occasional theatricals I believe, the last [a] novel of Edna Lyall or "Modern Society" I believe; and a general and very striking want of any kind of intellectual or poetic atmosphere—none of your poetry here, Mr. Symons: it is commonplace prose; so commonplace; but they are a simple, hearty, jolly set of people, and they *exist*—and are happy; I like them. But Hartlepool has its charm, a wonderful charm—and I am in a continuous state of ecstasy. Just in front of the house stretches a wild, bleak, historic moor, and beyond—the sea—the gray sea! When all the house is asleep at midnight, I draw up my blinds and in a passionate rapture, half of terror, half of mystical, fantastic, ineffable delight, I stand and look across the moor at the magical waters, magical! The rush of the surging waves in my ears—and in my soul, such an "intolerable agony" of something I cannot express.

Now I want to talk to you about the *Savoy*. I like it very much—this new number—you have some good writing in it: but I want to tell you specially about your own things. The "Causerie" I like extremely; it is charming, but do you know I got a shock when I saw the words "almost colourless" applied to Ernest Dowson's verses. Do you really think they are almost colourless? Now the first thing that struck me was the vague *richness* of colour; it is mystical, evasive, delicate, but rich it is—at least to me.

"Stella Maligna" whatever it may mean, and I have not grasped its meaning yet, is very beautiful; nearly everything you write is distinctly beautiful in some way—(except three or four things in *Silhouettes*) but I wonder how many people will understand it?

Your "colour study" is very well written, but I think I like the charming "Causerie" best of all. Do you think it "cheek" of me to criticize?

What is Yeats doing? With those deep Druid eyes of his does he draw spirits from out the vasty deep of Past and Future and wrest the secrets of eternity? How does his new drama get on?—I have met many interesting and extraordinary people in my life: but do you know that Mr. Yeats is decidedly the most fascinating and curious personality except my father, who is a glorious mystery, an incarnation of unique paradoxes.

Tell me of your new work: how does the prose volume get on, and have you been able as yet to triumph over the perverse [publisher] Fisher Unwin's? And how many new and lovely poems have you written? Ah, *that* is your real life, that is what is so intensely fascinating and marvelous; the other is not so real; at least to me it cannot seem so essentially your own!

Have you read Alice Meynell's *Rhythm of Life?* I have just been reading it and want you to tell me what you think of her as a prose writer. I know what you think of her as a poet—I should like to know Alice Meynell and I also want you to tell me what you think of Olive Schreiner's *Dreams*—And I want you to tell me such a lot of things. O dear! You will get tired even of reading the questions I ask! But as I have already told you, you must tell me directly I bore you, and you needn't answer a single question unless you like.

Do immortal spirits like you, most magical poet, know aught of mortal suffering—then, write me something *very* kind, because I am, apart from the wild sea-ecstasies, in a state of most awful disgust with myself, and—well, I am feeling that I've made my life an utter failure—you can never have felt that, because it wouldn't be true—but I—I have given myself over to despair; and assure you would not find me a charming companion just now. By the way, do you know Mathilde Blind wanted me to go down for a week with her somewhere in Surrey and read poetry to her under the pine trees—don't you think the dear lady should be grateful I don't take her at her word?—I've sent her a really charming companion instead and that is Ernest Dowson in the shape of his poems. I have only about two copies left of *Verses* now—haven't I been quick?

I return to town on the 7th. Don't know where I'm to stay till the 12th when Miss Tagart returns from her little holiday and we leave for the continent. I've thought of such a nice plan for myself. There's a poor dear little Swiss governess I know, overworked, and badly in need of a holiday; I am taking her with me, and she'll get her holiday, and I shall have some nice excursions of my own account with her to go about with me—I'm sure she'll be very keen to come.

But you, poor patient martyr, you have actually yawned three times already in spite of yourself! I am sorry—will you forgive me: I shan't keep you any longer: This is "the end, the end."

Good bye. To the dear "Singer of Scents" many good wishes and many kind messages from,

His true friend,
Sarojini Chattopadhyay

Have I written very indistinctly?

From a Letter to Edmund Gosse

33 BLOMFIELD ROAD, MAIDA HILL, LONDON
6 October 1896

Dear Mr. Gosse:

I did not dare to trust myself to thank you for what you said on Sunday. You cannot know what those words meant to me, how they will always color my life, how, when I am in the very depths of self-disgust and despair —as I so often am—they will give me new hope and new courage—no you cannot know! Poetry is the one thing I love so passionately, so intensely, so absolutely, that is my very life of life—and now you have told me that *I am a poet*—I am a poet! I keep repeating it to myself to try to realize it. Will you let me tell you a little about myself, because I want you to know how you have been an influence in my life—ever since I was eleven years old!

Beautiful and romantic and remarkable as were the circumstances amidst which I was brought up, there was nothing to directly encourage poetry—indeed, the strongest influences that were brought to bear upon us were scientific and mathematical. I always loved poetry but nothing could be further from my mind than trying to write verses myself, it never once occurred to me why, till one day, when I was about eleven, while I was trying to do a dull problem—Algebra it was I think—quite suddenly three verses came into my head and I wrote them down—of course they were worthless, but that day marked a new era in my life: I was going to be a poet! I did not tell any one about my new "adventures," but went on writing—things began to come with great ease and rapidity—weak and

sarojini naidu

childish no doubt—I have no records left to tell tales!—and somehow my father got hold of them and soon everybody got to know and I was of course the most marvelous thing in creation and everything I did henceforth was wonderful, divine, etc.—I was fully on the way to have my head turned with all that flood of sincere but remarkably blind and injudicious praise and flattery. About this time, I don't know how or why the name of Edmund Gosse began to be a sort of magical legend to me—legends were more real than realities then—and in a dim, vague kind of way I began to feel that somehow this magical name was to be one of the strongest and most inevitable influence[s] on my life. I went on writing, and Hyderabad began to get more and more mad about what I did—indeed I think nearly all over India I began to be looked on as a phenomenon—but the more they praised the more disgusted I got with myself, and longed, O how passionately—for somebody who could really criticize. I knew my verses were very poor, but I wanted to know whether they had even a grain of promise of better things to come. At last in despair I wrote you a letter— (it must have been very childish I suppose—this was when I was about 14 or 15)—but I burnt it the next day!

Then I had a long and terrible illness which nearly killed me and I believe for a time half-paralysed my faculties—everything seemed gone— except the love of poetry and the longing to do better. Then I came to England—I was about sixteen then—I must have been singularly ignorant for sixteen, because I knew that England to me meant Shelley and Keats, who were dead—and Edmund Gosse who was alive and certainly made up by far the greater part of England!—(I think Westminster Abbey and the Thames made up the rest!) Well, I made up my mind that I must know Edmund Gosse! For the first six months I did not, could not write a single line or indeed do anything, and then suddenly the fountains were unsealed and I began to write, write, write! In the three months I wrote I think nearly *45* pieces—horrible! but the verses had I thought less strength than some of my earlier ones—the first batch I sent you were selections from this extraordinary outburst of bad verse!—

Well, in January I first saw you: the magical legend had become a reality —and I was not disappointed—indeed I shall never forget that day—because with one great bound I seemed to wake into a new, large life—the life I had always longed for and so long in vain. From that day I seemed an altered being. I seemed to have put off childish things and put on the garments of a new and beautiful hope and ambition, and I have gone on growing and growing. I feel it—seeing more clearly, feeling more intensely, thinking more deeply—and loving more passionately, more unselfishly that beautiful Spirit of Art that has now become dearer than my life's blood to me—and all this I owe to you. I know I have not expressed myself at all well, but you will understand me I think, and you will not mind my telling you all this.

To Rabindranath Tagore (1912)

HYDERABAD, DECCAN, INDIA
16 November 1912

Beloved and honored Poet:

You were so gracious to my first little book of songs, *The Golden Threshold,* that I venture to send you all the way to your temporary alien home a copy of my new book *The Bird of Time* in token of my profound reverence for your genius. If you will do me the great honor to read and approve of my simple, sincere little verses, I shall indeed consider that I have achieved fame: the most exquisite and fruitful fame; for your praise would be like a garland of pearls hung around my spirit. I have been so proud, so rejoiced to hear of the ovations you have received in England, I am so glad that my old friend Yeats, the most subtle and delicate poet of modern Britain, has had the privilege of meeting you. More than any other man or woman in Europe, except Maurice Maeterlinck, Yeats has that mystic quality of imagination, that fervor and ecstasy of the spirit, that could alone make a true comrade for you. It is indeed good news that you have chosen him to edit the English versions of your poems. To the European world they will be a revelation of the beauty and rapture of the Indian genius at its best. And I am sure that hundreds of yearning souls will drink deep and find peace through your work, made accessible to them in such a gracious manner.

I wonder what your impressions of America will be; but I know what America will feel about the divine magician that carries to them the golden

and immortal gift of his lyric joy and spiritual bliss. May all find blessing and refreshment, who come within the sphere of your beautiful influence. Om!
Shanti! Shanti! Shanti!

I am your
Most sincere and reverent admirer,
Sarojini Naidu

To Rabindranath Tagore (undated)

HAROLD FINK PRIVATE HOSPITAL
17 PARK LANE, W. LONDON
[Undated; but probably December 1913]

Dear Poet:

I am writing from my sick bed on the very eve of my operation to tell you that your *Gardener* fills my room with the fragrance and beauty of immortal flowers; your *Crescent Moon* bathes me in the tender golden ecstasy of its illumination, and the world-wide recognition of your genius shines like a crown on the brows of Bharat Mata, the dear land of your heart's desire....

And before I go down into the darkness, for a few hours maybe or for ever, I want to tell you that because I am a woman, a poet, and patriot, I rejoice in your exquisite work, in your exquisite fame, your exquisite service to India: and I offer my threefold homage and love.

Your friend,
Sarojini Naidu

PREMCHAND (DHANPAT RAI)
1880–1936
(Hindi)

Munshi Premchand was born Dhanpat Rai in a village outside Benares. His mother died when the child was seven, and his father, a postal clerk who remarried, died when the young man was a student. In a memoir piece, Premchand writes of the poverty of his early days and his struggles to keep writing. He managed to earn a living as a teacher, a government job that he gave up in 1921 in response to Gandhi's call for noncooperation with the colonial powers. As a child Premchand received an Urdu education, and his first stories were composed in Urdu, though he later turned to Hindi, the latter allowing him a broader audience. His earliest collection of short stories, Soz e Vatan *(*Lament for the Motherland, *1908), was considered seditious by the colonial government. In addition to being a writer, Premchand ran his own publishing business, the Saraswati Press, and edited the literary journal* Hans. *He was able to shift fiction in Hindi away from the use of romance to a literary realism capable of great psychological insight, well able to probe the injustices of the world.*

His sensitive realism brought him many readers, and his evolving nationalism led him to take an active role in the Progressive Writers Union. In his presidential address in 1936, he addressed his fellow writers arguing for a literature that was written in the language really spoken by people: "I have no hesitation in saying that I judge art from the point of view of its utility." It seemed to Premchand that the best definition of literature was "a criticism of life." And he argues that "unless literature deals with reality it has no appeal for us." In one of his best known short stories, "Sadgati" ("Deliverance," *1931*), the protagonist, an Untouchable, is treated so cruelly by the Brahmin Pundit that he dies. Premchand probes the interior life of the tanner, his name Dukhi, connoting sorrow. The fear of pollution in a caste-driven society and the degradation enforced by unjust caste laws comes through powerfully in this story. In other stories such as "Widows with Sons" and "Secrecy," Premchand's women characters chafe at the societal strictures that inhibit their freedom, and we glimpse the complex emotions that drive their actions. Premchand was prolific, and when he died at the age of fifty-six, he left behind twelve novels and almost three hundred short stories, as well as film scripts and other writings. His important works include the novels Nirmala *(1927)*, Gaban *(*The Stolen Jewels, *1931)*, and Godan *(*The Gift of a Cow, *1936)*.

"Two Autobiographical Sketches"

I

My life is a level plain. There are pits here and there but no cliffs, mountains, jungles, deep ravines or desert wastes. Those good people who have a taste for mountaineering will be disappointed here.

I was born in 1880. My father was a postal employee, my mother an ailing woman. I also had an older sister. At the time of my birth my father was earning about twenty rupees a month; by the time he died his salary was forty. He had been a very thoughtful man, moving through life with his eyes wide open but in his last days he had stumbled and even fallen and brought me down with him: when I was fifteen he had me married. And scarcely a year after the marriage he died. At that time I was studying in the ninth grade. In the house were my wife, my stepmother, her two children and myself, and there was not a pice of income. Whatever savings we'd had were used up in my father's six-month illness and funeral expenses. And my ambition was to get an M.A. and become a lawyer. In those days jobs were just as hard to get as now. With a great effort you might find some post with a salary of ten or twelve rupees a month. But I insisted on going on with my studies. The chains on my ankles were not just iron but of all the metals together and I wanted to walk on the mountain tops!

I had no shoes and no decent clothes, and there were the high prices—barley was half a rupee for ten pounds. I was studying in the High School of Queens College in Banaras, where the headmaster had waived the fees. The exams were coming up soon. When I left school at half-past three I would go to the part of town known as Bamboo Gate to tutor a boy there. I'd get there at four and tutor until six, then leave for my house, which was five miles away in the country. Even walking very fast I could not get there before 8 o'clock. And I had to leave the house at eight sharp in the morning, otherwise I couldn't get to school on time. At night after supper I studied by the light of the oil lamp. I don't know when I slept. Nevertheless I was determined.

Somehow or other I passed my matriculation exams. But I made only second division and there was no hope left of being admitted to Queens College since fees could be remitted only for the first division. By chance Hindu College opened up the same year. I decided to study in this new institution. A Mr. Richardson was the principal. I went to his house and found him in full Indian dress—kurta and dhoti—sitting on the floor writing something. But it had not been so easy for him to change his personality—after listening to me only long enough for me to get half my request out he said he didn't discuss college business in his house and I should go to the College. Fine, I went to the College and he saw me there but our meeting was a disappointment. He could not remit the fees. What could I do next? If I presented suitable recommendations then perhaps he might consider my request. But who in the city would know a country boy?

Every day I set out from home to try to get a recommendation from somewhere, and after an arduous twelve miles return in the evening. Who was there to ask? Nobody was concerned about me.

But after several days I found someone to recommend me, Thakur Indranarayan Singh of the board of directors of Hindu College. I had gone to him and wept, and taking pity on me he'd given me a letter of recommendation. In that instant my happiness knew no bounds. Blissful, I returned home. I intended to go see the Principal the next day, but as soon as I reached home I came down with a fever. I couldn't get rid of it for a week. I kept drinking concoctions made from neem leaves until I could barely stand it. One day I was sitting at the door when my old family priest came along. Seeing my state, he asked for details and then immediately went off into the fields. He dug up a root and when he brought it back washed it and ground it in with seven grains of black pepper and made me drink it. It had a magical effect. After no more than an hour the fever broke. It was as if the herb had taken it by the neck and throttled it. I asked Panditji many times for the name of the root but he wouldn't tell me. He said that if he did its effectiveness would vanish.

After a month I went again to see Mr. Richardson and showed him the letter of recommendation. Giving me a sharp look he said, "Where were you all this time?"

"I was ill." "What was wrong with you?" I wasn't ready for the question. If I told him it was a fever perhaps the Sahib would think I was lying. In my estimation a fever was a very light matter, insufficient to explain so long an absence. I felt I should name some disease which by its gravity would draw his sympathy. At the moment I could think of the name of none. When I'd gone to Thakur Singh he'd mentioned that he suffered from palpitations of the heart. And that was the word I thought of. I said in English, "Palpitation of heart, sir."

Astonished, the Principal looked at me and said, "Are you completely well now?"

"Yes, sir."

"Very well, fill out the entrance application form."

I assumed that the worst was over. I took the form, filled it out and brought it back. At that moment the Principal was in one of his classes. At three o'clock I got the form back. Written on it was: "Look into his ability."

Here was a new problem. My heart sank. I could hope to pass no subject except English; I shivered at the thought of algebra and geometry. Whatever I'd learned I'd completely forgotten. But what else was there to do? Trusting to luck, I went to class and presented my application. The Professor, a Bengali, was teaching English; the subject was Washington Irving's "Rip van Winkle." I took a seat in the back row. In a few minutes I saw that the professor was competent in his subject. When the hour was over he questioned me about the day's lesson and then wrote on my form "Satisfactory."

The next hour was algebra. The teacher here was also a Bengali; I showed him the form. Most often the students who came to a new school have not been able to find admittance elsewhere, and that was the case here; the classes were full of incompetent students. Whoever came in the first rush had been enrolled—to the hungry the meanest gruel tastes good. But now the stomach was full and students were chosen only after careful selection. This professor examined me in mathematics and I failed; in the box marked "maths" on the form he wrote "Unsatisfactory."

I was so disappointed that I didn't bring the application back to the Principal. I went straight home. For me mathematics was the peak of Mount Everest, I could never reach it. In Intermediate College I'd already failed it a couple of times and, discouraged, gave up taking the exam. Ten years later when it was made optional I took another subject and passed easily. Until that time who knows how many young people's aspirations have been finished off by mathematics! Anyway, I went home disappointed, but the desire for learning was still strong. What could I do sitting at home? How to improve my maths and get enrolled in college was the problem. For this I would have to live in town.

By luck I got a post tutoring a lawyer's sons with a salary of five rupees. I decided to live on two rupees and give the other three to my family. Above the advocate's stable there was a rather small, unfinished room. I got permission to stay there. A piece of canvas was spread out for my bed, I got a very small lamp from the market and began my life in town. I also brought some pots from home. Once a day I cooked *khichri* and after washing and scouring the pots I'd set out for the library—maths was the pretext, but I would read novels and the like. In those days I read Pandit Ratannath Dar's *Fasana-e-Azad* (*The Romance of Azad*) as well as *Chandrakanta-Santati* (*The Descendants of Chandrakanta*), and I read everything of Bankim Chatterji's that I could find in Urdu translation in the library.

The brother-in-law of the advocate's sons had been a fellow student of mine for the matriculation. It was on his recommendation that I'd got this post. We were very good friends, so when I needed money I'd borrow from him and settle the account when I got my pay. Sometimes I'd have only two rupees left, sometimes three. On the day when I had two or three rupees left from my pay I'd lose all restraint—a craving for sweets would draw me towards the candy shop. I'd eat up two or three annas worth at once. On the same day I'd go home and give my family the two or two and a half rupees. The next day I'd begin to borrow again. But there were times when I was embarrassed about borrowing and day after day I'd fast.

premchand (dhanpat rai)

In this way four or five months went by. Meantime I had taken two and a half rupees worth of clothes from a draper on credit. Every day I used to walk by his place—he had complete confidence in me. When after a couple of months I hadn't been able to pay him I gave up going that way and took a detour. It was three years before I could pay off this debt. In those days a laboring man who made his home in the back of the advocate's house used to come to me to learn a little Hindi. He was always saying, "Know this, little brother!" and we had all come to call him that by way of a nickname. One day I borrowed eight annas from him too. Five years later he came to my house in the village and collected that half rupee from me.

I still longed to study, but every day I grew more and more despondent. I wanted to find a job somewhere but I had no idea of how and where to find one.

That winter I hadn't a pice left. I had spent a few days eating a pice worth of the cheapest cereal each day. Either the moneylenders had refused to loan me anything or from embarrassment I couldn't ask. One evening, just at dusk, I went to a bookseller to sell a book—"The Key to *Chakravarti's Mathematics,*" which I had bought two years before. I had held on to it until now with great difficulty but today in complete despair I decided to sell it. Although it had cost me two rupees I settled for one. Taking my rupee I was just about to leave the shop when a gentleman with big moustaches who had been sitting there asked me, "Where are you studying?" I said, "I'm not studying anywhere but I hope to enroll somewhere."

"Did you pass your matric exams? Then don't you want a job?"

"I can't find a job anywhere at all."

This gentleman was the headmaster of a small school, and he needed an assistant teacher. He offered me a salary of eighteen rupees; I accepted. Eighteen rupees at that time was beyond the highest flight of my pessimistic imagination. I arranged to meet him the next day and left with my head in the clouds. I was ready to cope with any circumstances and if mathematics didn't stop me I would certainly get ahead. But the most difficult obstacle was the university's total lack of understanding, which then and for several years afterwards led it to treat everybody in the manner of that thief who made everybody, tall and short, fit one bed.

premchand (dhanpat rai)

2

I began to write stories for the first time in 1907. I had read Tagore's stories in English and had Urdu translations published in the Urdu newspapers. But as early as 1901 I had begun to write novels. In 1902 one of my novels came out and a second in 1904, but until 1907 I had not written one short story. The title of my first story was "The Most Precious Jewel in the World," published in *Zamana* in 1907. After this I wrote another four or five stories. In 1909 a collection of five stories was published with the title "Sufferings of the Motherland." At this time the partition of Bengal had taken place; in the Congress the radical faction had developed. In these five stories I praised devotion to the country.

At that time I was a deputy inspector in the department of education in Hamirpur district. One evening, six months after the stories had been published, while I sat in my tent I received a summons to go at once to see the District Collector, who was then on his winter tour. I harnessed the bullock-cart and travelled between thirty and forty miles through the night and reached him the next day. In front of him was placed a copy of my book. My head began to throb. At that time I was writing under the name of Navabrai. I had had some indication that the secret police were looking for the author of this book. I realized they must have traced me and that I was being called to account.

The Collector asked me, "Did you write this book?"

I told him I had.

He asked for the theme of each one of the stories and finally losing his temper said, "Your stories are full of sedition. It's fortunate for you that this is a British government. If it were the Mughal Empire, then both your hands would be cut off. Your stories are one-sided, you've insulted the British government." The judgment was that I should give all copies of the book into the custody of the government and that I should not ever write anything else without the permission of the Collector. I felt I'd got off lightly. Of the thousand copies printed hardly three hundred had been sold. The remaining seven hundred I sent for from the *Zamana* office and had them delivered over to the Collector.

I assumed the danger was past. But the authorities could not be satisfied so easily. Afterwards I learned that the Collector had discussed the matter with the other officials of the district. The Superintendent of Police, two deputy collectors and the deputy inspector—whose subordinate I was—sat to consider what my fate should be. One of the deputy collectors, using quotations from the stories, asserted that in them there was nothing but sedition from beginning to end, and not just ordinary sedition but a contagious variety. The demi-god of the police said, "So dangerous a man ought to be severely punished." The deputy inspector was very fond of me. Afraid lest the affair be long drawn out he made the suggestion that in a friendly way he would sound out my political opinions and present a report to this committee. His idea was to explain to me and to write in his report that the writer was violent only with his pen and had nothing whatever to do with any political disturbance. The committee accepted his suggestion, although the police chief even at this moment was still blustering and threatening.

Suddenly the Collector asked the deputy inspector, "Do you expect that he'll tell you what he really thinks?"

"Yes, I'm intimate with him."

"By pretending to be friendly you want to find out his secret views? But that's spying! I consider it vile."

Losing his wits the deputy inspector stammered, "But I . . . Your Excellency's order . . ."

"No," the Collector interrupted, "that's not my order. I had no intention of giving any such order. If the author's sedition can be proven from his book, then he should be put on trial in an open court, otherwise dismiss the case with a warning. I don't like the idea of a smile on the face and a knife in the hand."

When the deputy inspector himself told me this story several days later, I asked him, "Would you really have done this spying?" He laughed. "Impossible. Even if he'd given several hundred thousand rupees I wouldn't have done it. I just wanted to stop any legal proceedings, and they've been stopped. If there'd been a court case, you would definitely have been sentenced. You would have found no one to plead your cause. But the Collector is a noble gentleman."

"Very noble indeed," I said.

NIRAD C. CHAUDHURI

1897–1999

(English)

Nirad C. Chaudhuri was born into a middle-class family in Kishorganj in what is now Bangladesh. As a young man with literary ambitions he moved to Calcutta and got involved in the literary skirmishes of the day, working as a critic for Bengali magazines. After years of involvement in the literary debates and currents of Bengali writing, he shot to fame with the 1951 publication of The Autobiography of an Unknown Indian. *Years later, in a second, massive autobiographical work,* Thy Hand Great Anarch! India 1921–1952, *he reflects on the genesis of that first work. As so often in Chaudhuri's writing, a species of auto-fiction that he created and mastered, the "I" holds forth, a subjectivity clinging to the complicated currents of an often violent history within and through which he must craft a self. It is no accident that in the midst of the turmoil of Partition the idea for the book clarified: "As I lay awake in the night of 4–5 May, 1947, an idea suddenly flashed into my mind. Why instead of merely regretting the work of history you cannot write, I asked myself, do you not write the history you have passed through and seen enacted before your eyes." He worked on the manuscript in the early hours of the morning, scraping together the time to write: "I worked steadily, typing on an average 2500 words a day, and in order to spur me on, I dated what I wrote."*

The Autobiography, *which earned him what he so earnestly desired, renown in the English literary world, also cut him off from his earlier life and ready acceptance by an Indian readership. Many in India took to heart his torment at not being utterly English, and read into his quotations of large swathes of French and English literature a craven attempt to become a brown sahib, a man who slavishly imitated what they could never become. It was as if with the persona Chaudhuri created, Lord Macaulay's desire had taken flesh and blood—what Macaulay famously defined in his 1835 "Minute on Indian Education" as the colonial need to create a "class of persons, Indian in blood and color but English in taste, in opinions, in morals and in intellect." Chaudhuri's dedication in* The Autobiography *inevitably drew the ire of patriotic Indians—"To the Memory of the British Empire in India which conferred subjecthood on us but withheld citizenship: To which yet every one of us threw out the challenge 'Civis Britannicus sum' because all that was good and living within us was made, shaped and quickened by the same British rule."*

But this allusion to Cicero and the praise of imperial life, pierced through by the pain of its enduring racism, should not blind us to the coruscating complexities of a master stylist and the beauty of his tender evocations of Indian childhood contained in those pages. It is instructive to read of how the child first encountered the English landscape, through the pages of a picture book, its images so vivid to the imagination, that longing for that other life quite overpowered him, an elsewhere of the imagination that took root in and through the ravages of the imperial project. In 1970, Chaudhuri and his family settled in England, never to leave it. In 1997, at the age of one hundred, he published his last work, Three Horsemen of the New Apocalypse, *a rhetorical essay on the decadence he saw swarming all around. The pen becomes a sword with which to slash the fallen world, to create a new Jerusalem.*

From *The Autobiography of an Unknown Indian*

✸

FROM "MY BIRTHPLACE"

Towards the middle of November we celebrated the formal passing of the wet season and the coming of the cold by lighting bonfires. For ourselves we wished good to come and evil to depart, and for the flies, mosquitoes and other insects the most humiliating discomfiture. Then we witnessed a succession of happenings which revealed to us the inexorable process of the seasons. First of all, the municipal workmen cleaned up the ditch which ran from one end of the town to the other separating all the houses from the road. This ditch had to be spanned in every case by a small bridge, made in some instances of brick but more generally of bamboo and beaten earth. The weeds which had grown in it during the rains were torn up and then the sides and the bottom scraped til the soft brown earth stood exposed. The drain, about three feet wide and only slightly less in depth, was never filthy, for it carried nothing but rain water. We always crept along it in our games, and after the annual cleaning it was our favorite resort.

A similar weeding was given to our grounds, and, as at this time large droves of swine were passing through the town in their journeys from their monsoon quarters to their winter quarters (we had no precise idea where they were), we requested the swineherds to bring their animals into our grounds and get them to dig up and destroy the bulbous arum plants which had grown so plentifully during the rains. We did not, however, allow the pigs to plough up our inner courtyard. This square of some forty feet by as many feet was entrusted to a special workman who tore up every blade of grass individually. It was *de rigueur* in every self-respecting household to keep the inner yard free of grass. To have even short stubbles of green showing there was as improper among us as it is to wear two-day-old stubbles of beard in English society.

About the same time one or two women were requisitioned to recondition our earthen floors. All our huts were built on platforms of beaten earth, about three feet high, the tops of which, without any kind of additional covering, constituted our floors. These floors were rubbed every morning with fresh mud and water in order to keep them firm and clean, and the sides too were given the same treatment almost every day. But during the monsoon the sides could not receive the same attention, if any at all, and so, at the end of the rains, they became rough, peeled, and in extreme cases even pot-holed. Ordinarily the senior servant or even my mother did this daily smearing, for it called for considerable skill and practice if the whole place was not to be made utterly messy. But my mother could hardly be expected to carry out the extensive renovation and the senior servant was a busy man, having to see to cooking and the meals. Accordingly, professional "mud-smearers" were sent for and they saw the job neatly through for a few annas.

These floors of ours call for some explanation but certainly no apologies. Although in our childhood, so far as the houses of the gentlefolk were concerned, mud floors were to be found only in our district and in one or two adjacent ones, we were carrying on a venerable tradition once established all over Bengal and very solidly. In later life, I read an old Bengali tract written to promote the cause of "female education," which unconsciously provided a mud floor for a royal palace. The pamphlet was written and published in 1822 and has thus a just claim to be called a Bengali incunabulum. Its writer was concerned with citing instances of female literacy from ancient Bengali history and chose no less an example than that of the daughter-in-law of the famous king of Bengal, Vallala Sena, and wife of the last independent Hindu king of Bengal, Lakshmana Sena. Lakshmana Sena as heir apparent, the story ran, had been sent on some expedition by his father and separated from his wife, and one rainy day the love-lorn princess could repress her anguish no more. So, while smearing with water and mud the place where the king, her father-in-law, was to have his midday meal, she forgot herself completely and scratched a few lines of verse on the mud floor. The quatrain was in Sanskrit, but here is a rough translation:

> "Rumbling cloud and rustling rain,
> Peacock's call: the same thing say—
> Lord of Love shall crown this day,
> Or Lord of Death shall end the pain."

The princess forgot to rub out the lines, and when the king came in to dine he read the verses and immediately understood the situation. He sent for his son and united the unhappy pair.

That was decisive enough in its day to prove that the last Hindu queen of Bengal knew her three R's, but to me, when I read the passage, the most valuable point was the historical justification the polemist had provided in it for our mud floors. What old Bengali tradition considered good enough for the palace of Vallala Sena was good enough, if not too good, for us. Incidentally, I found my Bengali ladies, including my mother, given to the habit of scratching on the mud floor. I never saw my mother scratching any poetry but I often saw her drawing very fine little designs of florets, peacock heads, elephants, or horses on the mud floor with her nails or with a bamboo pin, when she was abstracted either from vexation or some other mental preoccupation. We, the children, however, were never allowed to tamper with the floor, which, to tell the truth, if given a free hand, we would fain have dug up like the wolf in Webster's poem.

To conclude the story of the pigs, occasionally they and their men encamped on the low meadow before our house. I particularly remember one big camp, in which there were women and children as well as men and, of course, the pigs, and which was pitched so elaborately that it had bamboo screens all around it. I have no recollection why the party stayed in the town but I have a vague feeling that it remained for about a week and did some business with the sweepers of the town, who took this occasion to replenish their piggeries. Despite the severest warning against going anywhere near the unclean animals we felt the profoundest interest in the sucking-pigs which were carried in bamboo baskets and were perpetually squealing. We were always hanging about the camp, and when a particularly shrill chorus of squeals reached our ears we threw ourselves with desperation on the screen in order to peer and find out what was happening inside. The word went round that the sucking-pigs were being killed and roasted. Thus, even without knowing anything about Charles Lamb's Chinese boy or Mrs. Beeton's recipe for roasting sucking-pigs, we were taking the road which led to the first and through the first to the second.

There was another encamping we very much looked forward to seeing in the cold season, but which, throughout the years of my childhood spent at Kishorganj, I saw only twice. It was the encampment of the gypsies. We looked upon them with fascination and fear not only because extra police were posted to keep an eye on their comings and goings, but even more because it was reported to us that they caught and ate the malodorous animal which was almost legendary with us and which in our dialect was given a name which indiscriminately meant the civet as well as the polecat. And one day I saw with my own eyes a gypsy coming in with a hairy animal, swinging it by a striped tail, and flinging the furry bundle on the ground before his tent.

There was another thing in the gypsy camp which perhaps we admired even more, certainly not less. It was the ass. Asses are not native to East Bengal, nor are they kept or used there as domestic animals, so we never had a sight of asses before the gypsies brought them to our town for the first time. They were a delight to child and adult alike, and no okapi even could cause greater sensation. Their braying was listened to with even greater pleasure, and we should not have been surprised if like the oryx of legend the asses had stood in mystical ecstasy before the rising sun and sneezed. I have read that when the Hyksos brought the horse into Egypt, the Egyptians, previously unfamiliar with that noble animal, gave it the name—Ass of the East. We were disposed to call the ass the Horse of the West.

Many years afterwards my friend Tridib Chaudhuri confirmed to me this fact of general ignorance of the ass in East Bengal with a most interesting anecdote. One day, when I casually mentioned to him that we in East Bengal had no asses, he immediately remarked that he had been given conclusive proof of that unfamiliarity when he was in Deoli detention camp in Rajputana as a political prisoner. That was the camp where, between 1932 and 1937, some hundreds of Bengali young men had been kept in detention without trial for suspected complicity in terrorist activities. The first day Tridib Chaudhuri arrived there some previously arrived fellow-prisoners, who were from East Bengal, told him that at night they could hear the roaring of the lions at Kotah, kept in the menagerie of the Maharao, a famous Rajput prince.

My friend was naturally surprised, for Kotah was fifty-four miles away. But his new friends promised to wake him up at night and make him hear the lions. A little after midnight the tired young man was shaken to wakefulness and his companions whispered: "There, listen!" Tridib Chaudhuri, whose home was in West Bengal, was stupefied at first, then he cried out, "Why, it's only an ass braying." For this remark, taken as an unseasonable flippancy, he got only icy looks to begin with; had he not been a newcomer things would have gone very much farther. But the next morning brought his vindication. While he was walking with his companions near the edge of the camp, which was on a hill, he saw down below the hut of a *dhobi* or washerman, with a number of asses grazing nearby. As good fortune would have it, just at that moment one of the animals began to bray, and the enigma of the Kotah lions was finally solved.

That reminds me of our general ignorance about animals. Anything with a feline look and dashes of yellow and black in it was, and still is, a tiger of some sort or other. With inexplicable perversity we persisted in calling the common hare found at Kishorganj "spotted deer." In the fine zoological gardens of Calcutta not the least part of the entertainment is provided by the visitors with their imaginative wealth of observations. Listening with an appearance of unconcern, I have heard all kinds of names applied to the puma and the jaguar and all sorts of mythical attributes set down to the credit of the brown bear, the orang, and the hippopotamus. But the story which deserves to be classical is about a father and son and a zebra, and was told to me by another friend. The little boy was standing before the zebra enclosure and he asked his father what the animals were. The father replied that they were African tigers. The boy, who apparently had more wits than he was born with, protested: "But father, they look like horses." The father began to scold the boy, when my friend, unable to bear it any longer, intervened: "Sir," he said, "why are you scolding the boy? You must be familiar with the shape of that animal, although it has not got exactly your coloration." The father got more angry still and moved away growling that he was not going to be insulted before his son.

Another outstanding experience of the cold season was a folk-ritual which was performed every day for one whole month from the middle of January to the middle of February. It was a ritual for little girls, but it was very elaborate and if one was to draw the fullest benefit out of it it had to be performed for twelve years in succession. Therefore the girls began quite early in life, even at the age of three or four, so that they might see a substantial portion through before they were married off. But of course one could not speak of standards of performance before they had done it for some six or seven years, because the designs which had to be executed required skill in drawing. About twelve feet square or even more of the inner courtyard had to be covered with figures of the sun and the moon, floral decorations of various sorts, and big circles which had to be truly drawn. The palette was similar to that used by the Cromagnon man—dull red, black, and white, with only a greater preponderance of white. The actual coloring material used was, however, simpler than that at the disposal of later palaeolithic society, namely, brick dust instead of red peroxide of iron, charcoal dust instead of pyrolusite, and rice powder for white. The girls took the powders in handfuls, closed their fists, and released the colors through the hole formed by the curled little finger, regulating the flow by tightening or loosening their grip. It was wonderful to see how quickly they filled up the space. The sun was a staring face about two feet in diameter, the moon slightly smaller. The first was laid out mainly in red and black, producing a fiery effect, while the moon was for the most part in rice powder which very successfully brought out its blanched appearance. The floral decorations were of course motifs on which Bengali women had practiced no one knows for how many generations, and they came out as quickly and neatly as if they were being done from stencils.

Two girls of the house next to ours, whose parents we called uncle and aunt following Bengali custom, performed this ritual. At dawn they had their plunge in the cold river and came back singing and shivering. We, the boys, quickly collected twigs, dry leaves, bamboo scrapings, even a log or two, and made a fire for them. After they had got a little warm the girls set to work and it went on till about ten o'clock. The girls chanted hymns to the sun and the moon which could be called a crude and rudimentary version of the canticles of St. Francis. We could not go near or touch them because, being unbathed, we were unclean, but we did our best to make ourselves serviceable in every possible way.

This account of the process of the seasons at Kishorganj should now be closed. The campings and the rituals I have described were the rubrics of the year. Simultaneously, the ordinary text, though less colorful, was not unrolling itself less absorbingly. We were almost wild with excitement when the trees bought to supply the year's firewood arrived on the shoulders of men or on carts. The boles and the branches with leaves, buds, and even fruit were piled high on the wayside, on the riverside slope of the road, to dry. We climbed on them, heaved the whole green mass up and down, suddenly let go, and slid down to the ground. This lasted for about ten days, by which time the leaves withered and dropped off, and then the branches were cut up into logs.

After the firewood it was the turn of the year's supply of straw for our cows. Newly cut straw is lighter in color, stiffer, and more hollow than dry straw. It is also sharp. After a bout of climbing and rolling on straw we had very fine invisible scratches all over the body, and these smarted when we entered water. That was why we were usually warned off the straw. But we did not rate too high the price which we had to pay for making free love to it at its most lovable age.

The oranges from the Khasi Hills, which are rather small in size, besides being smooth, thin-skinned, and very sweet, were our regular winter visitors. They were quite plentiful at Kishorganj, and the cold season was for us a season marked by the flavor, fragrance, and color of oranges. Those were pre-vitamin days, when the eating of oranges was a pleasure and not a duty. The color of the oranges was taken up by the gorgeous borders of African marigold (*Tagetes erecta*) or *Gainda*, as we called them, which was the most common and in my childhood the only cold-season annual we had. By chance I and two of my brothers had bright orange-colored overcoats, and we stood in the sun in these overcoats every morning eating oranges. Perhaps I ought to explain here that from the bare skin of summer we passed to more adequate clothing in the winter.

As soon as the cold was passing off, our typical flowers began to come out. In addition to the marigold we cultivated another annual, the balsam, which, however, was a flower of the rainy season. In the meanwhile one glorious cycle of our prized blooms had come and gone. It was a remarkable thing that both the opening of the flowering season in spring and its final closing in the late autumn were marked by the same two flowers, two of the most deliciously scented flowers we had. They were the Night-blooming Flower of Sadness (*Nyctanthes arbortristis*), called *Sewlee* in Bengali, and the *Champa* (*Michelia champaca*). Whiffs of their heavy scent came borne on every little breeze to us. Starting from the spring we had, in a steady stream, all the kinds of jasmine, also the so-called Cape Jasmine which was not a jasmine at all but our *Gandharaj* (*Gardenia florida*), the China Box or *Kamini* (*Murraya exotica*), the ravishing *Bakul* (*Mimusops elengi*) with its creamy green flowerets, and the exquisite Tuberose, *Rajanigandha* or *Gul-shabu* (*Polianthes tuberosa*). All these flowers, with the exception of the *Bakul* whose color I have mentioned and the *Champa* which was pale golden yellow, were pure white, with scents which would be considered overpowering by many. The great floral attraction of the rainy season was the *Kadanwa* (*Anthocephalus cadamva*), which one could regard as the link between our white scented flowers and colored unscented flowers. It had only a very mild fragrance and its spherical flowers could be easily plucked bare of the innumerable white stamens to expose the orange core. The tall and large-leaved tree which bears this flower is famous in legend as that under which Krishna used to play his flute on the banks of the Jumna.

Among colored flowers we had, of course, the highly perfumed Bussora rose, and the scentless hibiscus—the red, the light pink, and the pendulous; also the *Hibiscus mutabilis,* which we did not look upon as a hibiscus at all but called "land lotus," the ixora, and the canna. Curiously enough, we never had oleanders. What passed as oleander or Karavi with us was a yellow, nectar-bearing, bell-shaped flower, to whose mildly poisonous fruit hysterical women bent on spiting their husbands by committing suicide sometimes had recourse. We, the children, loved all the flowers equally well. But our elders never thought much of any of the colored flowers except the red hibiscus which was indispensable for worshipping the goddess Kali. Even the sweet-smelling Bussora rose was out of court because it was looked upon as an Islamic flower. China had got accepted at our hands, but neither Iran nor Araby.

It was an essential part of our education to be able to weave garlands of three kinds of flowers—the jasmine, the Night-blooming Flower of Sadness, and the Bakul. We sat still with needlesful of thread pricking our way through the fine stalks of all these minute flowers. But when this task of infinite patience was over, we put the garlands round our neck for a few minutes and then tore them and threw them away on the ground to be trampled under foot. Our floors and inner courtyard in the summer were almost always strewn with the loose ends of garlands.

FROM "ENGLAND"
From "The English Scene"

However scrappy and simple our ideas of English life and society might have been, they could not exist at all without the accompaniment of some visual suggestion. Everything we read about the British Isles or in English evoked pictures of the external appearance of the country even when not avowedly descriptive. But we had plenty of verbal descriptions, and in addition to these we had pictures to go upon. [. . .]

Two colored pictures seen in a school text-book printed in England made a profound impression on me. One of them was the picture of a cricket match, showing not only the batsman, the wicket-keeper, and some of the fielders, but also the pavilions in the background. Cricket was our favorite game, and in Bengal at that time it had not been ousted in public affection by football. Football we also played, but we regarded it as a game on a rather plebeian level, while there was not the least room for doubt about the refinement and aristocratic attributes of cricket. An extra reason which inclined us to cricket was that one of its early pioneers in Bengal was a man from our district, who came of a wealthy family whose seat was a village only six or seven miles from Banagram. His full name was Sarada Ranjan Roy, but he was known in Calcutta and all over Bengal as Professor S. Roy, for he was a university teacher and ultimately rose to be the Principal of his college. He taught mathematics, but was a greater Sanskrit scholar, and in the department of sport he was a keen angler and a competent cricketer. It was from the shop run by him in Calcutta that we got our sports goods.

Years later, when I was at college in Calcutta and staying in a hostel run by the Oxford Mission, Father Prior (a descendant of the poet Prior), who was in charge of us, asked me one day if I had ever played any games. He had noticed that it was very difficult to make me play even badminton without dragging me out by main force, and that was the reason for his question. "Yes," I replied, "I used to play cricket when I was a boy." "You call that cricket, do you?" observed Father Prior very justly. But whatever might have been the quality of our cricket there was no dross in our enthusiasm. Our school team, composed of the teachers and the boys, was not quite despicable. We had some good players, and all the accessories—bats, balls, leg pads, gloves, stumps were by the best English makers. Some of the more fashionable boys even went into flannels. But our show, proud as we were of it, seemed to be reduced to total drabness by the side of the cricket world revealed in that colored picture. The game was transformed, it was cricket suffused with the colors of the rainbow.

The other picture was of a battleship which, so far as I can recall its outlines, seems to have been a ship of the 1895 *Majestic* class, or might have been even one of the 1901 *Formidable* class. Under this picture was the caption: "Hearts of Oak are our Ships, Hearts of Oak are our Men." The colored illustration fascinated me not only because I had an inborn liking for ships, but also because it gave me an impression of the seas being an appanage and projection of England. I could never think of England, as I thought of Bengal and of India, as a stretch of land alone. Combined visions of land and sea were always fleeting through my mind and before my eyes whenever I tried to think of England. Of only one other country in the world did I ever think in that way when I was a boy, and that was ancient Greece.

This characteristic vision of the physical aspect of England as half land

and half sea was confirmed in me by my reading of English poetry. The first piece of real English poetry which I heard was Colley Cibber's "O say what is that thing call'd light," read out to me by my brother from his text-book. But it was illustrated with a picture showing a blind Indian boy and therefore called up no associations of English life. English life proper struck me with the full force of its romance when about a year later I saw in my brother's new text-book, a woodcut showing a high cliff, at its foot the sea, at the edge of the narrow beach a boat, near the boat a boy and a girl, and above and below the picture the following eight lines:

"Break, break, break,
On thy cold gray stones, O Sea!
And I would that my tongue could utter
The thoughts that arise in me.

"O well for the fisherman's boy,
That he shouts with his sister at play!
O well for the sailor lad,
That he sings in his boat on the bay!"

I did not understand half of it, but to me the lines distilled a yearning to which not even the magic casement of Keats about which I read three or four years later could stir me.

I had a serious grievance against my brother. He was always having more interesting text-books than I had, and that was due to the fact that in my time a change had come over the theory of teaching English to Indian boys. Formerly, Indian boys were being taught English mostly from text-books meant for use in England, or from the English classics. But when I was young the educational authorities had had a sudden inspiration that it was too much of a burden for young Indian boys to have to cope with English ideas in an English background in addition to having to master the intricacies of a foreign language. In pursuance of this theory our English text-books were being Indianized as the administration of India was Indianized later. Thus it happened that while my brother read things like:

"O Brignall banks are wild and fair,
And Greta woods are green . . ."

or,

"Why weep ye by the tide, ladie?
Why weep ye by the tide?
I'll wed ye to my youngest son,
And ye shall be his bride . . ."

and also read fine stories from books like Andrew Lang's *Animal Story Book* and Kipling's *Jungle Book*, I was being forced to repeat:

"The fox sat on the mat"
"The dog is in the well"

—and at the next higher stage to read about three Mussalmans eating chilly and rice. I, however, tried to make amends by reading all my brother's text-books two years in advance of him, for in the school and by age he was two years my senior. I am still unconvinced that inflicting "fat cats sitting on mats" on little Indian boys is the best method of making them learn English.

English poetry was to me and to my brother, even before we could understand it fully, the most wonderful reading in the world. We read the usual things, Wordsworth's "Lucy Gray," "We are Seven," and "Daffodils," for example. We liked them, but we were too young to understand all their subtlety. The poem by Wordsworth which moved me most strongly at the time was "Upon Westminster Bridge." As I read:

"Earth has not anything to show more fair . . .
This City now doth, like a garment, wear
The beauty of the morning; silent, bare,
Ships, towers, domes, theatres, and temples lie
Open unto the fields, and to the sky;
All bright and glittering in the smokeless air."

—the heavenly light of dawn with its purity and peace seemed to descend on us.

There were two other poems which made an even greater impression on us and they were placed one above the other in Palgrave's *Children's Treasury*, which was one of my brother's text-books. The first of them was Shakespeare's "Full fathom five . . ." and the second Webster's "Call for the robin-redbreast and the wren. . . ." Again that juxtaposition of land and sea. The combination, as well as the contrast, was heightened in our mind by Palgrave's note in which Lamb was quoted, which we read very carefully without, however, taking in much beyond its general drift. But it was not necessary to understand more for the poems to set our imagination bestirring. What a magic country it was where the drowned were transformed into pearl and coral and where the robin and the wren covered the friendless bodies of unburied men with leaves and flowers, and the ant, the field-mouse, and the mole reared hillocks over them. Reading these lines of Webster, our hearts warmed up with a faith that could be described as the inverse of Rupert Brooke's. He was happy in the conviction that if he died in a distant land some part of that foreign soil would become forever England. We had a feeling that if we died in England what would become forever England would be a little foreign flesh, and with that faith there was happiness in perishing in an English glade, with the robin and the wren twittering overhead. But when we read the last two lines: "But keep the wolf far thence, that's foe to men, For with his nails he'll dig them up again," our boyish animalism got the better of us. Going on all fours on our earthen floor and stretching and spreading out our fingers as a cat stretches out and spreads its claws, we fell to scratching the ground.

If Webster's lines brought to us a very subtle realization of the quality of English land life, Campbell's "Ye Mariners of England" gave us a wholly straightforward initiation into the spirit of British maritime enterprise. We recited the simple lines, not with the half-perplexed, half-intuitive appreciation we had for the two poems by Shakespeare and Webster, but with great gusto and complete understanding. The climax of my own initiation into English seafaring life was reached when as a boy of eleven I read about the battle of Trafalgar and saw a colored picture of Nelson standing on the deck of the *Victory* with Hardy. Nelson's signal kept ringing within me and I shouted out time and again, "England expects every man to do his duty" (that was the form in which I first learned the signal). On one of those days I was coming up from the river towards the road in front of our house, shouting at the top of my voice "England expects every man to do his duty," when I saw some gentlemen passing along the road on an elephant. The most elderly gentleman had the elephant stopped and, leaning out, asked me who I was. I replied that I was

Upendra Babu's son. Then he asked me if I knew what those words were about. I said that they were Nelson's signal at Trafalgar. He seemed to be satisfied and went away on his elephant. I came to know later that he had spoken to my father about this meeting. It was my father who told me this.

From "The Englishman in the Flesh"

It must on no account be imagined that in regard to English life and the English spirit we were always floating in the empyrean. In actual fact, we were as ready to walk on earth, and more often descend to the underworld, as to soar up to heaven. Our ideas of the Englishman in the flesh were very different from our ideas of his civilization. To be quite frank, our ignorance of the one remained quite unrelieved by our knowledge of the other, and it is this difference which I am now going to illustrate.

The normal reaction of the unsophisticated Indian villager in the face of an Englishman is headlong flight. I and my elder brother, as young boys, jumped into a roadside ditch. We did not do so, however, from any ignoble motive of self-preservation, but to save a precious cargo which we were carrying and which we believed to be in danger from the Englishman. The plain story is this. I and my brother had been sent to buy some bananas from the bazaar and were returning with a bunch when we saw an Englishman coming up the road from the opposite direction. I have no clear recollection who exactly he was, but he may have been Mr. Stapleton, the Inspector of Schools, whom I met with greater self-confidence some years later. As soon as we caught sight of him we hid ourselves in the ditch, because we had been told that Englishmen were as fond of bananas as any monkey could be and that they swooned on the fruit wherever and whenever they saw it. So we crouched in the ditch among the nettles until the Englishman had passed. This incident took place when my brother was only learning his English alphabet and when his sole source of knowledge about Englishmen was oral tradition. I was guided wholly by his example. Thus our behavior on that occasion may be called behavior appropriate to a state of innocence untinctured by any taste of the fruit of knowledge.

But this monkey analogy had deeper and less innocent antecedents. In our time it was trotted out rather jocosely. None the less I heard an old teacher of ours asserting it in the class with accents, not only of conviction, but of passion, and declaring that the English race were of a she-monkey by a demon born. The prevalent attitude towards Englishmen of our people was one of irrational and ineradicable cringing and equally irrational and unconquerable hatred. Grown-ups reserved the first for the Englishman present before them and the second for the absent Englishman. Our great moral and intellectual leaders of the nineteenth century were perfectly aware of this weakness in their parishioners and tried to cure them of it. Bankim Chandra Chatterji has written a satirical piece on the Englishmen whose most sardonic and barbed point is reserved for his countrymen. A meeting of Englishmen is represented as a meeting of tigers, but the indigenes are shown as monkeys discreetly hiding themselves among the branches and leaves. When the tigers disperse, the monkeys swagger out and declare that they will now hold their meeting and abuse the tigers, and they do so. Finally, the meeting is closed with the observation from monkeys that after getting such a fusillade of bad language all the tigers must be dead in their lairs.

The remarkable similarity between the spirit of this satirical piece and the spirit of the passage about the *bandar log* in Kipling's story of Kaa's hunting has always intrigued me. Yet I can think of no explanation for it. Any possibility of borrowing on either side appears to be out of the question, for Bankim Chandra Chatterji died in the year in which *The Jungle Book* was published, and he had written the piece some years before his death, while Kipling could not have known anything about the Bengali skit since to my knowledge it has never been translated into English.

But the efforts of these manly and clear-sighted teachers of ours have been vain. The servility and malice ingrained in every fiber of our being which made us indulge in grotesque antics of alternating genuflexion and defiance before the Englishman persist to this day, and a most striking proof of this persistence was furnished by Mahatma Gandhi himself only one day before the announcement of the final British plan for transferring power to Indians, that is to say, on 2nd June 1947. After bestowing fulsome praise on Pandit Jawaharlal Nehru as the uncrowned king of India and emphasizing with what appeared like a licking of lips that he was a "Harrow boy," "Cambridge graduate," and "Barrister," Mahatma Gandhi went on to declare that "our future presidents will not be required to know English." The disappearance of the Englishman from the Indian political scene has not seen the end of this combination of servility and malice. Rather, as Mahatma Gandhi's pronouncement foreshadowed, the two-fold manifestation of homage and hatred has been transferred from the real to the imitation Englishman. I am thankful to my parents that they inculcated a saner outlook in their children and taught them, Indian gentlemen to be, to treat Englishmen as English gentlemen, no less, no more. But we could not help coming in contact with the debasing tradition.

JIBANANANDA DAS
1899–1954
(Bengali)

Jibanananda Das was born in Barisal, in what is now Bangladesh, into a family of modest means. His father was a schoolteacher, and his mother, Kusum Kumari, was a housewife who wrote poems. She passed her love of the word on to her son. His poetry, dark and sometimes biting, was filled with a melancholic sense of life's finitude, but through fragmented surfaces the longing for transcendence shines through. It is said that the poet was crushed by Tagore's response to the poems Das had sent him to read—it seemed to Tagore that the young man's work was marred by a singular lack of tranquility. There was little there of the exquisite equipoise Tagore valued so deeply. It was Jibanananda, however, who is credited with ushering the modern era into Bengali poetry. The lush pastoral landscape of the sonnets in the early composition Rupasi Bangla *(Bengal the Beautiful) gives way to the gritty, urban life of Kolkata with its streetcars and hydrants and anonymous lonely figures walking the streets. Yet even there, a cosmopolitan sensibility allows the speaker to reach out to distant lands he has never seen: China, Egypt, and the mythic Babylon. In an essay on poetry published in 1938 in the journal* Kavita, *Jibanananda wrote, "All are not poets, some are. And they who are, are so because in their hearts there is the autonomous substance of imagination. [. . .] In the rough and tumble of this disjointed world of man [. . .] the heart begins to glow like a candle and slowly the genius and faith of poetic creation becomes manifest." With Partition of India, the poet and his family moved to Kolkata, choosing to leave their ancestral home. This dislocation marked him deeply. He was often unable to find gainful employment. He struggled with an unhappy marriage and his own resolutely melancholic nature. In several poems the poet broods on death. In 1954, after a visit to the Calcutta Book Fair, Jibanananda Das was fatally struck by a tram car. It is not clear if he deliberately walked into the path of the oncoming car or if this was a tragic accident. Several of his poems were found after his death in notebooks and subsequently published. His works include* Banalata Sen *(1942),* Shreshtho Kobita *(Best Poems, 1954), and the posthumously published sonnet cycle* Rupasi Bangla *(composed in 1934, published in 1957).*

"The Professor"

With a wan smile I said:
"Why do you not with your own hand
Pen the poem?"—The shadow made no reply.
And small wonder, for he was no poet.
But only the timeless Prologue
Seated on a gilded throne
Of ink, Mss, and notes of his own.

No, no poet, only a toothless professor
Seeking eternity, drawing fifteen hundred a month
For picking to the bone fifteen hundred poets
Once living, but now altogether dead,
Scattering the flesh and the wriggling worms
To the four winds; though once they had sought
To warm their hands at the fire of life,
Felt pangs of hunger and of love,
And swum with sharks on the seas.

"Name Me a Word"

Name me a word
Great, simple, vast as the sky
A word that has, like the intimate hand
Of the woman I have loved forever,

Washed the dirty innards of history
And all its tired, wounded and dead
In blood; blood of the ones fed on
Food left out for hungry animals.

Like that starlit night stirred by the wind
Like that day agog with engine-driven wings
Of the bird that sees all the thirst of all birds
As the last pure flame of the dying candle.

"Poetry"

Knowing we have pristine joy
Implanted deep in our bones
We float along the dirty surfaces of time—
Or else all would be drained out.

And you sky, you were once
The flow of the dawn's stream
But now belong to the frozen seas on
Polar nights. Hence, neither the morning bird
Nor the dusky insect misreads the path of light.

The beggar, with female monkey
—Or lone goat—in tow,
Finds the answer to his question
In the still water held in his palm.

The bat sails out into the dark,
The eternity of the field asserts its power
Over the persistent rise of provincial grass;
The worn brick of the age-old grave
Discovers
The passion of the golden-eyed crickets for each other
As they lie amidst the unwanted reeds;

O sky
Once you were as the silent, frozen sea

Of the polar night
Now but the pale prospect
Of the river at dawn.

"The Windy Night"

The night was windy last night—and full of stars.
The whole night the wind played on the net over my head
Sometimes swelling it like the monsoon-tossed sea
Sometimes tearing it away from the bed
And wafting it away towards the stars.

At times—half-awake—I felt
The net was no longer overhead
It was flying like a white balloon over the blue sea past the stars.

All the dead stars had come to life last night—
There was no room in the sky to hold them all
I saw the faces of all the beloved dead among the stars
Stars shining in the dark like the dew-moist eyes of the
Love-laden kite upon the banyan tree;
The whole wide sky was glittering like a leopard-skin shawl
Flung across the shoulders of some Babylonian queen;
Such a marvelous night was last night.

Stars that had died many thousands of years ago
Peeped in through the window last night
Carrying with them each its own dead sky;
The damsels whom I had seen perish in Assyria, Egypt and Vidisha
Stood there, spear in hand, in rows across the misty edge of the
                                                                sky.

To conquer death? To celebrate the victory of life?
To raise awesome monuments to love?

I feel torn, crushed, dazed by the torment of the night;
Under the ceaseless widespread wings of the sky
The earth was brushed away like a fly

jibanananda das

And from the depths of the sky descended the wild winds
Screaming through my window
Like a thousand zebras in the flaming yellow steppes
Leaping to the roar of the lion.

My heart is filled with the smell of the green grass of the veld
Of the burning sun stretched across the endless fields
And with the hairy, wild, huge ecstasy of the darkness
Like the roar of the mating-mad lioness
And with the blue, tearing madness of living.

My heart tore itself from its moorings on earth
And flew like a swollen, drunken balloon across the blue sky
Like a distant star-mast flung across space,
Heady as an eagle.

R. K. NARAYAN

1906–2001

(English)

R. K. Narayan was born in Madras to a well-placed family. He lived most of his adult life in the princely city of Mysore. His father was the headmaster of a school, and as a child Narayan was able to spend a great deal of time in the library. His grandmother taught him reading and writing, in Tamil and Sanskrit, and mythology and classical literature, which he learned to love. In later life, Narayan edited and translated abridged versions of the two great Indian epics, the Mahabharata *and the* Ramayana. *There is a connection between his love of the classics and the imagined world of Malgudi that he created in several of his best-known novels. The powerful simplicity of the human passions is always apparent in what he writes, and the voice is driven by a clarity of purpose that reveals the intricate emotions of those who gather in houses and market places—a peopled world from which divinity is never exempt.*

In his memoir, My Days *(1973), he speaks of how the imaginary world of Malgudi entered his consciousness: "As I sat in a room nibbling my pen and wondering what to write, Malgudi with its little railway station swam into view, all ready-made." Graham Greene, who was a friend and mentor to Narayan, writes of how when closing a novel set in Malgudi, he immediately imagines who he might next meet from there, so vivid was that world. Narayan evokes the lives of his women characters with great empathy. In* The Dark Room *(1938), he writes of the days and nights of Savitri, a woman tormented by her unhappy marriage, the dark room where she seeks solitude and comfort, and how she tries to kill herself. In* The Guide *(1958), we see Rosie, torn between her husband and her lover, finally able to find the equipoise she needs in her own work as a classical dancer.*

The death of Narayan's beloved wife due to typhoid in 1939 left him depressed and unable to write for many years. In the work that followed this period, there is a darker tinge to the lives of the characters. Still, Narayan's humor often lightens what might otherwise take a tragic turn. He speaks of his youthful love of tragic endings: "I looked for books that would leave me crushed at the end." A book that fit the bill was Mrs. Henry Wood's East Lynne, which "left [him] shedding bitter tears." He was also deeply moved by his early reading of Charles Dickens, who he counted as a major influence. Narayan was a prolific writer of fiction, short stories, and essays. For many in the West, his work was a window into the previously dark and exotic world of India—his characters, with all the comical turns of their daily lives, were instantly recognizable as fellow human beings. His other important books include Swami and Friends *(1935)*, Malgudi Days *(1942)*, and The Painter of Signs *(1976)*.

From *My Days: A Memoir*

Being the headmaster's son, I had extraordinary privileges in the school library. During summer vacation the library clerk threw open the shelves at all hours, on all days, although he made it nearly impossible with his rules and his form-filling for an ordinary student to take any book home. He thought, perhaps, that he would earn a word of commendation from the headmaster for the privilege shown to his son, although I doubt if my father would have approved of any special treatment for us (my elder brother also obtained these facilities). On holidays, I spent the afternoons at the library, read all the magazines on the table, and had all the shelves opened. I took out four books at a time and read them at a stretch. A passage in one of our textbooks from Scott's *The Bride of Lammermoor* had whetted my taste for the mists of the Highlands and the drama and romance occurring in that haze. I read *The Bride of Lammermoor* and six other novels by Sir Walter, and relished the strong doses of love and hate that agitated the Highland clans. I admired Scott so much that I searched for his portrait and found one in a second-hand bookshop—a copper engraving as a frontispiece to a double-column edition in a microscopic type, containing three novels in one volume, with many illustrations that brought to life all those strong-willed men and forlorn women in their castle homes. After Scott I picked up a whole row of Dickens and loved his London and the queer personalities therein. Rider Haggard, Marie Corelli, Molière and Pope and Marlowe, Tolstoy, Thomas Hardy—an indiscriminate jumble; I read everything with utmost enjoyment.

I and my elder brother shared a room outside the main house but in the same compound, and there we competed with each other in reading. He read fast, noted in a diary his impressions of a book, and copied down passages that appealed to him. Sometimes, he read aloud a play—Shakespeare or Molière—and compelled me to set aside my own book and listen to his reading. For days on end we stayed at home and read, hardly aware of the seasons or the time passing. At eating time we would make a dash into the main house in which my parents and brothers lived, and returned by the back door to our room to resume our reading. We were in a world of our own. In addition to fiction, part of the time I enjoyed reading the history of English literature. A minor work on this, Long's *English Literature*, fell into my hands and I found it interesting right from the facsimile of Magna Carta in the frontispiece. It became my ambition in life to read at least two books from each literary period, starting with the Anglo-Normans. But it didn't work. Although Long's summaries of early literature were fascinating, I realized that the actual work in each case was unreadable. *Beowulf* I found baffling. Spenser confounded me. I could only begin from Ben Jonson, and allotted an hour a day for a methodical study of English literature. I imposed on myself a profound discipline and went through it heroically. At the end of sixty minutes, I returned to fiction with relief.

I loved tragic endings in novels. I looked for books that would leave me crushed at the end. Thus Mrs. Henry Wood's *East Lynne* left me shedding bitter tears, and I read it again and again. The heroine, the lady of a well-to-do family, committed adultery, ran away, was deserted by the seducer, was left for dead in a railway accident, but surviving it came to work as a menial in her own home, and looked after the children. Of course, she was not recognizable, her chief means of disguise being a pair of blue spectacles, so that her children and husband treated her as a servant throughout; when she was dying of "consumption" and coughing her misguided life out, she revealed herself in a harrowing manner. Reading and rereading it always produced a lump in my throat, and that was the most luxurious sadness you think of. I deliberately looked for stories in which the heroine wasted away in consumption (unless it was the sort of end that befell a lovely woman stooping to folly and finding too late that men betray). I found a lot of it in Dickens, but the most satisfying book in this category was *Passionate Friends* by H. G. Wells (though I cannot recollect if "consumption" ended the heroine's career, or strychnine). One book which I discovered with a whoop of joy was by Victoria Cross (Who was this? Never came across a second book by this author), in which the good lady dies of plague or cholera, leaving the man who loved her shattered and benumbed with grief for the rest of his life. Marie Corelli appealed to me most. I have recently tried to reread some of her books without much success, although one could still accept the synthetic atmosphere she could create of Norway, Egypt, or the English countryside. In a state of juvenile innocence, the mind absorbs the essence through all the dross. But at that stage of my literary searching I read about a dozen of her novels, and felt a regret at the end of each book that it was not longer than five hundred pages! Her overcharged romanticism and her pungent asides about English society and literary critics filled me with admiration. I cut out a portrait of her from *Bookman* and mounted it on my bookshelf.

My father utilized to the utmost all the library budget and any balance left over from other departments such as sports; the result was that the high-school reading-room had on its table magazines from every part of the world. Week-ends, when foreign mail arrived, were an exciting time. Magazines in brown wrappers were brought home straight from the post office in a mail-bag by a servant. They were opened and heaped up on my father's desk—every magazine from *Little Folks* to *Nineteenth Century and After* and *Cornhill*, published in London, was there. My father did not mind our taking away whatever we wanted to read—provided we put them back on his desk without spoiling them, as they had to be placed on the school's reading-room table on Monday morning. So our week-end reading was full and varied. We could dream over the advertisement pages in the *Boy's Own Paper* or the *Strand Magazine*. Through the *Strand* we made acquaintance of all English writers: Conan Doyle, Wodehouse, W. W. Jacobs, Arnold Bennett, and every English fiction-writer worth the name. The *Bookman* gave us glimpses of the doings of the literary figures of those days, the scene dominated by Shaw, Wells and Hardy. I knew precisely what they said or thought of each other, how much they earned in royalties, and what they were working on at any given moment. *Obiter dicta*, personal tit-bits about the writers and their world, the Chesterton-Belloc alliance against Shaw or someone else, the scintillating literary world of London was absorbing to watch. From our room, leaning on our pillows in obscure Bojjanna Lines of Mysore, we watched the literary personalities strutting about in London. Through *Harper's*, the *Atlantic*, and the *American Mercury*, we attained glimpses of the New World and its writers. [. . .]

After a month's stay at Bangalore, my uncle returned to Madras, persuading me to go with him and try my luck there. And so I was back in Purasawalkam. Our old house was still there, but much changed; my uncle (senior) was married and had many children. My grandmother was bed-ridden with cancer; and her garden and space had been parcelled and sold out to meet the expenses of running the house. My uncle had given up all lucrative activities on principle and was dedicated to bringing out a literary weekly to revive Tamil classics, and all his resources were utilized for it.

I was introduced to another character at Madras, who was planning to bring out a "Matrimonial Gazette." His editorial office was situated at an obscure and inaccessible spot in George Town. The man sitting at a desk cluttered with dusty bundles of paper straight away came to business. "I hear from your uncle that you want to be a writer. Good. But don't expect to become a millionaire in a day. Remember that the world is not waiting to read your stuff, whatever it may be. People have better things to do. But you must work hard and by sheer persistence, draw their attention to yourself—which means write, write and write." After this gratuitous advice, he made his offer. "At the moment, I have no notion what you write or how. But your uncle is a dear friend and I'll take his word." He paused to sweep aside the papers on his table and shouted through the window, "Hey, bring two colours immediately." And immediately on his table were placed by an urchin two bottles of some red aerated water fizzing and hissing like a cobra. "You must be thirsty, drink that *colour*. It's good." He set an example by tilting his head back and practically sucking the water out of the bottle, which he thrust between his lips. He put it down, belched loudly, pressed his nostrils with his fingers and said, "I want to start a magazine solely devoted to matrimonial themes. Marriage is the most serious situation everyone has to face sooner or later, and few give the subject enough thought. Many are the problems that arise before, during and after a marriage. Two strangers come together and have to live for the rest of their lives. Our journal will be devoted solely to this subject. We want jokes, stories, philosophies, and reflections all on this theme—of women who suffer, of men who are callous, and so on and so forth. You may write anything on these lines. Come back with some material as soon as you can and then we'll talk further." My head was in the clouds when I returned home that evening.

For the next three days, sitting beside my grandmother, I wrote and soon produced several pages of interesting anecdotes and a variety of imaginary stories centering around matrimonial life: about wife-beaters, husband-baiters, a live-and-let-live couple who faced some calamity, young runaways, elopers and elopees, and every kind of permutation and combination of man and woman. The tone, for some reason, emphasized misery—if not tragedy. It seemed so hard to find a happy couple in this world. Probably I felt that there was monotony in a contented, harmonious married life, nothing to write about. It was only a broken marriage or one at a breaking-point that offered literary material. I had no facility for typing and wrote everything in the best calligraphy I could manage, pinned the sheets neatly, wrapped them into a package, and carried them to the editor with no doubt that he would accept them with joy. My junior uncle, who was hardly at home but was in and out at certain specific hours for a wash or a change of dress, admonished me constantly, while passing, to write suitably and try and please the editor and forget all that damn-fool stuff about Malgudi and such things. So one day I took the literary package to George Town and placed it before the editor. He offered me a seat, and glanced through the sheets. I had managed to fill about thirty or forty pages. After studying them, he said, "You have a flair for writing, definitely, but you will have to understand our needs and aim at satisfying them. We should first take you as an apprentice in our office." (Suddenly he had switched on to the royal "we," although I did not notice a second person in the establishment.) "During the probationary period, you will not be paid. In fact we charge a fee, generally for training people. But in your case, I'll exempt you, being a nephew of my friend. I'll put you through every branch of the journal, and after three months, will consider paying you an honorarium commensurate with your aptitude."

"What about these?"

"Of course we will use them as and when we find an opportunity after editing them suitably."

"You will pay for them?" I asked timidly.

"Of course by and by, but not at present." I didn't understand what he meant. All that I could gather was that he was looking for a free assistant blackmailer, as I found that he was proposing to subtitle his publication *True Tales* (of matrimony) and needed a researcher in social life.

I had to drop this man and look for other possibilities. I offered samples of my writing to every kind of editor and publisher in the city of Madras. The general criticism was that my stories lacked "plot." There was no appreciation of my literary values, and I had nothing else to offer. *Malgudi* was inescapable as the sky overhead. "You have a command of the language, but . . ." was the almost routine statement made.

I stayed at Madras for three months during that year and pursued the editors of newspapers and magazines indefatigably. My junior uncle was at first wildly angry with me for letting down his matrimonial-gazette friend. But he still helped me to meet and talk to whomever he thought would be in my line, although most of them had only the English alphabet in common with me. Racehorse analysts, almanac-makers, film-writers, and so forth—most of them being my uncle's bar associates too. My senior uncle devoted most of his time to editing his literary weekly. He sat up all night in his attic (where I had once concealed myself) and wrote seventy-five per cent of the eight-page weekly himself under different pen names and in different styles, edited and rewrote others' contributions, corrected proofs, prepared copy, and studied voluminous ancient Tamil poetry. Also he conducted night schools for slum children, and left his desk for a couple of hours in the evening on this mission. A hard-working intellectual who spurned the idea of earning money but somehow carried on. He had, of course, discarded his old hobby of photography; his cumbrous camera lay gathering dust on the top of a shelf, along with many other discarded things.

I showed him some of my writing. He read them and said, "Good start, but you must study a lot more Shakespeare, for instance, and above all *Ramayana* by Kamban. Try to read his version, and try to understand it with the help of the commentaries you will find in my journal. You will profit by it. Your writing will gain seriousness and weight. There is no hurry to seek publication yet. Keep writing, but also keep reading . . ." I could not quite accept his advice. I was setting out to be a modern story-writer, and he tried to make me spend my time poring over tough old classics. I listened to his suggestion out of politeness but rejected it mentally.

He wore himself out trying to establish his journal, and was on his deathbed in 1938 from a damaged heart, after running the weekly for eight years single-handed. I was in Mysore at the time and was summoned by a telegram to Madras to his bedside at the General Hospital. He lived for a couple of hours after my arrival, but had clarity of mind and speech. He gave me an advice with his last breath: "Study Kamban's *Ramayana*." I said, "Yes, I will," out of consideration, but with no conviction that I would or could ever be interested in Kamban; we were poles apart. I was a realistic fiction-writer in English, and Tamil language or literature was not my concern. My third novel, *The Dark Room*, was just out in London; and when I was leaving Mysore, the postman had handed me an envelope from my press-cutting agency containing all the first reviews, which were most enthusiastic. There was no reason why I should now perform a literary atavism by studying Tamil. So I rejected his advice as being the fancy of a dying man. Strangely enough, three decades later, this advice, having lain dormant, was heeded. I had totally forgotten my half-hearted promise, but in 1968 I became interested in Kamban, spent three years in reading his 10,500 stanzas, and found it such a delightful experience that I felt impelled to write a prose narrative of the *Ramayana* based on Kamban as a second volume to a work of Indian mythology. Strangely, I had completely forgotten the words of my uncle, until Marshall Best, my editor at the Viking Press in New York, asked just before I left for India if I had anyone in mind to whom I wished to dedicate the book. We had completed all the editorial work on my manuscript, and it was ready to be sent off to the printer. I suddenly recollected my uncle's injunction. I wrote out the dedication and handed it to Marshall at Kennedy Airport, where he had come to see me off.

My free-lance efforts at Madras bore fruit to the extent that I was given a book to review. Its title was *Development of Maritime Laws in 17th-Century England*. A most unattractive book, but I struggled through its pages and wrote a brief note on it, and though not paid for, it afforded me the thrill of seeing my words in print for the first time. The same journal also accepted a short story and paid ten rupees less money-order charges. My first year's income from writing was thus about nine rupees and twelve annas (about a dollar and a quarter). In the second year there was a slight improvement, as *The Hindu* took a story and sent me eighteen rupees (less money-order charges); in the year following, a children's story brought me thirty rupees. I handed this cheque to my father and he was delighted. He remarked, "Your first and last cheque, I suppose!" I objected to his saying "last" and he at once apologized. "I don't know what made me say 'last.' Don't mind it."

VAIKOM MUHAMMAD BASHEER

1908–1994

(Malayalam)

Vaikom Muhammad Basheer was born into a Muslim family in the village of Thalayolaparambu in Kerala. A truly original writer, he fashioned the Malayalam vernacular into a pared down, polished medium where the sometimes absurd intricacies of ordinary life could find a place. In novellas, his favored form, voices flow with startling immediacy, laying bare the vividness of village life with its birds, beasts, and fruit trees. His writing, which sometimes displays a bitter wit, often reveals characters driven by a longing for love. Balyakaalasakhi *(*Childhood Sweetheart, *1944) brought him acclaim, and his work was translated into many languages. As a young man, Basheer was inspired by Mahatma Gandhi, who had traveled south to Kerala to spearhead the Vaikom Satyagraha, an attempt to open up the Hindu temple to Untouchables who were ritually barred entry. Basheer continued as a follower of Gandhi and suffered imprisonment twice at the hands of the British—the first time for distributing nationalist pamphlets and then again in 1942 when he took part in the Salt March. One of Basheer's celebrated novellas,* Mathilukal *(*Walls, *1965), is set in a men's prison and evokes the protagonist's longing for a woman who is herself imprisoned on the other side of the wall.*

In his early days Basheer wandered all over the country, doing odd jobs to make ends meet—working in a mill, as a hotel peon, proofreading, even doing bits and pieces of teaching. At first he published his work himself and would go door to door trying to sell his writing. Later, he set up a bookstall and sold books from there. Suffering intermittently from mental illness, he was hospitalized more than once and has written candidly about his struggles with depression and what he experienced as a terrible fragmentation of the psyche. His existential fictions are often based in details of his autobiography. Later in life he married and settled down to a quieter domestic life, enjoying great acclaim as a writer. Among his best known works are the stories "Ntupupapaakoraanaendaranu" ("Me Grandad 'ad an Elephant," 1951) and "Pathummayude Aadu" ("Pattumma's Goat," 1959). What follows is a prefatory comment by Basheer as he turns his acute, acerbic gaze onto his own fortunes as a writer.

From "Pattumma's Goat"

Some time ago I wrote a book with the title "Me Grandad 'ad an Elephant!" As soon as it came out in book form, two remarkable things happened. One, the Congress Government gave me five hundred rupees or something, saying that it was the best novel of those years. (Don't misunderstand this. It was not the Congress Government of Kerala, but of Madras.) The second remarkable thing was that the Communist Party criticised the book unmercifully, saying that it was against the ideals of communism. One of those who criticised it was the Finance Minister of the Kerala Communist administration, Mr Achuta Menon. After that, the book was awarded the M.P. Paul Prize. After that, it was selected by the Sahitya Akademi in New Delhi to be translated into fourteen or fifteen Indian languages. Although this has no great significance, the President of the Sahitya Akademi is Jawaharlal Nehru. Some time passed by like that and then the Communist Party came into power in Kerala. Whether to my good fortune or bad, "Me Grandad 'ad an Elephant!" was prescribed as one of the texts for non-detailed study in school examinations. (After the revered Parasuraman made Kerala, this is the first such incident. That is to say, an incident when a Muslim's book was accepted as a non-detailed text. It was the Communist Government that did it. So this must be taken a wee bit seriously. So conveniently forget all the other books that were accepted and oppose this one!) So opposition started.

Let me record a pitiable truth. I did not request anyone to accept this book for non-detailed study. As a matter of fact, I was opposed to it. I had even drafted a letter to exempt this book from being prescribed for non-detailed study, when the Government order came. The reason is that the price of the book has to be reduced by a rupee and a half. And 25 per cent commission goes to the Government. If I consented to this, the Government would take about seventy-five thousand copies. I did not feel like consenting. At two rupees it had gone into a seventh impression. Moreover, paper had become very expensive. I thought it would end in a loss. But it was at the insistence of Mr Karoor Nilakanta Pillai that I agreed to it and sent a favourable reply to the Government. It was the Sahitya Pravarthaka Co-operative Society, Kottayam, that published it from the beginning. I think this is the first co-operative society of its kind in the world. Anyway, it is definitely the first one in India. Mr Karoor Nilakanta Pillai is its Secretary. If you wish to know how many copies of this book were sold, you can ask either the honourable Communist Government, or Mr Karoor.

The book had to face opposition. Some friends told me that Catholics were going to oppose it. I do not know what the reason is for the opposition. Anyway, everybody opposed it—the Catholic Congress, Praja Socialist Party, Congress, Muslim League. If what I saw in the papers is true, they all told me plenty of lies about it. I am an old Congressman, a dutiful soldier who has taken a lot of beatings and punchings and gone to jail several times. When I hear talk of Congress, I think of Mahatma Gandhi, Indian Independence and the like. Congress, which is supposed to represent non-violence and truth, need not have stooped so low. I read in the papers that the Congress members in the Assembly said that the book sold for eight annas. The Indian Congress need not have told that white lie. I mentioned above that the book was published by the Sahitya Pravarthaka Co-operative Society. They have given me royalties on a price of two rupees a copy for all of the seven impressions. Messrs Karoor Nilakanta Pillai, Vettoor Raman Nair, P. Kesava Dev and others—writers and members of the S.P. Co-operative Society—who know more about books as regards price and so on, made statements. I do not intend to quote them here. It is unfortunate that people think that, just because they get a few more votes than somebody else, they know everything.

I see it in the papers that the opposition made me a Communist Party member. Great! I also see that, according to the opposition, this book will bring me four lakhs of rupees. Come to think about it, why do I need so much money? The opposition is requesting the Communist Government to consult with the Sahitya Pravarthaka Co-operative Society which published the book, and then give them the amount they spent on it, give me about fifty thousand rupees and give the opposition the remaining three and half lakhs or more. Long live the opposition!

"Oh Creator of the World! They know not what they do; forgive them!"

I completed the story "Pattumma's Goat" on 27th April, 1954. I thought I would copy it out and publish it with an introduction. Days passed by as I kept putting it off till tomorrow.

Five years!

Up to now I have not copied out the story. Almost all that I have published before this, I have written and rewritten more than once. This is coming out without being copied, without any corrections, just as I wrote it. I read it through and did not feel it should be corrected or copied. It is a gay story. Still, when I wrote it, I was burning all over. I must forget the pain of the past. Write! So the mind. . . .

Yes . . . at that time my mind . . . like a tiny island that is starting to sink into a bottomless ocean. . . . I don't know whether that makes any sense or not. Anyway, the mind gets drowned in darkness filled with frightful dreams. I myself am the mind. When I look up, there is only a small patch of light. In darkness and in light. . . . Oh God! Where am I? What is true? What is false? Light! . . . Light. . . . I want only light. But, . . . darkness filled with terrible dreams . . . is approaching from all the eight directions, roaring and booming.

Will I drown in this for ever?

No! I won't let my life be thrown into disarray. I must get well! I must get well! Gathering all the strength I have, I must make a powerful effort!

Goodness. Keep the attention only on that! Concentration! . . . Let it be kept on that . . . that pinpoint. The mind . . . the mind . . . is breaking up into hundreds of thousands of pieces of darkness. . . . In each of those pieces . . . what is it that I see and hear?

Don't lose your reason; find out the cause. Everything has a cause. Courage . . . courage to try to find out. Superstition is comfortable. If you take refuge in that . . . ! This is nothing like that. All the beliefs you now have—from childhood . . . from days gone by . . . from before history began—analyse them all, and accept only what is good. Evil is a sickness. If you treat it, you can cure it. There is no sickness that you cannot cure. If you think there is one, it is through ignorance; never make ignorance a permanent abode.

When you think properly, what actually is wrong here?

Nothing. Turbulent thoughts. Sleepless nights. Hard-working days. I loathed the days, the nights, the work, the place and everything. No food, no sleep; just dreams. Nothing but fear!

What happened? Hopeless heartache. Talking incoherently. That is how I came under the treatment of Mr P.C. Govindan Nair. I was taken to Trichur in a car belonging to Kuttappan Nair, owner of the Krishnan Nair Watch Company, Ernakulam. It was Kuttappan Nair who was driving. In the car were artist Raghavan Nair, editor of "Narmada," Mr M.P. Krishna Pillai, owner of the M.P. Studio, and Mr Perunna Thomas. You must remember that Vaidyaratnam P.C. Govindan Nair is a specialist in madness and related sicknesses. When I arrived at my destination, there were about thirty mad people there. They were in different stages, some in chains, some handcuffed. I think everyone was following the same treatment. I shall tell you about mine.

After bed coffee, I go to the latrine. After that, as soon as I get back from washing my hands, feet and face, they put some oil on my head. It is very cooling. (I have heard that Mr Perunna Thomas had this oil on his head and slept for three days or something like that.) He is staying with me to look after me. There are others, too, to look after me. Mr K. Parameswaran Nair, Mr M.M. Khadar and Mr Paremmal Vasudevan. Mr Parameswaran Nair runs the Shobhana Studios of Trichur. He is a very good photographer. He is also an actor and an art director. I call him Paramu. The only person who read the manuscript of this book is Paramu. In those days, his main occupation was to write letters. I would dictate; and Paramu would write. I used to write to all the people with whom I had even the slightest acquaintance. I used to dictate all those letters just to forget my heartache. Later it was introductions to books. That was how I came to write the introductions to the two books, "Hunger" and "Life's shadows." During those days many interesting incidents took place. It was arranged that Mr Perunna Thomas would write down whatever I said or did from the time I got up to the time I went to bed. He was given a big fat notebook for the purpose. I spent ten or twelve days reading it. Then I tore it into small pieces and burnt it. I have told Paramu many funny stories. I remember them all very well even now. I had thought of including all that in this introduction. Let me digress a little. Any sickness can be cured. But for that, medicine alone is not enough. The patient must have the will, too. I had a hundred percent will. I do not have time now to write all the details in this introduction. (Didn't I tell you I was going through the turmoil of getting a house built. Moreover, I have been promoted to the rank of husband. My wife's name is Fatimabi. She is the eldest daughter of Koyakutti, a teacher from Cheruvannore, near Calicut. I call her Fabi. I have narrated all the interesting incidents of my sickness to Fabi. When I have time, I shall set it all down on paper.) So we were talking about the oil. It is very cooling. Suppose twelve elephants ran amok. It is said that if you put some of this oil on the head of one of them, all twelve will go to sleep! They put that on my head. Then they pour some sort of potion into my mouth. To get the full effect of the oil, I sit like that for half an hour. After that there is the medicinal bath. That, too, is cooling. I lie on my back on a bench. The medicinal bath will go on for at least an hour. It is after this that two famous treatments come.

I am lying on my back.

I can hear voices. Birds are chirping. I can hear motor horns. (Because it is near the national highway.) The sun is shining brightly. Meanwhile, a cone made from a jackleaf is put into one of my nostrils. Then they pour about three ounces of liquid into it. I start to get a powerful burning sensation. Wow! Does it burn! The liquid in the right nostril explodes like an atom bomb and jumps out with a bang through the left nostril. By that time the sun has burnt out; there is no sound of people, birds or cars. The world is silent. Earth alone is left. By this time, they have put the cone into my left nostril and also poured the medicine into it. Wow! It really burns. With a crash and bang the earth has been shattered into pieces.

In actual fact, of course, nothing has happened in the world. All the uproar took place inside my head. Just because I can see properly, they have put some salve on my eyes. Something that is a thousand times stronger and that burns a thousand times more than what was poured into the nose, is put into my eyes. Wham! I can't see. Some kind person leads me by the hand and sits me beside a big copper pot. Then starts the bath. Wait! It isn't just a bath, but a continuous pouring of water. That is to say, some-one pours ice-cold water on my head. Anybody will start shivering within ten minutes. But this will go on for at least an hour. Luckily, by that time I can open my eyes. Yet that burning and fuming have not gone completely.

All this that I have just described will be repeated at four o'clock. In between I get potion, pills, medicinal ghee, and such-like. The most interesting part of the treatment is what is done in the nose and the eyes. Within a few days I reduced the potency of the salve. This is how I did it: as soon as they put the salve on the eyes, I would open both of them. It is as if I said with all the courage and strength I could muster, "Let's see who wins!" I would keep my eyes open. If air gets in for a minute, then it isn't too bad. For that one minute you must have strength and courage. That's all. During those days and even after that, I used to insist on rubbing salve on the eyes of all those who came to see me. I give the names of those whom I remember. Against the names of those I am doubtful about I have written "doubtful" in brackets. If they let me know, in the next edition I'll remove the brackets and the doubt, and, if they want, the name also.

K. PARAMESWARAN NAIR
PAREMMAL VASUDEVAN
PERUNNA THOMAS
M.A. KHADAR
GOVINDANATHA PANIKKAR
R.S. PRABHU
S. SANKARAN (AIYAR)
SATYAN *ex-police inspector & film star*
RAMU KARIAT
A.C. GEORGE
K.A. JABBAR
S.K. POTTEKKATT

TIKKODIYAN

P. BHASKARAN

N.V. KRISHNA WARRIOR (*doubtful*)

V. ABDULLA

M. ABDURAHIMAN

M.V. DEVAN (*doubtful*)

M.P. KRISHNA PILLAI

P.K. BALAKRISHNAN

D.M. POTTEKAT

K.A. RAJAN

KOCHAPPAN

JOSEPH MUNDASSERY (*doubtful*)

PONJIKKARA RAFI

VAYALAR RAMA VARMA

M. GOVINDANN (*doubtful*)

BHASKARAN NAIR, N.K.

K.K. THOMAS, B.A., B.L.

PONKUNNAM VARKEY (*doubtful*)

FABI BASHEER (*doubtful*)

In addition to these I have also put salve on the eyes of some women. Now that I am married, I have forgotten their names. No matter how hard I try, I cannot remember them! Satis verborum!

It was during this period of treatment that I wrote the story "Pattumma's Goat." When I got tired after writing for about an hour, I would go and interview some of the mad people. There was one madman, Padmanathan by name, who used to be with me like my beloved disciple. He used to call me "Swamiji." He believed that I was a brahmin. He used to bring a pot of clean water and sprinkle my room with it to purify it. He even purified the path I walked on. He was a Sanskrit pandit. He recited a lot of Sanskrit slokas to me. Meanwhile, he would drink the tea that I had sipped at and he would smoke the beedi that I had puffed at. There have been two religious teachers with the name Shankara. He would talk to me about both of them. Then he would ask which of the two I was. I would say, "My name is Vaikom Muhammad Basheer. I am a heathen!" He would ask, "Swamiji, why do you hide?" Because he was rather afraid of salve, I would say, "Let's put a little salve on our eyes." Immediately he would go to purify another room.

Another was always silent. He was a Christian. I think he was a Catholic. It was after I had tried for many days that he talked to me. Usually, after the treatment at four o'clock, he would go to the verandah on the eastern side, turn west and laugh twice. Then he would light a beedi and come away. When we became friends, this chap told me the secret of his life. I asked him, "What was your job?"

"Soldier," he said. "Five years ago I died in Syria."

"And then?" I asked.

"Now God has sent me down to Earth."

I did not ask him why. Another one was a fat madman who had only one wish in life—to eat an elephant!

I said to him, "Me grandad 'ad an elephant!"

"Did anyone eat it?"

"No," I said. "He is walking around outside."

"Is it possible to catch him?"

"I don't know," I said.

There are many funny stories like this to write. But there is no time. One thing I must say, before I let loose "Pattumma's Goat." Last November three gentlemen, by name V. Abdulla, M. Abdurahiman and Tikkodiyan, had come to Thalayolaparambu from Calicut. They wanted to make the novel "Me Grandad 'ad an Elephant!" into a play. They wanted to give the first performance for the Kerala Arts Festival. There was no time for delay.

Right.

I went along with them to Calicut, made it into a play, and their performance was first-rate. The play was a success. I did not go to see it, for I was spending my honeymoon at "Chandrakantam," Mr S.K. Pottekkatt's house in Pudiyara, after marrying Fabi.

I shall now bring this introduction to a close. "Pattumma's Goat" is not just a story. All the characters in it are still living, by the grace of God; I mentioned before that it is five years since I wrote it. Many new characters have come into being since then. You must remember that this is the story of my family. When I wrote the story, I purposely omitted some of the things in this introduction. Reminding you of that, I am letting loose Pattumma's goat before you.

Best wishes.

VAIKOM MUHAMMAD BASHEER
Thalayolaparambu
1st March
1959

RAJA RAO

1908–2006

(English)

Raja Rao was born into a Kannada-speaking family in the small town of Hasan in what is now Karnataka, South India. From early on the boy, whose mother tongue was Kannada, revealed himself to be a writer. In a memoir piece he writes of how in the small school in Hyderabad where he was sent to study, he quickly picked up English models for writing. His first novel, Kanthapura *(1938), published when he was only thirty—composed some years earlier while he was a student in Montpellier—uses the narrative structure of folk tales where myth and actuality mingle. At the heart of the novel is the narrator, an old woman born and brought up in the village who in a clear, lyric voice tells the story of a Mahatma, clearly modeled on Gandhi, and the turbulence that comes in his wake. In his foreword to the novel, Raja Rao evokes the notion of* sthala-purana, *the mythology of place out of which forms of life emerge. In the same foreword he writes, "The telling has not been easy. One has to convey in a language that is not one's own the spirit that is one's own." But English, he continues, far from being alien, "is the language of our intellectual make-up—like Sanskrit or Persian was before—but not of our emotional make-up." What can this mean? It means for Raja Rao that the language he uses bends and turns to the undertow of both Sanskrit and Kannada. To add to this complexity, it was in the crucible of French literary culture that he started to perfect his literary language, a finely sculpted English that he was able to craft only after he plunged early into writing in his mother-tongue, Kannada —a "holy dip" that returned him refreshed to the English language.*

In the years before Indian independence, Raja Rao was active in the Quit India movement and served as a coeditor, with Ahmed Ali, of a nationalist magazine. His travels continued back and forth to France, and then to the United States where he settled in Texas. His major novel, Serpent and the Rope *(1960), is a tour de force of lyric inventiveness, braiding together history and mythology, India and Europe in the narrative of an Indian husband and a French wife, each searching for the mystical meaning hidden in the twists and turns of everyday life. The title of the novel plays on the philosophical conundrum prevalent in Indian epistemology, concerning the nature of the real. Raja Rao was able to achieve a lyrical clarity of language even as the metaphysical and the erotic blur into each other in the consciousness of his characters, and landscapes of ancient myth come alive in elegant gestures reminiscent of sculptural friezes. The great Polish poet Czeslaw Milosz dedicated a poem to Raja Rao (one of the few that Milosz wrote in English). Milosz's poem, which is simply called "To Raja Rao," was composed in Berkeley in 1969. It evokes the tensions of a life lived among continents, cities, civilizations, languages, the crucible out of which each writer forged his art:*

> *I learned at last to say: this is my home,*
> *here, before the glowing coal of ocean sunsets,*
> *on the shore which faces the shores of your Asia,*
> *in a great republic, moderately corrupt.*

Raja Rao's other works include The Cat and Shakespeare: A Tale of India *(1965),* Comrade Kirillov *(1976), and* The Chessmaster and His Moves *(1988). In 1988, he was awarded the Neustadt International Prize for Literature.*

"Entering the Literary World"

✦

I was born in a dharmashala, room number 1, in (the town) Beautiful, Hassana, whose goddess, the Lady Beautiful, Hāssanakkammā, saw her devotees only once a year, and again for just nine days, while an ancient worshipper, that lone and cursed girl, because she never did come on appointed time, became a rounded long stone, and you can still see where she started from and where she now is, there, in the large courtyard of the temple, for she goes but the pace of a rice-grain, one rice-grain step a year, so that when she finally reaches the sacred Feet of the Lady Beautiful, not only this town but the whole world will be dissolved, till, when the waters have stayed quiet for Brahmā's requisite aeons (432,000,000 man years) and the karma of the world, lying asleep for all this while, curled deep under the waters, will wake again, and the world will revolve in its own rhythm, and man and beast will go their conditioned way, and the Goddess Beautiful too will emerge from the earth, and the accursed girl also will, no doubt, go a single rice-step a year, till the world dissolves once more—unless one goes beyond the real, the mental, the essential, that is, beyond cause and effect, and this one, he, he will have, as you well know, neither birth nor death.

I heard all this, not that I understood it, when I was a boy four or five years of age, from my grandfather, a convinced Vedāntin (from a family that can boast of having been Vedāntins at least since the thirteenth century, and again brahmin advisers to kings, first in Rajputana, another thousand years earlier, and yet again brahmins to other kings, maybe the Greco-Indian ones in Gandhara, earlier yet—at least such our mythical genealogy tells us)—and my grandfather taught me *Amara*, that wonderful thesaurus which, like a grave and good brahmin boy, I had to learn by heart, and thus never have to ask who the Two-mothered One is, of course he is Gaṇeśa, or Kārttikeya, his brother, who is of course Commander-in-chief of all the armies, et cetera. Life would not be worthwhile if you did not know which God was what, and if you will not have understood that Śiva is so awesome, you could see him only between the two ears of his vehicle, the bull, such as I did every evening at our family temple while the women chanted hymns to Pārvatī, his bride, so richly adorned in gold, silk, sapphire, ruby, gifts that came from generation after generation of the family. Some kings of Mysore had given us privileges (for carrying the Royal Post, and also collecting the fee when a concubine girl first "tied on her bells") and thus the lands we had, while the Maharaja of Mysore, when he came to Hassana, had perforce to stop first in front of the Post Office House, which now explains why my mother, not finding enough room in our ancestral home for lying-in, had to be transported to the dharmashala, room number 1, and hence when my father was offering the prescribed "half-cut lemon on the knife" to His Highness (and this was Krishna Raja Wodeyar, the Vedantin-king), my mother was so vitally shaken she threw me into the world, hence instead of being named Ramakrishna, like my grandfather was, I was simply called Raja.

Now then, I had also to be educated in the modern manner, consequently every summer (duly accompanied) I started going to my father who was in Hyderabad, five hundred long miles away—and Hyderabad, because one of my grand-uncles (I should not even talk loudly of it), a handsome man, loved a beautiful concubine, and to give her joy pilfered bits of royal money from the local treasury of which he was the guardian; therefore with the help of my grandmother who gave him some of her own jewels, he slipped out of Mysore State before the Law came to his door, and being handsome and very clever, he became Prime Minister in a neighbouring state, where again, having seduced the queen, and followed by the wrath of the king, my grand-uncle, as courageous as he was handsome, escaped on his white charger, followed by his brave Sikh bodyguard (who, the family says, slew ten soldiers before my grand-uncle was across the river and safe)—and thus on to Hyderabad, where he became a lawyer, and an adviser to many of the Hyderabad rich, so that my father came to him to stay with and to study, and I went of course in the wake of my father.

And this was how a South Indian brahmin boy entered the Madrasa-e-Aliya, a school meant mainly for Muslim noblemen, the only Hindu in my class. But when summer rose, and the heat began blinking on the black boulders of Hyderabad, the family took the long trip back from the city of Lakṣmī (for the real name of Hyderabad is Bhagyanagar, "City of Riches") to the town of the Lady Beautiful. And from there we went further still by bullock cart to the Malnad hills, where amidst rice fields and coffee plantations, we lived under the protection of Goddess Kenchammā, on the bank of the virgin Hemavathy. And when summer ended, we came by bullock cart to Hassana, and by horse cab to Arasikere, where we took the metre-gauge express to Bangalore, and again after a night here, the train took us down the ghāts, and then on to the parched and cotton lands of Andhra, while the broad-gauge rains, going so fast and looking so big, took us to Wadi, and here we changed trains again in the middle of the night, and by morning we saw the dust and the minarets of Hyderabad. And I would now go back to my Madrasa-e-Aliya, whose headmaster was a burly Englishman called Durand, but above him was the great principal,

Kenneth Burnet, so mysterious, and, for an Englishman, riding a bicycle! I was to learn later that he had to divorce his wife, and with two or three sons at school, he could not afford more than this green BSA. When my father, who was teaching English under him, bought me a bicycle, Burnet was surprised. "Oh, and I cannot even buy one for my sons," said Burnet. But I was mighty proud of my shining slick machine of locomotion.

Though the Goddess Lakṣmī was so generous to us in Hyderabad, and the school kind (for the children of Hyderabad nawabs were well groomed and intriguing, but not really interested in studies—there was too much palace gossip to be serious with books and teachers), I developed some chest trouble, and the doctors asked me to go back to my home-mountains, where I went, and this time to my sister, to that hallowed place of pilgrimage, Nanjangud, on the river Kapila—I lived just behind the temple, among priestly brahmins, I a student of Durand (who taught us *The Prisoner of Zenda*) and Burnet, who, later, taught us Aristotle. And such the play of karma that in the Mysore city library, which still stands there, yellow, bright yellow and long—I discovered (in the Indian *Who's Who*) the address of an English friend of our family, Eric Dickinson, a minor poet, and from Oxford, who taught English at Aligarh, and had come to India because he was a good friend of my cousin Shama Rao (a theosophical discovery of Mrs. Annie Besant, this cousin an adept for the apostle to be). Shama Rao went to Oxford to study, but died there of the Spanish flu. Thus from Oxford, Dickinson, in memory of Shama Rao, came a pilgrim to India, and I having started to write, naturally, to him I sent my first pieces. But since the doctor again advised I should go as far away as possible from the sea, and also, because I was interested in writing—my karma, or certainly more august forces, took me to Aligarh and to the Muslim University. There I was once more a student in an Islamic institution (my karma had certainly something to do with my Muslim connections), and here it was from Dickinson I first heard of Aries and Avignon, of Michelangelo and of Santayana. Poor Mr. Burnet must have known only Kent (from where he came, I think) and Oxford, and maybe he'd seen Flanders during those terrible war years (1914–18), though I never really knew. Jack Hill from Oxford taught me French in Aligarh— we were both staying with Dickinson—and later when I went back to Hyderabad, I continued to be involved with literature till one day, a letter came in a blue envelope (I still remember) from Sir Patrick Geddes, who said he had established an international college at Montpellier, and since he liked what little he'd seen of my writing, "So, why not come?" The government of Hyderabad and good Burnet were duly impressed with this exalted invitation, and as such with their blessings and money, straight I went to Montpellier, that ancient Greek and Saracenic town, so close to Sète where Valéry was born, and Béziers where there are still charred walls (so they said) at the place the Albigensians were burnt by the Pope's helots.

And France was so much like India, formal, friendly, and full of the *beaux désordres*—the Indian *désordres* were not even *beaux*. I was impressed too by the self-reflectiveness of the French language, by its severe musicality while I continued to read (alas!) Tagore and W. B. Yeats, bad influences for a young man of nineteen. But I had met Camille by then, and we were to marry soon, and she and her ardour for precision and for structure (*la méthode*, after all) brought me many tears—she did not think my Tagore-Yeats English (with some Macaulay added to it) was at all literary. Now I went back to my Kannada, wrote a few things in my classic native tongue and published them in *Jaya Karnataka*, a literary monthly, and emerged out of this holy dip a new man, with a more vigorous and, maybe, a more authentic style. I later read Frank O'Connor and Sean O'Faolain, introduced to me by that perspicacious Irish poet Padraic Colum, whom I had met in Paris, and he even came to visit us in Soissons, where Camille taught Racine and Voltaire at the Collège de Jeunes, while every morning I sat down seriously to write. My first stories, "Javni" and "The Little Gram Shop," were written in Soissons, a medieval town where Abélard was imprisoned and condemned, where Jeanne d'Arc convinced the Dauphin he should be crowned, at Rheims, King of France, and where, much later again, the Germans and the French fought one another across the Aisne for four ghastly years. I lived thus with France, and France gave me back my India.

A South Indian brahmin, nineteen, spoon-fed on English, with just enough Sanskrit to know I knew so little, with an indiscrete education in Kannada, my mother tongue, the French literary scene overpowered me. If I wanted to write, the problem was, what should be the appropriate language of expression, and what my structural models—Sanskrit contained the vastest riches of any, both in terms of style and word-wealth, and the most natural to my needs, yet it was beyond my competence to use. To marry Sanskrit and Gide in Kannada, and go further, would have demanded an immense stretch of time, and I was despairingly impatient. French, only next to Sanskrit, seemed the language most befitting my demands, but then it's like a harp (or vina); its delicacy needed an excellence of instinct and knowledge that seemed well-nigh terrifying. English remained the one language, with its great tradition (if only of Shakespeare) and its unexplored riches, capable of catalysing my impulses, and giving them a near-native sound and structure. "We cannot write like the English. We should not," I was to write in the preface to *Kanthapura*. "We cannot write only as Indians. We have grown to look at the large world as part of us. Our method of expression therefore has to be a dialect which will some day prove to be as distinctive and colorful as the Irish or the American. Time alone will justify it." I will have to write *my* English, yet English after all—and how soon we forget this—is an Indo-Aryan tongue. Thus to stretch the English idiom to suit my needs seemed heroic enough for my urgentmost demands. The Irish, remember, had done it, not only with Yeats, but again with Frank O'Connor and Sean O'Faolain. Further, Joyce had broken in, as it were, from the side-wings, giving us sound and symbol structures that seemed made for almost the unsayable. So why not Sanskritic (or if you will, Indian) English?

In such a world of linguistic ferment, at that time there were also going on experiments with form. Kafka had broken the crust of realism and given fabled meanings to man's fears. The Surrealists having abolished the natural as the concrete gave earth wings upwards, and even more, bore blindfold downwards into subterranean fires. And suddenly Malraux burst in on the scene, upsetting all intellectual stratagems, and giving the world an international dialect or, as it were, pure gesture and metaphysic meaning. For an Indian therefore who wanted to forget Tagore (but not Gandhi), to integrate the Sanskrit tradition with contemporary intellectual heroism seemed a noble experiment to undertake. Thus both in terms of language and of structure, I had to find my way, whatever the results. And I continued the adventure in lone desperation.

When I published my first stories in *Europe* in Camille's fine translations, Romain Rolland and Stefan Zweig wrote enthusiastic letters to me about them. And *Kanthapura*, my first novel, was mostly written in a thirteenth-century castle of the Dauphiné in the heart of the Alps, and when it came out, E. M. Forster spoke so boldly of my rigour of style and structure, I had, so to say, entered the literary world.

LALITHAMBIKA ANTHERJANAM

1909–1987

(Malayalam)

Lalithambika Antherjanam was born into a Namboodiri Brahmin family in Kerala. An important Malayalam writer, she started as a poet, and the lyrical vein is clearly present in her evocations of the pastoral landscape. However, she quickly turned to short stories, which afforded a more muscular form, better suited to the social critique that animates all her work. She was profoundly shaped both by Gandhi's nonviolent movement and by the writings of Rabindranath Tagore. She speaks of how at the age of fifteen, after her father presented her with a copy of Tagore's Home and the World, *she quickly wrote a novel that she then kept hidden in a box. The teenager was struck by the figure of Bimala that Tagore had created, a woman torn between the safety of home and husband and desire for the restless, fiery Sandeep, a nationalist leader. In 1976, Antherjanam published her novel* Agnisakshi (Trial by Fire). *In the novel we find the rebellious figure of Tatri, a Brahmin woman cast out, her body "explosive" at the heart of a "great silence." In the memoir piece "Balyasmriti" ("Childhood Memories"), the writer evokes the great house (*tarawad*) into which she was born and the protection her father's progressive views afforded her. The child learned to write by dipping an ostrich feather into ink she prepared with kadakka nuts, copper sulfate, and petals of the hibiscus. But over the child hovered the "death" that puberty would bring on, seclusion in the* antahpuram, *the women's quarters. The two years before marriage that she was forced to spend in seclusion enforced a painful education. She writes of the "unfortunate souls" she encountered. Time and again in her fiction we* *hear the voices of women, filled with desire for a full life in the shared world but cast aside because of widowhood or some minor contravention of social decorum. There is a poignant connection with the younger writer Kamala Das. Antherjanam tells us that even as her own mother lay dying, she herself was immersed in reading Das's memoir* Ende Katha *(*My Story*), a work that bears witness to the younger writer's struggle for freedom from the psychic and sexual constraints imposed on women by strict societal codes. Antherjanam is an important figure in the evolving landscape of women's writing in India. Her other works include* Moodupadathil *(*The Folds of Seclusion, *1946),* Agnipushpangal *(1960), and* Atmakathakkoru Ammukham *(1979).*

"Childhood Memories"

CHILDHOOD

My very first memory of early childhood is of the sounds I used to hear when I woke up in the morning: the chime of holy bells blending with the chants. I usually lay in bed for some time and listened. When I rose and came out, the *nalukettu* was always enveloped in the smoke of the Ganapathi *homam*. The fragrance of tulasi and sandalwood and of foods prepared for the *naivedyam* would waft out of the thevarappura.

Amma rose very early in the mornings. She would have had a bath and begun the rituals of worship and the preparations for breakfast by the time I awoke. Many of the children would have had their baths. Because it was such a huge extended family, there was a certain lack of order in the routine of the household. But none of us were allowed to have breakfast till we had had a bath and said our prayers. I usually ran to the tank on the eastern side of the house, had a dip in it, dried myself rapidly, and rushed back. As a child of five or six, all I wore was a *konam* made of the spathe of a palm leaf or red cloth. I first went to the temple, then worshipped all the household deities and prostrated before them. After this I ate my share of the offerings: the milky sweet made for the worship that day, malar, *trimadhuram*, and slivers of coconut. Then came breakfast, for which I had hot *kanji* with ghee and roasted pappadams.

In the mornings we had lessons with a teacher. All we took to class were a quill pen and a few sheets of paper. Pens with nibs were not very common in those days. We wrote with sharpened ostrich feathers, and made our own ink. We pounded kadukka nuts, mixed copper sulphate into it, added water, and left it in the sun in a frying pan. Sometimes we put in hibiscus flowers to improve the consistency. When the mixture had been sunned for four or five days and grown thick, we strained it and stored it in bottles.

We sat on the floor and wrote on little low desks, which had drawers in them to hold pens and ink. Writing in copybooks was a strict requirement. We began with a lesson in Sanskrit. After that we studied the government textbooks of the period. They were chosen for us according to the class we were suited for. We did arithmetic, geography, and history. In the afternoon, we were free for an hour and started lessons again after lunch only at three. We continued until the sun set. The music teacher came occasionally, in the morning or the evening.

At dusk we said our prayers again. Achan sat with us after dinner, while we read the Puranams. All this left me very little free time. However, we managed to escape the watchful eyes of the grown-ups to run away and paddle and swim in the tanks, roam through the banana groves, and pick flowers. Wild rabbits played amongst the bushes. You could stand on the hill and watch the lovely sunsets and the green fields lying around. I have breathed the beauty of this landscape so often as a child.

There is a high school building on the hill now, and children instead of rabbits play on the hillside. Roads run all over and cars and buses go down them ceaselessly. Cement structures have been erected everywhere. I watch the children of the new generation and think that the human race has certainly made great progress, but is losing touch with nature. Is that part of progress? Who are the fortunate ones, they or we? But then concepts like good fortune and happiness are relative after all.

THE BEGINNING

There were three portraits in the front room of their guesthouse. The first was of Swami Vivekananda delivering the Chicago address [in 1894]. The next one was of Gandhiji in a big turban with a shawl around his shoulders. The third was a beautiful painting of Tagore, with eyes as wide as lotus petals, a long beard, and a loose robe. Her father's brother had brought the last two from Madras where he was a student. Discussions on the ideals and activities of the three persons in these portraits—on religion, nationalism, and literature—took place very often in the room where they hung. All three attracted her, but Gandhiji exerted the strongest influence over her. She began to think and write about him and about the freedom of India. She tore up most of what she had written, but one or two articles were published.

Disturbing news filled the newspapers: the Mapilla Rebellion, the satyagraha at Vaikkam, the protest against land taxes. I recall the little girl engrossed in K. P. Kesava Menon's biography of Mahatma Gandhi, bent almost double on the ground. She cried because she wanted to wear khadar. She bought a spinning wheel. She planted cotton and spun yarn. She put up pictures of the nationalist leaders on the walls of her room.

When she insisted she would wear nothing but khadar, her father asked, "What is so special about khadar?"

"It is a *swadeshi* product. Gandhiji has asked all of us to wear it."

Her father replied, "What about the mundus woven here, in Veliyath and Talachara? Aren't they swadeshi as well? Don't the weavers who make them have to make a living too?"

He was right. Her family always used mundus woven in the rural areas. She thought of the old weaver from Veliyath who usually brought them. His family lived on the paddy he received in exchange for the mundus.

She now perceives that most people who advocated khadar at the time were not truly interested in the ideals that inspired its manufacture, they wore it merely because it was in fashion. Around this time her father bought her a copy of Tagore's *At Home and Outside*.

THE TREASURES OF MEMORY

She hardly ever left the protective circle of her fortress home, except for an occasional visit to her uncle's house, or, more rarely, to the house of a relative. Such expeditions had to be made in stages. First, there was a tiring walk of three or four miles, and then a journey of nearly four days, partly in a closely covered bullock cart and partly in a country boat.

Her father could be described as a child of the mountains, while her mother must have been the offspring of a water goddess, for she loved water. As a little girl she often saw crocodiles as their boat glided slowly over the Pamba River. Red and white water lilies grew in the fields and lotuses bloomed in profusion in the channels between them. The sand lay knee-deep in summer, and during the monsoon water flowed everywhere, as far as the eye could reach.

Boat rides with her uncle, festivals in the temple, a grandmother who adored her: all these filled her life with novelty and happiness.

As a child she did not think of herself as different from others, and it was only much later that she noticed that the quality that set her apart had certain disadvantages. As if in response to her father's wish, her mother bore no more daughters. She grew up with her brothers for company, learned whatever they did, and behaved no differently from them. Wooden kuradus were not inserted in her earlobes to lengthen them in the customary manner and she never went bare-breasted. As she grew older, she was aware that people disapproved of the way she was being brought up. They thought that a growing girl had no right to so much freedom.

When she looks back now, she understands the meaning of the expression in her father's eyes every time she lingered in the room where literary discussions took place. He obviously could not bear to tell her to go to the inner rooms, to explain to her that she could no longer be with them now that she was growing up.

A CAGED BIRD

The event that her parents had dreaded took place at last. The day she reached puberty, the house looked and felt as if someone had died. Her mother wept, so did the rest of the family, and the servant women, and seeing them, she too could not help crying. Even her father, usually confident and assured, lamented: "I feel as if I have to cage a free bird."

She was like one dead now, as far as the outside world was concerned. She might not go to the temple, or play under the champakam tree. She might not talk to her favorite swami. She felt the impact of these changes very sharply over the next four days, and began to understand why her father had been so distressed when a daughter had been born to him.

Like everyone else around her, she had to submit to customs that had been observed strictly over many centuries. She knew that no concessions would be made for her, and that she had to bow to the dictates of destiny, no matter how deeply it hurt.

I feel that her real education took place during those two years, when she was confined to the *antahpuram*. She read a great deal during this period and wrote a little too. She reflected deeply and compassionately on the contradictions, the joys, and the sorrows, the ideals, desires, and experiences of all the people around her: her immediate and extended family, her society and the laborers in the village. The longer she thought about them, the more intensely she shared their joys and sorrows. She often asked herself, "What if I were in their place?"

Three of her grandfather's sisters, who were child widows, lived with them and she observed them closely. She had heard the story of yet another sister who had been unjustly cast out when she was fifty years old for the crime of having gone out of the house without her umbrella in the midst of a family quarrel. She had taken ill and died untended by the roadside.

Two or three young girls distantly related to her had been sold to people who came from north Kerala, on the pretext of being given in marriage. Nothing had been heard of them since.

She often thought that the souls of these unfortunate women inhabited her. What if I had been one of them, she would ask herself.

She wrote a novel in the narrative style of *At Home and Outside*. Poems, plays, and stories followed swiftly. She read them over and over again, cried over them, then tore them up. She had no companions of her age at all.

MARRIAGE

Her parents became increasingly busy with their domestic responsibilities. Her brothers had left home to go to the English school about seven miles away from their village, and now lived in the vicinity of the school. Once she finished her household duties, she read, wrote, and watched the happenings in and around the house through the doors of the *nalukettu*. She never regretted those two years of solitude, which gave her the opportunity to nurture her inner vision and to define her ideals.

Discussions that would eventually decide their daughter's future must have taken place during this period, in the outer rooms and the kitchen of the big house. And that was how a good-looking, gentle, affectionate young man came into her life one day, like a messenger from the gods. He held her hand over the glowing flames of the sacrificial fire and said to her,

"I take your hand in the certainty that it will bring good fortune to both of us. Will you follow me?"

She said yes silently in her heart. The priest said to them, "Your lives are now joined."

They have been mutually supportive companions now for forty-two years. There have been occasions when they felt too tired to go on, when they were lost and confused. But their griefs and burdens brought them closer together. When the dreamlike responses of the imaginative vision and the practical good sense of everyday reality go hand in hand, a new lineage is born.

Now that she had a comrade to help her achieve her aims and desires, she grew stronger. Her mind, free of its fetters, longed for complete freedom. It was a period when a group of young revolutionaries were actively engaged in trying to change society. They convened meetings, performed plays, and spoke on public platforms. Her village took part in these activities and organized public speeches and propaganda marches.

People began to see that art could be used as a powerful weapon. The waves of this impassioned social and national struggle swept through the darkest corners of the inner rooms and roused them into a new awareness of freedom.

WE CAST AWAY OUR UMBRELLAS

She remembers it perfectly, the day they decided to hold that important meeting in a nearby town. A group of courageous women who had decided to cast away their umbrellas were going to be there. She pretended she was going to a temple, started out with her umbrella and shawl, and threw the umbrella away as soon as she left the house. She then rearranged the mundu that covered her as a saree, and took a bus to the venue of the meeting.

It gives her great pleasure now to think of that inspiring event. But she came back that day to find her mother in tears, sorrowing as if her daughter had died. Her relatives wanted nothing to do with her, and even the servants avoided her. Senior members of the family declared that they could not perform a *shraddha* in a house where a woman had been cast out. Others counseled that she be forbidden to enter the kitchen. It began to look as if the matter might lead to a legal dispute, or even partition of the family property. However, her father remained unruffled. "All right," he said, "she and her husband went to a public meeting together. Is that sufficient reason to cast her out? People have done worse things and not been so severely punished." He refused to be intimidated. And society gradually changed its norms.

I believe that each era evolves its own ideas and goals, and that they also depend on how old one is, the stage of life one has reached. It is the combination of these factors that compels human beings to action. The young woman therefore surrendered to her destiny, which was to express the thoughts and feelings within her. But when she began to put them down in writing, she did not ever think that she might someday become well known in the literary world. A friend came across some of the pieces she had written in her notebook and insisted that she send them to one of the leading Malayalam weeklies, which published them. The editor then asked her for a poem. She gave them a poem and a story. And so it all began....

She was determined to fulfill her literary and domestic duties, as well as her commitments to society, with an equal degree of dedication. They were all integral parts of her life and she could not bear to neglect any of them. She did not realize at the time that this obstinacy would result in her being unable to accomplish any of her tasks completely.

Meanwhile, there were babies every year. She brought them up. She wrote, read, and made speeches. When I look back, I see the young mother crouched on the ground, writing as she rocks the cradle. I see the willful, ignorant young woman standing on a public platform, holding her baby close to her while she makes a speech—the impudent woman who opposed anyone who did not agree with her, who used her art as a weapon against her adversaries, who stoically accepted the blows and wounds that her enemies in the literary world aimed at her.

She dealt with the world around her solely on the basis of information gleaned from the newspapers, and her vision of life was directed purely by her imagination. She saw the world in the light of her own beliefs—beliefs that changed constantly with the changing pace of the times. Only much later did she see that even the great men of the twentieth century could do little to alter the corrupt nature of the prevalent goals and methods of action, and that truth and justice had no place in political conflict.

Those who use the pen as a weapon often lacerate their own hearts with its needle-sharp point. She became sensitive to criticism and found herself wondering whether readers would be annoyed with her, whether they would misunderstand her. She tormented herself endlessly with self-censure.

But she persisted in her chosen way of action with extraordinary self-confidence, even at the risk of being considered insolent. Human beings are an assortment of defects, misdeeds, and contradictions that they wish upon themselves. Their definitions of defects and misdeeds vary according to the period they live in, the beliefs that guide them, and the circumstances in which they are placed. Who knows what is right and what is wrong? There are religions that believe that all men and women are born sinners. How innocently, how trustingly, they call themselves sinners! I am not prepared to go that far. But I do know that we often bruise and slash each other in order to achieve what we consider good. But who can tell whether what we thus achieve is truly good and right? Sometimes when we try to eliminate what we believe is bad in us, we lose an essential part of our individuality. What we thought of as a defect might well have been our strongest point.

As time went by, her impudence and her outspokenness were repeatedly crushed, and she had perforce to learn humility. With that, however, the artistic skills she had acquired began to weaken.

lalithambika antherjanam

AGYEYA
(SACHCHIDANANDA VATSAYAN)
1911–1987
(Hindi)

The poet who called himself Agyeya ("the unknown")—the pen name given to him when his poems and short stories were smuggled out of prison—was born Sachchidananda Vatsayan in the town of Kushinagar on the northern border of India. His poems and prose works ushered in the era of "Nayi Kavita" (new poetry) in Hindi literature. His personal life followed the turbulent twists and turns of Indian history. He was imprisoned for his revolutionary, bomb-making activities by the colonial government and spent the years from 1931 to 1934 in solitary confinement. It is thought that this difficult experience shaped the silence and solitude which he viewed as essential to the creation of poetry. His poetry, short stories, and literary criticism were viewed as central to a movement that started with the publication of Tar Saptaks *(1943), an anthology of seven young poets who espoused differing forms of free verse. In his introduction, Agyeya writes of how these new poets "do not belong to any school. [. . .] There is no ideological unity among them." The contributing poets were as diverse as the Marxist poet Muktibodh and Agyeya himself. Later Agyeya served as the founding editor of the Hindi newspaper* Dinaman *where his progressive political views grew sharper.*

Agyeya's poems, however, turning away from overt political ideology, are based in the sounds and sense rhythms of human experience, in the mysteries of the affective life. In later years, deeply influenced by Zen Buddhism, he held a belief in the power of memory to lead us to a mystic horizon. Questions of identity, self-recognition, and love are central to his writing. In "From an Undated Diary" he writes, "And finally what is the relationship between words and the poet himself? Do the names of things flow from his consciousness to embrace and envelop things, or do they flow from things to engulf him?" Agyeya was a prodigious writer, and in addition to numerous volumes of poetry, he published novels, short stories, memoirs, and plays. Among his many important works we find the poetry collection Aangan Ke Par Dvar *(1961), the verse play* Uttar Priyadarshi *(1966), and* Nilambari *(1981), a collection of poems that he selected and translated into English. In 1978, he was awarded the Bharatiya Jnanpith Prize for Literature.*

"The Signs"

At every turn in the road, we were given signs
Which we didn't even notice.
The old ways of seeing blinded us.
Surely we were not blind at the start, but the old way of seeing
Is dazzling,
A blindfold of many colors.

We kept on getting those signs: they were wordless:
We were rolling in words.
"In the beginning there was the word, and it is secret"—
"The word is the thing in itself"—
And then we saw through the word.
We would still sit weaving garlands of glittering words
But for a novel form.
For this much we knew:
Form was the thing.

A silence was sweeping on past us
Sending up bubbles,
Its secret signs.
Each swell of a bubble thrilled us,

Each burst was a state of pain.
A thrill, a pain.
Silent and secret signs. Mere shame!

And we kept on getting these
Wordless signs;
We kept on grabbing at form.

But form is only the figure
Of something, some signal, just beyond words—
Some sign that living
Has given from far underneath.

Words,
Forms,
Then signals.
These signals on every side at every turn of the road—
So many signs from living
Which say beyond themselves
What is meant!
How many walls round nothing are yet to beat down,
So the word, released, can leap through
To take what is meant
To itself!
Will we ever command the sacred art to hold them as one?

What is meant! Give us that!
Don't rush us with a flurry of forms!
We know the sign that is given by living.
Carry us over:
Not form, but what is essential.

And so we found out our voice: we broke into speech.
We know the words: words were exquisite
And even true, and crammed with rich matter.
But our words
Did not comprehend the people.
Because what was in us and opening out
Was not of the people.

agyeya (sachchidananda vatsayan)

Our fineness of feeling
Kept us apart from the life we were in:
The road we had opened
Came out at nowhere.

Is that the place we have finished? Is it there, defeated,
Our signature means the end?
Has living used up the very last message
In the chronic book of signs?

They may bend us under—that load of books—
The old ideas, the old ways of doing.
Those massive manuals for living last year,
But something ahead insists that we meet it.

There is another turn in the road up there,
But who is that seeming to signal just at the turn?

"Words and Truths"

It is not that I have never found the truth,
Nor that I stumble upon the word only rarely, by chance;
I keep running into them every so often.
The question that abides is this:
The wall that these two always have between them,
How, when, catching them off guard
Can I breach that wall
Or blow it up with high explosive?

Let those who are the poets, let them keep doing what they do.
My simple concern is this:
These two who stand so rigid, one towards the other—
How, when, in what burst of light can I bring them together:
These two, my friends, my comrades, my companion always.

"Three Words to Make a Poem"

Three words to make a poem:
One not to be spoken;
The second, spoken,
Falling short of my meaning;
The third, true metal when struck, rings the question:
Can't I do without it then?
So, silence, though I have
Three words to make a poem.

"The Revolving Rock XVI"

I, as the poet,
Seer, discloser,
Explorer,
Bearer of signs and figures,
Prodigal spender,

I write the truth
And, writing,
Misconceive it.

You, as the poem,
Reality always swaddled,
Yet for ever stretching,
Grave without gravity,
Not to be spent,

You dissemble
But in each dissembling
Are the more precise, explicit
In your absolute difference.

agyeya (sachchidananda vatsayan)

"The Revolving Rock XXV"

Where sea met land
On that very seam
I sat.

Why the sea was silent
Why the land voluble,
I don't know.

On the line of meeting, absently, I sat
Watching the sea
And listening to the land;
What I could read on the sea waves
I wrote on the ruffles of sand.

I don't know
Why I sat there.

But all of this
Was by day:
Later,
When the sun, risen from the land,
Wasted with heat,
Fell into the sea,
A shaft of light cut through me,
Pinning me down to that line of meeting
Before it dissolved.

agyeya (sachchidananda vatsayan)

UMASHANKAR JOSHI
1911–1988
(Gujarati)

Umashankar Joshi was born in the village of Bamna in Gujarat. At an early age he joined Gandhi's freedom movement and was imprisoned twice, first in 1930–31 (in Sabermati jail) and then again in 1932. His first volume of poetry, Viswashanti *(World Peace), was published by Gandhi's Navajivan Press in 1931 just as Joshi was released from jail. The poet's staunch belief in nonviolence led him into the tumultuous heart of Indian public affairs. When asked how he could have written in the midst of a public life, he said he could not have been a writer without this existential involvement, and that all the while his poems were writing themselves "in the backyard of the mind." In an interview in the* Journal of South Asian Literature, *he speaks of his deep connection to the natural landscape, how as a young man he saw the full moon rise over Nakhi Lake and composed his first poem, a sonnet entitled "Autumnal Full Moon on Nakhi Lake" inspired by the loveliness of the landscape. The last line of the poem, with its invocation of beauty, was "a sort of mantra, a guiding idea that a young man in whom the creative principle was astir would lay his hand upon." His poetry gained in complexity but always retained the harmonies of sound as his powerful, exquisite lyrics ushered in the era of modernism in Gujarati poetry. A quarter century later, Joshi's long poem "I Am Fragmented" (1956) evokes the splintering of the psyche in sharp, disjunctive language that must have seemed shocking to readers at the time.*

During a trip to the United States he met Robert Frost and became friends with him. One can see a poetic connection between these two poets from very different cultures and languages—the clarity of the colloquial language and the ways in which the precisely documented event or natural object opens up to the horizon of the unseen, a subtle turn to the metaphysical. In Joshi's poem "The World of Birds," he evokes with precise, mellifluous detail the foliage of trees, the droplets of light, and the calling of birds: "Putch, mutchi, ritch, wutch, witch . . . / The birds recite, in one breath / The compact litany of Sanskrit verbs." In 1947, the year of independence, he established the literary journal Sanskriti. He was a prolific writer and in addition to numerous collections of poetry, he published plays, essays, novels, short stories, and academic writings. His important works of poetry include Gangotri *(1934)*, Nishith *(1939)*, and Abhijna *(1967)*. In 1967, he was awarded the Bharatiya Jnanpith Prize for Literature.

"My Four-Sided Field"

This, my four-sided field,
A piece of paper.
A storm blows from nowhere
And sows a seed.

The seed dissolves
In the alchemy of imagination;
Words sprout up, swelling sprigs,
Then flowers too.

Fruits with unearthly relish abound.
Sow a moment, reap eternity,
A harvest without end.

A horn of plenty, of bliss, ever full,
This, my four-sided field.

From "The World of Birds"

If ears were eyes
Sounds would be light to them

Before day-break, sounds, breaking
        through the drowsy night,
Shine on those who are half-asleep,
The thick dark foliage of trees
Seems to be leaking droplets of light all over.
From the dense mass of the leaves
Drip . . . "*Putch, mutchi, ritch, wutch, witch . . .*"
The birds recite, in one breath,
The compact litany of Sanskrit verbs.
The message is—Wake up, get up and get going
Through closed eyes, my mind recalls
The terse aphorisms of Panini, the grammarian
We learnt as students of Sanskrit.
The entire scholarly bounty of Panini's learning
Is revealed in a flash,
By brief, little notes of bird-song!

A small draught of light, poured out by a bird?
"*Putch, mutchi, ritch, wutch, witch*"
A stream of light, movement, and sound,
Gratifying the ears.

Men of letters can compose exquisite tomes
For scholarly academics to study
So early in the morning.
Words come to a poet, looking for him,
Whether words regulated by the canon of Panini
Or the patches of sunlight, spilling from birds.
If words could speak
They would certainly tell the poet—
"How ever could we become a poem on our own?
Scattered when in dictionaries and books on grammar

umashankar joshi

Together when spoken by men and women,
We were hardly like anything you saw in poems.
As soon as we see the world
We start hopping to and fro like frogs.
As soon as the author beckons to us
For his composition, we obey him,
Fascinated, as if by a spell.
We, words and sounds, sink into silence.
Our prattle about meanings subsides
Under the spray from waves of poetic emotions."

. . .

The song of the cuckoo soars up
Like a fountain of light.
The rasping of a gang of crows
Sweeps the expanse like a broom.
A whole flock of sparrows comes
And sprinkles it all over
With its twitter.

At the end of it all
The bulbul starts warbling
Shreeprabhu in two parts
Shreep . . . rabhu! . . . Shreep . . . rabhu!

At times
From some unknown depths
Of its diminutive body,
It sings, as if with the awareness
That the whole earth is balanced
Just on the spur of its song,
And is waiting,
Holding its breath in suspense.

. . .

Shall I tell you?
Each and every time I speak
In a group, in the class-room, in the garden,
Inside the home, in a railway carriage,
Going for a brisk walk or under a tree

Do I really feel that at all times
My voice sounds to me as my own?
I try to listen, sitting opposite,
On a bench in the class-room—saying,
What does this man really want to say?—
And turn my face aside once in a while.

Sleep—a time for rest to all living things—
Drenches my entire being and my eyelashes,
Drop by drop,
Mouthful after mouthful and wave after wave,
From the waterfront of darkness and light.
This is the time only for listening—
Not a word to be uttered.
Even so, I could not help saying—
—"My voice!"; it is only my voice
That I have to hear. . . .
That is when there is unbroken sleep
And complete rest for the mind
A breaker at high tide,

A punch of wakefulness
Which never misses its mark
And amplifies my voice
And opens up my awareness,
By dispersing both into the shapes of dreams.

My voice is the only thing being heard,
From within myself at one moment
From somewhere outside the next.
In the middle of the night, far away
Rousing every drop of my blood
With that untamed chant
Invoking, welcoming something.
. . .
A father I had, and a mother.
Yes, also the language my mother spoke.
There was the body nurtured in affection

And imbued with a soul.
A heart I had which had an ear
And a voice.
What is the work that I have to do?
And the name I am known by?
Moments full of life and tremors of bliss—
That is my work.
And it has now merged itself
With the vivacious odyssey of mankind
The word patterns I created,
Rather like ripples of emotion
Have now subsided into the hearts of others.
And my name?
It has fused itself with language
Wait-a-bit!
The last word has to be spoken by silence.

Ahmedabad, 1975, 16/18–3–1981

Acceptance Speech for the 1968 Bharatiya Jnanpith Award
VIGYAN BHAVAN
NEW DELHI
20 December 1968

I am indeed very thankful to the Bharatiya Jnanpith for selecting my book of poems *Nishīth*, also with *Shrī rāmāyana darshanam* by my friend, the great Kannada poet, Dr. K. V. Puttappa, for this year's literary award. I think this is one of those activities which can contribute to a fuller awareness of the living unity which is there deep down in the life of our people.

The poems were written when I was half my present age and was struggling hard to gain a footing in a vast modern city like Bombay, first as a student and then as a householder. The first line of the title poem "*Nishīth*" was taken down, I vividly recall, on the blank space of a letter I had received from the poet Meghani, while returning late at night on a suburban train. Apparently the meter of this "Ode to the Spirit of Midnight" was attuned to that of the Vedic invocations, but the undulating rhythm of the electric train did not fail to creep into the structure of the poem. Thirteen of the seventeen sonnets of the sequence—*Atmānā khander,* "Soul in Ruins"—were written in three days while I was deeply engrossed in the study of Indian banking as an undergraduate student. That was also the time when I felt the deep impact of Love and Death, the two great experiences of life—or shall I call them one?—for they present themselves as one to the poetic vision. I had returned to studies after four years of non-co-operation, and though it was Gandhiji who inspired us to court imprisonment and it was the British Government whose hospitality we enjoyed, we, the youth of the early 1930's, came out of jail with ideas of socialism. However, Gandhiji did remain the predominant influence for us. Such was the time-spirit that moved some of us who began writing in the 1930's.

How was it that I, a young boy from a village in northeast Gujarat, came to cherish the Word "like a bud of flame"? This is a question I have asked myself time and again and have yet found no answer to. All I am sure about is that to evolve as a poet is to get involved in an increasingly vaster social milieu.

Was it that my parents and the people around me in my village had a taste for words on their tongue—at least it seemed to me to be so—that I was drawn to the Word? The Word led me, before I was fully aware of it, to all that clamors for articulation in human life. It established an intimacy with things and creatures. The Word was the key with the help of which things opened up to me. It was the Word which eventually made much that was significant in the past a living presence and charted the ocean of the unforeseen future, and created a rich "within-ness" for me.

A poem is a word construct, and through the creative word the stirrings of a poetic soul are translated into joy in the consciousness, rather into the joy-consciousness, of his readers.

The poet's is a pilgrimage, with the Word as his guide. No, it is much more. The Word is the element through which and through which alone he can exist. And then sometimes one finds that the difference between the Word and the deed diminishes. The Word itself becomes the deed. I love the compound *kavi-kratu* in the *Rigveda.* The *kavi* is one who sees beyond, who sings of the beyond-scape, the poet. *Kratu* is the doer, the man of action. *Kavi-kratu* is the singer-doer, one whose song itself is an action. Yesterday Rabindranath was such a one. Today it is Octavio Paz.

I began with *Viswashānti*, "Peace in the Universe" (1931). In 1956, I turned out the Dissolution ode, "I Am Fragmented" (*Chhinnabhinna chhu*). If the most exalted thing I have seen with these eyes of mine is the pair of Gandhiji's sparkling eyes, out of which was welling up abounding love after twenty-one days of his fast, the most gruesome spectacle that I have witnessed is that of a lump of mortar and cement through which was gleaming the white of bones that were melted and made one with them in the infernal heat of the atom bomb in Hiroshima. Only the poetic word can unify experiences which are opposed to each other.

What was realized as an outward manifestation in *Atmānā khander* (1935), "Soul in Ruins," is inwardly visualized in "I Am Fragmented" and "The Search" (the two poems which may run into a series). It seems the creative spirit sometimes goes spiraling up. The sonnet sequence worked itself up into reality. This new series of odes attempts to lay a hand on the creative principle which would help integrate a fragmented personality.

And this is perhaps what the present human situation demands of at least the creative artist, who, if he succeeds in achieving art, does vindicate the hope for an integrated life. The techno-structuring of contemporary society is fast leading to the drying up of the channels of love. Man feels lonely in crowded cities and is denied inward aloneness, a center of peace from where he can function as a human being. It is for poetry, now more than at any other time before, to highlight the network of relationships of interdependence and through insights and intuitions point to a rich reconciliation of the human and the non-human, of the body and the non-body, of the inevitable cruelty that there is in living, and the perennial flow of love. It is for poetry, indeed, to point out to Paradiso from Inferno via Purgatorio.

What goes into the making of an Indian poet in the present-day world? His sharing the global anxiety and agony too. Paradoxically enough, the more worldminded he is, the more Indian he will be, as one could see in the case of Tagore.

The poetic drama, with its focusing of attention on human destiny, is bound to attract poets. But if an epic is written anymore, maybe the new epic might well concentrate not only on a particular national or cultural theme, but on one-world-ness, on the total human situation today.

A poem just happens. Poems are islets of Being in an expanse of Becoming. A poem is a fulfilment.

The still-unopened eyes of a child in the womb
shine in the mother's face.
Did you ever see a poem
shine so in my being?

A poet leaves a poem behind and moves along, ever in search of a new thing, for a fresh beginning. With the birth of every poem he is reborn as a poet. With every poem that he creates, there is for him a spiritual ripening.

SAADAT HASAN MANTO

1912–1955

(Urdu)

Saadat Hasan Manto was born into a Kashmiri Muslim family in Samrala, Punjab. His fierce, brilliant short stories mine the life of the streets and the bazaars, and evoke the sexual life of people caught up in violent events beyond their ken. He began his literary life as a translator of French and Russian writers, including Victor Hugo, Guy de Maupassant, Anton Chekhov, and Leo Tolstoy among others. With the Partition of India, Manto moved from Bombay, where he was writing for the film magazine Musawwir, to Lahore, a city he learned to embrace. From Lahore he penned a series of "Letters to Uncle Sam," biting, darkly humorous, poking fun at the West as well as Pakistani communists. In 1919, as a seven-year-old child, he witnessed the Amritsar Massacre—peaceful civilians, on a day of the Baisakhi festival, having gathered in defiance of a British order, gunned down at close quarters by colonial soldiers. Manto's first short story, "Tamasha" (1934), draws on this autobiographical material and is told from the point of view of a boy who witnesses another child bleeding after the gunshots.

Time and again the ravages of Partition and the senseless violence it engendered enter into his crystalline stories. His last and perhaps most celebrated story, "Toba Tek Singh," is set in an insane asylum at the time of Partition. When asked if he will go to India or to Pakistan—for in Manto's fabricated world, the inmates of the madhouse are given this choice—one man clearly understands that neither country will do. Very simply, he says, "I wish to live *in this tree." He picks a single tree and installs himself there, his limbs dangling, sensing in a green cage the only safety he will ever find. Then there is that other mad creature who speaks in the babble that no one can follow. He stands stock still on his swollen legs, refusing to move, until he falls, flesh upon dirt, marking an untouchable zone, a no man's land. Six times, both by the colonial and new nationalist governments, Manto, whose work was often sexually explicit, was indicted for obscenity, and time and again he was hauled into court to defend himself. His friend Ismat Chugtai has written of how they once stood trial side by side in Lahore. In addition to many collections of short stories, Manto published essays and radio plays. His important works include "Naya Quanun" ("New Constitution," 1938) and "Kali Shalwar" ("Black Shalwar," 1942).*

"First Letter to Uncle Sam"

31 LAXMI MANSIONS,
HALL ROAD,
LAHORE
16 December 1951

Dear Uncle,

Greetings,

This letter comes to you from your Pakistani nephew whom you do not know, nor does anyone else in your land of seven freedoms.

You should know why my country, sliced away from India, came into being and gained independence, which is why I am taking the liberty of writing to you. Like my country, I too have become independent and in exactly the same way. Uncle, I will not labour the point since an all-knowing seer like you can well imagine the freedom a bird whose wings have been clipped can enjoy.

My name is Saadat Hasan Manto and I was born in a place that is now in India. My mother is buried there. My father is buried there. My first-born is also resting in that bit of earth. However, that place is no longer my country. My country now is Pakistan which I had only seen five or six times before as a British subject.

I used to be the All India's Great Short Story Writer. Now I am Pakistan's Great Short Story Writer. Several collections of my stories have been published and the people respect me. In undivided India, I was tried thrice, in Pakistan so far once. But then Pakistan is still young.

The government of the British considered my writings pornographic. My own government has the same opinion. The government of the British let me off but I do not expect my own government to do so. A lower court sentenced me to three months hard labour and a Rs 300 fine. My appeal to the higher court won me an acquittal but my government believes that justice has not been done and so it has now filed an appeal in the High Court, praying that the judgment acquitting me be quashed and I be punished. We will have to see what the High Court decides.

My country is not your country which I regret. If the High Court were to punish me, there is no newspaper in my country that would print my picture or the details of all my trial.

My country is poor. It has no art paper, nor proper printing presses. I am living evidence of this poverty. You will not believe it, uncle, but despite being the author of twenty-two books, I do not have my own house to live in. And you will be astonished to know that I have no means of getting myself from one place to the other. I neither have a Packard nor a Dodge; I do not even have a used car.

If I need to go somewhere, I rent a bike. If a piece of mine appears in a newspaper and I earn twenty to twenty-five rupees at the rate of seven rupees a column, I hire a tonga and go buy locally distilled whiskey. Had this whiskey been distilled in your country, you would have destroyed that distillery with an atom bomb because it is the sort of stuff guaranteed to send its user to kingdom come within one year.

But I am digressing. All I really wanted to do was to convey my good wishes to brother Erskine Caldwell. You will no doubt recall that you tried him for his novel "God's Little Acre" on the same charge that I have faced here: pornography.

Believe me, uncle, when I heard that this novel was tried on an obscenity charge in the land of seven freedoms, I was extremely surprised. In your country, after all, everything is divested of its outer covering so that it can be displayed in the show window, be it fresh fruit or woman, machine or animal, book or calendar. You are the king of bare things so I am at a loss to understand, uncle, why you tried brother Erskine Caldwell.

Had it not been for my quick reading of the court judgment I would have drunk myself to death by downing large quantities of our locally distilled whiskey because of the shock I received when I came to know of the Caldwell case. In a way, it was unfortunate that my country missed an opportunity to rid itself of a man like me, but then had I croaked, I would not have been writing to you, uncle. I am dutiful by nature. I love my country. In a few days, by the Grace of God I will die and if I do not kill myself, I will die anyway because where flour sells at the price at which it sells here, only a shamefaced person can complete his ordained time on earth.

So, I read the Caldwell judgment and decided not to drink myself to death with large quantities of the local hooch. Uncle, out there in your country, everything has an artificial façade but the judge who acquitted brother Erskine was certainly without such a façade. If this judge—I'm sorry I don't know his name—is alive, kindly convey my respectful regards to him.

The last lines of his judgment point to the intellectual reach of his mind. He writes: "I personally feel that if such books were suppressed, it would create an unnecessary sense of curiosity among people which could induce them to seek salaciousness, though that is not the purpose of this book. I am absolutely certain that the author has chosen to write truthfully about a certain segment of American society. It is my opinion that truth is always consistent with literature and should be so declared."

That is what I told the court that sentenced me, but it went ahead anyway and gave me three months in prison with hard labour and a fine of three hundred rupees. My judge thought that truth and literature should be kept far apart. Everyone has his opinion.

I am ready to serve my three-month term but this fine of three hundred rupees I am unable to pay. Uncle, you do not know that I am poor. Hard work I am used to, but money I am unused to. I am about thirty-nine and all my life I have worked hard. Just think about it. Despite being such a famous writer, I have no Packard.

I am poor because my country is poor. Two meals a day I can somehow manage but many of my brothers are not so fortunate.

My country is poor, but why is it ignorant? I am sure, uncle, you know why because you and your brother John Bull together are a subject I do not want to touch because it will not be exactly music to your ears. Since I write to you as a respectful youngster, I should remain that way from start to finish.

You will certainly ask me out of astonishment why my country is poor when it boasts of so many Packards, Buicks and Max Factor cosmetics. That is indeed so, uncle, but I will not answer your question because if you look into your heart, you will find the answer there (unless you have had your heart taken out by one of your brilliant surgeons).

That section of my country's population which rides in Packards and Buicks is really not of my country. Where poor people like me and those even poorer live, that is my country.

These are bitter things, but there is a shortage of sugar here otherwise I would have coated my words appropriately. But what of it! Recently, I read Evelyn Waugh's book "The Loved One." He of course comes from the country of your friends. Believe me, I was so impressed by that book that I sat down to write to you.

I was always convinced of the individual genius found in your part of the world but after reading this book, I have become a fan of his for life. What a performance, I say! Some truly vibrant people do indeed live out there.

Evelyn Waugh tells us that in your California, the dead can be beautified and there are large organisations that undertake the task. No matter how unattractive the dear departed in life, after death he can be given the look desired. There are forms you fill where you are asked to indicate your preference. The excellence of the finished product is guaranteed. The dead can be beautified to the extent desired, as long as you pay the price. There are experts who can perform this delicate task to perfection. The jaw of the loved one can be operated upon and a beatific smile implanted on the face. The eyes can be lit up and the forehead can be made to appear luminous. And all this work is done so marvellously that it can befool the two angels who are assigned to do a reckoning once a person is in the grave.

Uncle, by God you people are matchless.

One had heard of the living being operated on and beautified with the help of plastic surgery—there was much talk of it here—but one had not heard that the dead can be beautified as well.

Recently one of your citizens was here and some friends introduced me to him. By then I had read brother Evelyn Waugh's book and I read an Urdu couplet to your countryman that he did not follow. However, the fact is, uncle, that we have so distorted our faces that they have become unrecognisable, even to us. And there we have you who can even make the dead look more beautiful than they ever were in life. The truth is that only you have a right to live on this earth: the rest of us are wasting our time.

Our great Urdu poet Ghalib wrote about a hundred years ago:

If disgrace after death was to be my fate,
I should have met my end through drowning
It would have spared me a funeral and no headstone would have
    marked my last resting place.

Ghalib was not afraid of being disgraced while he was alive because from beginning to end that remained his lot. What he feared was disgrace after death. He was a graceful man and not only was he afraid of what would happen after he died, he was certain what would happen to him after he was gone. And that is why he expressed a wish to meet his end through drowning so that he should neither have funeral nor grave.

How I wish he had been born in your country. He would have been carried to his grave with great fanfare and over his resting place a skyscraper would have been built. Or were his own wish to be granted, his dead body would have been placed in a pool of glass and people would have gone to view it as they go to a zoo.

Brother Evelyn Waugh writes that not only are there in your country establishments that can beautify dead humans but dead animals as well. If a dog loses its tail in an accident, he can have a new one.

Whatever physical defects the dead one had in life are duly repaired after death. He is then buried ceremoniously and floral wreaths are placed on his grave. Every year on the pet's death anniversary, a card is sent to the owner with an inscription that reads something like this: In paradise, your Tammy (or Jeffie) is wagging his tail (or his ears) while thinking of you.

What it adds up to is that your dogs are better off than us. Die here today, you are forgotten tomorrow. If someone in the family dies, it is a disaster for those left behind who often can be heard wailing, "Why did this wretch die? I should've gone instead." The truth is, uncle, that we neither know how to live nor how to die.

I heard of one of your citizens who wasn't sure what sort of a funeral he would be given, so he staged a grand "funeral" for himself while he was very much alive. He deserved that certainly because he had lived a stylish and opulent life where nothing happened unless he wished it to. He wanted to rule out the possibility of things not being done right at his funeral; as such, he was justified in personally observing his last rites while alive. What happens after death is neither here nor there.

I have just seen the new issue of "Life" (5 November 1951, international edition) and learnt of a most instructive facet of American life. Spread across two pages is an account of the funeral of the greatest gangster of your country. I saw a picture of Willie Moretti (may his soul rest in peace) and his magnificent home which he had recently sold for $55,000. I also viewed his five-acre estate where he wanted to live in peace, away from the distractions of the world. There was also a picture of his, eyes closed, lying in his bed, quite dead. There were also pictures of his $5,000 casket and his funeral procession made up of seventy-five cars. God is my witness, it brought tears to my eyes.

May there be dust in my mouth, but in case you were to die, may you have a grander farewell than Willie Moretti. This is the ardent prayer of a poor Pakistani writer who doesn't even have a cycle to ride on. May I beg you that like the more farsighted ones in your country, you should make arrangements to witness your funeral while you are alive. You can't leave it to others; they can always make mistakes, being fallible. It is possible that your physical appearance may not receive the attention it deserves after you have passed away. It is also possible that you may already have witnessed your funeral by the time this letter reaches you. I say this because you are not only wiser, you are also my uncle.

Convey my good wishes to brother Erskine Caldwell and to the judge who acquitted him of the pornography charge. If I have caused you offense, I beg your forgiveness. With the utmost respect,

Your poor nephew
Saadat Hasan Manto,
Resident of Pakistan

(This letter could not be mailed because of lack of postage)

ISMAT CHUGTAI

1915–1991

(Urdu)

Ismat Chugtai was born in Badayun to a Muslim, Urdu-speaking family. Her father was a remarkably progressive man who took pains to ensure that both his sons and daughters were educated. In an interview Chugtai spoke of how in her family, the women never had to sit apart from the men and how she was given reading and writing lessons and learned horseback riding and how to use a gun. Her extreme frankness about female sexuality made her a controversial figure, but she never relinquished her belief in the need to express what the heart felt. Her short story "Lihaaf" ("The Quilt") was published in 1941 and caused a storm. It is written in the voice of a woman who looks back on her childhood and recalls how when she was a small girl, she lived briefly with Begum Jaan, the lonely wife of a rich nawab. Tormented by her sexual needs (her husband was given to finding his pleasure with good-looking young boys), the Begum strikes up an affair with her maid. The lesbian relationship is evoked in rich, sensory detail through the child's voice. It begins with the child's bewilderment at seeing the quilt on the Begum's bed change into an elephant-like creature that wiggles and humps. Only later is it revealed to the uncomprehending child that the Begum and her maid were making love under the covers. When the story appeared, the colonial government charged Chugtai with obscenity, and the writer traveled to Lahore to stand trial. A memoir piece describes the time in Lahore and how both she and her friend, the short story writer Saadat Hasan Manto, stood trial together, each facing charges of sexual perversion in their writing. At about the same time Chugtai joined the Progressive Writers' Movement and spoke out strongly for women's rights. She was married to the filmmaker Shahid Latif. They lived in Bombay and wrote and codirected many films. Her novel Terhi Lakir *(The Crooked Line, 1943), widely considered a masterpiece, is a passionate, often searing novel that gives us the intimate world of a woman, her rage, her sexual longings in a time of tumultuous historical change. Chugtai was a prolific writer and in addition to short stories and novels, she wrote novellas, essays, and film scripts. Her important works include the novel* Ziddi *(1941) and the short story collection* Choten *(1943).*

"We People"

I don't know whom to blame for my being so impressionable. My paternal relatives believed that I had taken after the maternal side of my family entirely. These poor wretches are Sheikhs, consumers of watery daal. On the other side, my maternal relatives were positive that I had taken after my paternal family. The same sharp, biting tongue that my aunt has. What else could one expect from the descendants of Changez Khan?

But if someone asked my mother, "What happened to your daughter?" she would sigh deeply and say, "It's neither the fault of the paternal side nor the maternal. This is all a trick of fate."

Under these circumstances who can I blame? The seed responsible for bringing me into the world was certainly not deformed but somewhere along the line a mistake had definitely been made in the nurturing process.

Personally, I have no complaints about the environment in which I was raised and nurtured. In the midst of several children of all ages and sexes I received a foot-soldier's training. No one spoiled me or tolerated my histrionics, no amulets were made for me, no one ever offered supplications to rid me of the evil eye, nor did I ever feel I was an important part of anyone's life.

Since my sisters were much older, I found a place for myself in the row of brothers. My early childhood was spent playing gulli danda, football and hockey with them and I also shared their lessons. Come to think of it, the real culprits were my brothers, it was their company that enabled me to think freely. The shyness that is considered to be an indispensable quality in young girls from middle class families was not given a chance to flourish in my case. Because they constantly teased me, my brothers prevented me from developing the habit of wearing a dupatta at a young age, bowing sedately to offer salaams, and blushing at the mention of marriage and weddings. Except for Azim Bhai, everyone else in the house was very lively and talkative. The whole family was well-informed and boisterous conversations were commonplace. We constantly played word games, devising original and novel phrases, and it was customary to tear one another apart with criticism, to the extent that you would think every child in this family was born with a whetstone on his tongue.

When Abba retired and began receiving his pension, all of us moved back to the ancestral house in Agra. After flying high all this time we now suddenly had to deal with a stifling, oppressive atmosphere. What a leap from football and gulli danda to the company of those timid girls who, frail and jaundiced from being raised in the squalid, suffocating streets of the muhalla of Agra's Panja-e Shahi, were startled by the sound of their own heartbeat. I couldn't get along with these girls at all and I also clashed with the elderly women who were horrified to see me leaping across rooftops.

"Heaven forbid! Is Nacho's daughter a girl or a *maujbijar?* May god help us!"

Overcome by embarrassment, my mother Nusrat Begum (whom everyone lovingly called Nacho) would break out in a cold sweat. She felt quite uncomfortable when hemmed in by family members.

For the first time, in those streets of Agra, I regretted being a girl. Why had god created woman? What was the purpose of this dejected, helpless, captive being? The washerwoman was beaten every night, the sweeperess received a walloping from her husband every other day, and in the adjacent neighbourhoods, husbands often thrashed their wives. And every day I would plead with god. "O god, please turn me into a boy so I don't get a beating for flying kites on the roof, so I can play kabaddi in the streets and run after monkeys without fear." Not only were the streets in Agra filthy, but living in these streets were close and distant relatives who terrified Amma. As long as we were in other cities we lived as we pleased, but the moment we arrived in the midst of our family it was as if our feet were bound by chains.

I was forced to be friends with the bashful Agra girls and I soon discovered that these very girls who appeared so innocent on the outside were, in reality, very shrewd. God help us, they had such surprises up their sleeves. In a matter of seconds they would successfully dodge the elderly women and then proceed to flirt with the boys in the street. I was revolted by this life of deception.

However, we were soon rid of the loathsome environment in Agra. Abba moved us to Aligarh. Surrounded by its liberating atmosphere, our old life made a comeback. We had the same thatched bungalows, the same riverbank, the same open fields and, stealing cucumbers and climbing trees again, I shed my disappointment at being a girl. As a matter of fact, I began to see some advantages to being a girl. For example, Abba had ordered that the girls' plaits were not to be pulled and that their earrings were not to be yanked off. Also, if the girls resorted to hitting or slapping this was to be reported to Abba and he alone would devise an appropriate punishment. Actually there were no "girls," there was just one girl, namely me. Complaints about my behaviour were constantly presented in Abba's court, but my brothers were so notoriously naughty that I usually received no punishment at all, while they, on the other hand, were censured endlessly.

After our arrival in Aligarh I became increasingly conscious of my brother Azim Bhai's presence. God knows why he had suddenly developed an interest in me. I preferred Nasim Bhai, who was older, and I enjoyed getting a beating from him because he also gave me money and sweets. Azim Bhai never gave me any, nor did he ever box my ears. In fact, he treated me as if I was someone important.

It wasn't long before he started teaching me history and geography. I can't remember how it all began, but I do remember that when he returned tired and exhausted from work in the evening, he would lie down in the veranda and ask me to read aloud. Then he would correct my translations, give me dictations, and finally engage me in discussions. I don't remember what exactly we talked about in the beginning, but later he told me about the Quran and the Hadith. His method of teaching was very odd. He would hand me a novel and say, "Translate this." This was done from English to Urdu and Urdu to English. Ten pages or more at a time. There were several advantages to translation. For one thing I had to read the novel in its entirety before I started translating anything and this was when I developed a passion for reading. All night I would devour novels and short stories, even though I did not understand the novels I read during this period and had to re-read them later. Hardy was the first novelist who, in the words of Azim Bhai, I "stirred well and drank deep."

I was so influenced by Azim Bhai in those days that I became an echo of his voice. The family maintained that "God speaks through Mansur." When I said something the others would tease me by insisting that it wasn't me, it was Azim Bhai speaking. Azim Bhai took advantage of my naivete. What he couldn't say himself, he would cleverly whisper in my ear and I would immediately blurt it out. According to the rest of the family members, he instigated me often during this time and my disposition, which was obstinate and headstrong to begin with, received encouragement from him and spun completely out of control.

He was studying law, working in a factory at the same time and also writing articles. After working so hard he would tutor me for several hours at night. Sometimes he would run a temperature, and have aches and pains in his chest, hands and feet. His wife and daughter would warm his chest and he would be teaching me. He never asked me to press his head or his feet and I never thought it necessary to do anything for him. He was my older brother, it was his duty to tutor me.

One day he suffered a violent coughing attack. Two hours passed and, still coughing, he hadn't finished going over the translation with me. I became annoyed.

"I'm not going to study any more, you cough too much," I said angrily.

"You silly girl, I'm not coughing deliberately," he said with a laugh and then promised he wouldn't cough again.

I don't know why he was so interested in my future. When I passed my matric exam he was happier than he had been at the birth of his son. At this time he was practicing law in Jodhpur. During the vacations he invited me to his house and helped me read the Quran and Hadith in translation.

He also wrote *afsaanas* and I'm certain that after reading them that I secretly started writing myself. A little later when I read the *afsaanas* of Hijab Ismail, Majnun Gorakhpuri, and Niaz Fatehpuri, I felt that their writing reflected my personal experiences. And then, imagining myself to be the heroine of such stories, I began writing exciting ones myself.

For example: I'm very beautiful, just like the Hijab Ismail heroine, with golden hair, blue eyes . . . I'm reclining on a bed under a crimson coverlet . . . the hero walks in—my first hero was always a doctor, because perhaps in those days the only male outsider who could come into your house and feel your pulse was the doctor. This doctor was of course very handsome. All night he would sit by my bedside and would weep when my condition deteriorated, kiss me agitatedly, and wail uncontrollably at my youthful death, or, better still, commit suicide.

How interesting these stories were! Writing them was as much fun as reading them. Just as the reader feels excitement when the hero kisses the heroine on the lips in a romantic novel, in the same way the writer of such stories also experiences great excitement. Usually I tore up my stories soon after I had written them because I knew they were "filthy" and also that if anyone read them accidently I would be severely punished.

But I don't know why it was so pleasurable to write these stories and read them again and again. It seemed as if someone else had written them. As a matter of fact, they weren't really my creations or an account of my daily life; they were, instead, the essence of all the stories that had led me astray.

A collection of such stories accumulated at my bedside and what I was afraid of finally came to pass.

One day, my brother Shamim, who is a year and a half older than me, came to my room and lay down on my bed while I was in the bathroom. When he felt the crinkling of paper under his pillow, he pulled out my papers and started reading.

"Ahha . . . what filthy stuff the witch has written, god help us!"

Shamim, the wretch, then began reading the story aloud.

"Dr. Jamil placed his fair-skinned hand on my chest, and my pink lips . . ."

I was in the bathroom next to my room and had already put *besan* in my hair. Oh god! You can't imagine how I was tormented. God, if he reads another line I will have no choice but to drown myself!

Filled with terror, I began screaming at the top of my lungs. The whole house was in an uproar. People thought a snake had appeared from somewhere and bitten me. Poor Shamim flung aside the papers and ran to help me. I hurriedly threw on some clothes, rushed out of the bathroom, and clawed Shamim's face. He was bewildered and confused. Fearful that I had been bitten and was perhaps dead, he hadn't read another line. I immediately burnt the entire manuscript. Shamim did his best to broadcast the fact that I had been writing filthy stuff, but I said it was only a translation. The poor boy was known to be a liar so no one took his allegation seriously.

Even now I'm terrified by the thought that if one of my other brothers had stumbled upon my stories all hell would have broken loose. From that day on I vowed never to write such dirty stories and I decided that even if I did write them I would tear them up immediately. Now the memory of those days makes me laugh. There was nothing in those stories except a shallow ardour that, after some time, seemed very superficial.

And then for many years I didn't write anything. The world changes after you complete your B.A. In four years you grow up so much. I was forced to read assigned course texts. From Greek drama and Shakespeare to Ibsen and Bernard Shaw—I read so much. Bernard Shaw had my heart in his fist. *Fasaadi*, my first play, was influenced heavily by his writing. I drew the subject of the play from my environment and Bernard Shaw provided the bricks and mortar. In my B.T. classes Azra Haider, one of my classmates, teased me by calling me Bernard Shaw, and that was when I decided to liberate my writing from his clutches.

During this period in my life I encountered a dynamic personality who really shook me up. Was there anyone alive who could meet Rashid Apa of the bright eyes and smiling, fresh face and not be overwhelmed by her?

I saw her for the first time at a meeting. Begum Bhopal was chairing it. Wearing heavy shawls and coats, the women in the audience were shivering on this cold, blustery day while Rashid Apa, dressed in a sleeveless blouse and sari, was delivering an impassioned speech. Her black, curly hair was blowing in the air because the window across from her was ajar. The women in the audience were muttering, complaining about her short hair, her sleeveless blouse and the bitterly cold breeze blowing in from the open window. But perhaps her speech was no less biting, because afterwards Begum Bhopal scolded her severely. That day her boldness caused a furor and, without understanding very much of what she had said, I gathered her words to my heart as though they were pearls.

In 1937 Rashid Apa became Rashid Jahan of *Angare*. Now children, too, could read her smoldering words.

And then my handsome doctor-hero of the long slender fingers, the orange blossoms and crimson coverlets, all disappeared in a puff of air. The Rashid Apa who was cast in clay destroyed all my marble statues.

Life appeared before me in all its nakedness. Those who have met Rashid Apa know her well. If those very people encounter the heroine of my stories they will assume that she and Rashid Apa are twins, because I simply picked Rashid Apa and placed her on the shelf of my *afsaanas;* she is the only one who could have been the heroine in the world of my imagination. But when I think carefully about my stories I realize that I have only been able to seize Rashid Apa's boldness and her candour. Her rich, overwhelmingly impressive personality has evaded my grasp. I always hated the griping, weeping, whining womanhood that bore bastards. I regard as a curse that loyalty that exists for the sake of loyalty alone and loathe all those other qualities that are considered to be an eastern woman's adornment. I am exasperated by sentimentalism. Passionate love is not at all the fire that "doesn't ignite when ignited and is inextinguishable when one tries to extinguish it." To be obsessed with the beloved, to commit suicide when thwarted, to make a fuss—all these things are forbidden in my religion. Love is ruled by the heart and the mind, it's not a disease of the soul.

I learned all this from Rashid Apa and I was convinced that one woman like Rashid Apa was far superior to ten ordinary women.

After the division of the country one's mind was emptied of everything save communal riots. The country became fragmented and so many beautiful and precious values were shattered as well. Calls for purposeful literature proved to be even more distressing and the predicament created by questions like, "Why should we write? And what should we write?" further obscured our paths. The Progressive Writers' Movement gave us a great deal but also took away a lot. We found many new companions, lost so many old friends. And then, in the words of the poet, "The branch on which we had built our shelter is no more . . ."

The Movement was blown apart. Films deluged the Bombay group, on whom people had depended heavily. It's obvious that one cannot make a living just by writing for magazines and journals, nor can novels and collections of short stories provide the sole means of support in Bombay, although a secure livelihood is assured if one can put one's talent to work in films.

When we began writing for films we realized that the force of boldness and candour do no good here. What is required is that which will make you rich instantly; you will have to walk along a predetermined path. And so it happened that regardless of what it took, those who walked that path continued to walk.

My experience of communal riots didn't go beyond what I had heard. I couldn't feel or write more than "Dhani Bankpan" and "Jaren." But while I was writing these two narratives my heart took a big tumble. Till now all the stories I had written didn't have any fathers and mothers, or if they did, the parents were not dynamic characters. It was my view that one could gain victory over parents by ignoring them. What more are they except obstacles in one's path? "Don't do that" was still stuck in my head. But it was only when I wrote these two essays that I really saw my mother.

Everyone had gone to Pakistan, leaving her alone. I went to Jodhpur to meet her. Amma had moved into a small room across from our ancestral home. Our own expansive house had been taken over by the army.

When I arrived, I saw her sitting all alone in an empty desolate room. Amma had never had the time to coddle or kiss us. I don't recall that she had ever expressed her love before. But this time when she saw me she began weeping uncontrollably, like a child. During my stay I saw her gazing silently again and again out of her window at the house where we had all lived once as a large happy family, where children ran about, and where fights followed by reconciliation were a common occurrence.

I considered her age. I thought about her aloneness. Even after delivering ten robust children, she was alone.

A storm of love raged in my heart. My maternal instincts were aroused. I looked at my mother, then looked at my daughter and found myself bound between the two. When I saw my mother, I was moved with love for all the old women in the world, women who populate it, give birth to children in pain and agony, nurture them, endow them with whatever they have, and in return ask for neither a sealed statement nor a receipt on legal paper. Their offspring are regarded as obedient if they take care of their parents in their old age, and deemed unfortunate if they have nothing left for their parents after providing for their own families. In ancient times the old were considered to be useless beings and were buried alive. How horrifying the desolation of old age is.

It was just a coincidence that I met my mother and some strings that had been silent all this time were plucked. There are so many other strings that are dead, that are still slumbering. Who knows when those *mizrabs* will be created which, when struck, will shatter other slumbers. Moss gathers on standing water. A tiny pebble falls into the water . . . the moss is disturbed . . . the reflection of a glimmering world sparkles on the surface of the water, man takes a step forward.

Bombay, January 2, 1970

AMRITA PRITAM

1919–2005

(Punjabi)

Amrita Pritam was born in Gujranwala in the Punjab, in what is present-day Pakistan. In 1947, at the time of Partition, she came as a refugee to Delhi. The violence she witnessed haunts all her writing. Pritam wrote in her mother tongue, Punjabi, but because she felt there was no audience for Punjabi writing, she often had her work translated into Hindi before first publication, so it could gain a wider, national audience. Her celebrated poem "Waaris Shah Nuun" ("To Waris Shah"), from the 1948 collection Laamiyan Vaatan, *evokes the figure of the Waris Shah, the eighteenth-century poet of Punjab who wrote of the love and sufferings of Heer. In the aftermath of much bloodshed, Waris Shah must return from the grave to inscribe a fresh page in the Book of Love. Pritam lived an unconventional life, divorcing her husband and traveling all over the world to give poetry readings. She had several intense love affairs that fueled her art. One was with the Urdu poet Sahir Ludhianvi, whom she met in Delhi in 1944. In her memoir Pritam speaks of how she used to smoke the cigarette butts he left behind in her house as a way of getting closer to him. For several decades she edited the Punjabi journal of new writing,* Nagamani, *and in this task she was helped by her companion, the poet Imroz.*

The high cost of Pritam's personal and sexual freedom was also something about which she was never afraid to write. A prolific writer, she worked in multiple genres—poetry, fiction, and autobiography. In an interview with Carlo Coppola Pritam said, "I started writing very early, earlier than even fifteen. I was less than that. My father was a writer, and I was the only child. My mother died when I was eleven. I was absolutely alone, so out of loneliness, I started writing and my father encouraged me." Although not officially a member of the Communist Party, she was deeply involved in the left-wing politics of the post-independence era and counted many of the Progressive Writers as her friends. Her important works include Pinjar (The Skeleton, *1950*) and Kagaz te Canvas (Paper Was My Canvas, *1973*). In Rasidi Ticket (The Revenue Stamp, *1976*), she writes in a journal-like form of the pleasures and pains of a writing life. In *1981*, she was awarded the Bharatiya Jnanpith Prize for Literature.

"To Waris Shah"

Today I asked Waris Shah:
Speak from your grave;
Open a new chapter
In the Book of Love.

A daughter of the Punjab once wept;
You wrote her long story for her.
Today millions of daughters weep,
Waris Shah. They're calling you.

O Friend of sorrow,
Look at the Punjab.
The village square heaped with corpses,
The Chenab flooded with blood!

Someone mixed poison
In the five rivers;
Their flow
Watered the Punjab.

Poison has sprouted
From this fertile land.
Look, how far the red has spread.
Curse how far the red has spread!

Poisoned air
Floated into the jungles
Turning all bamboo flutes
To snakes

Biting everyone's lips;
Their tongue tips rose up
And quickly all parts
Of the Punjab turned blue.

Song is crushed in every throat;
Every spinning wheel's thread is snapped;
Friends parted from one another;
The hum of spinning wheels fell silent.

Oars have left all boats
And float in the current;
Peepal branches with swings
Lie broken.

Where is the grove where love songs
Used to echo, where the flute?
All Ranjha's brothers
Have forgotten how to play the flute.

Blood keeps falling upon the earth,
Oozing out drop by drop from graves.
The queens of love
Weep in tombs.

It seems all people have become Kaidos,
Thieves of beauty and love—
Where should I search out
Another Waris Shah.

Waris Shah!
Open your grave;
Write a new page
In the Book of Love.

From *The Revenue Stamp*

MY SIXTEENTH YEAR

Came my sixteenth year—like a stranger. Inside me, there was an awareness I could not explain.

Except for Father, there was no one else in our house. He wrote away and sometimes would keep at his work all through the night and sleep during the day. Had Mother been alive, my sixteenth year would have been different; it would have come like a friend, a near relative.... But without Mother, there was a great deal missing from my life. To shield me from outside influences, Father thought it right that I should have no familiarity with anyone: not with any girl from school nor with any boy from the neighbourhood.

Like a thief came my sixteenth year, stealthily like a prowler in the night, stealing in through the open window at the head of my bed....

Our house was full of books. Most of them were on religion, about *rishis* and about meditation. There were a few books of history but into these too, *apsaras* sometimes intruded—like Menaka or Urvashi, out to seduce the meditating *rishis*. It was reading them that my sixteenth year broke through the age of my innocence....

Every *apsara* disturbing the meditations of a *rishi* was, mythologically speaking, the commissary of Lord Indra. My sixteenth year must also have been Lord Indra's work, invading the purity of my childhood. It was now that I began to write poetry, and on every poem I wrote, I carried the cross of forbidden desires. Just as the *rishis* became restless as each *apsara* appeared, so my rebellious thoughts pursued me, giving me no peace....

And yet that year established no kinship with me. It was a clandestine relationship. Like me, it was scared of Father. As it stood away from me behind a door, every poem I wrote I tore to bits and appeared before Father, an innocent, dutiful child.

Not that he objected to my writing poetry. He had himself given me my first lessons in metrical composition. But what he expected from me was religious verse, orthodox and conventional in style.

That was how my sixteenth year came and went. Nothing very significant happened. Yet life took on a different meaning. It was the beginning of the uneven road of life with all its hairpin bends, its ups and downs. It was also the beginning of curiosity. I questioned parental authority, I questioned the value of doing my work at school by rote. I questioned what had been preached to me and I questioned the entire stratified social scheme. What I had so far learnt was like a strait-jacket that gives way at the seams as the body grows. I was thirsty for life. I wanted living contact with those stars I had been taught to worship from afar. What I got instead was advice and constraint which only fed my rebellion.

I suppose everyone goes through this phase. But it happened to me with three times greater impact. First, there was the drabness of middle-class morality; then the dosage of "don'ts" thrust down my throat which I somehow felt I would have been spared, had my mother been alive. There was the overbearing presence of my father, a man of religion. Poor Father. He wanted me to be an obedient, self-effacing daughter and here was I in my sixteenth year bearing my cross like a pang of an unfulfilled love. I was sixteen and memory creeps into every phase of my life. . . .

I caught its spirit again and again. At the time of the partition of the country in 1947, when all social, political and religious values came crashing down like glass smashed into smithereens under the feet of people in flight . . . those crushed pieces of glass bruised my soul and my limbs bled. I wrote my hymns for the suffering of those who were abducted and raped. The passion of those monstrous times has been with me since, like some consuming fire—when I wrote later of a beloved's face; of the aggressors from neighbouring countries; of the crime of the long Vietnamese night, or, at one stage, of the helpless Czechs. . . . In the haunting image of beauty and in the anger at wrong and cruelty, my sixteenth year stretches on and on. . . .

I thank the fates that conspired to break through the years of my innocence. That conspiracy relates not only to that one year alone but to the whole of my life.

Each thought of mine year after year intrudes upon those innocent years. I pity the patience and resignation of those who come to terms with wrong, I am happy I have not had the solace of peace as I go alone on my restless quest . . . except, perhaps, that I have since acquired the sense to discern. And like in my sixteenth year, I do not negotiate my walls by stealth. I do not avoid confrontation. As I begin my fiftieth year my feelings have the same intensity. Even now, everything around me seems to constrict the soul just as the clothes one grows out of during adolescence.

The lips are parched with the thirst for life; desire comes back to stretch the hand and touch the stars. Wherever in the world a wrong is done, I continue to feel a deep sense of outrage.

A SHADOW

A deep dark shadow walked along my side for as long as I can remember. It gradually came on me that much was layered into it: the face of my ideal lover, and mine, that I imagined growing wiser, stronger, more mature. The layer deepest down was of the freedom of my own and other lands.

Whatever I wrote was inspired by this shadow, to which I gave flesh and blood, a vague mass in which I sought to reveal something luminous in quality.

Was this out of a longing to embody God—a God with so many faces? The moments of my life expand to reveal beauteous concepts and forms. . . . Those moments were painful, like the bird song in the morning, heard one moment, lost the next. I remember writing once, "I have many contemporaries, only I am not contemporaneous."

It was well if someone gave ear to my songs. I had no right to claim it.

I was yet a child when I heard those myriad voices of hate and abuse. There were flags of so many denominations and so many flagstaffs on which they fluttered. They thought I too wanted to fly on my own. I wanted to cry out to them all, "My friends, have no illusions. You're welcome to your faiths and your flags. I want nothing." But did anyone care? Would a time come when they would hear? Not when it came to my own language. This is as true today as it was thirty years ago.

This was my first painful experience. I did not know it would last a lifetime.

A few elders of the earlier generation in the field of Punjabi letters—Gurbux Singh, Dhani Rama Chatrik, Principal Teja Singh—merely smiled. Two of them passed away. Gurbux Singh decided to create a world of his own—which had little to do with all that was happening around him.

Deep down in the layers of my mind, was the first impact of a religion against which I had risen as a child, when I had seen that glass tumbler touched by someone with a different faith became impure.

This broadened the outlook of my innermost eye, and even after having suffered so much from the partition, I found it within me to deplore dispassionately the holocaust caused by the devotees of the two religions. Thus it was that I came upon that painfully sensitive face around which my novel *Pinjjar* (Skeleton) was written.

I had hardly stepped out of my teens then. I saw in that face, the embodiment of the man of my dreams. (I wrote about him at some length in *Akhri Khat*.) It was like leaping into the flames every day. I was worn out by the effort and when someone telephoned to give me the news of the Akademi Award in 1957, my first thought was: "Lord! I didn't write *Sunehre* for an award! If the one who had inspired me hadn't read the book, did it matter at all to me if this entire world had?"

Late that evening came a reporter and a photographer from the press. The photographer wanted me to pose as one engrossed in the act of writing. I put a sheet of paper on the table in front of me and, pen in hand, began writing, in a trance, the name of the one for whom I had written *Sunehre*. "Sahir, Sahir, Sahir. . . ." I had completely filled the sheet with that name.

When the pressmen had gone and I was alone, it struck me: "What if in the photo that would appear in all the papers next morning, the incantation 'Sahir, Sahir, Sahir . . .' would show?"

It was like living through the classical romance of Manju madly calling out "Laila, Laila, Laila. . . ."

But in the photograph my hand had obscured the sheet of paper on which I was writing. Not a squiggle of what I wrote was to be seen in the morning papers. Momentarily, I was relieved. But then a cry of anguish when . . . God knows it wasn't true . . . it wasn't!

I have carried a little more of Sahir into the novels *Ashoo, Ik Si Anita,* and again in *Dilli Diyan Gallian* through the character of Sagar.

I wrote also, poems. Sunhere till then, was the longest—longest in fact of all those under the title *Chetter*. After an exile as it were of fourteen years, I felt at long last that I was through with this phase of my life.

Yet the years one has lived through are not like the clothes one wears. Constrictive corsets leave marks that might mar the beauty of a sensitive complexion, but the scars left by the years that one lives through, are infinitely deep. . . .

Much later, when I was at Varna, a city south of Bulgaria, flanked by the sea on one side and mountainous forests on the other, my wild imagination conjured up a ship sailing towards the shore and from the ship he seemed to have alighted and entered through the window of my hotel room. . . .

The real and the illusive so intertwined, I sat up and wrote the poem beginning with the line:

Long have thoughts of you lain in exile.

The curse of my lonesome state has been broken through . . . by Imroz. But before I met him, I had the privilege of a friendship with a wondrous soul. Sajjad Haider had come into my life before the partition. I had, however, never so far come across anyone who had not brought complications and misunderstandings in his train. Bitterness had been shed all around by litterateurs . . . barring, of course, Sajjad. He was perhaps the first real friend I had.

As long as I was in Lahore, we met often enough and talked—yet only as occasion demanded. He carried with him always an air of respectability. Soon after the riots began, dusk-to-dawn and then all-day curfews followed. But at whatever time the curfew was lifted, he would come—no matter for how brief a while. In between came April 23 and my little daughter's first birthday. With arson and rioting all around, there was no thought whatsoever of a celebration. Yet whose was that knock at the door? Sajjad's. He had braved all and come with a birthday cake for her.

The riot-torn month of May 1947 took me for safety to Dehradun. Letters from Sajjad came regularly nonetheless. Then, at about the time my son was born, Sajjad also became a father at Lahore. I named my son Navraj; Sajjad found a name sounding nearly alike for his, Navi. We saw each other's sons through the photographs we exchanged.

One day Navraj had fever. My anxiety grew with the days. When I found the time to reply to Sajjad's letter, I happened to mention something about the little one's fever. The letter I received by return post is still engraved in my memory. He had written: "I have been praying all night for your son. There is an Arabic saying: 'when the enemy prays, the prayer is bound to be granted.' In the eyes of the people I am an enemy of your country at this hour. . . . God forbid that I ever become one of yours or your child's. . . ."

My poem about the partition—*To Waris Shah*—came after I had written *Neighbouring Beauty*. This poem I had sent to Sajjad. As chance would have it, I lost the Punjabi version. That explains why it has never been published in my language; Sajjad, however, translated it into English and had it published in *The Pakistan Times*.

NISSIM EZEKIEL

1924–2004

(English)

Nissim Ezekiel was born in Bombay to a Jewish Bene-Israel family. He has spoken of how as a child he used to go to the synagogue with his parents, but on completing school he decided to abandon religion. After a few years of studying philosophy in London, he worked his way back to India as a deck scrubber on a boat that was traveling to Indo-China. He experimented with drugs, and it took an LSD trip (during a visit to America) to blow his mind and turn him into a "believer." Many of his poems, with their ironic clarity of voice and their elegance of form, turn on a tussle with God. The tension between the life of the spirit and that of the flesh, between metaphysical longing and fleshly desire, animates his poems. Gathering inspiration from Modernist poets such as T. S. Eliot and Ezra Pound, Ezekiel moved away from what he felt was the tired Romanticism of a generation of poets before him. He believed that the English language had to be tuned to the Indian landscape and the crowded, multicultural realities of the city of Bombay. Time and again he evokes his outsider status as a Jew in India, but an Indian nevertheless who has made his choices: "My backward place is where I am." The line is a dig at Naipaul, who in his Area of Darkness *heaps scorn at the backwardness of India. In the mid-1960s, Ezekiel worked on a series of poems that he called "Very Indian Poems in English." Their satirical tone with lines like "Visit please my humble residence also. / I am living just on opposite house's backside" garnered a good deal of controversy, with people saying that he was making fun of the* way his fellow citizens spoke English. Ezekiel defended himself by replying he was just putting into poems what he actually heard coming from the mouths of others. In addition to his eight volumes of poetry, Ezekiel has written numerous essays, published a collection of plays, and translated poetry from Marathi. He also founded a literary magazine and wrote columns for the newspapers. His important volumes of poetry include The Unfinished Man *(1960)*, The Exact Name *(1965)*, Hymns in Darkness *(1976)*, *and* Latter-Day Psalms *(1982)*.

"Background, Casually"

I

A poet-rascal-clown was born,
The frightened child who would not eat
Or sleep, a boy of meager bone.
He never learnt to fly a kite,
His borrowed top refused to spin.

I went to Roman Catholic school,
A mugging Jew among the wolves.
They told me I had killed the Christ,
That year I won the scripture prize.
A Muslim sportsman boxed my ears.

I grew in terror of the strong
But undernourished Hindu lads,
Their prepositions always wrong,
Repelled me by passivity.
One noisy day I used a knife.

At home on Friday nights the prayers
Were said. My morals had declined.
I heard of Yoga and of Zen.
Could I, perhaps, be rabbi-saint?
The more I searched, the less I found.

Twenty-two: time to go abroad.
First the decision, then a friend
To pay the fare. Philosophy,
Poverty and Poetry, three
Companions shared my basement room.

2

The London seasons passed me by.
I lay in bed two years alone,
And then a Woman came to tell
My willing ears I was the Son
Of Man. I knew that I had failed

In everything, a bitter thought.
So, in an English cargo-ship
Taking French guns and mortar shells
To Indo-China, scrubbed the decks,
And learned to laugh again at home.

How to feel it home, was the point.
Some reading had been done, but what
Had I observed, except my own
Exasperation? All Hindus are
Like that, my father used to say,

When someone talked too loudly, or
Knocked at the door like the Devil.
They hawked and spat. They sprawled around.
I prepared for the worst. Married,
Changed jobs, and saw myself a fool.

The song of my experience sung,
I knew that all was yet to sing.
My ancestors, among the castes,
Were aliens crushing seed for bread
(The hooded bullock made his rounds).

nissim ezekiel

3

One among them fought and taught,
A Major bearing British arms.
He told my father sad stories
Of the Boer War. I dreamed that
Fierce men had bound my feet and hands.

The later dreams were all of words.
I did not know that words betray
But let the poems come, and lost
That grip on things the worldly prize.
I would not suffer that again.

I look about me, now, and try
To formulate a plainer view:
The wise survive and serve—to play
The fool, to cash in on
The inner and the outer storms.

The Indian landscape sears my eyes.
I have become a part of it
To be observed by foreigners.
They say that I am singular,
Their letters overstate the case.

I have made my commitments now.
This is one: to stay where I am,
As others choose to give themselves
In some remote and backward place.
My backward place is where I am.

"Poet, Lover, Birdwatcher"

To force the pace and never to be still
Is not the way of those who study birds
Or women. The best poets wait for words.
The hunt is not an exercise of will

But patient love relaxing on a hill
To note the movement of a timid wing;
Until the one who knows that she is loved
No longer waits but risks surrendering—
In this the poet finds his moral proved,
Who never spoke before his spirit moved.

The slow movement seems, somehow, to say much more.
To watch the rarer birds, you have to go
Along deserted lanes and where the rivers flow
In silence near the source, or by a shore
Remote and thorny like the heart's dark floor.
And there the women slowly turn around,
Not only flesh and bone but myths of light
With darkness at the core, and sense is found
By poets lost in crooked, restless flight,
The deaf can hear, the blind recover sight.

MAHASWETA DEVI
1926–2016

(Bengali)

Mahasweta Devi was born in Dhaka (the present-day capital of Bangladesh) into a literary family with strong roots in social activism. Both her parents were Bengali writers, and the celebrated filmmaker Ritwik Ghatak was her uncle. As a young woman she joined Santiniketan, the university founded by Rabindranath Tagore, and her studies there helped consolidate her love of beauty and a belief in its efficacy when confronting situations of violence and degradation. Her life as an activist pours into her writing. Indeed, the question of social justice, the difficult lives of the tribals, those forgotten indigenous people of India who have endured the destruction of their natural dwellings in the forest lands, enter into much of her work. Her life as an investigative journalist took her to remote villages, and what she saw and heard entered into the coruscating density of her writing. In the grassroots journal Bortika, *which she edited, the dispossessed tell their own stories. In a conversation with Gayatri Spivak, Mahasweta evoked the destruction of Native American lives and land and likened it to what has happened to the tribal peoples of India: "Only in the names of places the Native American legacy survives. Otherwise entire tribes have been butchered. Their land has been taken away." In clipped, unvarnished prose, capable of great complexity, she evokes the destruction of forms of life, both human and ecological, in an India that has become an ambitious nation-state sucked into the maw of globalization.*

In her short story "Douloti the Bountiful," a young woman from an Out-

caste family is sold into bonded labor. Her father, who is burdened by debt, is tricked into marrying the girl, Douloti, off to the money-lender, and she, cut away from home and family, is forced into prostitution. She struggles to survive, and her brief moments of inner freedom are set against the backdrop of the remembered village with its fireflies and stars. At the very end of the story, in a fierce indictment of the new nation, Douloti's wasted, abscess-ridden body lies spread-eagled across a map of India colored in chalk that schoolchildren have made for the Independence Day celebrations. As so often in Devi's work, it is the female body in all its generative power and suffering that lies at the heart of things.

In an interview we have included here with Naveen Kishore, Mahasweta Devi speaks of her great love of words, how she collected them, jotting those that struck her in her notebook, letting their sense and sound irradiate her so that her mind moved in a web of associations, granting flesh to the story. It is in this manner that she speaks of her process of writing about sati, the ritual self-immolation that was decreed for Hindu widows. There were words and phrases that haunted her, detailed accounts she found of the expenses that had to be paid by the head of the household: "The master of the house is calculating and dictating the costs of this particular celebration. Ghee. To burn along with her. Teen tala. Three rupees. Oronparon bastra. Ek taka. One rupee. That is the cloth to cover her with. The girl is possibly eight years old. Or somewhere around that age. Sati bastra ek joda. A pair of saris." Later she points out that this ritual death sentence passed on the living breathing child widow was something that was clearly sanctioned by scripture. She clarifies that it was also possible to find in the ancient Hindu texts an interdiction on this practice.

In a keynote address for the 2013 Jaipur Literary Festival, three years before her death, Mahasweta Devi looked back with great delicacy at the atmosphere of words in which she had always lived and moved ("The air I breathe is filled with words"). She spoke of her own budding sexuality as a young woman in an extended family and the crucial importance of dreams: "The only way to counter globalization, just a plot of land in some central place, keep it covered in grass, let there be a single tree, even a wild tree [. . .] small things, small dreams." Mahasweta Devi has numerous collections of short stories, novels, plays, and nonfiction; her important work includes Aranyer Adhikar (Rights of the Forest, *1977*), Bashai Tudu (*1993*), Imaginary Maps (*1995*), and The Book of the Hunter (*2002*).

"So Many Words, So Many Sounds"

NAVEEN KISHORE: When you're actually sitting down . . . do you see things in pictures? Do you worry about form and content in a certain way? Do you actually get preoccupied with the craft of writing? Do you just let it flow? Or is it a conscious plan?

MAHASWETA DEVI: No, no, nothing flows that easily. I have lots of things scribbled down . . . let me see . . . my notebooks are scattered . . . there was a time when I would write down words I came across. Here, for example. *Parnanar*. Made of *polash* leaves. This refers to a strange ritual. Say a man has died in a train disaster. His body couldn't be brought home. His relatives then, using straw or other materials . . . the area I speak of is full of the flame of the forest tree . . . the *polash*. So they use its leaves to make a man. There's another extraordinary word. *Subhhikshma*. You've heard of *durbhikshma*. Or famine. When one describes a year as being *subhhikshma*, it means there was no crop failure that year. *Su* means good.

Paap purush. Something out of folk belief. Doomed to eternal life. He keeps vigil over other people's sins. He appears. Doesn't appear. He has not sinned himself. But he keeps account of everybody else's transgressions. Of their *paap*. Ceaselessly. And so he walks the earth. Taking note of the smallest things. A goat. Punished. Tethered to its post under the blinding sun. Unable to reach water or shade. Then the *paap purush* leaves behind his words. "That is a crime. What you have done is wrong." "*Tui ja korli ta paap.*"

Actually it is not a person. Merely the embodiment of an idea.

NK: Yes, I realize that. But just imagine. Say I was entrusted with the job of keeping an account of all the *paap*. What sort of qualifications would I have? In the sense that, am I taken because I am trusted or because I am being punished? Because it is a very punishing task.

MD: It might be a punishment. He may have committed some grave crime. *Shey hoyto kono paap korechhilo*. Some unforgivable sin. And so now, he is doomed to be a *paap purush* through all eternity. And

mahasweta devi

in fact, there is never just one *paap purush*. There are many. Just as there are many places that believe in this.

And there are so many more beautiful words. Bengali words. *Chorat*. Meaning planks. Then, *dak shankranti*. This refers to the *Chaitra shankranti*. *Dak maaney dekey dekey jai*. Those selves who are extremely conscientious, vigilant . . . only they can hear this call. Of the old year as it leaves. Questioning. The old year ends today. And the new one begins tomorrow. What have you not done? What have you still left to do? Finish it now.

Thakuri kolai. It is a kind of dal . . . like rajma. It is used only as an offering for the gods. During pujas.

Garbha daan. This is very interesting. A woman is pregnant. Someone promises her that if a daughter is born, she will be given this and this. If a son is born, then something else. *Garbha thaktey daan korecchey*. The gifting has happened while the child is still in the womb. This legend claims that the unborn child can hear this. And can remember. And record it in its mind. Later, he or she may ask that person about the promise. About the *garbha daan* that is still due.

Our India is so very interesting. Take for instance the pardhi tribe of Maharashtra. Denotified tribals. Because they are tribals, girl children are in great demand. The husband of a pregnant woman can easily auction off or sell the unborn child. *Pet ki bhaaji*. *Petey ja aacchey*. What's still in the womb. *Nilam korey dicchey*. Auctioning the fruit of the womb.

Then, another word. *Jayoti patra*. That which is drawn up at birth. The horoscope.

Hell has many names. *Narak-er onek gulo naam acchhey*. One name which I like in particular is *oshi patra bon*. There are so many kinds of hell. *Oshi* means sword. And *patra* is a kind of plant with sword-like leaves. An entire forest of such plants. And the dead soul must walk through this forest. The sword-like leaves tearing into him. You are in hell, after all, because of your sins. And so your soul must now suffer this agony.

Whenever I come across an interesting word, I write it down. All these notebooks. *Koto katha*. So many words, so many sounds . . . I've just been collecting them wherever I came across them.

See here, these are the detailed accounts of the expenses of conducting sati. In the early nineteenth century. Think about it. A girl is tied up in a corner of the house. She will be burned. Her husband is dead and now she too will be killed. But the rest of the household is abuzz with activity and excitement. In the same manner in which they would bustle and plan and arrange for a marriage or any similar celebration. The master of the house is calculating and dictating the costs of this particular celebration. Ghee. To burn along with her. *Teen taka*. Three rupees. *Oronparon bastra. Ek taka*. One rupee. That is the cloth to cover her with. The girl is possibly eight years old. Or somewhere around that age. *Sati bastra ek joda*. A pair of saris. The sari that the sati will wear. There were no blouses or petticoats in those days. Only a sari. The pair amounts to two and a half rupees. *Adhai taka. Kath*. Wood. *Teen taka*. Three rupees. The priest will also take three rupees. The sati has to give to the others before she dies. *Sati ke daan ditey hoy*. That is a rupee. *Ek taka*. Which means she would distribute small change. *Chaal*. Rice. *Ek anna*. What the price of rice was in those days! *Supuri. Du poisha*. Betel nuts.

In those days, *du poisha* was a half of *ek anna. Phool. Ek anna. Tokhon to sholo anna ek taka*. Sixteen annas made a rupee. The currency of the times. It started from pai. *Teen pai-te ek poisha . . . shiki-te ek taka. Du shiki-te ek adhuli.*

A *shiki* is what would be 25 paise today. Or 4 annas of yore. In those days you had a pai. Very small coin. Adhla. Or half of *ek poisha. Ek poisha* was rather large. Larger than our one-rupee coins of today. Like a two-rupee coin. Made of copper.

Anyway, to return to the accounts. *Korpur*. Camphor. For *ek anna. Shiddhi*. Also for *ek anna*. This is very important. *Shiddhi* is bhang. It would be used to intoxicate the girl. *Holud. Ek anna*. Turmeric, required for all auspicious occasions. *Chandan, dhoop, aar narkel*. Sandalwood, incense and coconut, *shob miliye ek poisha*. All together one poisha.

There's more. *Behara*. The men who will carry her in the *palki*, the palanquin. Five annas. Four plus one anna. *Dhuli*. Those who will beat the drums. Eight annas. And the *naptani*, she will get—

NK: *Naptani?* Who was that?

MD: We have seen such women even in our childhood. Like the barber or *napit*, she would visit the houses to trim women's nails,

mahasweta devi 131

clean their feet, put *alta* . . . and the *tabaldar* . . . to play the tabla. Three annas. The total came to 15 rupees, five annas, three paise. *Ponero taka. Paanch anna. Teen poisha.* And there you are. There's a satidaha for you. And your seat in eternal heaven is guaranteed.

Here, I had noted the source. *Satidaha.* By Kumudnath Mullick.

There are two categories of sati. *Sohagun* sati and *dohagun* sati. *Sohagun* is when the wife is actually with the husband when he dies. *Dohagun* is when the husband is somewhere else and the news is brought of his death.

So in the Rigveda it says, *imanari raho vidhaba shu patni / ragna eno sharpisha shamprit shantan.* This should read *samprishantan.* "*Ei shokol nari, boidhobbey klesh bhog kora opekkha, ghrito o anjon lupto— poti ke prapto hoiyya uttam ratna dharon purbak agnimoddhey asray lau.*" *Agun.* Take shelter in fire. Addressing the widows. Instead of suffering the hardship of widowhood, pour sandalwood paste and ghee on your husband's body, and then, wearing your finest jewellery, take shelter within the (funeral) fire.

The second part says *anasraya anamiva su seva aarohontu janaya joni magne. Hey nari, shongshaarer dikey phiriya cholo.* Woman, return to the family. *Gathrothhan koro. Tumi jahar nikat shoyon koritey jaitechho, tini got-ashu hoiya giyacchen.* He has died. *Choliya aaisho.* Come away. *Jini tomar pani grohon koriya garbhadaan koriyachhilen, shei potir patni hoiya jaha kicchu kartabya chhilo, shobi tomaar kora hoyiachhey.* Your obligations are over.

Thus, both pro-sati, and anti-sati. You get both in the scriptures. I found this very interesting. I used this in my *Amritashanchaar.* Just for a page and a half. I have always done fieldwork like this before writing any of my works. Suddenly the thought will strike me. And I will then have to read up something. Or write it a particular way.

NK: It's beautiful, like listening to folk tales. Every word has a tale around it.

MD: This is also very interesting. *Gandharba bibaher joto shontaan krura karma, mitthabaadi, aar tara dharma o bed birohi hoy.* This is anti-love marriage. Claiming that the offspring are wily lying heathens.

Niyog karta jokhon shaami, shei chheley kshettraja putra. That means, if the child is by the husband it will be regarded as a *kshettraja putra*. A legitimate child. A "correct" child. *Nija grihey agyato shwajatiyo dwara utpanno chheley guratpanna*. If the child is the result of relations between the wife and some other male relative in the household, such a child is regarded as *gurutpanna*. *Goponey jaakey utpadon kora hoyecchey*. One who has been conceived in secret. He'll never have a proper identity.

NK: Where is this from?

MD: I don't have all the sources written down. Can't remember them all.

NK: But they have been used by you?

MD: Yes. Somewhere or another. They have come in use. Fitted in.

Ma o baba-r ubhoyer ba ekjoner parityakto putra ke putra roopey grohon korley she hoy apaap pitta put-ra. Abandoned by either the father or the mother, or by both, he will be called *apaap pitta*. Blameless.

Kumari kanya gopone shabarna purusher (a man from within her own clan) *putra janma diley* that child is called—*kaneen*. It's a very common word. I have used it in some of my stories. Kunti had once said, "Each of my sons is justified. None of them is *kaneen*." But *kaneen* was quite an acceptable form.

NK: But acceptable in what way?

MD: In some places . . . with a feudal system . . . the child of the first night used to be called *kaneen*. Such sons received a certain respect. The concept was that they were the offspring of the royal family.

Kono kammmatya brahman, shudrar petey shontan utpaadon korley jeebito thekeyo takey shob boley gonona kora hobey. A child conceived by a brahman out of lust in a low caste woman, is to be regarded as a corpse by his father. That man has no right over the child.

Jodi bidhobar petey baccha koraar jonye kaukey nijukto kora hoto. If someone in particular is appointed to impregnate a widow. The appointed male had to apply ghee all over his body before going about his task. He was to remain silent. And his job was to produce one male child. He was to fuck her only once. She would be impregnated thus, and overnight, be announced as pregnant. She would therefore be allowed to live. All this would occur within the household. For property reasons.

NK: You've used all this in your stories too?

MD: Yes. In many bits and pieces. So many stories can emerge from these scraps.

NK: The whole process is very interesting.

MD: And I have to bring in the process.

If the wife gives birth after the death of her husband. *Shekhaaney poti golakdhaamey jaabey.* That is, the man will go to heaven. But if the husband is alive, *aar streer shontaan holo . . . shekhaney* ordinary. Nothing special.

Brahman, kshatriya, vaishya, *teen barneyi heena jata*—that is scheduled caste—*ramani garbhey putra utpadan korley shey chheley kintu babar naam pay na.* Children born in scheduled caste homes, fathered by brahman, kshatriya or vaishya males, do not get to avail of their father's names, titles, or castes.

These are vessels and utensils of long ago. *Bashon. Bogno.* A flat *dekchi.* Of my mother's time or even in my childhood. Made of bell metal. Round. Now you may get them in steel. Larger. To cook rice in. *Jambaati.* A large bowl. *Baily.* A small something to put vegetables in. *Kanshi.* Like this, but made out of bell metal. To pour the fish curry into. *Paonli.* A sweet word. My mother drank water out of a *paonli ghoti.* A small *ghoti.* My mother never used a glass. *Chumkir ghati.* Made out of copper or bell metal. With little round sequin-like things stuck on them. *Chunnuni bati.* Small bowl to put *chandan* in. *Patil.* A cooking vessel. Kind of *handi. Deg.* It's something that we still use. *Beri.* Something like a *sharanshi,* tongs. Used to remove the *handi* from the fire. *Dao.* Large *bonti.* Used to cut vegetables while sitting on the floor. Even to cut fish.

See here, these are the details of "Shesh Shamanin," a story I had written. About the last shaman in the saora tribe. The child's grandmother tells stories to the unborn child. That is what a *shamanin* does. Is supposed to do. She tells it about *ittalan* which is a painting but is also god. The form of *ittalan* no longer exists among the saoras. But among the rathoa bhils, they have *pithoro* paintings which are ceremoniously and traditionally painted all over the walls. The area in front of it is supposed to be very sacred. Say you are about to sow your crop. You will place the seeds on the floor. In that space. Before you sow your crop. Your first crop you will place there too. Very few persons are entitled to paint these. The saoras are among those tribes where painting is religion. It's very interesting. These are the eastern zone saoras. And those are of the western zone. The rathoas. It is painting. But it is also god.

NK: But isn't that an interesting concept? That painting is bringing god into existence. That the painter is actually painting god.

MD: And what is most interesting about the *pithoro* paintings is the predominance of the horse. It's a lot like the dang pictures which are made into blocks and printed on bedcovers. The entire life is depicted. The gods who are drawn, are supposed to communicate through the painter.

NK: Almost like a medium.

MD: Yes. All these things are very interesting about the saoras. These spirits are called *soom*. The *pahari soom*. Then there are the sahib *sooms* also. For there were foreigners there, then. Suddenly, the painter is painting a cycle. A horse. The owner of the house points and silently queries the drawing. The painter says it is the need of the *sooms*. It is what they have asked for. If they can ride horses so can we. If the foreigners can ride cycles, so can we.

NK: So these are demands made by the spirits while the picture is being painted?

MD: Yes. They can have policemen too. The dailiness of creation. Depicted with explosive joy. Children playing. Women fetching water. A group singing and dancing. Others going off on a hunt.

NK: A lot to do with celebration. Happiness.

MD: In the case of both the saoras—the eastern and the western lot—there is no greater joy than the daily joys of life. That is the greatest joy. This festival carries on eternally.

I write here about the girl who is still an unborn child. Her nani had told her while she was still in the womb: which *ittalan* to draw to appease which *soom*.

NK: A conversation . . . communing with the unborn child.

MD: And the child in the womb understood every word. And remembered. The story goes like this. The child is born. She heard the story in her childhood. About how the saoras were forced to leave their village. She pleaded with her *shamanin*—her grandmother—to draw an *ittalan*. To drive away the outsiders. The saoras were peace-loving people. This is a fantastic description. An immense wall. Splashed with paintings. In the Orissa hills. But by the time it is completed, the outsiders have entered.

And what has been the final outcome? Those motifs are now block-printed on bedcovers. Saris. Curtains.

But the saoras had prayed there before they left their village. For a long time it remained theirs. After they left, their flowers still lie, strewn before the wall. The chickens they had sacrificed, their blood still splashed on the wall. The outsiders did not try to protect that place but nonetheless stayed in awe of it. It is something that inspires fear. And gradually it crumbled to ruins.

The old woman who had told her all this is forgetting, now. Everyone has now become contracted labour. She suddenly gets up and tells the girl that she had a dream. That the outsiders were driving away all the *sooms*. Now that she has had that dream, she is forced to draw. There are no *shamanins* left. Everyone has gone away. Then the girl says that she will do it.

NK: The one who heard the story in the womb?

MD: Yes, yes. So she begins to wash and plaster the wall. Using red earth. Pounds rice. Says, "Dadi, to what god?"

The old woman says, "Child, all the gods are spirits now. I have to provide them with courage, draw separate houses. So that they can stay there. But what to offer? There's only bad rice, country liquor."

Then the granddaughter asks, "Are they demanding?"

Dadi replies, "No, the gods too are about to die." With the final depiction of the hill on top of which these two will stay, Dadi instructs "Sacrifice the last hen."

"I will. I'll draw the *ittalan*." She calls upon her tutelage and ancestors and the *sooms*. "See, this is the last act I do, so do not take away the dreams from me."

The gods' house is high. A ladder for the gods to climb up. Surrounding saoras guarding them.

And finally, after so many years, the place becomes a bazaar. The wall is seen as a marketable curio but they could not demolish it due to the vehement opposition of the people; it became the temple of all *sooms* or gods. Thus it stayed till a big man came and photographed it in detail and carried it to the mills where they block-printed the designs. And minted money.

And this place was called *shakal shumera gruha*. The house of all *sooms*. All the gods have a place there.

Now an alley of liquor shops is known as *shumera gali*. After painting, the *shamanin* dies. Before dying she tells the girl the details of the *ittalan*. This whole story is beautiful.

NK: Tell me more. What're these jottings about?

MD: About the market within a jail. In 1993. This was when we were trying to release the women. Rice, two rupees a kg, masur dal, six rupees a kg, eggs, three for two rupees, costliest fish, 20 rupees a kg, meat at 12 rupees a kg, mustard oil 10 rupees a kg, double-toned milk from the Haringhata dairy, half a litre for two rupees, sugar at eight rupees per kg, tea, 10 rupees per kg, and biscuits, 100 gm for Rs 2. This was purchased for lifers and under-trial prisoners, sold at the above prices to the jail sepoys. They would either send the supplies home to their families or sell them off and pocket the profits. The under-trial prisoners and lifers have no chance of getting these commodities at these prices or in these quantities. I got this information when I was visiting the jails. We cooked according to the quantities prescribed and then showed it to the prisoners. Then we asked them if they got that much. Never!

Then, this *buro angul*. The thumb. Cut off in the case of Ekalavya. By way of *gurudakshina*. Details are provided about this. Ekalavya. A *bisheshan*. Adjective. *Lavya* means *chheda*. Sliced off.

Take the word *Drona*. *Purush*. This is the origin—*utpotti*. This is Sanskrit grammar, *tika*. One of the meanings of *drona* is *dogdho*—scorched. The raven or *dar kak* is also called *dron*. So is the scorpion or the *brishchik*. And the *chatusshoto dhonu*, a kind of bow, is also called *dron*. *Dron* also means *brihat jolashoy*, a vast waterbody.

Megher nayak or *meghbishesh*. When the rain clouds appear, there is always one cloud leading them. That too is known as *dron*. And when that cloud appears, a good crop is foretold. *Dron* also means the acharya or chief of the *Dhanurveda*. The book of archery. *Dron* also means mountain. Also a utensil to measure the crop.

A limit. I may say, I will give you one dron of crop. Or grain. So a unit of measurement. In the table of land measures, it is equal to 16 *kanees*. That too was a land measure. Like *bighas* and *kathas*. *Kanee* was applicable not to homestead land but to agricultural land.

Dron kheera is the name of a fruit.

Also, 32 seers of cow's milk boiled down into *kheer* will give you *dron kheer*.

So *dron* is associated with might and power, milk, food and so many many things. I'm greatly fascinated by such things.

NK: Why do you find this interesting? People ask me such questions about my photographs also. Yesterday I was walking along Camac Street. The drizzle. I was looking down to protect my spectacles. And whatever I was seeing on the road, I could see either in vertical or horizontal frames. A leaf. A stone. If you make them still, they become frames. When they become still, then I am able to explain what I find interesting and why. But I cannot explain otherwise. It's like taking what I can with my eyes closed.

MD: It's maddeningly fascinating.

I'll tell you about the kolhati tribe of Maharashtra. I wrote a story about them, "Jhuku Jhuku Railgadi." Jhuku jhuku railgadi aa gila re. In the kolhati tribe, the first girl child is not married off. This is also the custom in the dombari tribe, on the borders of Andhra Pradesh and Karnataka. The dombaris have a tradition of ceremoniously and officially marrying off their first daughter to Venkateshwar Shiva. After that marriage, the father and uncles and brothers build her a hut adjacent to their home and she begins to prostitute openly. She has to give her parents all her earnings. But such women are not hated by the community. When they walk into public spaces like the market, for instance, people tend to fawn over them. For they are the Venkateshani. They are the wives of Shiva. This goes on and on. But when she can no longer sell her body, she is provided with a hut in a far off spot, and then she is free to entertain any and every man who seeks her services. She has to survive in whatever way she can.

This is a time-honoured custom in those parts. It struck me as extremely peculiar. This happens in Telengana, where the famous Telengana battle was fought, where the people's war is still being waged. I realized that the women's side of it has never been heard. Never been considered. We read that book called Women of Telengana which Susie Tharu and K. Lalita edited... There they mention how these women are used afterwards.

In Maharashtra. The kolhati tribe. Kishore Shantabai Kaley, author of the book Against Odds, has written of this feature of the kolhatis. *Chheda nahi utaarne ka*. That means the first female child will sport bangles from childhood. Then one day her father, the panchayat pradhan and others will come and auction her. To the highest bidder.

NK: At what age?

MD: As soon as she attains puberty. The man who buys her will be the one to first take off her bangles. He will have paid 5,000 or 10,000 to her father. This custom is present among the *kolhatis*, the *dombaris*. These girls are also those who participate in the local tamasha, their form of rural theatre. Maharashtra has the highest number of kolhatis.

This girl's name is Manda Hiraman. Her parents auction her for the first time. She gets pregnant. After her son is born, she no longer has any claim on him so she must leave. Then she is auctioned for the second time. Another son. Walks away again. The more sons she delivers, the more her price goes up. People come to know that she delivers male children. The third time, what Manda did was... I met Manda. Went to her house. Talked to her. The third time, at the auction, Manda was carrying a vicious whip. She held onto it.

mahasweta devi

In secret. A whip that could slash the skin. Her father, the pradhan, the so-called client, all the men were there before her. Her mother also. When money matters were being discussed and haggled over . . . By then Lakshman Gaekwad had built his organization . . . there were branch offices here and there . . . Manda pulled out her whip and lashed out at all those around her. And then, running out, she climbed onto a cycle and fled to one of those branch offices of Lakshman.

In the meanwhile, a huge *panchayat* had met and begun its session. A terrible scandal. That a kolhati girl should act this way. They decided to burn her with *tejaab*. Acid. That was the ultimate punishment. And hang her upside down. That is, they would insult her as much as possible. Lakshman enters with Manda and says that from now on, she is the superintendent of all the social work in that entire area. "Anyone touches her and they'll have to deal with me." Then all her former clients were brought before them. Money was wormed out of them. The father who had collected a neat stash of his own was also made to pay up. And then Manda was provided with a two-storeyed wooden house in far off Jamkheda. The ground floor had a stage and Manda lived upstairs.

And now that Manda had money of her own . . . these people have a tradition of worshipping the Tuljamata. Also known as Bhabani. (She was worshipped by Shivaji too.) Every year her puja is auctioned. If you bid the highest, then all the offerings that come to the temple are yours. Manda took over that puja. Not only did she take it over, but built a temple for Bhabani right next to her own house. And then she said, speaking in her husky voice, "Amma, everyone who despised me, they all have to come here now. They have to pay here now. And whatever they offer in puja, I'll get." And the people in question were quite enraged about it.

Then Manda purchased a Bullet motorcycle. And riding that motorcycle, brandishing her whip, she rides all over the place, keeping a vigil on the rest of the people.

NK: What does she wear?

MD: The sari in the way that the Maharashtrians wear it. With pleats like the dhoti. Very womanly. Smiles. Speaks in a low voice. Not loud. Her voice is very husky. Manda managed to get many other kolhati girls to her temple. Around her. "Why do you wait here to be auctioned? Come to me." So this group of 16–17 girls would perform their traditional tamasha but weave in these themes. Bring in these issues through dance and song. And the clients are told strictly that they are merely paying for their tickets. They are to watch the performance and then make themselves scarce. The whip hangs near the door. One wrong move and you know what Manda will do to you. She's a terror.

NK: How old is she now?

MD: About 30, 32. She told me . . . when I asked her, "You are so young but you have two sons? Where are they?" She replied that she had sent her boys off to boarding school. And yet when I told her, go talk to the people in your *maikey,* your maternal home, she said, "Oh no, I couldn't."

NK: There's no question of her having a *sasur badi,* I guess. No in-laws.

MD: No question of it, she's never been married! She feasted me on *puranpuri,* which is a luxury, and *bhakri,* their usual bread. Wonderful! They have a custom among the kolhatis in Maharashtra, that if an unmarried girl has a child, and if she dies, the child gets an LIC benefit, from Life Insurance Corporation. There's just no end to this kind of interesting stuff. Life is very interesting, isn't it?

I have lots of notes and scribbles here, as you can see. Marathi lullabies, songs, lines . . .

NK: These are notes to yourself?

MD: My writing process is anything but haphazard. Before I write, I think a lot, mull over it, till it forms a crystal-clear hard core in my brain. I do all the homework I need to do. Take notes, talk to people. Find out. Then I start expanding it. After that I don't face any hitches, by then the story is in my grip. When I write, all my reading, memories, direct experience, acquired information, come into it.

Wherever I go, I jot down things . . . the mind remains alive . . . and I forget things too. I'm actually very happy with life. I don't

mahasweta devi

owe anything to anyone, I don't abide by any rules laid down by the society, I do what I want to, go wherever I want to, write down whatever I like, roam around . . . but when I come back to Calcutta I feel claustrophobic. Anyway, life has been very much worth living.

NK: Good. Now give me one last strange word, to leave with.

MD: Let's see . . . I'm telling you a theme I'm going to write on when I have time, at leisure. I've been thinking about this for a long time. The only way to counter globalization . . . just a plot of land in some central place, keep it covered in grass, let there be a single tree, even a wild tree. Let your son's tricycle lie there. Let some poor child come and play, let a bird come and use the tree . . . small things. Small dreams. After all, you have your own small dreams, don't you? Like you were saying, as you walk, you see strange frames. Rainwater pooled on the street, a leaf floating there . . .

People do not have eyes to see. All my life I have been seeing small people and their small dreams. I feel as if they wanted to lock up all the dreams, but somehow some dreams have escaped. A jailbreak of dreams. Durga, watching the train. An old woman who simply craves sleep. An old pensioner who finally gets his pension. The people evicted from the forests, where will they go? Common people, and their common dreams. Like the Naxalites. Their crime—they dared to dream. Why shouldn't they be allowed even to dream?

NAYANTARA SAHGAL

b. 1927

(English)

Nayantara Sahgal was born in Allahabad, to a renowned family, intimately tied to the freedom struggle against the British. Her mother was Viyalakshmi Pandit, the first woman president of the United Nations General Assembly, and her uncle was Jawaharlal Nehru, the first prime minister of independent India. In her memoir Prison and Chocolate Cake *(1989), Sahgal writes of how at the age of three, enjoying the pleasures of a slice of chocolate cake, she was startled to see policemen arriving at her home. Her mother was forced to explain that the police had come to take papa away to prison. Ever after the delight of chocolate cake was intermixed with the fear of prison. Both her parents were jailed by the British for their adherence to nonviolent resistance, and in 1943 Sahgal was sent with her sisters to America. She spent several years at Wellesley College where she studied Russian with Vladimir Nabokov. The powerful cosmopolitanism in her work, perhaps a result of her early upbringing, is wedded to a fierce attention to the details of political reality in India, the corruption, the mismanagement of funds, the oppression of women, the growing gap between rich and poor. But far from being merely rhetorical, these concerns are embedded in the lives of characters, women and men caught up in the turmoil of historical events over which they have no control. The stories of women trapped in a traditional, patriarchal society struggling for a measure of independence have haunted her writing.*

The novel Rich Like Us *(1989) is set during the Emergency, the era when*

Indira Gandhi, Sahgal's first cousin, took away civil liberties and imprisoned many dissenters. The protagonist Sonali, a bureaucrat who has been unjustly fired for her job, finds she must fight both for her place in society and for a measure of personal happiness. At the back of Sonali's head is the memory of a piece of writing she accidentally discovered that describes how her paternal grandmother was forced to commit sati (a ritual immolation of widows) at her dead husband's pyre. Later the novel evokes the words of the Hindi poet Dinkar—"Vacate the throne for the people are coming." In the novel, in a satirical gesture, the lines are bent from their original anticolonial sense and made to extol the power of "Madam"—Prime Minister Indira Gandhi in her new incarnation as dictator of India. Sahgal could not bear the thought that the democratic ideals so painfully gained during the anticolonial era might be destroyed in such a cavalier fashion. In recent years she has been a powerful and fearless advocate for democratic values and the rights of free expression in India.

In "Rejecting Extinction," Sahgal writes that while literature teaches us to value our diversity and rejoice in what binds us together, "the actual world, to our sorrow, has often taught us very different lessons." In the same essay she draws attention to the fact that whether it was the colonial era, or during the postcolonial disaster that was Mrs. Gandhi's Emergency, or even in her own personal life as a divorced woman struggling for happiness, she often found herself "on the wrong side of the establishment." Her important works include the novels Mistaken Identity *(1988),* A Situation in Delhi *(1989), and* Lesser Breeds *(2003), as well as several volumes of nonfiction.*

"Rejecting Extinction"

We start life as readers, not as writers. It is the chords that other writers have touched in us and awakened in us through words written perhaps in another country, another language, another century, that have given us entry into worlds not remotely like our own, and involved us in feelings and experiences we would otherwise never have had—long before we ourselves began to write—that have much to do with what we ourselves write later. In this sense there is a world of literature where we meet and touch and influence each other, and it is far removed from the actual world we live in which divides and separates us in so many ways. The world of letters teaches us to recognize our common humanity but to value our diversity and to realize that our differences are worth preserving. The actual world, to our sorrow, has often taught us very different lessons. If literature has any function it is to convey our differences to each other through our individual visions, and in doing so there is no "clash of civilizations," only a comradeship between civilizations. So I am making a distinction here between the freewheeling life of the imagination that we inhabit as writers, and life on earth where we are confined to, and operate within, specific circumstances of location and community and nationality—or of displacement from these—all of which factors have been responsible for shaping us and making us what we are.

I think it is very hard for a writer to speak in terms of generalities, like the themes this seminar will be addressing. One can only speak of what one knows from one's personal experience. In that respect I run counter to your theme of Borders and Crossing Borders—in other words a literature brought about largely by the experience of migration. I have not migrated, nor have I been part of the cross-cultural experience as it is understood today. I think of myself as having been invaded, occupied and colonized because these are not just words to me, nor a chapter in a history book. They have overshadowed my lifetime, and whatever culture-crossings have taken place in me have been a result of these and not of decision or choice. Today's border-crossings—whether of necessity or choice—strike me as being largely one-way traffic. It is my culture that must cross and change and merge. Traffic does not flow the other way. And in the process it is as if past history is best forgotten. A few years ago Mr. Naipaul was invited to a writers' get-together at Nimrana in Delhi. On the last day there was to be a discussion for which the agenda had been laid down and the topic was colonialism and other related issues. It fell to me to make the opening remarks and as soon as I started Mr. Naipaul said he was tired of colonialism and didn't want to hear any more about it. So that was that. Forgive me for not using his title but I am a republican and my tongue lapses into mister. Personally I don't think recent history can be brushed aside so casually when many living imaginations and situations worldwide are still products of it. Therefore, I was interested to see from the program that this seminar will be exploring the Concept of Self as it emerges through interaction with politics and memory.

Again, contrary to much of today's thinking, I have a hard time be-

nayantara sahgal

lieving this is One World. It is certainly a better connected world but the nation state is very much, and very aggressively, with us. Nations are not about to pool their resources or surrender their identities or give up their separate deadly stockpiles of weapons of mass destruction. Some nations think nothing of making war on other sovereign nations and occupying them. And as always, it is the powerful who lay down the agenda that others must follow. So as long as there are nations there are going to be national literatures, each arising out of its own soil and its own collective consciousness. Jawaharlal Nehru, a writer himself, has expressed India's collective consciousness in these words: "For we are very old and trackless centuries whisper in our ears." This sentence vividly evokes a distinct and unique identity, not to be confused with other national identities which are as distinct and unique. Art, of course, crosses national borders, but nothing has yet eliminated borders. It seems to me they are here to stay for a long time. And much as I would like to believe otherwise, the global arrangement I am looking at is still the one that empires brought into being by those 300-odd years of European exploration, conquest and colonization that mythologized Europe as the centre of the world, inhabited by a master race, and bestowed upon it the monopoly of civilization—all of which gave it the right to impose its mindset on the rest of creation. Those empires wound up long ago but new empires of occupation have taken their place, and so far, as essential human affairs are concerned, the West is still in charge, politically, militarily, financially, and therefore, culturally. Absurd imperial terms like the Middle East, the Near and Far East are still in use though they were concocted to indicate how Near or Far these areas were from the British Foreign Office in Whitehall, and had nothing to do with their actual position on the map as East or West Asia. Then, in the kind of globalization we have been conscripted into, we are required to subscribe to the curious economic philosophy that the world is a supermarket and the purpose of our life on earth is to go shopping. It is this mindset that tells us cross-cultural connections are more relevant today than roots, and this may well be true according to the prevailing fashions and priorities that govern us. But fashions need not be taken seriously when they are laid down for us by think-tanks and experts thousands of miles away. It makes more sense to evolve one's own criteria, relevant to one's own circumstances.

If I fit anywhere among the subjects you are going to explore it would probably be under writing as resistance. At one time or another I have been on the wrong side of the establishment—whether of the accepted power structure; or of accepted conventional morality; or of what was considered to be the sort of books Indians should be writing about India. I was brought up by rebels against the established order—people who had committed their lives to overthrowing British rule. Later, when I began to write, and was being published in Britain and America, my American agent told me, "Honey, readers don't want to read about people like themselves. They want contrasts." I had something quite different in mind which I proceeded to do. I wrote novels with contemporary Indian political settings, novels which in sequence have turned out to be about the making of modern India. When I have set a novel in the past, as I did *Mistaken Identity*, the 1920's setting related to what anguished me then about contemporary India, which in this case was the growing tide of Hindu fundamentalism. When I went back to the early 1900's in a part of *Rich Like Us*, it was to highlight the nightmarish contemporary theme of the novel, in this case the dictatorship known as the Emergency of 1975. My fiction did not rise out of the proverbial heat and dust seen through the lenses of the Raj or the post-Raj, because inside of me there was an Indian, buried for centuries, who was struggling to come out, looking and behaving like an ordinary human being—as villainous or as virtuous as any other—and not like an ethnic curiosity or an exotic oriental specimen. Just as we had come to know the English, Irish, French, Russians and others by reading their literatures—which means seeing them as they saw themselves—so others would have to see us as we saw ourselves, and not expect us to fit into their imaginings of us.

In common with all writers who write from their soil I did not feel surrounded by the presence or constant awareness of another culture to measure myself up against. At one time I was advised against politics as material for fiction. Arranged marriage, joint family, quaint customs, local colour, maharajas etc. were the favoured themes. But one does not pick and choose one's material. One works with the material one has and in my case politics was my natural material. I had no other, having grown up in a climate filled with the sound and fury, and overflowing with the passion of the fight for freedom when every issue, from the cloth you wore to the school you went to, to the company you kept, was a political issue, and when politics was not something "out there" but an intimate part of family life. But leaving aside my own case, politics—which is only another name for the conditions we live under—is very much the material of fiction, as it is of all art. The artist, above all, is a political animal, acutely sensitive to the environment she lives in. We would not have understood the times we have lived through but for the political consciousness of European, Asian, African, American and Latin American writers. In our own time politics has become increasingly inseparable from private life, and the line between public and private has been a continually disappearing one all over the world as vast numbers of people have had to face the consequences of political events in their personal lives.

Politics is about power, and not only in the public domain. For me it has been a constant presence in gender relations, in the unequal equation between husband and wife which takes the wife's subordinate role for granted. I notice as I look back on my writing that the hesitant and powerless women of my earlier novels—who are not even convinced of their right to be individuals—get more confident in the later novels, and in the last two they step out to become confident individuals. I suppose this has something to do with my own stumbling progress from virtual voicelessness as a wife to acquiring a voice and persona of my own.

Asian writing comes out of several continents now and its cross-currents of racial experience have added a new dimension to literature. Black immigrant literatures have enlarged the vistas of writing in English, transformed the English language and spun new life and lyricism from it. But it is a special genre occupying its own imaginative space, and it does not conflict with, nor can it take the place of those who write from home. Staying home makes for its own kind of writing. It is where we are located on the map that gives us our particular angle of vision along with the insights and, above all, the point of view that flow from it. This gut vision grows out of the cauldron of ideas, emotions, and physical sensations —sounds, sights, smells, food, drink—that assail us every day of our lives. As opposed to the recurring migrant theme of exile, and the pains, problems and rewards of adjustment, the daily business of living in India literally assaults us with our own realities: the ugliness of caste, corruption, female foeticide and religious fundamentalism, and alongside these, computers, satellites and a sexual revolution. We live in co-existing time zones, among tremendous contrasts, and with paradoxes of a kind that allow us to defecate without shame in public but forbid us to kiss in public. To whom can this tumultuous scene possibly matter but to the lives that are affected by it, the people who enjoy or must suffer its consequences, and those among us who feel compelled to do battle against it? The ultimate battles for a new world must be fought on one's own soil and part of every battle is putting it into words. Our stories are gut-bound to our own society. They mirror what concerns us: the things we take pride in as well as our fears and anxieties. They question our values and the direction we may be taking. In this respect my own fiction bears witness to my faith in secular political ideals, cultural and religious pluralism, and the rightness of non-violence. My last novel *Lesser Breeds* revives the decades when non-violence was used for the first and only time in history as a weapon in a fight for freedom. I meant *Lesser Breeds* to be a tribute to a heroic period, and to the continuing relevance of non-violence, but now I think of it more as an epitaph. With military might growing mightier all around us, including our own, what chance would satyagraha have against it?

The value of staying rooted, as opposed to migration, is that it preserves the wholeness of a point of view that has not had to trim itself in order to make itself understandable to another society. This organic wholeness matters, if only because the world we are living in is not even-handed on the question of identity. It is taken for granted that some identities have a right to exist while others must be surrendered. Taken far enough this would be cultural genocide. So it makes good sense to reject this form of extinction and for us, or any culture, to hold on to what makes it original and exceptional on a scene that is fast becoming standardized, and in danger of being reduced to a monoculture. By what makes us exceptional I do not mean the religious fundamentalism, here or among the diaspora, that masquerades as culture. Point of view is crucial to life and literature, the pivot on which a story turns. It is the very spine of the story. Narrative depends on it. Style is the frills you clothe it in. Character, action, inaction, what happens or doesn't happen, are the result of it. And in its larger meaning, as an angle of vision that derives from its own history, geography and regional memory, it ensures that a culture—along with the literature that can arise only from it—will remain alive. The only differences worth keeping among peoples are cultural, and if this diversity is reduced to a one-culture hegemony, then literature itself cannot survive. Great things happen, great creative energy is released in life and ideas, in language and literature, in art and science, only when cultures interact and flow into each other.

It is a mark of great literature, whether written on home ground or elsewhere, that it has a resonance beyond its time and borders. There are states of mind and feeling that reflect the human condition everywhere. One does not have to migrate to feel exiled or alien. As a child in British India I felt like a foreigner in my own home town, Allahabad, because it had so few reminders of anything Indian. All the roads were named after British generals and governors, the cinema showed English films, and every establishment catered for a British clientele. I had to learn my own language outside school and discover India outside my stifling colonial confines. Some of this is reflected in *Lesser Breeds* when a nationalist family hires a teacher in the 1930's to un-teach their daughter what she is being taught in her convent school. He wonders how to do this and discovers he can do it simply by shifting her point of view to give her an entirely different perspective of the same event.

In reverse, a migrant can feel securely rooted to the ground where he has settled because it is human nature to put down roots, and natural to adapt to one's surroundings and be influenced by them. So there is no hard and fast divide between the condition known as exile on the one hand and roots on the other. Nor can story-telling be divided into these categories. But if one thing distinguishes home-grown writing from writing elsewhere, it is the home-grown sensibility for which there is no substitute. And that is a priceless possession, not to be argued out of or given up, at least as long as there are nation states and national literatures.

My own background has set me down in a shifting landscape between exile and roots in spite of having stayed rooted. Some years ago I described my imagination as schizophrenic and invented my own definition of schizophrenia as a state of mind and feeling that is firmly grounded in a particular subsoil, but above ground has a more fluid identity that does not fit comfortably into any single mould. Nowadays I also feel like a stranger in a world whose political arrangements, economic priorities and military solutions are not of my choosing. What I am and what I write is the end result of these bits and pieces.

Earlier I referred to having been on the wrong side of conventional morality. In 1994 I made a border-crossing of my own when I published a personal correspondence titled *Relationship* that tracked the growth of a relationship outside marriage. It seemed important to bring a woman's experience—my own—to light in a country where family honour is sacrosanct, silence is the law for women, and any attempt to break it brings on merciless punishment. Border-crossings of this kind need to be made. Sometimes courage fails, as in a case I know of a Sri Lankan writer who told me she had, after much agonizing, changed the ending of a story she had written because her husband was shocked and upset that the heroine leaves her husband for her lover. To avoid upsetting her husband, endangering her marriage, and ruining her reputation, she re-wrote the ending. I asked her if the artistic outcome of the story did not require its own natural ending. She agreed it did but said she could not take the risk. If these are still the impossible terms most women have to surrender to in life and literature, then surely we who write must reject them by having our say through fiction, poetry and autobiography.

Recently I was interested to hear from a social activist who was interacting with rural women on the subject of domestic violence, that she had used an extract from *Relationship*, translated into Hindi, in a discussion with them. It had led to a lively question and answer session. My border-crossing into forbidden territory has more than served its purpose if it has found a response among rural women with whom I can share this common ground.

(Talk delivered at the University of Rajasthan, September 20, 2007)

QURRATULAIN HYDER

1928–2007

(Urdu)

Qurratulain Hyder was born in Aligarh into a literary family. Her parents were writers, and her father was also a translator from Turkish. Her mother, a short story writer and novelist, was active in the struggle for the education of women. Hyder speaks of how as a small child she spent a year with her parents in the Andamans, the Indian Ocean island where the colonial government sent their political prisoners. In 1947, both mother and daughter fled the riots of Partition and sought shelter across the border in the newly formed Pakistan, where Hyder found work as a journalist and translator and also as an editor of documentary cinema. Among the works she translated into Urdu were Henry James's Portrait of a Lady *and Truman Capote's* Breakfast at Tiffany's. *She subsequently left Pakistan for Britain and from there in 1961 returned to India. She is one of the few people to have written from both sides of the border about the massive upheavals caused by Partition. Her characters are often travelers searching for an impossible love. But even those who stay at home discover that they have become internal exiles, bound to a fitful, changing place. Hyder's writing reveals the syncretic culture of Indic civilization with its multiple religions, languages, and communities. Still her characters have to face up to terrible fissures in their day-to-day lives. The mode of collage that Hyder developed, using samplings from classical texts in swift cut-and-paste motions, allowed her to create a mosaic-like whole. Fragments of both internal and shared life are pieced together in cinematic fashion. In this way, as disjunctive historical moments are set side by side, time turns spatial and the metamorphic possibilities of identity emerge. At times her writing has the rhythmic intensity of prose poetry.*

The novel Aag ka Darya *(*River of Fire, *1959), her magnum opus, created a stir when it appeared. Forty years later she "transcreated" it, the verb she uses, from Urdu to English. The novel takes the whole of the subcontinent for its material and cuts through historical epochs, starting in Pataliputra in the fourth century* BCE *and ending in India in the mid-twentieth century. It is possible to read her aesthetics of fragmentation as a response to the violence of Partition, a powerfully inventive way of transmuting the pain of dislocation and the experience of traumatic flashbacks into the fictive delight of a literary text. The critically acclaimed novella* Sita Haran *(*Sita Betrayed*) with its restless protagonist, a woman who searches for love in an all-too-unstable world, was first published in 1960 in Karachi, in the Urdu magazine* Naya Daur.

Its fabular quality allows us to read it almost as if it stemmed from our own globalized world. Hyder's important works include Patjharki Awaz *(1965),* Raushniki Raftar *(1982), and* Aakhir-e-Shab ke Hamsafar *(1989). In 1989, she received the Bharatiya Jnanpith Prize for Literature.*

"Beyond the Stars"

SUKRITA PAUL KUMAR: A lot of thinking and writing has been done by philosophers and literary critics on the specific experience of the loneliness of a creative artist. I should like to begin our discussion by focusing your attention on the peculiar sense of loneliness that you may have encountered for you are not only a creative writer but also one who happens to be writing in Urdu in India—a language which has a comparatively limited readership here. Possibly, therefore, you may have been pushed into a greater sense of exclusiveness. How conscious are you about this "situation" of yours?

QURRATULAIN HYDER: You have asked two questions; one is regarding the loneliness of the creative writer. Though this may sound rather pompous, let's face it, it is very much there. It has always been there with an artist anywhere in the world. A writer writes in isolation. The loneliness of a Western writer, of course, has a sociological aspect. There is also another point—the loneliness of a woman writer. Well, a woman writer, whether in the West or here in the East, is more or less in an identical situation. In the East, perhaps, it's slightly worse. And then, to make it even more accentuated, you say, loneliness of a woman writing in Urdu. Writing in Urdu in India makes no difference because writing in Urdu in Canada, Pakistan or anywhere else, according to me, would not change the situation. And then, a woman writing in Urdu in India or a man writing in Urdu in India would also be the same. Women have been writing in Urdu for the last hundred years. You know that the first woman novelist wrote in the same period as the first male novelist. The point is: a woman writing self-consciously is a situation common to women all over the world.

SPK: But don't you think that there's bound to be a difference since it would depend upon the cultural context in which the writer is firmly entrenched? George Eliot or the Brontë sisters had to pose as male writers to escape the critical bias against a woman writing in nineteenth-century England. Till about 15 to 20 years ago, the situation in India was perhaps the same. Didn't the evaluation of your work depend, till a few years ago, on the fact that you were a woman writer? Also, did this cause any self-consciousness that you may have experienced or may have had to get rid of while you were writing . . . perhaps, in selecting the theme of your creative venture or the taking of a particular stance?

QH: It may come as a surprise to many that there has never been any segregation of man and woman in Urdu literature, as you may expect in a society based on the principle of segregation. I think we must understand this peculiar phenomenon at the outset. There have been women writing fiction and there have been women writing poetry in Urdu. There was a slight male chauvinistic patronisation at times, which one may encounter anywhere in the world. It was, I think, never very emphatic and the woman did not get affected enough to be disturbed as a writer. She didn't have to worry at all. For instance, my own mother started writing at the age of 13 or 14 and there was no question of any criticism, as there would have been, for instance, in the case of a woman coming out of *purdah*. Women have been writing romantic short-stories and novels for quite some time now.

As for me, what I am perturbed about is not this self-consciousness of being a woman writer, but the fact that critics are generally not attentive to what is happening in Urdu fiction. No serious critical evaluation has ever been done on fiction in Urdu. My own writing suffers due to this obvious neglect.

SPK: Does that place you in an exclusiveness of sorts?

QH: No, I don't feel that at all. I am not an isolationist, nor am I a celebrator of loneliness. That is not my problem at all. My only concern is that my work suffers from the lack of any active and lively literary give-and-take—you know, a literary life, as it were. There is a general indifference. I don't mean that I *need* critics. Only, I feel bad about the neglect that Urdu fiction suffers from as a result of this indifference.

SPK: Do you think that the creativity of the fiction writer gets thus affected?

QH: Yes, indeed. The wrong kind of approach, group mentality and group politics which promote bad and mediocre literature can do a lot of harm. I have mentioned, a number of times, really outstanding fiction writers in my writings and interviews. Most people have not even heard of them but there's never a follow-up. No one has asked me who they were or what they wrote. In Urdu, there is a strong tendency to attach one's self to a single writer. For example, a critic would start what he calls "specialising" on one writer, say, Premchand. He'd go on writing about him, his characters, the bulls in his fiction, his village scenes. Everything else in literature becomes of secondary importance for him. His total devotion to Premchand blinds him to everything else. Another one may be devoted to Iqbal and yet another to, say, modern poetry. I think this is an easy way out.

SPK: Do you think you could, perhaps, explain this tendency by trying to understand the complexity of the Indian society wherein each great writer constitutes a category in himself? There is a diversity or rather a diversification of concerns and multiplicity of perspectives available to us through our rich heritage and tradition, through exposure to a variety of cultures and religions down the ages on the one hand and, on the other, advent of high technology and progress-oriented modern civilization. In the West, there are movements and categories to classify the writers (Primitivism, Naturalism, etc. and literature of cruelty, literature of silence and so on), while here, it becomes far more difficult to "group" writers.

QH: Perhaps, but what I'd like to emphasise strongly is the *lack* of original thinking in critical writing here. It is so repetitive. I can close my eyes and repeat to you from the word "go" that the Progressive Movement began in 1936 and till today they are busy writing *reports* rather than criticism, producing more or less surveys. This goes on year after year. There is no criticism worth its name and their thinking is so confused. For instance, a group of writers made such a hullabaloo about ten years ago over the so-called abstract and symbolistic writing. Yet today the same people are condemning it. At that time there was supposedly a revolution in Urdu fiction and all earlier writing was rejected as backward and stupid. A lot of bad stories were suddenly recognised as reflecting *real* intellectual thinking, real inner life, etc. All those cliches were used for stories which were not even riddles, for riddles can be much more interesting. The same critics who had promoted that kind of writing are now condemning it. The point is that there is no clear thinking and perhaps there is no clearly developed critical faculty.

SPK: Shall we take up another point of discussion? It is a known fact that your father, Sajjad H. Yaldrum, was himself an established short-story writer writing in the conventional style before the emergence of modernistic techniques or perspectives. A generation later, you have been producing a very different kind of fiction, both long and short. Would you accept that there has been a progress in literature and that you've taken the short-story forward? Or, is it just a question of how the writer confronts his own reality and gives his own kind of fictional representation to his experience?

QH: I think there's definitely a progress in literature which is after all influenced by the progress or the advancement of the human mind. For instance, writers who were writing before the philosophical probes into the concept of reality or the discovery of the theory of relativity would have had a different world-view. The general advancement of knowledge is bound to affect the sensibility of the writer. My father's generation was reading Tennyson and my generation was brought up, as it were, on T.S. Eliot and that itself makes all the difference. Of course, great literature would always be great irrespective of the age it is produced in. As Hazlitt says, the writer captures the spirit of his age; it does not matter what technique he might use.

SPK: There are more and more tools available to comprehend the various dimensions of reality now and the writer, with his ingenuity, finds newer modes of creative expression. I am reminded here of the frustration of some of the Western writers such as Samuel Beckett with the inadequacy of language vis-à-vis the expression of the creative experience. And this, mind you, is with the English language, where there has been a tremendous emphasis on the development of the science of language. Urdu has not experienced the similar attention of scholars. The English language has more or less developed hand in hand with the human psyche. Despite that or perhaps because of that, the cacophony produced by the explosion of words and the revolution in the tools of language, some writers are experimenting with the literature of silence. There is a growing lack of faith in the semantic potential of the "word" as a meaningful unit of expression. I wonder if you take a similar position as a writer in Urdu?

QH: No, that is not my problem at all. Urdu is so rich. There is a tremendous range of meanings for each word in Urdu. In fact, I am often not able to cope with one single area of expression or a single dialect.

What concerns me, or rather disturbs me, is the gradual deterioration in the use of the language. I'm very bothered about the purity of language wherein lies its beauty. I feel upset when I hear unwieldy Hindi being used on Doordarshan because Hindi is also a beautiful language. And they use ungainly expressions like "*Mausam chipchipata rahega.*" Well, that's against the aesthetics of the language.

But as a writer in Urdu, I don't feel the inadequacy of the language at all because I am aware that the Urdu language has a lot to offer.

SPK: Well, the linguistic theoretician should take a cue from this and help evolve the science of the language if only to make it retain its purity. It is, however, heartening to see your faith and confidence in Urdu and its potential power of expression.

Having gone through some of your works, specifically the well-known novel, *Aag ka Dariya*, it is striking to see your perceptive concern for history. You make large expanses of time, huge chunks, as it were, of history available in the "present" through your novels. Tell me, when you are writing a short-story, do you feel constricted in any way because the form of the short-story does not allow one to spread out over that kind of length of time?

QH: Yes, but I think many of my stories dwell over a long period of time. Some are about the whole life of a character, some about the life of a family. They tend to cover a number of phases of a lifetime, not just one little piece or facet.

SPK: I find that your novels carry very poignant points of stasis and it gives me a feeling that you are far more comfortable writing a novel. I wonder if I could ask you as to what prompts you to choose the form of the short-story then? Is there any theoretical position that you take regarding the form you choose to write in?

QH: I think this whole business of theory doesn't mean anything to me. You write because you feel like writing—there is an idea you want to express.

SPK: But sometimes the writer does make a conscious effort to intellectually understand the form he is choosing.

QH: Maybe they do, but I have been basically interested in history and I have been using it in my fiction. Techniques and theories don't mean anything to me. What I feel interested in, I spontaneously write. I have been trying to explain to many people over and over again that technique comes naturally when one sits down to write. One does not have to consciously think about it. *It just happens*. With a musician, it is different. He has a *raga*. Though he may take a different variation, the constraints of the *raga* have to be adhered to. For me it is different. For me, mostly some little scene, an image from my memory starts me off. And then the technique evolves by itself. I will give an example from my recent novel, *Gardish-e-Rang-e-Chaman*. I remember a scene from my childhood. My mother was a pioneer of sorts in education and was very happy to meet educated women, particularly if a lady had gone abroad to study. Well, there was this lady who came to Lucknow as an inspector of schools. My mother and I went to see her. Her house was hidden in a garden with thick, huge trees. There were two ladies there, two middle aged unmarried sisters, and the younger one (who was quite good looking) was the Inspector who'd been to England. At that time this was quite a novelty. I'm talking of the 1930s. On the mantel piece inside the house, there were some little ceramics. Strangely, we were told by the older woman that they were made by her when she'd joined an arts school in England while she was chaperoning her younger sister in that country.

That scene remained in my mind. I never met them again. Here were two ladies, simple folks from a middle-class Muslim family. Who were they and what happened to them, I don't know. But that scene stayed with me. And years later I started off this novel with two ladies in a house in Lucknow. But they are mother and daughter. They've been to England; the younger one is a doctor and the mother says, "I did those paintings when my daughter was studying." You see, this is how anything like that is a starting point for a writer. I didn't sit down to work out the theme or the technique. I just started writing—the plot developed and the characters came to life. I called it a semi-documentary novel because I brought in a lot of real people.

SPK: This is interesting—how a small image or a little happening was the kernel for a huge novel. Actually, come to think of it, even a casual reader notices the use of the visual in your stories. It is almost cinematic, this concern for the *image* and also the dramatic handling of time, the constant going back and forth and the use of the montage.

QH: It is cinematic. I indulge in a little bit of painting too, so the concern for colours is also there.

SPK: One notices that your use of the stream of consciousness technique mingles with the narrative style. I think writers in this sub-continent have adopted this practice rather than the use of the pure stream of consciousness technique as handled by Virginia Woolf. There's the linear sense of time and there's the dive *into* time. To move on to another question: how do you respond to your contemporaries in Urdu literature? Do you feel particularly curious about some and are you specifically attracted or influenced or even disturbed by them? Do you discriminate between the Western writer and one writing in Urdu? There are some writers who seem to be working in isolation, deliberately disregarding the work of their contemporaries.

QH: Oh, that'd be very sad. Not only do I read my contemporaries with interest, I have also been translating some of them into English. It'd be carrying one's smugness a bit too far to deliberately not read one's contemporaries. You are enriched by looking around. There are four or five very significant writers in Urdu who've been actively writing as my contemporaries and I always read them.

SPK: How would you define modernism?

QH: It is very difficult because what you call modern today may sound dated later . . . well, Shakespeare too may have called himself modern as compared to, say, Chaucer. Modernism is very relative. In the nineteenth century, from Baudelaire onwards, they were moderns. Among the people writing in the earlier period . . . well, Pope was modern in his time.

SPK: Let me be a little more specific. In the early twentieth century there was a cultural crisis in the West. The prevailing climate of doubt, a breakdown of faith in the context of industrialisation and scientific probes into the fundamental nature of things and a questioning of some established ideas pertaining to religion led to a collapse of the "old" and the "conventional." The fragmented human psyche groped for newer forms of expression to match the new creative concerns. All this has been broadly termed as modernism.

QH: The conventional forms of expression were broken even earlier in France towards the late nineteenth century. This change came to us much later. But I would not compare our situation with that because then we'd appear as Rip Van Winkles or, worse still, merely imitative. T.S. Eliot's *The Waste Land* was translated in Urdu about 1935 while it was written much earlier. Baudelaire was introduced to the reader about a hundred years after his time as a "modern" poet of France. The point is, when we use the term "modern" we automatically relate it to something that has come to us from the West.

SPK: Don't you think that modernism in the West came with such a bang that it had a tremendous impact on the writers' consciousness even in the East, particularly in India where the British had entrenched English as a common language for communication?

QH: But you know that even in our painting, what Amrita Shergil, who became our first "modern," was doing had been done earlier in Europe. So when we talk of modernism in India, it is a delayed reaction that we notice here, that is, if it is the 'fifties we are talking of. I am certainly not part of it. In fact, I started all this—monologue, interior monologue, stream of consciousness, abstract thinking—in the 'forties when I was a teenager. So, I am a pioneer which is, of course, not acknowledged. My short-stories in *Sitaron ke Aage* would bear me out. They demonstrate all those ideas which writers of the second generation in Urdu are experimenting with. I did all that in my second year of graduation. All this is old hat for me. I've been through it long ago. And I did it unconsciously, not as following a fashion.

SPK: As a writer who's reviewing what you had written so many decades earlier, even if some of those modernistic characteristics were developed decades later by other Urdu writers, what I'd like to determine is whether you think something new has been added to what already existed? Or is our modern literature a mere borrowing? Did you yourself feel that you were writing under the influence of such and such writer? Did the inner compulsion of the Urdu writer in the forties and fifties determine his literary techniques? The "new writer" hadn't yet come of age. The historically important happening, the Independence of the country, hardly seems to have inculcated a spirit of confidence and freedom. In fact, it is the gruesome phenomenon of the Partition of the country that captured the sensibility of the writer. The modern short-story, I'd say, in Hindi and Urdu reached maturity in the sixties and seventies. The reason for this would, perhaps, lie in the fact that the form of the short-story is itself not indigenous.

QH: It's a rage these days—this business of writing consciously. You'll be surprised to hear that when I was in Sweden recently for a seminar, a professor read a bit from the Penguin reproduction of my novel *Aag ka Darya*. (I'm quite sick of this novel and try not to mention it.) Well, what he said set me thinking about my total lack of interest in what I do. He read one chapter and said that I had written a "total novel" much earlier than this American writer. And I didn't even know what this "total" novel was! Well, that apart, I feel shocked by the fact that our critics are not examining fiction in the way a new piece of writing is taken up elsewhere in the world. Our fiction suffers from a total neglect and the whole critical effort is concentrated on poetry. Our critics seem to have nothing original to say. They go on quoting—this has been happening for the last forty years now. A long string of words and very little genuine analysis, jumbled and obscure thinking!

I should think that the fundamental problem with our critics is that they don't read at all. What do they read? Some new books on criticism borrowed from the British Council or the USIS from where they read up some new sensational stuff and then they start quoting left and right. Once they get important posts and chairs in the Universities, then all they have to do is repeat themselves.

JAYANTA MAHAPATRA
b. 1928
(English)

Jayanta Mahapatra was born in Cuttack, a town in Odisha, a coastal state in eastern India. He was educated in the local schools and in Ravenshaw College, where he majored in physics. He spent many decades of his life as a physics professor in the college. His mother tongue is Odia (Oriya), but like several other Indian poets of his generation, including Kamala Das and A. K. Ramanujan, he fashioned English, the language of his learning, into a supple instrument for the expression of an intricate inner world. Mahapatra was over forty when he published his first book, Svayamvara and Other Poems *(1971).*

In Mahapatra's work, the self is always bound to the land, to its rocks and stones and trees and sky. The massive floods and hurricanes that strike the Odisha coast with such regularity enter into the cruel instability of the elements that he frequently evokes. His work is distinguished by an exquisite lyric line that often turns elegiac. Mahapatra broods on the transience of desire, the pain of history, the harsh realities of life in a place of poverty and difficulty. He has also written essays, memoir pieces, and short stories. His travel to the International Writing Workshop in Iowa was a defining moment. It was there he met the Japanese poet Kazuko Shiraishi to whom he dedicated his long poem "Relationship," which won the Sahitya Akademi Award in 1981. More recently from time to time he has turned to writing in Odia, his mother tongue. He says that it gives him the pleasure of a face-to-face audience, a reading community right where he lives. In an autobiographical prose piece and also in the poem

"Grandfather," he writes of the old notebook that his father brought home one day, its pages written in a script used by country folk. It was a piece composed by the poet's grandfather at the time of a devastating famine that struck Orissa and tells of how he converted to Christianity so that he could get food that was offered by the missionaries. Mahapatra's important books include A Rain of Rites *(1976),* Burden of Waves and Fruit *(1988),* A Whiteness of Bone *(1992), and* Land *(2013).*

From an Autobiographical Essay

One evening on his brief visit home, Father brought out an old, tattered notebook from somewhere and called us near him. A faraway look kept flitting in his eyes; of something unbound, something of distances that appeared to edge his usual fatherly bliss with gloom. We watched him as he opened the book gingerly and pointed to the already-yellowed first pages on which a childish scrawl was beginning to turn brown. The Oriya [Odia] alphabet on the page was difficult to read; the letters were in a script mostly used by rural, unlettered folk. Father pointed at the writing again and said simply, "Your grandfather's."

Soon, what Father wanted to convey to us became clear. The ancient-looking notebook was indeed a diary or record of some significant events that concerned Grandfather's life. Words he had wanted posterity to know.

In the year 1866, a devastating famine had struck Orissa. Though the English, who ruled the country, made frantic efforts for the movement of food grains into the province, no rice was available, especially in the villages. There were no roads, and communication on a few pitted pathways was only by the help of bullock carts. Even the tamarind trees were stripped of their tender leaves as people began pouncing upon whatever they could find. Many managed to subsist on unknown roots and tubers; these, in turn, caused epidemics of typhoid and cholera which reached unmanageable proportions. Thousands died, and corpses by the hundreds were literally strewn on the riverbeds to be devoured by equally starving jackals and vultures. And Grandfather, who was then a mere seventeen, starving and in a state of collapse, staggered into a mercy camp run by white Christian missionaries in Cuttack, where he embraced a new religion urged by the Baptists.

I could imagine Grandfather, the thin, callow youth he must have been, walking the still-unmade paths of the land, the long, hot afternoon floating down into the pit of his stomach—as death made him stretch his emaciated hands out, and out into the unknown.

The terrible famine ran its predetermined course. Grandfather staked his claim to his place in a new social order. To the same camp had arrived a girl from another village in Orissa, a girl of another caste, younger than Grandfather. But this child, called Rupabati, had been brought there against her will; and once she began living in the camp, partaking of food from the "free" kitchens, her people wouldn't take her back. This is how it happened: The caretaker of a cartful of children making its way to Cuttack discovered suddenly that one child from the total number under his charge was missing. Perturbed, he didn't know what to do. To his good fortune, the caretaker noticed Rupabati playing by herself on the road as his cart ambled through the village. He forcibly picked up the child and brought her along to the camp.

A few years later, Grandfather got married to Rupabati. They must have been a devoted couple. They were not staunch Christians, and they had six children: four sons and two daughters. My father, the youngest, was named Lemuel. I presume the white missionaries must have given him this unusual name.

So, as children, we grew up between two worlds. The first was the home where we were subjected to a rigid Christian upbringing, with rules my mother sternly imposed: the other was the vast and dominant Hindu amphitheater outside, with the preponderance of rites and festivals which represented the way of life for our own people. Two worlds then; and I, thinking I was at the center of it all; trying to communicate with both, and probably becoming myself incommunicable as a result throughout the years.

Grandfather's diary, torn and moth-eaten, is one of my most prized possessions. It is history. Memory too, and communication. And it was that very scroll of despair (what else, I ask myself?) which prompted me to write one of the poems dear to me. The poem was titled "Grandfather" and appeared first in the *Sewanee Review*. It began:

The yellowed diary's notes whisper in vernacular.
They sound the forgotten posture,
the cramped cry that forces me to hear that voice.
Now I stumble in your black-paged wake.

Today my brother is a faithful Christian, a leader of the local community.
I am not. I hear Grandfather's cry, welling back, torn in the air.

"Grandfather"

(Starving, on the point of death, Chintamani Mahapatra embraced Christianity during the terrible famine that struck Orissa in 1866.)

The yellowed diary's notes whisper in vernacular.
They sound the forgotten posture,
the cramped cry that forces me to hear that voice.
Now I stumble in your black-paged wake.

No uneasy stir of cloud
darkened the white skies of your day; the silence
of dust grazed in the long afternoon sun, ruling
the cracked fallow earth, ate into the laughter of your flesh.

For you it was the hardest question of all.
Dead, empty trees stood by the dragging river,
past your weakened body, flailing against your sleep.
You thought of the way the jackals moved, to move.

Did you hear the young tamarind leaves rustle
in the cold mean nights of your belly? Did you see
your own death? Watch it tear at your cries,
break them into fits of hard unnatural laughter?

How old were you? Hunted, you turned coward and ran,
the real animal in you plunging through your bone.
You left your family behind, the buried things,
the precious clod that praised the quality of a god.

The imperishable that swung your broken body,
turned it inside out? What did faith matter?
What Hindu world so ancient and true for you to hold?
Uneasily you dreamed toward the centre of your web.

The separate life let you survive, while perhaps
the one you left wept in the blur of your heart.
Now in a night of sleep and taunting rain
my son and I speak of that famine nameless as stone.

A conscience of years is between us. He is young.
The whirls of glory are breaking down for him before me.
Does he think of the past as a loss we have lived, our own?
Out of silence we look back now at what we do not know.

There is a dawn waiting beside us, whose signs
are a hundred-odd years away from you, Grandfather.
You are an invisible piece on a board
whose move has made our children grow, to know us,

carrying us deep where our voices lapse into silence.
We wish we knew you more.
We wish we knew what it was to be, against dying,
to know the dignity

that had to be earned dangerously,
your last chance that was blindly terrifying, so unfair.
We wish we had not to wake up with our smiles
in the middle of some social order.

"The Abandoned British Cemetery at Balasore"

This is history.
I would not disturb it: the ruins of stone and marble,
the crumbling wall of brick, the coma of alienated decay.
How exactly should the archaic dead make me behave?

jayanta mahapatra

A hundred and fifty years ago
I might have lived. Now nothing offends my ways.
A quietness of bramble and grass holds me to a weed.
Will it matter if I know who the victims were, who survived?

And yet, awed by the forgotten dead,
I walk around them: thirty-nine graves, their legends
floating in a twilight of baleful littoral,
the flaking history my intrusion does not animate.

Awkward in the silence, a scrawny lizard
watches the drama with its shrewd, hooded gaze.
And a scorpion, its sting drooping,
two eerie arms spread upon the marble, over an alien name.

In the circle the epitaphs run: Florence R. . . , darling wife
of Captain R. . . R. . . , aged nineteen, of cholera . . .
Helen, beloved daughter of Mr. & Mrs. . . . , of cholera,
Aged seventeen, in the year of our Lord, eighteen hundred . . .

Of what concern to me is a vanished empire?
Or the conquest of my ancestors' timeless ennui?
It is the dying young who have the power to show
what the heart will hide, the grass shows no more.

Who watches now in the dark near the dead wall?
The tribe of grass in the cracks of my eyes?
It is the cholera still, death's sickly trickle,
that plagues the sleepy shacks beyond this hump of earth,

moving easily, swiftly, with quick power
through both past and present, the increasing young,
into the final bone, wearying all truth with ruin.
This is the iron

rusting in the vanquished country, the blood's unease,
the useless rain upon my familiar window;
the tired triumphant smile left behind by the dead
on a discarded anchor half-sunk in mud beside the graves:

jayanta mahapatra

out there on the earth's unwavering gravity
where it waits like a deity perhaps
for the elaborate ceremonial of a coming generation
to keep history awake, stifle the survivor's issuing cry.

"Hunger"

It was hard to believe the flesh was heavy on my back.
The fisherman said: Will you have her, carelessly,
trailing his nets and his nerves, as though his words
sanctified the purpose with which he faced himself.
I saw his white bone thrash his eyes.

I followed him across the sprawling sands,
my mind thumping in the flesh's sling.
Hope lay perhaps in burning the house I lived in.
Silence gripped my sleeves; his body clawed at the froth
his old nets had only dragged up from the seas.

In the flickering dark his lean-to opened like a wound.
The wind was I, and the days and nights before.
Palm fronds scratched my skin. Inside the shack
an oil lamp splayed the hours bunched to those walls.
Over and over the sticky soot crossed the space of my mind.

I heard him say: My daughter, she's just turned fifteen . . .
Feel her. I'll be back soon, your bus leaves at nine.
The sky fell on me, and a father's exhausted wile.
Long and lean, her years were cold as rubber.
She opened her wormy legs wide. I felt the hunger there,
The other one, the fish slithering, turning inside.

A. K. RAMANUJAN
1929–1993
(English)

Attipat Krishnaswami Ramanujan, poet, scholar, and translator, was born in Mysore. He was educated at Mysore University where he read English literature. His father was a famous mathematician and astronomer, and his mother a housewife who loved reading and writing. Both parents had a powerful influence on his work. Ramanujan's life as a translator continued even as he created finely chiseled stanzas of his own poetry in English. His poetic language is compressed, aphoristic, influenced by the traditions of classical poetry in Tamil and Kannada. Questions of memory, ancestry, and the nature of dislocation mark his work. His important theoretical work on Indian aesthetics, translation theory, and folklore opened up realms of possibility for the poets and thinkers who came after him. More than a decade after his death, his essay "Three Hundred Ramayanas"—a celebration of the pluralistic traditions of Hinduism—came under fire from a right-wing group. The essay was discarded from the syllabus of Delhi University, and for a short while, in spite of protests, his Indian publisher, Oxford University Press, suppressed his work.

Ramanujan spent much of his adult life in Chicago, and we see how the gritty, urban life around him in that bustling, sometimes violent city, enters into the symbolic landscape of his poetry and marks the jeweled precision of his work. The loss of place runs like a bloody thread through his writing and with it the phantom force of forgetting. Often memory is layered onto the present and ancestry onto the body of the forgetful self. In the poem "Saturdays," the lived body becomes an almanac, a multicolored map essential to the worlds that have beckoned it into being. Tragically, his life was cut short. He died in Chicago in 1993 under anesthesia during a surgical procedure. Ramanujan's first book of poetry, The Striders, *was published in 1966, and it was followed by* Relations *in 1971 and* Second Sight *in 1986.* The Black Hen *was posthumously published in 1995 as part of his* Collected Poems. *In 1983, he received a MacArthur Fellowship.*

"Elements of Composition"

Composed as I am, like others,
   of elements on certain well-known lists,
father's seed and mother's egg

gathering earth, air, fire, mostly
   water, into a mulberry mass,
moulding calcium,

carbon, even gold, magnesium and such,
   into a chattering self tangled
in love and work,

scary dreams, capable of eyes that can see,
   only by moving constantly,
the constancy of things

like Stonehenge or cherry trees;

add uncle's eleven fingers
   making shadow-plays of rajas
and cats, hissing,

becoming fingers again, the look
   of panic on sister's face
an hour before

her wedding, a dated newspaper map
   of a place one has never seen, maybe
no longer there

a. k. ramanujan

after the riots, downtown Nairobi,
   that a friend carried in his passport
as others would

a woman's picture in their wallets;

add the lepers of Madurai,
   male, female, married,
with children,

lion faces, crabs for claws,
   clotted on their shadows
under the stone-eyed

goddesses of dance, more pillars,
   moving as nothing on earth
can move—

I pass through them
   as they pass through me
taking and leaving

affections, seeds, skeletons,

millennia of fossil records
   of insects that do not last
a day,

body-prints of mayflies,
   a legend half-heard
in a train

of the half-man searching
   for an ever-fleeing
other half

through Muharram tigers,
   hyacinths in crocodile waters,
and the sweet

twisted lives of epileptic saints,

a. k. ramanujan

and even as I add,
   I lose, decompose
into my elements,

into other names and forms,
   past, and passing, tenses
without time,

caterpillar on a leaf, eating,
   being eaten.

"Saturdays"

Enter a five-cornered room.
See yourself as another,
an older face in the sage
blue chair, the whole room
turning a page:
white words in black stone,
you know without knowing how
death will fog
a Saturday at three-fifteen
at home in a foreign place
where you jog,
as gold needles of rain
scatter the Art Fair in the park.

Not on Thursday, not in Paris
at nightfall,
not in a local train as you'd like
but on a day like this,
three weeks into a garbage strike,
a Dutch elm dying against a redbrick wall
that you'll remember but not know why
looking into a sawtooth
sky in a sequoia forest.
The two fingers you learned to pop

a. k. ramanujan

on your sixth birthday
crook and ache now,
like mother's on her sixtieth.
She died in the kidney wing, hallucinating.

A brother's briar pipe chatters
between his teeth,
as his heart comes to a stop,
accepting failure
that first Saturday in April,
mouth filled with bile
in a green-walled hotel room
within earshot of the Bombay sea
after a meeting under a slow ceiling
fan, red tea, letters
melting in alphabet soup
in the Reserve Bank,
his last thoughts like coils of brown rope
down his village well, sand, rope of sand.

The body we know is an almanac.
Saturdays ache
in shoulder bone and thigh bone,
dim is the Saturday gone
but iridescent
is the Saturday to come:
the window, two cherry trees,
Chicago's four November leaves,
the sulphuric sky now a salmon pink,
a wife's always clear face
now dark with unspent
panic, with no third eye, only a dent,
the mark marriage leaves on a small forehead
with ancestors in Syria, refugees
from Roman Saturdays.
The kettle's copper, mottled with water spots,
whistles in the kitchen. You

a. k. ramanujan

stir and leave the five-cornered room,
left foot wronged in a right-foot shoe,
imprisoned in reverse
in the looking-
glass image of a posthumous twin.

Turn around
and see the older man in the sage
blue chair turn around
to walk through the hole in the air,
his daily dying body
the one good omen
in a calendar of ominous Saturdays.

From "Is There an Indian Way of Thinking? An Informal Essay"

Walter Benjamin once dreamed of hiding behind a phalanx of quotations which, like highwaymen, would ambush the passing reader and rob him of his convictions.

I

Stanislavsky had an exercise for his actors. He would give them an everyday sentence like, "Bring me a cup of tea," and ask them to say it forty different ways, using it to beg, question, mock, wheedle, be imperious, etc. My question, "Is there an Indian way of thinking?," is a good one for such an exercise. Depending on where the stress is placed, it contains many questions—all of which are real questions—asked again and again when people talk about India. Here are a few possible versions:

Is there an Indian way of thinking?

Is there *an* Indian way of thinking?

Is there an *Indian* way of thinking?

Is there an Indian way of *thinking*?

The answers are just as various. Here are a few: There was an Indian way of thinking; there isn't any more. If you want to learn about the Indian way of thinking, do not ask your modern-day citified Indians, go to the pundits, the *vaidika*s and old texts. On the contrary: India never changes; under the veneer of the modern, Indians still think like the Vedas.

The second question might elicit answers like these: There is no single Indian way of thinking; there are Great and Little Traditions, ancient and modern, rural and urban, classical and folk. Each language, caste and region has its special worldview. So, under the apparent diversity, there is really a unity of viewpoint, a single supersystem. Vedists see a Vedic model in all Indian thought. Nehru made the phrase "unity in diversity" an Indian slogan. The Sahitya Akademi's line has been, "Indian literature is one, though written in many languages."

The third question might be answered: What we see in India is nothing special to India; it is nothing but pre-industrial, pre-printing press, face-to-face, agricultural, feudal. Marxists, Freudians, McLuhanites, all have their labels for the stage India is in, according to their schemes of social evolution; India is only an example. Others, of course, would argue the uniqueness of the Indian Way and how it turns all things, especially rivals and enemies, into itself; look at what has happened to Indo-Europeans in India, they would say: their language gets shot with retroflexes, their syntax with nominal compounds, they lose their nerve—the British are only the most recent example (according to Nirad Chaudhuri). Look what happens to Buddhism, Islam, the Parsis. There is an *Indian* way, and it imprints and patterns all things that enter the continent; it is inescapable, and it is Bigger Than All of Us.

The fourth question may question whether Indians think at all: It is the West that is materialistic, rational; Indians have no philosophy, only religion, no positive sciences, not even a psychology; in India, matter is subordinated to spirit, rational thought to feeling, intuition. And even when people agree that this is the case, we can have arguments for and against it. Some lament, others celebrate India's un-thinking ways. One can go on forever.

We—I, certainly—have stood in one or another of these stances at different times. We have not heard the end of these questions—or these answers.

II

The problem was posed for me personally at the age of twenty in the image of my father. I had never taken a good look at him till then. Didn't Mark Twain say, "At seventeen, I thought my father was ignorant; at twenty, I wondered how he learned so much in three years"? Indeed, this essay was inspired by contemplation of him over the years, and is dedicated to him.

My father's clothes represented his inner life very well. He was a south Indian Brahmin gentleman. He wore neat white turbans, a Sri Vaisnava caste mark (in his earlier pictures, a diamond earring), yet wore Tootal ties, Kromentz buttons and collar studs, and donned English serge jackets over his muslin *dhoti*s which he wore draped in traditional Brahmin style. He often wore tartan-patterned socks and silent well-polished leather shoes when he went to the university, but he carefully took them off before he entered the inner quarters of the house.

He was a mathematician, an astronomer. But he was also a Sanskrit scholar, an expert astrologer. He had two kinds of exotic visitors: American and English mathematicians who called on him when they were on a visit to India, and local astrologers, orthodox pundits who wore splendid gold-embroidered shawls dowered by the Maharajah. I had just been converted by Russell to the "scientific attitude." I (and my generation) was troubled by his holding together in one brain both astronomy and astrology; I looked for consistency in him, a consistency he didn't seem to care about, or even think about. When I asked him what the discovery of Pluto and Neptune did to his archaic nine-planet astrology, he said, "You make the necessary corrections, that's all." Or, in answer to how he could read the Gita religiously having bathed and painted on his forehead the red and white feet of Viṣṇu, and later talk appreciatively about Bertrand Russell and even Ingersoll, he said, "The Gita is part of one's hygiene. Besides, don't you know, the brain has two lobes?"

The following poem says something about the way he and his friends appeared to me:

Sky-man in a man-hole
with astronomy for dream,
astrology for nightmare;

fat man full of proverbs,
the language of lean years,
living in square after

almanac square
prefiguring the day
of windfall and landslide

through a calculus
of good hours,
clutching at the tear

in his birthday shirt
as at a hole
in his mildewed horoscope,

squinting at the parallax
of black planets,
his Tiger, his Hare

moving in Sanskrit zodiacs,
forever troubled
by the fractions, the kidneys

in his Tamil flesh,
his body the Great Bear
dipping for the honey,

the woman-smell
in the small curly hair
down there.

NIRMAL VERMA

1929–2005

(Hindi)

Nirmal Verma was born in Shimla in the mountainous state of Himachal Pradesh. He crafted a clear, pristine prose style in Hindi and used it to forge his haunting, probing short stories, novels, and essays. With the publication of his story collection Parinde *(1959), he shot to the forefront of what became known as the Naya Khahani Movement in Hindi literature. The writer coupled political activism—he was both a member of the Communist Party (an affiliation he later renounced) and a great admirer of Gandhi's nonviolent way—with a focus on the longings and isolation of the individual self, adrift in the circumambient landscape. Early in his life, Verma spent a decade in Czechoslovakia at the invitation of the Oriental Institute in Prague. There he was involved in the translation of Czech writers, including Karel Capel and Milan Kundera, into Hindi. Verma's first novel,* Ve Din *(Days of Longing, 1964), was set in Prague.*

He traveled widely in Europe, and his cosmopolitan outlook allowed him to turn in a fresh, incisive way to the roots of Hinduism. In his celebrated short story "Deliverance," a man comes up to the mountains to find his brother, who, having fled the family, has taken on the garb of a holy man and now lives in a tiny cell cut into the rock. The narrator, a writer, has brought papers for the sale of the family house where the aged mother still lives, and we watch how the unspoken grief of the past flows into the shared present. In his essay "The Self as Stranger," Verma begins with the question of human estrange-

ment and continues, "So the past is not something dead and gone-by, it co-exists with man's present. To be uprooted from one's past, as Simone Weil has pointed out, is the worst form of self-alienation. It deprives man of the only thing which connects him to his ancestors, his memory." In later years, Nirmal Verma forged a friendship with the Dalai Lama and became actively involved in Tibetan causes. Verma's essays, collected in several volumes, establish him at the forefront of literary thinkers. His important works include the novel Antima Aranya (The Last Wilderness, *1979*) and the volume of essays Bharat aur Europe (India and Europe, *1991*). In *1999*, he was awarded the Bharatiya Jnanpith Award for Literature.

"Returning to One's Country"

The foreigner's pleasure is not mine. He sees it all for the first time—the women, the sunshine, the swaying saris on rooftops hung up to dry. He stops everywhere in the joy of new discoveries. I, too, stop; my eyes smarting with a particle of recognition which will neither come out nor get dissolved. I do not have the satisfaction of the native who skirts around this endless waste, this interminable poverty. Nor do I have the foreign tourist's love for India who can take in everything while he remains untouched himself.

I am a native stranger who has come back. I am an alien Indian who is suspect everywhere, most so to himself.

When I return home, my host in Allahabad asks, "Did you go to the Sangam? What, in this scorching heat and swirling dust storm? It must be after a long time for you." But, ever since I have come back, the years spent abroad seem either like a gossamer web or a plant which closes upon itself when you touch it. It is as if the needle, that got stuck on the record when I left, has now started moving again from exactly the same place. The music is resumed just where it had stopped at the point where my age had paused. The time I spent abroad was like a night spent on the railway platform waiting to listen to the rest of the record which is all about dust and summer nights.

"How do you feel after all these years?" Whenever I am asked this question I remember that burning afternoon at the Sangam. Everything else recedes—I vividly recall only the small figure of a sadhu and his thin crazy-looking disciple waving a fan over his head. Stale pieces of *batashas* and a few dusty coins lay scattered in front of him on a soiled *durree*. "What are you staring at, Babu?" The young disciple points to the sadhu. "He is a direct avatar of Shiva. He never sleeps at night."

Shiva's avatar peered at me. I stared at him. In the background spread the dry expanse of the river bank. A line of huts with coloured pennants flying above them looked like a Jewish ghetto, closed within itself. Between the dry Ganga and Shiva's avatar blew swirling dust, that special Indian dust which deposits a film. And there was the howling sound of the wind. He never sleeps at night. I thought of my own nights spent in pools of perspiration on the rooftop where I could hear the whispers of the people in the adjoining houses.

When I was leaving, Shiva's disciple gave me a complaining look. "You won't understand, Babu. People from *vilayat* come and sing his praise."

My steps faltered at the mention of *vilayat*. Was he going to show me his certificates? And why not? If our Hindi writers do not tire of lecturing on Gandhi's greatness in American universities, it would be quite natural for a sadhu to produce foreign testimonials as evidence of his worth.

I looked at the deformed man again, the ash-smeared midget, that avatar of Shiva. For a moment I felt like sitting down beside him and quietly telling him: you are as wonderful as he is—overlaid in dust, sitting with closed eyes by the Ganga. You do not need any certificate, either from Indian babus or from Indophile American women. But I did not have the courage to say anything to the sage who never slept at night.

The water of the two adjoining rivers divides my body between them. Half of my weariness is washed away by the Jamuna and the other half by the Ganga. Withered flowers are floating on the murky water. The accumulated fatigue of my years abroad is slowly cleansed by the rivers of my land. Perhaps, the Aryans washed their dust and weariness in these very waters thousands of years ago. I remembered what the Icelandic writer, Harold Laxness, said: The Indians are strange people—they will not believe that the Ganges water can carry germs.

If you ask me, I cannot believe it either. How can you believe in something you cannot see? We are a very physical people. I wonder if there is any race in the world attached to the body in a more palpable and fleshy way than we are. Who can deprive us of the pleasure of seeing with naked eyes, eating with bare fingers, making love with unsheathed organs, sleeping in public places? Our forefathers might have conceived the theory of transmigration because of this deep and abiding attachment to the body. They must have found the thought of death as the ultimate end of the body, the final annihilation of self, quite terrifying and unbelievable.

You see the body being displayed everywhere in this country. Others might find a contradiction in such shameless exhibitionism in a closed and inhibited society like ours, but we have got quite used to it. Eyes peep from one house into another. No tender personal secret can be hidden from the greedy and prurient gaze of the neighbours. From the morning bath to sleep at night—every act is performed in public view. Families may be rigid in their concepts of status and position but their daily lives are like the pages of an open book. When a sister enters a brother's room or a wife enters a husband's, she does not feel the need to knock. There is no word for "privacy" in Hindi, because Indian families have never felt any necessity for it. Leonard Woolf was perhaps the first to notice it when he had gone to see Jawaharlal Nehru in an apartment house in London. He thought it odd that Nehru should sit with the doors wide open. People walked in, talked to him, and went away. In Europe it is quite different. There is freedom in the society and easy mobility among classes, but inside the house each individual keeps his body and soul inviolate from his friends and relatives.

I have always found this concept of mutual concealment in European families slightly ridiculous. But this concealment is linked to a deeper bond, which, without undue exposure and baring of selves, can turn a house into a home, a home with memories clustered within its walls. Perhaps, these dark accumulated memories helped in the emergence of the distinctive genre of the novel in Europe. If we do not find excellence in our prose fiction (a mere four hundred pages of prose do not necessarily make a novel) it could be because our climate has no use for privacy and there is no mystery in the dark corners of people's individual lives. There is no enveloping memory carried from generation to generation, which can build a nest capable of containing both life and death. There is too much sun here. A *Mahabharata* may be written in the midst of open spaces and the sun washed ruins of centuries, but never an *Anna Karenina* or a *Buddenbrooks*.

I remember an afternoon long ago in Burgen, Norway, when the guide told me that the most important sight in the city was the house where a wealthy merchant lived centuries ago. I was mildly surprised. The house had been preserved like a valuable museum. Old furniture, family pictures, the piano, everything had been embalmed intact, only the residents were no more. These long rooms seemed resonant with memory; with perhaps Ibsen's haunted characters still roaming in the maze of the dark corridors. Solemn literary critics might laugh at this, but I had a strange illusion that the snow outside, the stillness of the lonely rooms and the span of time and space between childhood and death—these were slides which literature, like a magic lantern show, projected on a wall. To lose them is to be deprived of one's memories and be left in barrenness where there was no place for Virginia Woolf's *A Room of One's Own*.

It is this barrenness that bewildered me when I roamed the streets of my city again after these long years. Is there any word to capture this oppressive malaise which envelops every Indian city like a thick layer of dust? Every city seems to suffer from a slow consuming fever of about ninety-nine degrees. Above these cities, simmering in the sunlight, kites and vultures hover like figures in a nightmare. Down below one hears the shrill and sharp city sounds—the same in Delhi, in Lucknow, in Allahabad scratching the invisible sores under the sad scabs of interminable boredom. I used to be afraid of these sounds years ago. Now, years later, no matter how much I have changed on the surface, that old fear still haunts me, lurking somewhere in the serpent-like coils of these sounds.

Can one capture these sounds and weave them into a pattern as Joyce wove the incessant rambling city sounds of Dublin in a pulsating breathless prose epic? That is not possible here because our cities are mere collections of houses. The connecting link of memories dried up years ago. They lie on the fringe of the villages looking like advertisements of cheap and shoddy goods. Our cities have attempted to grab all the material props of western prosperity, but none of its saving graces. Hardly any "culture" in the world, as it has developed in India after independence, is as shallow as that of the affluent urban Indians. In spite of the polish and plaster on top, every now and then, tawdry tastelessness from down below leaks out. One can invite Le Corbusier to build a Chandigarh but one cannot import the values that turn a concrete structure into a home. The matrix of memories makes a city out of a conglomeration of homes, connecting it not only to the past but also to the vibrant living present. Without this, every Chandigarh turns into a modern ruin and every ancient ruin becomes merely a cluster of mounds without memory.

There is a great deal of difference between poverty and destitution. What strikes one most sharply after returning to India is not poverty—the West has poverty too—but the sanctimonious smugness of the Indian educated class. Gandhiji was the first to notice its amazing "heartlessness."

Perhaps this is one reason why I blush with the shame even in the darkness of a movie hall when the commercials are shown before a feature film starts. To me it is an excruciating experience to watch the smooth-faced healthy children being fed cornflakes by their smiling mother. All the three elements seem to me equally obscene—the children, the mother and the cornflakes. I have had occasion to see many blue films in Europe, but this naked feeling of crude vulgarity has never hit me like this before. I cannot bear to look at healthy children any more after seeing these films. Their mothers I can stand even less.

At first this aversion seemed abnormal even to myself. Now I am beginning to understand the reason in a vague sort of a way. The gap between the streets and the movie screen is nowhere as wide as it is in our country. Children on their way back from school wait for hours at the bus stop—tired, thirsty and hungry. On the one hand, we have these wilted faces under the merciless sun; on the other, there are the glowing children of the cornflakes ad. I find it difficult to reconcile the images.

A gap like this must exist in every country, but in India it assumes the proportions of a surrealist fantasy. I am afraid to touch the morning newspaper for this reason. Things happen in the bureaucratic strata of the society but they never affect the reality of daily life around us. Theirs is a strange charmed world—the meditating peon sitting in front of an office, the clerks absconding from work to see a film in the afternoon, the poets who can outdo Nero by writing humorous and satiric verses, the intellectuals who seem quite indifferent to the commercialisation of life around them and yet get excited about obscenity in literature. These are the healthy, modern, educated people on whom we pride ourselves. And rightly too. Which mother would not be proud of her lively, healthy, cornflakes-eating children?

Each one of us has his own Chandigarh—Le Corbusier's town walls painted with the pointillistic blobs of paan spittle. Where else can one come across a stranger amalgam of modernity and Indianness? There is hardly any part of our inner or outer life where the shadow of this dichotomy does not fall.

Perhaps I am wrong here. Part of us does remain untouched like virgin glass. Even if we spend half a lifetime abroad, there are lights that give out signals on our return and call us to them. Drinking beer on the rooftop one evening, or even without the beer, you can see them. In India, as soon as night falls the fever of the cities subsides. The flocks of dust-filled yellow wings descend from the sky. One can look up from the rooftop to see the clear sparkling frill of stars stretching far into the dome of the sky, something one never sees in the skies of London, Prague and Paris. The shrill edge is taken off the day sounds of the city. One hears peals of laughter from the girls in the street, reminding one of other evenings, other faces and other times. It is strange, how girls in all warm countries, be it Spain, Italy or India—all laugh in a similar open manner at this point in the evening. We may not have the mysterious houses surrounded by layers of time, but our lanes and street corners have their own special existence at night—an attraction that draws people out of their houses.

And, then as the night advances, even the streets become empty. Wind rises and the wistful sound of *kirtan* wafts from one rooftop to another. The sudden sound of collective shifting of beds when it begins to rain on a July night, the dripping sound of water leaking from the walls . . .

The dust-begrimed children sleep in the lanes. They suddenly remind one, not of the glowing faces in the cornflakes ad, but of Mahadevi Verma's moving pen-portraits of her childhood. A vacant wayside stone seat reminds you that years ago Gulki Banno, in a well-known Hindi short story by Dharmvir Bharati, must have sat here on her tattered rug. Our novels might appear lifeless, but our Hindi stories have come out of these damp houses, rooftops clustered together, crossings of lanes, haunted doors behind which waiting eyes hide themselves, the sound of an unfamiliar peal of laughter in the darkness. These are with us forever.

But many things disappear. From the rooftop, I look down at the lane and see the girls scattered here and there near the lamp-posts and wonder where the girls I had seen years ago are. Indeed, where are they?

K. AYYAPPA PANIKER

1930–2006

(Malayalam)

K. Ayyappa Paniker was born in the village of Kavalam, Kerala. The early death of his mother marked him deeply, and there is often, in spite of the sometimes biting wit, a melancholy tinge to his poems. Paniker was a crucial figure in the modernist turn in Malayalam letters. The journal Kerala Kavita, *which he cofounded in 1968, published new Malayalam poets as well as poets who write in other Indian languages, such as Jibanananda Das. Paniker also published a wide array of international poets—Zbigniew Hebert, Pablo Neruda, Eugenio Montale, and others—whose works were made available for a Malayalam audience. Ayyappa Paniker was a mentor to the poet K. Satchidanandan, who speaks of how the senior poet encouraged him to go to literary festivals and counseled him to make sure that his work had a cosmopolitan audience. Malayalam, Paniker felt, was to be construed as a world language, and through his dazzling erudition, wit, and sharp irony, Paniker moved the language away from the somewhat heavy Romanticism of an earlier era into a new global consciousness. One thinks of the poem "Passage to America," where the bardic presence of Walt Whitman with his fluid, epic consciousness lies just below the surface, but America is now a land of dynamite and mind-altering substances, "this ancient newborn land." Even toward the end of his life, Paniker was active in helping younger poets, many of whom were now publishing their work online. He told me that he thought of the internet as a new frontier for poetry. The poet's intellectual work was broad ranging,* and he wrote on American and British literature as well as medieval Indian literature and classical texts of Indian aesthetics. He developed the concept of "Interiorization" (Antassannivesha), a difficult and somewhat elusive idea that he relates in part to Gerard Manley Hopkins's notion of inscape: a hidden and essential selfhood, unique to a person or thing, and in the last analysis beyond the grasp of words. Paniker's works include Kurukshetram (1957); Ayyappa Panikarude Kritikal (1974); and the posthumous collection of his poetry, Ayyappa Panikarude Kavitakal (2011), as well as the three volumes of his collected essays, Ayyappa Panikarude Lekhanangal (1982, 1990, 2005).

"Why Write?"

"Because I cannot help it" would be the answer one might give to this query, implying perhaps that the writer in question has nothing else to do, or is good at nothing other than writing. That one writes is the sole truth behind this exchange. If one were to set aside grand philosophies, one might think of a few more reasons. One might say, for example, that one often writes to make money. That one writes *also* to make money will be a more charitable way of saying the same. Other possible answers are: one writes to reform others; one writes to reform oneself; one writes to while away the time; one writes for one's own pleasure; one writes as part of one's profession; one writes to earn fame; one writes at the behest of one's friends. In truth, a writer might be able to justify all these answers at the same time. Perhaps it is not imperative that only one of these reasons need be right.

The above answers apply as a rule to almost all writers. If confronted with the pointed question as to why he writes poetry, the author of this essay—"the present writer," as they used to say in the past—would be prepared to recognize the inadequacy of each of the answers suggested. There is an element of inspiration behind all good poems. One is being dishonest to oneself if one claims that there is no craving for fame behind writing. And one is being dishonest to others too if other people start believing that claim. It is also important to remember that readers will have to be schooled in certain things. All this—and a lot of other things as well—would go to motivate and strengthen writing. All works of all the writers need not be focused on a single object. It is possible that each work of a writer has a different object.

Let me cite the example of my poem "Gopikadandakam." I copied it out on paper after the entire poem had been composed in the mind, recited several times and then transcribed on to the electronic tape. It was a poem that had grown with me from my early childhood—right from the days when I was an avid reader of the Bhagavatam and was moved by the soulful entreaties of the Gopikas to god Krishna, who I had thought was somewhat insensitive to their appeals. I therefore was trying to speak to the Gopikas on Krishna's behalf in that poem. This poem, one might say, drives Krishna to the understanding that knowledge is not a limited entity, but is a sequence of accumulated experiences. Let Krishna know that if he were ever to respond to the Gopikas, he might do so in the way conceived here. In that sense the poem's implied targets are not the Gopikas. It is aimed at Krishna himself who is expected to speak to them. The poem in this sense can be read as an instance of ghost writing—or dubbing—undertaken on behalf of the god who could be deemed heavily preoccupied with other matters. I am convinced that he too must have found this interpretation sufficiently convincing.

There are friends who ask me why I make matters so complicated. Can't I give a straightforward answer to the question why I write? Only when you are driven to a corner and forced to make an appropriate choice from a given set of answers—A, B, C and D—as in multiple choice questions would you care to give precise answers. And the answers you give in such situations need not always be correct. What literary history teaches us is that for most great works of art there might be multiple goals. The real object of art need not be visible to the poet who might be carried away by the poem's superficial goal. Good readers on the other hand will invariably arrive at the real goal.

Since the speaker in "Gopikadandakam" adopts Krishna's persona, one could assume that the poem narrates what a person leaving the village for the city tells his girl friends from the village. One might say that the poem articulates the sentiments of good old Krishna as well as of his modern counterparts. Would that be a fair assessment? It was quite accidental that it acquired a specific rhythmic and verse structure and was assimilated to the "dandaka" form. Its eternal, trans-historical perspective was also accidental. It is foolish of an author to talk about his or her intention in composing a work or to imagine that a work becomes the author's property after it has been published. There is an element of vagueness about all works of art. Even in the appreciation of art there might be elements that one cannot fully understand and share with another. It is in art's nature to become vaguer as one attempts to bring greater clarity to it. The appreciation of poetry is like love and affection. If one goes on talking about it, one starts wondering whether one is telling the truth after all.

There are people who write with a personal object in mind as well as those who write with a social object. There are also others who write at the instance of other people. Such observations certainly apply to me too, as they do to most other writers. But my best works are all written at my own instance—for sheer pleasure, with little premeditation.

>   Acts performed for one's own cheer,
>   Of cheer they should be to others too.

I believe that the above dictum of Sri Narayana Guru could be extended to the art of literary writing as well.

It is not enough that the poet swears he has been motivated by poetic inspiration. There should be proof for that in the poem. And the reader should feel convinced about it too.

Why write, then?

"Upon My Walls"

Look at the picture my hands have drawn on my walls:
why do you stare? Look carefully, you fool!

Nerves that stretch from the navel and the eyes
thirst and burn in the brain;
copper dreams blossoming on the dead volcano
blaze and flow around;
tears unfrozen, ears unstopped,
the veins keep glowing: is it creation or destruction?

Look at the picture my hands have drawn on my walls:
why do you stare? Look carefully, you fool!

"Epitaph"

Here lies the body of Mister Panicker
who at the end of his panicking days
agreed to lie still for a while.
It's not known what happened to his soul
if indeed he ever had one.
He wasn't quite unlike any of us while he lived:
his flesh to tell the truth often revolted
and upset his delicate sensibility.
Space he could never control to his liking;
his sense of time you know wasn't strong either.
He had of course in his wallet many a theory;
the things he could touch however
told him a different story.
All his life he was patiently
learning how not to live at all.
Who knows perhaps
given another chance
he might do a better job of it than before.

And you who pass by
do not stop here for long
but move on quietly to the nearest graveyard
that may be waiting for you.

From "Passage to America"

I

on the day of the feast
death had its celebration
the teevees and the movies
told us the same story

death in the morning death in the evening
death in the cellar death in the alley

death on the highway the boy returning from the rally
death in the cornfield the girl going to the grocer's
death in the valley and high on the mountain
death from pollution and the great disillusion
death in the mind in the womb in the cradle
death from belief and its comic relief
the winds from the north and the winds from the south
sowed the seeds of death and waited for the harvest
death was riding nightmares
on the streets of civilization
someone had coughed in the women's room
and Kleenex caught her vaginal sneeze
while history knocked at the door
and waited in the winter outside
the computer counted the errors
and discounted others
a woman had died but it was a mistake
someone wanted to undo it
learned it was too late
and walked to the seashore
and watched the tidal waves
death was riding in the receding waves
death was roaring in the generation gap
and lying in history's lap
was sucking its sap
on the day of the feast
death had its celebration
knocked out of sleep by the casualty list
someone was still groping in daylight
but it's christmas and new year
time to stop worrying over those that are dead
time to start thinking of living yet
while the sun is still hot and the day not done
perhaps a mistake to suppose it so
it's easy enough to suppose it so
and it's easy enough to die in these circumstances
but think of the horror and the glory of having to live

k. ayyappa paniker

11

my sitar
my guitar

from east to west
i do not care
whatever i dare
is for the best

fingers of the left
tripping on nipples
fingers of the right
strumming the ripples
around the lotus bud
as we sit on the bed
each petal quakes
as the *raga* awakes
raises in dizzy spirals
towers and gyres
steeples and spires
domes and minarets
pagodas pyramids

fabled hoofs
trot on gabled roofs
as the *tala* quickens
we rocket to the heavens
to gather the starlust
and then we fall
falter and fall
like flakes of feathered snow
sprinkled with stardust

o my guitar
o my sitar.

k. ayyappa paniker

ARUN KOLATKAR

1931–2004
(English/Marathi)

Arun Kolatkar was born in the town of Kolhapur but lived most of his life in Bombay, and his work is intimately bound to the knotted cosmopolitanism of the city. He attended the J. J. School of Art and worked in a series of advertising agencies to earn his living. He lived a café life, cultivating friendships with other poets—Dilip Chitre, Ashok Shahane, Dom Moraes, Nissim Ezekiel— and the painter M. F. Husain. Like several other Indian poets of his generation, he met and befriended Allen Ginsberg and Peter Orlovsky, who were visiting India. Kolatkar's volume of poetry Jejuri, *published by the small press Clearing House, won the Commonwealth Poetry Prize in 1977. The intense detail of his poetry benefits from tight syntax and clarity of image, which allow him to figure forth the trajectory of the actual. Sometimes those details spin out into a visionary zone.*

The question of language haunted him, and he felt that he had been in some measure unhoused from his mother tongue, Marathi. His poem "Irani Restaurant Bombay" was composed in Marathi and then translated into English with an additional stanza. In his prose piece "From an Undated Sheet," Kolatkar says that the writing of the two versions "could almost have been simultaneous." In "Making Love to a Poem," he muses about his identity as a poet who writes in two languages, saying, "My pencil is sharpened at both ends / I use one end to write in Marathi / the other in English." He even alludes to how he sometimes writes in a third—one imagines this to be the patois of Bombay. But linguistic tensions only serve to highlight the imaginative power of his lines and the inner life of a man who thought of himself as a world-poet. In the circle of invisible friends he counted the medieval bhakti poets of India, Tukaram and Eknath and Kabir; twentieth-century European poets such as Federico Garcia Lorca, Marina Tsvetayeva, and Paul Celan; as well as the American poets Allen Ginsberg, William Carlos Williams, and Ezra Pound. For that matter, access to American culture, gangster films, and the language of the blues gave Kolatkar a way to forge his fierce originality. Important works include two volumes in Marathi, Bhijki Vahi *and* Chirimiru, *both published in 2003. In 2004, a year of great creativity for him, he published three books:* Dron *in Marathi and* Sarpa Satra *and* Kala Ghoda *in English. His* Collected Poems *were edited by his friend Arvind Krishna Mehrotra and posthumously published in 2010. In 1977, Kolatkar was awarded the Commonwealth Writers Prize.*

"From an Undated Sheet"

I wrote all the poems that Dilip has translated originally in Marathi. The majority of them were written between 1955–57. I also wrote English parallels for most of them at the same time but abandoned them as hopeless efforts.

I wrote "Make Way Poet," "Woman," "Teeth," "Suicide of Rama," "Dreaming of Snakes," originally in English.

"Three Cups of Tea" is a translation of a poem I wrote not in Marathi but in some kind of street Hindi or "Bambai" Hindi.

2 of my English versions have their Marathi equivalents. "The Hag" I probably wrote first in English and "Irani Restaurant Bombay" probably in Marathi. In fact, the writing in both cases could almost have been simultaneous.

"Irani Restaurant Bombay": While doing it in English I overtook the original Marathi version by adding one more stanza. The last stanza (in the English version) is absent in Marathi. To anyone reading it in both languages, it would appear as if the English version was the more complete one.

"Teeth" is an interesting case. In a way, I wrote it first in Marathi or started writing it, and although I have the rough drafts lying around somewhere to this day, in the hope of getting back to it, I never completed it. After completing the English poem, I took up the theme in Marathi again. More than once. But every time I found a new variation and came up with 3 different poems in Marathi. I won't be surprised to find more Marathi poems coming out of it when I go back to it, as I keep promising myself.

Whenever I have written a version in both languages, I like to think of them as two original poems in two different languages rather than one a translation of the other.

From "Making Love to a Poem"

I

Translating a poem is like making love / having an affair

Making love to a poem / with the body of another language

You may meet a poem if you like

Getting to know the poem carnally
   gaining carnal knowledge

A consenting poem
   having made sure that the poem is above the age of consent

Varieties of the experience
   if the poem is ready / game / willing
   it may need as much skill, patience, delicacy
   to consummate the act

Having got the poem into bed
you may discover you're not up to it
or that it's just not your day / or night

it follows that translating your own poems
   is like making love to one of your daughters
   it ought to be a cognisable offence
   taboo
   carry a stigma

arun kolatkar

there ought to be a law against translating your own poems
(unless the law against incest already covers it)
since it would be like seducing your own daughter

2

I can't translate a poem until I've got the feeling that I possess it
I must take possession of a poem before I can translate it

3

Tilak and Gandhi were bilingual writers

Some of the finest poetry in India, or indeed in the world, has come from a sense of alienation

It is the central experience of a lot of bhakti poetry for instance
   It's at the bottom of a lot of Dalit poetry
   it has given us poems like "Cold Mountain"
   folk poetry   where women sing about their lot

4

"Only in one's mother-tongue can one express one's own truth. In a foreign language, the poet lies."—Paul Celan

"By submitting the German language to so intense a reduction that he [Paul Celan] is, in effect, writing German like a foreign language."—Katherine Washburn and Margaret Guillemin, *Parnassus*, Spring/Summer 1981.

"Celan took German poetry through a process of willed decomposition."

5

Ever since I began to write poems I have written in 2 languages (on occasion in a 3rd language)
but I don't think I have written a bilingual poem in my life

arun kolatkar

A poem written in 2 languages
like Eknath did in the 16th century   Hindustani & Marathi
& Ram Joshi in the 19th century   Sanskrit & Marathi

I generally try not to let my left hand know what my right is doing

Bilingual poets may exist
a bilingual poem doesn't

I have a pen in my possession
which writes in 2 languages
and draws in one

My pencil is sharpened at both ends
I use one end to write in Marathi
the other in English

what I write with one end
comes out as English
what I write with the other
comes out as Marathi

6

Whether half of my work will always remain invisible
like the other side of the moon
whether a reader in one language will have to be content
with the side facing him

Whether my work is 2 bodies of work   in spite of their common origin
which have developed independently of each other
each with its separate history
ecology   life forms
spin   rate of spin   temperature   tilt   tilt of axis
atmosphere
each moving in its own orbit

occasionally influencing each other   causing anomalies
in motion   or occasionally eclipsing one another
causing tidal waves   tides

arun kolatkar

A pencil sharpened at both ends   the bilingual poet waits
will he write his next poem in English
will he write it in Marathi

which language will he write the next poem in
will depend on which way his pencil points at the piece of paper
before him

what will he do if he wants to write a poem in Chinese
find a pencil which points three ways
buy a new pencil   brush

There is a neural selector switch in my brain
                first I press the on button
                when I see the light   pilot light
                I press the selector switch

How do I write in 2 languages? On alternate days

Am I two different animals   or just one with a striped skin
                                        A piebald

                                7

I've written in 2 languages from the start
I was writing what I hoped were poems
switching from the one to the other freely
without asking myself whether I had
the right to write in either
                                and riding rough shod over both
            or the qualifications
qualifications I knew I had none

I didn't have to ask myself what qualifications I had
for I knew the answer to that one   I had none

I went merrily along
writing one poem in Marathi after another in English
sometimes starting one in Marathi and finishing it in English

or vice versa
writing one in English and then rewriting it in Marathi
or the other way round
and abandoning many ideas

writing ten in one language   then a few in another
sometimes writing 3 altogether new poems
in an attempt to translate one
        or indulge in cannibalism

or sometimes constructing one poem
out of material taken from 10 discarded poems
stolen / salvaged / plundered
from rubbish heap / junkyard / graveyard

You need a double barreled gun to shoot a bilingual poet
one bullet in the head will never be enough to kill me
you need 2 bullets to kill me   for I'm two beasts
        you're hunting / tracking not one but 2 beasts
            though our tracks may crisscross
and we may come to the same waterhole to drink
        and to the same saltlicks
            there are two distinct scents we use
to mark the boundaries   we hunt in different parts of the jungle
        though our territories may overlap
or sometimes when our paths cross we may pass through each other
exchanging some of our characteristics in the process

8

32 ways of skinning a bilingual poet

9

Or whether it's only a reflection
of cultural schizophrenia
creative schizophrenia   split personality

arun kolatkar

Whether I'm just one poet writing in 2 languages
or in fact 2 poets writing in 2 different languages

whether I present one profile in one language
and another profile in the other

whether I'm a double agent
stealing the secrets of one language and selling them to the other
and vice versa

whether I practice a kind of psychological double-bookkeeping

whether I'm truly ambidextrous
or whether I reserve / relegate one language for certain restricted /
                                            unclean functions

which would be taboo in the other

whether I wipe my arse with one   eat with the other
                use one to wipe my arse   one to eat with
or whether my use of 2 languages can be likened
to the way I use my 2 hands
relegating one to minor jobs or certain taboo functions

and leaving the other free to *[left incomplete]*
reserving one to do all the dirty work
and leaving the other free to do pretty well what it likes / wants to
           a simple twist of mind
or whether the 2 sides of my creative personality
represented by work in 2 languages run into each other
to form a single continuous surface like a Möbius strip
   or whether my work taken in its entirety forms a Möbius strip
   the 2 sides running into each other and forming
   a single continuous surface

10

Or whether I've done the sensible thing

I've bought plots in two cemeteries   graveyards
        booked space for myself

arun kolatkar

      dug my grave in 2 cemeteries
      I'll be buried in two coffins

      placed orders with 2 funeral parlours
            2 tombstones with epitaphs in 2 different languages

      why have I been digging my grave in 2 cemeteries
            a trick I learnt from Kabir
      when they look for my body they'll find flowers
                     before they come to blows
they'll only find some flowers   2 handfuls of flowers
which they will divide equally among   between them
and the 2 handfuls   they'll carry the 2 handfuls
to be buried in 2 separate graves

                       I I

For an Indian robbed of his mother tongue
                  who has been robbed   disinherited
by his education   family background   cheated out of his
                                                inheritance
there may be no alternative to writing in the only
language he knows   English
but why a person   someone like me who doesn't even have
that excuse should bother to write in it
may seem a mystery if not a crime   a cognisable offence
                since there is at least as yet
                no law against it
effectively preventing [him]
      from getting access   cultural inheritance
and cutting him off from much of daily life   the life   around him
shutting him out   depriving him

    a cultural bypass operation
opening wide windows   picture windows
in one wall   with sea view westerly breeze
out of which   for him to look out of
boarding up another

arun kolatkar

so as to keep him from looking at what is happening in his own
                                                backyard

a window to the world   wide world
cutting off his lifelines

12

"To create a poem means to translate from the mother tongue into another language . . . No language is the mother tongue. For that reason I do not understand when people speak of French or Russian poets. A poet can write in French, but he cannot be a French poet . . . Orpheus exploded and broke up the nationalities, or stretched their boundaries so wide that they now include all nations, the dead and the living."—Marina Tsvetayeva in a letter to Rainer Maria Rilke

U. R. ANANTHAMURTHY

1932–2014

(Kannada)

Udipi Rajagopalacharya Ananthamurthy was born into a Brahmin family in the village of Melige in what was to become Karnataka state. He came into prominence with the publication of his novel Samskara *(1965), composed in Kannada when he was a graduate student in England. The writer has spoken of his hunger for his mother tongue, how it seemed to him that the novel "wrote itself," and as he wrote he seemed to hear the voices of the great writers of the past.* Samskara *casts a fierce light on the hierarchies of a small village and the fear of pollution faced by the Brahmins there, a fear so acute that one of them is left without a proper cremation. The spreading fear is that the dead man's sexual bond with an Untouchable woman has rendered his body Outcaste and that anyone who touches him to prepare the body for cremation would themselves become polluted. This fear of touching another human being who might pollute, as well as the inner transformation of its protagonist, is brought out powerfully in this short novel.*

In a memoir Ananthamurthy writes of how the sense of touch, with all its erotic reckoning, is important to him—a powerful emotional current that runs through his work. Kannada for him becomes a vehicle for exploring the knotty, intertwined issues of erotic desire and social justice, and the ensuing complexities that the writer faced growing up in a world in upheaval. As a young man Ananthamurthy felt that Gandhian nationalism was as important as the socialist promise of equality. His writing, far from being programmatic, is rich and sensual, shot through with the details of the natural world he was so close to as a child. Ananthamurthy was part of the Navya, or Modernist, Movement of Kannada literature and had deep connections with Mysore- and Bangalore-based writers such as the poet A. K. Ramanujan (who translated Samskara *into English), the playwright Girish Karnad, and others. Of the writers of the Navya school, Ananthamurthy comments, "Our inspiration came from the great poetry of Gopalakrishna Adiga who had interiorized the one-thousand-year-old-Kannada tradition and opened out to the influence of modern European and English writers." Ananthamurthy has written poems, a play, short stories, and novels. His important work includes the novels* Bharathipura *(1973),* Avasthe *(1978), and* Bara *(1994), as well as the collection of short stories* Stallion of the Sun *(1988). In 1994, he was awarded the Bharatiya Jnanpith Prize for Literature.*

From "Five Decades of My Writing"

My writing has a humble but mysterious, and also a seemingly silly beginning, as I see it now. The title of my talk should really be Seven Decades of My Relationship with Literature for I am running seventy-five now. I was famous for a simple sentence I spoke when I must have been hardly five years old. Did I really speak it? My mother must have repeated it many times in her fondness for me. (She died three years ago, aged about 86 years). I was her eldest child and I had done well and my mother delighted in reminding me how simple I was and yet how I could say something clever and sweet to the ears.

The obviously silly sentence makes no sense unless it is contextualized. There was a woman called Abbakka—literally, sister Abba—who came to our large tile-roofed house in the midst of a jungle. Each large house like ours, a kilometre apart at least, had the name of a village and it had a few thatched huts in the vicinity where the peasants who worked for the land-owners lived. One of them was Abbakka and I remember she had twin children whom she carried in her arms tucked in her armpits. They clung to her neck. Abbakka had jasmine flowers in her oiled and tightly-plaited hair and a large kumkum on her forehead and turmeric powder on her cheeks. I think I remember her kind and mischievously smiling face and the fragrance of the jasmine flowers in her hair and the tobacco she shared secretly with my mother.

She was familiar and yet mysterious to me. This ordinarily smiling friendly domestic help who gossiped endlessly with my mother about her well-to-do and not so well-to-do relatives, broken marriages and miscarriages, her waywardly yet fond husband, her twins who clung to her always and didn't let her cook, was transformed on some nights, once a week. She would turn into a Devi whom the neighbours came to propitiate. She would then hold bunches of areca flowers, and wave them in the air, with her eyes closed or staring into empty space and her freshly washed, wet, dark hair gleamed over her shoulders in the light of burning torches respectfully held in front of her. Her forehead was covered in kumkum and the whole face in saffron. Her whole body swayed rhythmically and she made an ecstatic moan as she swayed. People fell at her feet as if she was not the everyday Abbakka. She was no longer a low caste woman but a Devi who advised you where to look for your lost cow, where to get medicine for your child, how to set right the young daughter-in-law who strayed from the path of wifely duties. My grandfather, himself a priest who consulted the almanac and cowrie shells and found the right star and date for auspicious occasions, would be a witness of this Abbakka with me on his shoulders. "Abbakka has power when the Devi possesses her, which I don't have," he would tell me.

After one such night Abbakka came home to work as usual for Mother in the morning. This is how my mother used to tell me the story of my gift with words. Abbakka stands there with her twins tucked in her armpits under a pomegranate tree in the back of our house and I, standing beside the well, cry out this sentence: Ábbakkanna *gubbakka kachchikondu hoytbu*. It appears Abbakka was so delighted with my gibberish that she went near a drain and emptied her full mouth of half-chewed tobacco—a real sacrifice—for she wanted to hug and kiss me. What had I said after all? It was just a silly rhyme of Abbakka and *gubbakka*. *Gubbakka* is an expression of fondness for the bird gubbi, a sparrow—a small bird. Abbakka was large and *gubbakka* was small but I had ventured to imagine that the big Abbakka was carried off by *gubbakka* in her small beak which picked up seeds and worms. Had I tried to match a supernatural sight of our Abbakka becoming a Devi with another fantastic happening of a small bird carrying her away? I must have done this not as an idea but as a sheer delight in rhyming a word.

I remember this, thanks to the love and pride of my mother, and I wonder: don't I work even now to balance a sentence and get the right kind of rhythm in my prose and thereby admit into my writing, from an unknown source, meanings that I did not consciously or deliberately pursue? It is like a sudden gift when you get it in your language. Only in your language spoken by your people, can you do this. This is indeed a primitive kind of source, and, however intelligent and sophisticated you are in your meaning, if you lose this primitive, magical gift you can't be a poet. You can only be a theoretician. Our great poets—Bendre, Adiga and Kambar—have this gift of making a play of words, a *leela* of *shabd*, create great meanings. But as a writer I am aware it can't be done deliberately and self-consciously.

My early education was not in a school, for it was too far away and therefore in my fifth year my mother initiated me to writing, on the patch of sand spread on the floor, in the open veranda of the house with large carved pillars of jackfruit tree-wood; with my forefinger she made me write on the sand my first alphabet, praying to Goddess Saraswati. My father and grandfather took care of my education. I remember one poem that my father read out to me, for there were tears in his eyes as he read it out to me. I have seen my mother cry, even the Devi Abbakka cry. I have never seen my father cry, except when he read this poem which we call "Govina haadu"—The Song of the Cow. The poem begins, revealing the whole globe first as if a camera in the sky catches a vast space, and then the poem moves from a long shot to a close up. In the centre of the globe is Karnataka. In Karnataka lives a cowherd called Kalinga. He calls all the cow-mothers. What are their names? Ganga, Gowri, Tunga Bhadra—two of them are rivers, tells my father.

Our cow Punyakoti, while grazing, strays accidentally into the territory of a tiger. The tiger is hungry. It is the dharma of the tiger to eat whatever comes into its territory. Punyakoti has to yield herself to the hunger of the tiger but begs permission of the tiger to let her go back to the shed and feed its young calf, which is hungry too, and after fulfilling her motherly duty, she promises that she will come back to become food to the tiger. There is a moving passage as Punyakoti feeds her calf and advises her never to stray into a territory which is not rightfully her own and bids a tearful farewell requesting her other companion cows not to butt her child if she comes in front and not to kick her if she goes behind them and thus to mother her orphaned child.

The tiger waiting hungrily cannot believe that Punyakoti is there before him offering her all, her hot, flowing blood, her strong muscles, her soft flesh as food to be eaten. There is a sudden change of heart in the tiger. Our anonymous Kannada poet knows that the tiger's heart may change but not its nature. In a Sanskrit original, it seems, the tiger after undergoing a change of heart becomes a *tapaswi*. But our Kannada poet is a realist and therefore makes the tiger jump off a precipice and kill himself.

It is one of the great poems extolling non-violence and truth—a cow triumphing over a hungry tiger. It is a surreal poem. A surreal Gandhian poem, I should say.

Ever since I got to know this poem, Karnataka is in the centre of the globe for me. No language is ethnic or just regional only because it is bound within a geographical space. The first known author of Kannada, Srivijaya, who wrote *Kavirajamarga* a thousand years ago, defined Kannada as a language spoken from Kaveri to Godavari, and the people living in such a land as a *janapada* conceived in the language Kannada. (More precisely, in *that* Kannada, thus importing to the language a metaphysical and abstract dimension. My late friend K.V. Subbanna writes movingly about this in his classical work which the Akademi honoured.)

No writer in the past in my language thought that he was limited because he did not write in a cosmopolitan language like Samskruta. Our first Mahakavi Pampa knew his Kalidasa and admiring him tried to do better. Our great Vachana poets of the 12th century were original thinkers and spiritual seekers and recreated the Upanishadic search on their own terms. Kuvempu, a writer of our times, invokes the epic poets of the world and says that *Ramayana* has created the Kuvempu-poet. I do not mean to say that everything in Kannada is worthy to be termed as world literature; such a claim is meaningless for any language. Srivijaya of *Kavirajamarga* has both the qualities of humility and self-confidence when he says Kannada is unique and at the same time partakes of the larger world. [. . .]

I must now move away in time and then come back to the days of my youth. This was in the sixties and I was a doctoral student in Birmingham and my first guide was the famous novelist and critic, Malcolm Bradbury. He was my age and I admired his learning and his curiosity and openness. We together saw in the University film society Bergman's Seventh Seal. The film shown had no subtitles. What you misunderstand or barely understand can be very stimulating and productive when you are also ready for such stimulation. I barely understood the film as a story of crisis—a crisis of belief in medieval Europe which encountered its mysterious "other" in the Crusades.

I remember telling Professor Bradbury after the film as we had a draught beer in the student union bar, the following:

When a European has to recreate the medieval ages, he does so through learning and research. But for me the medieval is immediate; it is present in my relatives and in some of my deep feelings along with the present. My marriage could have taken place according to the viewpoint of my medieval grandmother while the job I do may be in an office belonging to the modern world system. I live in several worlds at the same time. Centuries co-exist in our consciousness for our history has not moved in a straight line forward as in the case of Europe. Chaucer telling Canterbury Tales during a pilgrimage is as contemporary for us as Dickens writing in an industrializing London and Camus with his metaphysical questions.

I was thinking then of a typical day in my high school—meeting Sinha in a clinic and a teacher criticizing the Bhagavad-Gita and listening to an argument which was long ago settled by Galileo. Bradbury said that I must find a way of reflecting this in my creative writing.

This served as a good excuse for me for I could delay my next chapter of the thesis. Also, suddenly I remembered the story of the sleeping princess I had trickily retold in the manuscript magazine. In less than a week I wrote my novel Samskara.

I must say the novel got written by me. I was fatigued having to speak English all the time, and when I sat down to write all my Kannada, alive from my childhood and boyhood memories—mostly from the whispered secrets I had heard in the backyard of my house, as well as from the front yard where men sonorously recited morally ennobling Puranic stories—came back to me and the characters entered into my novel on their own. All the great, older writers in my language communicated their strength to me in a silent manner. I must also add here that I belonged, in all my earlier stories like "Ghatashradha," to the Navya School of writing and our inspiration came from the great poetry of Gopalakrishna Adiga who had interiorized the one-thousand-year-old Kannada tradition and opened out to the influence of modern European and English writers.

KAMALA DAS

1934–2009
(English/Malayalam)

Kamala Das was born in Punnayurkulam in what was to become Kerala state. Her mother, Nalapat Balamaniamma, was a celebrated poet in Malayalam, the mother tongue Das used for her own prose—fiction, memoirs, and short stories. But her poetry was composed only in English. Perhaps this was a way of separating herself from her mother, marking even more clearly the disjunction between Balamaniamma's delicate, haunting lines often focused on domestic or mythological themes and Das's own passionate stanzas, frequently in the voice of a woman who needs an illicit sexual passion to set her soul free. Kerala has a powerful matrilineal tradition and lines of female descent. Even as these elements feed into Das's poetry, allowing for creation of intense female ancestors, there still remains a desperate need to free the intimate self, to permit the "I" to move to the rhythms of desire no one else will acknowledge. The Old Playhouse and Other Poems *(1973) broke fresh ground in the field of Indian English letters with readers marveling at the poet's honesty in speaking of sexuality. As for the choice of language, it was something Das felt compelled to defend. In her poem "An Introduction," she points out that the English she uses "is as human as I am human." She argued that any choice of language rendered it inalienably her own. Until the very end she wrote copious prose in Malayalam, both fiction and nonfiction, under the pen name Madhavikutty.*

Her autobiography, My Story *(Ende Katha, 1976), with its frank revelations of a girl's blossoming sexuality, caused a controversy in Indian literary circles. In* My Story *she writes, "Poets, even the most insignificant of them, are different from other people. They cannot close their shops like shopmen and return home. Their shop is their mind and as long as they carry it with them, they feel the pressures and the torments. A poet's raw material is not stone or clay; it is her personality."* Later in the same book, she speaks of writers as *"those dreaming ones, born with a fragment of wing still attached to a shoulder."* Her conversion to Islam late in life, inspired by a love affair with a younger Muslim man, took her readers by surprise. In response to death threats from the Hindu right, she moved to Pune, where her son lived. She took the name Kamala Surayya and continued writing and appearing in public, including on Indian television, but instead of the bright silks she previously favored, the poet dressed in a black burqa and covered her head. For many in the women's movement her conversion was seen as a retrograde step, but for Kamala Das, always the individualist, this seemed to be simply another turn in the ongoing theater of life. Her important works include the volumes of poetry Summer in Calcutta *(1965),* The Descendents *(1967), and* The Annamalai Poems *(1985); the collection of short stories* Padmavati the Harlot and Other Stories *(1992); and the novel* Neermathalam Pootha Kala *(1994).*

From *My Story*

"THE BOUGAINVILLEA"

On our way to school on some privileged days the cook used to get for us the narrow limp strips of Nestle's chocolate which came in wrappings of glazed and red paper with a coloured photo of the British royal family tucked inside its second layer. We collected enough to be able to demand an album from the dealer.

We had also the habit of collecting cuttings from the newspapers for a political album. This contained all the photographs of Hitler and Mussolini who were undoubtedly the greatest heroes in our eyes at that time. The newspapers gave their speeches maximum coverage, built them up into supermen. We secretly hoped to be like them when we grew up.

At this time my brother thought it a good idea to start a manuscript magazine. None of our contemporaries could turn out essays or poems because they felt diffident about their spelling. So the responsibility fell on my shoulders.

I was six and very sentimental. I wrote sad poems about dolls who lost their heads and had to remain headless for eternity. Each poem of mine made me cry. My brother illustrated the verses and wrote faintly political articles.

We had two tutors. Mabel, a pretty Anglo-Indian, and Nambiar, the Malayalam tutor. The cook was partial to the lady, served her tea on a tray with tiny sandwiches laid out on a quarter-plate, and to Nambiar who came much later in the evening he only gave a glass tumbler of tea and a few sardonic remarks. Nambiar, in our house, moved about with a heavy inferiority complex and would hide behind the sideboard when my father passed through the dining room where we had our Malayalam lessons. We learnt our vernacular only to be able to correspond with our grandmother who was very fond of us.

One day all the children of our school were taken to the Victoria Gardens for a picnic. We were given sugar-cane juice and ham sandwiches which, being vegetarian, I threw away behind the flowering bushes. The young schoolmistress kept shrieking out, "Oh Archie, Oh Archie," every now and then to the dark history teacher while he tried most unsuccessfully to grab her and kiss her. She ran round the trees escaping his clutches, all the while laughing gaily as though it was a big joke.

I went away to the farthest fence and lay near a hedge of Henna which had sprouted its tiny flowers. The sun was white that day, a white lamp of a sun on the winter sky. I was lonely. Oh I was so lonely that day. No one seemed to want my company, not even my brother who was playing a kind of football with his classmates. Helen, the only girl who could dance, was telling the others of the film called *The Blue Bird*. I wondered why I did not join the girls who crowded around her.

I wondered why I was born to Indian parents instead of to a white couple, who may have been proud of my verses. Then suddenly like the clatter of pots and pans, harsh words attacked my privacy. "What on earth are you doing here, Kamala?" shouted the teacher. "Why don't you join the others? What a peculiar child you are!" And the white sun filled my eyes with its own loneliness. The smell of Henna flowers overwhelmed me. Sobbing, I rose and walked towards my teacher. The children stared at me. The teacher laughed. As though it was a signal for them to begin laughing too, they broke into high laughter. The birds on the trees flew away . . .

In the afternoon occasionally I slipped out of the gate while the fat watchman slept soundly on his charpoy and walked to the old cemetery. The tombstones were like yellowed teeth and even the writing had faded with the rains of half a century. But it was thrilling to read the words that had not faded and to know that Elizabeth Hardinge was born in 1818 but died in 1938. Who was Elizabeth? Who was Roger Upton who died only at the age of eighty-three? Who was Rosamund? Except for monkeys I was the only living creature there, but the red bougainvillea, gaudy as spilt blood, that had climbed the minarets, swung in the breeze. The marigolds dipped their heads in curtsy. The monkeys ignored me and suckled their young.

I was too young to know about ghosts. It was possible for me to love the dead as deeply as I loved the living. I could even go up to the unknown Rosamund and confide in her. From the dead no harshness could emanate, no cruelty . . .

FROM "THE P.E.N. POETRY PRIZE"

In the year 1963 I won P.E.N.'s Asian Poetry Prize and had for the first time in my life a bank account of mine from which in two days' time I withdrew almost half the amount for outfitting myself. I have always ignored fashions, being fully aware of their disability to help me look chic, but I have wanted to dress aesthetically.

I grew fond of lungis with floral prints and shirts of black poplin that concealed the heaviness of my upper torso. I like strands of red beads and red glass bangles. I disliked the foreign perfumes with their alcoholic base but I liked to pour attar in my bathwater. Instead of soap I used the powdered bark of the Vaka tree which had an abrasive action on the skin.

I had an oily skin which made me look younger than my years. This endeared me to old men who were weary of sophisticated ladies and the fragrances of their elaborate toilet. I was drawn to old people for they seemed harmless and they had charm. They smelt clean. They knew how to put a girl at ease just by paying her a simple compliment.

One of the old ones who used to visit our family on Sundays had a face that resembled Stan Laurel's, and I was very fond of him. He made me laugh, clowning on our verandah, and with mimicry that delighted my son. He used to take us out when my husband was out touring, and get us ice cream and chocolates and carry us to little restaurants full of smoke and twilight.

We were grateful for the outings, for nobody else did bother about us. My husband was too busy to think of taking us out anywhere and he was not exactly rich either. This old man used to plant kisses on my cheeks leaving us at the door, slobbering kisses that had to be washed out in a hurry, and yet I was guilty of encouraging him because I wanted someone to take my little sons out and give them a good time. When he once brought me a pornographic book wrapped in brown paper, I decided to end the friendship. No reasons were given. He was shrewd enough to guess them.

Then there were the men who were either connected with my husband's occupation or were at one time my father's friends, the ones I used to call "Uncle" from intimacy, who had changed to such an extent that they gave me lecherous hugs from behind doors and leered at me while their wives were away. I hated them. Often I told my husband that we ought to run away from Calcutta and its corrupting atmosphere. But he paid no heed.

Poets, even the most insignificant of them, are different from other people. They cannot close their shops like shopmen and return home. Their shop is their mind and as long as they carry it with them, they feel the pressures and the torments. A poet's raw material is not stone or clay; it is her personality. I could not escape from my predicament even for a moment. I was emotional and oversensitive. Whenever a snatch of unjustified scandal concerning my emotional life reached me through well-meaning relatives, I wept like a wounded child for hours rolling on my bed and often took sedatives to put myself to sleep.

"The Old Playhouse"

You planned to tame a swallow, to hold her
In the long summer of your love so that she would forget
Not the raw seasons alone and homes left behind, but
Also her nature, the urge to fly, and the endless
Pathways of the sky. It was not to gather knowledge
Of yet another man that I came to you but to learn
What I was and by learning, to learn to grow, but every
Lesson you gave was about yourself. You were pleased

With my body's response, its weather, its usual shallow
Convulsions. You dribbled spittle into my mouth, you poured
Yourself into every nook and cranny, you embalmed
My poor lust with your bitter-sweet juices. You called me wife,
I was taught to break saccharine into your tea and
To offer at the right moment the vitamins. Cowering
Beneath your monstrous ego I ate the magic loaf and
Became a dwarf. I lost my will and reason, to all your
Questions I mumbled incoherent replies. The summer
Begins to pall. I remember the ruder breezes
Of the fall and the smoke from burning leaves. Your room is
Always lit by artificial lights, your windows, always
Shut. Even the airconditioner helps so little,
All pervasive is the male scent of your breath. The cut flowers
In the vases have begun to smell of human sweat. There is
No more singing, no more dance, my mind is an old
Playhouse with all its lights put out. The strong man's technique
Is always the same. He serves his love in lethal doses
For love is Narcissus at the water's edge haunted
By its lonely face, and yet it must seek at last
An end, a pure, total freedom, it must will the mirrors
To shatter and the kind night to erase the water.

From "An Introduction"

I don't know politics but I know the names
Of those in power, and can repeat them like
Days of week, or names of months, beginning with
Nehru. I am Indian, very brown, born in
Malabar, I speak three languages, write in
Two, dream in one. Don't write in English, they said.
English is not your mother-tongue. Why not leave
Me alone, critics, friends, visiting cousins,
Every one of you? Why not let me speak in
Any language I like? The language I speak

Becomes mine, its distortions, its queernesses
All mine, mine alone. It is half English, half
Indian, funny perhaps, but it is honest,
It is as human as I am human, don't
You see? It voices my joys, my longings, my
Hopes, and it is useful to me as cawing
Is to crows or roaring to the lions, it
Is human speech, the speech of the mind that is
Here and not there, a mind that sees and hears and
Is aware. Not the deaf, blind speech
Of trees in storm or of monsoon clouds or of rain or the
Incoherent mutterings of the blazing
Funeral pyre. I was child, and later they
Told me I grew, for I became tall, my limbs
Swelled and one or two places sprouted hair. When
I asked for love, not knowing what else to ask
For, he drew a youth of sixteen into the
Bedroom and closed the door. He did not beat me
But my sad woman-body felt so beaten.
The weight of my breasts and womb crushed me. I shrank
Pitifully. Then . . . I wore a shirt and my
Brother's trousers, cut my hair short and ignored
My womanliness. Dress in sarees, be girl,
Be wife, they said. Be embroiderer, be cook.
Be a quarreler with servants. Fit in. Oh,
Belong, cried the categorizers. Don't sit
On walls or peep in through our lace-draped windows.
     Be Amy or be Kamala. Or better
Still be Madhavikutty. It is time to
Choose a name, a role. Don't play pretending games.
Don't play at schizophrenia or be a
Nympho. Don't cry embarrassingly loud when
Jilted in love . . .

KEKI DARUWALLA

b. 1937

(English)

Keki Daruwalla was born in Lahore to a Parsi family in what was then an undivided India. At the time of Partition his family migrated to India. His poems draw on the great sweeps of history—Parsi, Moghul, and European as well as the violence of the new nation. All this is viewed as fit material for the lyric. His first volume of poetry, Under Orion, *was published in 1970. At the time Daruwalla was an officer in the Indian Police Service. In a career path unusual for a poet, he rose through the ranks, retiring as chairman of the Joint Intelligence Committee. In his essay "The Decolonised Muse" he writes of "my almost fierce commitment to place, site, landscape." He thinks of this as a way of forging the unique "soundscapes" of his poems, moving beyond the mellifluous diet of English Romantic poetry, John Keats, Percy Shelley, and others that he was fed in school. In the same essay he reflects on English, the language the British Empire bequeathed India: "You cannot choose your generation, your parents or your language, even a foreign one at times. If your father teaches English, and you have three thousand books in the house, all in the same language, you have precious few options. To become fully conscious of writing in the language of one's erstwhile colonial rulers, one must cross various thresholds of realization. To put it simplistically, a child thinks through language and feels through experience."*

In "Childhood Poem," dedicated to his friend A. K. Ramanujan, Daruwalla evokes his early acts of writing; the poet reveals how instead of "rondures /

and scimitar curves" that the Urdu required, the child was only able to create "serrations and smudges / charred centipedes on a wooden slate." English for the poet becomes the medium of self-translation, a language that for all its perceived shortcomings can serve to body forth the emotions of the multilingual self. In addition to his many volumes of poetry, Daruwalla is also a prolific writer in prose, having published several collections of short stories, a travelogue, and novels—one a historical novel on Vasco da Gama and Pedro Alvares Cabral entitled For Pepper and Christ *(2009) and another drawing on material closer to home,* Ancestral Affairs *(2015), about a Parsi family at the time of Partition. Daruwalla's important works of poetry include* The Keeper of the Dead *(1982),* Crossing of Rivers *(1985), and* The Map-Maker *(2002). His* Collected Poems *appeared in 2006. In 1987, he was awarded the Commonwealth Poetry Prize.*

"The Decolonised Muse (A Personal Statement)"

We are all trapped in history.[1] The Europeans came to trade, hung on to fight, intrigue and conquer, and stayed on to instruct. Their colonies became vast markets for their textiles and their language. Conversions followed, to another way of life and on occasions to Christianity. When they went back they left their language behind—and half-castes. In an alien land, language itself turns brown and half-caste.

English was introduced in India with commercial objectives in view. What was achieved was something much greater in dimensions. Colonial history shows that language can be as domineering as any occupation army. It supplants myths, whole iconographies, world-view, ideologies. It ushers in its own symbols, and its own values. An armada of new texts sails in. Old dogmas and bigotries are swept away—and exchanged for new ones.

You cannot choose your generation, your parents or your language,

---

1. A talk delivered at Internationale Literaturtage '88 held at Erlangen, West Germany, a beautiful Hugenot town with much of its old seventeenth century architecture still intact. A cursory attempt was made here to inform a German (and international) audience what Indian poetry in English was all about. This conference, known generally as Interlit 3, was held in 1988. Some of my views finding mention here have since changed. Writers deserve better than being held to account for views they held almost two decades back.

even a foreign one at times. If your father teaches English, and you have three thousand books in the house, all in the same language, you have precious few options. To become fully conscious of writing in the language of one's erstwhile colonial rulers, one must cross various thresholds of realization. To put it simplistically, a child thinks through language and feels through experience. The first school I entered was called Sacred Hearts. But World War II was raging, the Italian fathers next door were under house arrest, and even a string or two of barbed wire had sprung up around the school. Not the right type of atmosphere for a growing boy, my father thought. So I got transplanted to an Arya school, quite a different kettle of fish, really. Many of the boys came from a different social stratum. Urdu, Hindi, Sanskrit were given as much importance as English, and rightly so. The pronunciation of the school masters and the students bordered on the atrocious. My fluency (so called) in English was greeted with derisive laughter. Just because the grammar was correct, and the diction not too awful, one became an object of mockery.

The next threshold was crossed when one encountered boys from public schools. These were situated in the mountain sanctuaries of Murree and Simla and Nainital. The boys wore blue blazers and school neck ties. Their speech was more clipped, their smiles more condescending. They even spoke their *Hindustani* with an anglicized accent. They could hardly pronounce the names of the towns they lived in. Nainithal, as it is pronounced in Hindustani, got twisted to "Nainitoll." And they used slang. It was old slang of course, shipped some three decades ago, which had got lost on the seas, then lay rotting on the docks like dry fish, till it was dispatched by steam rail and later on mule back to those public schools in the mountains. But the fact is that they used slang and if you did not latch on to a phrase, you were held in contempt.

And then came my first conversation with an Englishman. He had to repeat himself three times to make himself understood. What an exotic accent, I thought. Why couldn't the fellow speak English as she ought to be spoken?

No other trauma intervened for the next fifteen years or so. Then as one started publishing poetry in English, critics shook their heads in disapproval. Yes, fiction, essays, articles, even pornography one could write in English, they said (though nothing like Punjabi for robust abuse). But poetry was another cup of tea. You could write it only in a language you had imbibed with mother's milk. This line of argument gave rise to what I chose to call the Lactatory School of Literary Criticism. Another august body called the Royal School of Dreamy Criticism asked me if I dreamt in English. The trouble was I dreamt in images mostly and seldom in language. My dreams were often silent movies. When once in a while they did turn into Talkies, they were like me, multi-lingual.

Exiles come to alien shores and write in the language of their adopted country. Joseph Conrad, Arthur Koestler, Nabokov are examples. An Indian writing poetry in English was an exile in his own country.

The handicaps were all too apparent. One is not merely speaking of an exclusive readership. Isn't poetry restricted to a class with a certain educational background? It could be said that 7,000 miles and quite a few years separated the Indian writer from the "living speech" of the language. But didn't millions speak English in India? Wasn't it at least the second language of most educated Indians? It was the language of the bank and the stock exchange, of the Parliament, the secretariat and the law courts. The writer was at home with it. What I am trying to refer to is the difficulties in writing poetry itself. You stuck to the straight and narrow path of textual English. You cut out linguistic heroics and hesitated taking liberties with the language. It was tough enough mastering (if that's the word) the idiom. To now start fragmenting it, chopping up the grammar and entering the slippery realm of the disjunctive seemed an unthinking indulgence. Sound, as poets know, is vital to poetry. At times I hesitated in giving a full phonetic charge to my verse unless the meaning was crystal clear and each line as a unit made sense.

Yet instinctively, one knew what to exclude: words like "deliverance" and "renunciation," expressions like "the wondrous mysteries of the divine," "the oneness of Brahma," "the stream of life," the self (both the small guy starting with an "s" in lowercase and the big fellow with the capital "S"), all talk of *moksha* (liberation) and *maya*[2] (appearance), all reference to infinity and eternity and expressions like "the womb of the void" or "the void of the womb"—have it any way you please. I avoided them like the plague. Not once, as far as I recollect, have I talked of the soul in a poem. It was by a conscious act of will. The stranglehold over the soul, this monopoly over the spiritual enjoyed by the earlier well-meaning

---

2. Since then I have written an entire poem on *maya*!

savants who passed off as philosophers, and the present batch of crooks who masquerade as godmen, is one of the intellectual scandals of this century.

Instinctively one made language slightly subservient to content. Those who think that the form is the poem would not take kindly to this. Literature concerns itself with the world of the spirit and the flesh as we know it. Passions, feelings, consciousness, the past and memories get thrown in. Language after all is just one of the dimensions that make literature what it is. So it was good literary strategy to give slightly more weight to content. All language and literature are in some way a translation: you render reality (dreams, perceptions, memories, the physical world around you) into words. Surely this reality is important, and a case can be made out for giving it a certain degree (however small) of primacy over language.

How would I define insight or truth? That, which in any other tongue, would have gone as swiftly to the heart.

Looking back I find that the compulsion to mark out an identity for myself must have been very strong. Since one was writing in English it should be all the more evident that it was an Indian writing. Just bringing an Indian sensibility to bear on a theme was not enough. The poem had to be securely fastened to an Indian setting; should seek freshly upturned earth under a monsoon downpour. Most, if not all of this, worked unconsciously within me. With hindsight, that is the only way I can explain my almost fierce commitment to place, site, landscape. (Not just in my poems but also in my stories, where I take great care to set the scene first, almost like a director visualizing the stage for a play). In my first book, *Under Orion*, one entire section was devoted to life in the marshlands (the *terai*). Another book dealt with the Ganga at Benares and with the purificatory myth of the river.

At the same time one could not close one's eyes to the filth at the ghats of Benares and the seeming chaos, the miasma of funeral pyres going up in flames a few yards from unconcerned pilgrims bathing in the river, offering obeisance to the rising sun. I accepted the notion that its swirling waters cleansed one of one's sins. But I could not shut my eyes to what was happening in front of me. This is where we come back to language. For languages erect their own outposts of sensibility—not that you can easily marshal arguments to support this kind of a nebulous statement.

Nor had this kind of perception anything to do with a colonial hangover (though critics might believe otherwise). One saw squalor and chaos for what they were. They registered themselves on the cornea. No alibis are needed here.

In university one had been brought up on a diet of Shelley and Keats. When you left the campus you faced harsh reality around you—drought, poverty and communal riots. One needed a harsh language, words with a saw-edge, words which rasped and got into you like the shards of a broken bottle. Slowly, almost unconsciously the poems developed a vocabulary and a soundscape of their own.

The question of patois comes up often, of the Indian contribution to the English language. Some of these experiments (in prose) have been very successful, for instance Desani's *The Mad Hatter* and Raja Rao's *Kanthapura*, both recognized as minor classics today. Novels are one thing, verse another. We have had no such triumphs in poetry. Admitted that the Indian has his own way with English syntax, but it is in no way comparable to the Caribbean patois. The Indian way of speaking English is to mix the languages—half a sentence in English and the other tattered half in Hindi or Marathi or Bengali. Writing in that manner could bring on numerous problems. Pidgin is fine but a half-Hindi–half-English amalgam becomes impractical.

Finally, while the poet endeavours to hone the language to his purpose, language also has a way with his poetry. If you have wielded an oriental scimitar all your life, you are used to whirling it about, making fearful whistling arcs in the air and generally slashing around. But give the same man a straight-bladed sword and willy-nilly, given some time, he will learn to thrust and stab.

ANITA DESAI
b. 1937
(English)

Anita Desai was born in Mussoorie to a German mother and Bengali father. She grew up speaking German to her mother, as well as Bengali, Hindi, and English. In her essay "On Being an Indian Writer Today" Desai writes of the hostility she sometimes experienced in her earlier days as an English language writer in the subcontinent and the loneliness she faced. She speaks of how she was forced to "retire to one's corner and scribble there as invisibly and unobtrusively as possible." But out of this enforced isolation, "that cave of solitude," came the materials for her crystalline art. Her delicate, probing, elegiac novels brought her great acclaim. Indeed, she was one of the earliest novelists in modern India to enter into the complexities of female lives, lives lived out in an upper-middle-class setting but bound ineluctably by social demands. Still, the emotions of someone who is displaced are never far from her. In an interview published in the Massachusetts Review *in 1988, she speaks of her sympathy with outsiders, a legacy perhaps of having a German mother and growing up in India but also an intrinsic part of what she sees as the condition of artists everywhere. "The element I most sympathize with is the one of being an outsider. I suppose most authors, most artists, confess to feeling outsiders to society to some degree or another." Later she speaks of a duality in herself faced with the tumultuous world of the subcontinent: "I feel about India as an Indian, but I suppose I think of it as an outsider."*

In the lyrical masterpiece Fire on the Mountain *(1977), Desai presents an elderly woman, Nanda Kaul, who retreats to her cottage in Kausali, clinging to the precious solitude she has finally discovered for herself only to find it abruptly shattered by the arrival of her difficult granddaughter. In the novel, Desai was writing of the Kausali hills she loved, a refuge from the abrasive city of Bombay. In* The Clear Light of Day *(1980), the family house in Old Delhi harbors the interlinked memories of generations of a family that survived Partition, only to be thrust abruptly into a sharply altered world. Her important books include her first work,* Cry the Peacock *(1963);* In Custody *(1984), which was turned into a movie by Merchant-Ivory; and* Baumgartner's Bombay *(1988), which tells of a German-Jewish refugee who fled the Holocaust to live out his days in that crowded metropolis. She now lives in the United States. Her novel* The Zigzag Way *(2004) is set in Mexico, a country she has visited for many years in the company of her daughter, the gifted novelist Kiran Desai.*

"On Being an Indian Writer Today"

The first time that I visited the USA, my publisher took me to dinner at his club in New York and asked me what it was like to be a writer in India. I thought over how best to describe my existence at home and finally told him "It is like being deep inside a dark cave, quite alone." "With no bou-oum?" he asked with incredulity. "No," I replied, "with no bou-oum at all." Inevitably we were using E M Forster's metaphor of a cave in *A Passage to India* since it was the English language and literary tradition that had brought us together.

I should explain what I meant. I was talking about writing in the 1950s and 1960s when it was an act of solitary confinement and the actual existence of writers no more than a rumour spread by their books. Yes, we had the mighty triumvirate of Mulk Raj Anand, Raja Rao and R K Narayan, as mythical and awe-inspiring to us as gods (I am confining myself to comments on the writing done in English in India) and, a long way behind, there was the triumvirate of women writers to which no one would have thought of attaching the label "mighty"—Attia Hosain, Nayantara Sahgal and Kamala Markandaya. One might find some dusty paperback copies of their novels in shabby bookshops, tossed in with cookery books

anita desai

and those collections of wise sayings and proverbs that publishers of the day liked to bring out.

In this distinctly discouraging atmosphere, one could only withdraw to write without any hope of there being publishers who might want to publish what one wrote, still less of readers who might wish to read it. Readers of the English language almost without exception preferred to read the English written in its native land, the only English considered pure and acceptable; P G Wodehouse and Jane Austen clubs flourished. I, too, grew up reading Henry James and D H Lawrence, Virginia Woolf and George Eliot. No Indian author had entered the school or college syllabi at that time (in my children's, a translation of one of Tagore's poems and Nissim Ezekiel's 'Night of the Scorpion' had been introduced; to this day they are able to recite them).

It dawned on me what a hopeless business it would be to make a living as a writer. No literary agents existed then and I made out a list of publishers from the books on my shelves and started sending out the manuscript of my first novel to one after the other. Finally it was accepted by a small independent publishing house in London that specialised in the work of international authors, often in translation. I was deeply grateful for the acceptance since it seemed to validate my existence as a writer. If I remember correctly, I made £300 from it. At one point the publisher sold translation rights to a Romanian publisher for ten pounds, and I was grateful for that too because they were willing to take a chance with an unknown writer living in India. R K Narayan, remember, was not published in England till Graham Greene endorsed his work. Why had I not gone to an Indian publisher? Well, there wasn't one interested in publishing fiction by a local author. The only books they published were text books that had a steady, reliable sale, and reprints of classics from abroad; even R K Narayan had to descend to the ignominy of publishing his own work.

Since it was clear that I could not live upon my earnings as a novelist, I tried breaking into a related field like journalism or editing but when a friend of the family who was an art critic at *The Statesman* took me along to introduce me to the editor, we were waved away like two annoying flies (this was long before the age of student internships). I next approached one or two publishers to ask for an editorial position. I can still see the dark, cluttered office of one who sat dispiritedly fanning himself during a power breakdown and his look of incomprehension when he asked "Why would you want to work here?" By then I too had lost my intention to do so and left without a protest.

There really was nothing to do but retire to one's corner and scribble there as invisibly and unobtrusively as possible. In those years my courage was kept up by a neighbour in Old Delhi, the writer Ruth Prawer Jhabvala. It was not so much what she said to me as seeing her live her quiet domestic life while turning out her marvellous portrayals of our Old Delhi world that made me think that solitude and the lack of response did not really matter if it allowed me to do the one thing that I wanted to do.

I imagined that writers of the indigenous languages lived richer, more active and involved lives, confident of their roles in the world. Unfortunately, I never met them. There was, in those years, an antipathy, an hostility even, towards writing done in English—that colonial language that should have been banned outright at Independence and that needed to be put in its place, a parasite that refused to go away and conveniently die. I tried to ignore the assumption that mine was the last generation in India that would write in English but shared in the sense that these were its twilight years.

The picture changed abruptly, dramatically, in 1981, when a book called *Midnight's Children* appeared on the scene like a thunderbolt and the author was sent to India on that until then unknown exercise, a book tour. It was the combination of a book that proved that Indian English was a language in itself, capable of presenting serious and important ideas with vigour and originality (G V Desani had done the same in *All About H Hatterr* but it had been a flash in the pan and led nowhere), and of the author as a personality, a living personality, that changed the Indian scene overnight.

Not only was a whole generation of younger writers like Amitav Ghosh, Vikram Seth and Upmanyu Chatterji energised and given confidence by the success of Salman Rushdie's book, its language and ideas, but all the discouraged, defeated publishers sat up and took notice of them. And the combination of these two phenomena—a new generation of Indian writers addressing Indian subjects and themes in a language taken from the Indian streets, newspapers, journals and films, and a class of enterprising businessmen who decided they were worth publishing—marked the 1980s and 1990s. It was a heady time, the climax being the spectacular moment when a British literary agent actually flew to India—did he charter a plane? Did he fly it himself? Never mind, he gave the *impression* that he did—to sign up an Indian author who went on to win the Booker Prize.

Things have never been the same since. By the number of manuscripts that arrive daily and hourly from India on the desks of British and American agents and publishers, I would guess no country has more aspiring writers than ours. And enough of them are published to fill glossy catalogues and whole sections of bookshops; it is hardly possible to enter one and not run into an array of books with Indian brides, Indian spices and Indian textiles splashed across the covers. In fact, there is now such a din in the publishing world that it is beginning to resemble that hoary cliché, the Indian bazaar.

In the clamour—agents! contracts! royalties! awards!—it might be easy to overlook the revolution that brought it about. While it is curious —and a little sad—that writing only became a "respectable" profession once it began making money, it is very gratifying to know that a young, talented person can make such a choice today and not be consigned to "loser" status. It is actually possible at last to make a living by writing, to be self-supporting and thus self-respecting. The importance of this cannot be stressed enough. As long ago as 1929 Virginia Woolf knew this and wrote of it in her seminal *A Room of One's Own*.

A side-effect has been the proliferation of book festivals and readings. I had never known a public event other than an occasional academic conference that might invite an author into its august gathering, but now writers can roam the world and bump into each other at the local wine bar and *adda* or at festivals in Jaipur, Hay-on-Wye, Toronto, Frankfurt, Brazil or Bali. A camaraderie has emerged where there had once been a lonely vacuum. Indian writers can meet and talk to writers from Australia or Cuba or Iceland and, as importantly, see their books placed on tables and shelves along with theirs. As my young daughter, herself one of the peripatetic generation, says, "It is a good time to be an Indian writer."

And maybe it is a good time to stop and look back at the long curve that has brought us to this point. Having looked, I must admit I find myself disconcerted, somehow disoriented and inclined to retreat, backwards, into that cave of solitude where I found writing came from, where one can think without interruption and take one's time, where no one is watching or waiting or even interested. After all, that contains a great and wonderful —if daunting—freedom.

GIRISH KARNAD
b. 1938
(Kannada)

Girish Karnad, who composed his plays in Kannada, was born in Mathern, a small town in what is now Maharashtra state. In his autobiography Aadaatha Ayshuya *(2011), he writes: "Kannada chose me." The language of his consummate literary production was not his mother tongue, Konkani. Instead, the mythic traditions of Kannada literature provided Karnad with a fertile field for his activities. His plays are grounded in ancient Indian legends and also draw on sources from world literature. Time and again he examines the self-division that afflicts the main characters, an internal drama that often emerges in heightened theatrical fashion.* Hayavadana *(Horse's Head, 1972) caused a great stir when it was first performed by the Madras Players. It was subsequently published in Rajinder Paul's journal* Enact *in a translation by Karnad himself. The play draws on the Sanskrit classic* Kathasaritasagara *as well as on the Thomas Mann reworking of the story in* The Transposed Heads. *Karnad uses elements of the traditional Yakshagana theater, with its masks and songs and ritualized dance, to present the existential quandary of the main figures. An important element of Yakshagana is the Bhagwata, a singer-speaker whose presence Karnad exploits to great effect. The play focuses on the trials of Padmini, who finds that her husband, a light-skinned man known for his powerful intellect, together with his best friend, a man who is dark and possessed of enormous physical strength, have made a pact and each committed suicide. Unrequited love for Padmini has driven each man to this dire end. Grief-*

stricken, Padmini transposes their heads and is left to ponder the metamorphic identities they presented her with. In Naga-Mandala *(1988), first performed at the University of Chicago—Karnad was visiting on a Fulbright—the central woman character is again torn between two men, her husband who neglects her and her lover, the king cobra or Naga, who comes in the shape of the husband and eventually takes refuge as a tiny new snake in the black coils of her hair. In addition to his plays, Karnad has directed feature films and several documentaries on the lives of poets. He composed the screenplay for* Samskara *(based on the novel by U. R. Ananthamurthy) and has often appeared on screen as an actor in Hindi and Kannada films and on Indian television. His other important plays include* Tughlak *(1964) and* Taledanda *(Death by Beheading, 1990). In 1998, he was awarded the Bharatiya Jnanpith Award for Literature.*

From Author's Introduction to *Three Plays*

My generation was the first to come of age after India became independent of British rule. It therefore had to face a situation in which tensions implicit until then had come out in the open and demanded to be resolved without apologia or self-justification: tensions between the cultural past of the country and its colonial past, between the attractions of Western modes of thought and our own traditions, and finally between the various visions of the future that opened up once the common cause of political freedom was achieved. This is the historical context that gave rise to my plays and those of my contemporaries.

In my childhood, in a small town in Karnataka, I was exposed to two theatre forms that seemed to represent irreconcilably different worlds. Father took the entire family to see plays staged by troupes of professional actors called *natak companies* which toured the countryside throughout the year. The plays were staged in semipermanent structures on proscenium stages, with wings and drop curtains, and were illuminated by petromax lamps.

Once the harvest was over, I went with the servants to sit up nights watching the more traditional *Yakshagana* performances. The stage, a platform with a back curtain, was erected in the open air and lit by torches.

By the time I was in my early teens, the *natak companies* had ceased to function and *Yakshagana* had begun to seem quaint, even silly, to me. Soon we moved to a big city. This city had a college and electricity, but no professional theatre.

I saw theatre again only when I went to Bombay for my postgraduate studies. One of the first things I did in Bombay was to go and see a play, which happened to be Strindberg's *Miss Julie* directed by the brilliant young Ebrahim Alkazi.

I have been told since that it was one of Alkazi's less successful productions. The papers tore it to shreds the next day. But when I walked out of the theatre that evening, I felt as though I had been put through an emotionally or even a physically painful rite of passage. I had read some Western playwrights in college, but nothing had prepared me for the power and violence I experienced that day. By the norms I had been brought up on, the very notion of laying bare the inner recesses of the human psyche like this for public consumption seemed obscene. What impressed me as much as the psychological cannibalism of the play was the way lights faded in and out on stage. Until we moved to the city, we had lived in houses lit by hurricane lamps. Even in the city, electricity was something we switched on and off. The realization that there were instruments called dimmers that could gently fade the lights in or out opened up a whole new world of magical possibilities.

Most of my contemporaries went through some similar experience at some point in their lives. We stepped out of mythological plays lit by torches or petromax lamps straight into Strindberg and dimmers. The new technology could not be divorced from the new psychology. The two together defined a stage that was like nothing we had known or suspected. I have often wondered whether it wasn't that evening that, without being actually aware of it, I decided I wanted to be a playwright.

At the end of my stay in Bombay, I received a scholarship to go abroad for further studies. It is difficult to describe to a modern Indian audience the traumas created by this event. Going abroad was a much rarer occurrence in those days; besides, I came from a large, close-knit family and was the first member of the family ever to go abroad. My parents were worried lest I decide to settle down outside India, and even for me, though there was no need for an immediate decision, the terrible choice was implicit in the very act of going away. Should I at the end of my studies return home for the sake of my family, my people and my country, even at the risk of my abilities and training not being fully utilized in what seemed a stifling, claustrophobic atmosphere, or should I rise above such parochial considerations and go where the world drew me?

While still preparing for the trip, amidst the intense emotional turmoil, I found myself writing a play. This took me by surprise, for I had fancied myself a poet, had written poetry through my teens, and had trained myself to write in English, in preparation for the conquest of the West. But here I was writing a play and in Kannada, too, the language spoken by a few million people in South India, the language of my childhood. A greater surprise was the home of the play, for it was taken from ancient Indian mythology from which I had believed myself alienated.

The story of King Yayati that I used occurs in the *Mahabharata*. The king, for a moral transgression he has committed, is cursed to old age in the prime of life. Distraught at losing his youth, he approaches his son, pleading with him to lend him his youth in exchange for old age. The son accepts the exchange and the curse, and thus becomes old, older than his father. But the old age brings no knowledge, no self-realization, only the senselessness of a punishment meted out for an act in which he had not even participated. The father is left to face the consequences of shirking responsibility for his own actions.

While I was writing the play, I saw it only as an escape from my stressful situation. But looking back, I am amazed at how precisely the myth reflected my anxieties at that moment, my resentment with all those who seemed to demand that I sacrifice my future. By the time I had finished working on *Yayati*—during the three weeks it took the ship to reach England and in the lonely cloisters of the university—the myth had enabled me to articulate to myself a set of values that I had been unable to arrive at rationally. Whether to return home finally seemed the most minor of issues; the myth had nailed me to my past.

Oddly enough the play owed its form not to the innumerable mythological plays I had been brought up on, and which had partly kept these myths alive for me, but to Western playwrights whom until then I had only read in print: Anouilh (his *Antigone* particularly) and also Sartre, O'Neill, and the Greeks. That is, at the most intense moment of self-expression, while my past had come to my aid with a ready-made narrative within which I could contain and explore my insecurities, there had been no dramatic structure in my own tradition to which I could relate myself.

One of the plays of post-independence India to use myth to make a contemporary statement was Dharamvir Bharati's *Andha Yug* ("The Blind Age"). The play is about the aftermath of the Kurukshetra War, which forms the climax of the epic *Mahabharata*. The entire epic is in fact a build-up to this great confrontation between Good and Evil, in which God himself participated in the form of Lord Krishna. It was during this war that Krishna expounded the Bhagavadgita, a discourse on the ethics of action and knowledge that had exercised the most profound influence on Indian thought through the ages. Yet this fratricidal war left in its wake nothing but desolation and a sense of futility. No "new world" emerged from the wholesale massacre of the youth of the country. Arjuna, the hero, became impotent. Lord Krishna himself meekly accepted a curse and died an absurd death. In his play, Bharati used the myth to give voice to the sense of horror and despair felt in India in the wake of partition of the country and the communal bloodbaths that accompanied it.

Although later Satyadev Dubey's production proved that it was genuine theatre, *Andha Yug* was actually written for the radio, as a play for voices. It was as if, at the time of conceiving the play, the playwright could imagine no stage on which to place it.

Indeed this contradiction haunts most contemporary playwrighting and theatre in India. Even to arrive at the heart of one's own mythology, the writer has to follow signposts planted by the West, a paradoxical situation for a culture in which the earliest *extant* play was written in A.D. 200! The explanation lies in the fact that what is called "modern Indian theatre" was started by a group of people who adopted "cultural amnesia" as a deliberate strategy. It originated in the second half of the nineteenth century in three cities, Bombay, Calcutta and Madras. None of these seaports built by the British for their maritime trade had an Indian past of its own, a history independent of the British. These places had developed an Indian middle class that in all outward respects aspired to "look" like its British counterpart. The social values of this class were shaped by the English education it had received and by the need to work with the British in trade and administration. [. . .]

The proscenium and the box office proclaimed a new philosophy of the theatre: secularism—but a commercially viable secularism.

The secularism was partly necessitated by the ethnic heterogeneity of the new entrepreneurial class. In Bombay, for instance, the enterprises were financed by the Parsis, who spoke Gujarati. But the commonly understood language was Urdu, popularized by the Muslim chieftains who had ruled over most of India since the sixteenth century. Naturally many of the writers employed by the Parsi theatre were Muslim. And the audience was largely Hindu!

The consequences of this secularism were that every character on stage, whether a Hindu deity or a Muslim legendary hero, was alienated from his true religious or cultural moorings; and myths and legends, emptied of meaning, were reshaped into tightly constructed melodramas with thundering curtain lines and a searing climax. Unlike traditional performances, which spread out in a slow, leisurely fashion, these plays demanded total attention, but only at the level of plot. Incident was all. Even in *natak* companies run entirely by Hindus, the basic attitude was dictated by this Parsi model. [...]

Yet there was no other urban tradition to look to, and in my second play, having concluded that Anouilh and Co. were not enough, I tried to make use of the Parsi stagecraft. This time the play was historical and therefore, perhaps inevitably, had a Muslim subject. (I say inevitably, for the Hindus have almost no tradition of history: the Hindu mind, with its belief in the cycle of births and deaths, has found little reason to chronicle or glamorize any particular historical period. Still, independence had made history suddenly important to us; we were acutely conscious of living in a historically important era. Indian history as written by the British was automatically suspect. The Marxist approach offered a more attractive alternative but in fact seemed unable to come to terms with Indian realities. Even today Marxist ideologues are lost when confronted with native categories like caste. It was the Muslims who first introduced history as a positive concept in Indian thought, and the only genuinely Indian methodology available to us for analyzing history was that developed by the Muslim historians in India.)

My subject was the life of Muhammed Tughlaq, a fourteenth century sultan of Delhi, certainly the most brilliant individual ever to ascend the throne of Delhi and also one of the biggest failures. After a reign distinguished for policies that today seem far-sighted to the point of genius, but which in their day earned him the title "Muhammed the Mad," the sultan ended his career in bloodshed and political chaos. In a sense, the play reflected the slow disillusionment my generation felt with the new politics of independent India: the gradual erosion of the ethical norms that had guided the movement for independence, and the coming to terms with cynicism and realpolitik.

The stagecraft of the Parsi model demanded a mechanical succession of alternating *shallow* and *deep* scenes. The shallow scenes were played in the foreground of the stage with a painted curtain—normally depicting a street—as the backdrop. These scenes were reserved for the "lower class" characters with prominence given to comedy. They served as *link* scenes in the development of the plot, but the main purpose was to keep the audience engaged while the deep scenes, which showed interiors of palaces, royal parks, and other such visually opulent sets, were being changed or decorated. The important characters rarely appeared in the street scenes, and in the deep scenes the lower classes strictly kept their place.

The spatial division was ideal to show the gulf between the rulers and the ruled, between the mysterious inner chambers of power politics and the open, public areas of those affected by it. But as I wrote *Tughlaq*, I found it increasingly difficult to maintain the accepted balance between these two regions. Writing in an unprecedented situation where the mass populace was exercising political franchise, in however clumsy a fashion, for the first time in its history, I found the shallow scenes bulging with an energy hard to control. The regions ultimately developed their own logic. The deep scenes became emptier as the play progressed, and in the last scene, the "comic lead" did the unconventional—he appeared in the deep scene, on a par with the protagonist himself. This violation of traditionally sacred spatial hierarchy, I decided—since there was little I could do about it—was the result of the authority which climaxed Tughlaq's times and seemed poised to engulf my own.

(An aside: whatever the fond theories of their creators, plays often develop their own independent existence. In his brilliant production of *Tughlaq*, E. Alkazi ignored my half-hearted tribute to the Parsi theatre and placed the action on the ramparts of the Old Fort at Delhi; and it worked very well.)

For the first two decades after independence, how traditional forms could be utilized to revitalize our own work in the urban context was a ceaseless topic of argument among theatre people. The poet Vallathol had given a new identity to *Kathakali*, Shivaram Karanth a new lease on life to *Yaksha-*

gana. Habib Tanvir has gone to areas in which the traditional troupes operate, taking with him his urban discipline. He has taught, lived, worked, and toured with the local troupes and evolved through them a work that is rich, vital and meaningful.

But what were we, basically city-dwellers, to do with this stream? What did the entire paraphernalia of theatrical devices, half-curtains, masks, improvisation, music and mime mean?

I remember that the idea of my play *Hayavadana* started crystallizing in my head right in the middle of an argument with B.V. Karanth (who ultimately produced the play) about the meaning of masks in Indian theatre and theatre's relationship to music. The play is based on a story from a collection of tales called *Kathasaritasagara* and further development of this story by Thomas Mann in "The Transposed Heads."

A young woman is travelling with her insecure and jealous husband and his rather attractive friend. The husband, suspecting his wife's loyalties, goes to a temple of Goddess Kali and beheads himself. The friend finds the body and, terrified that he will be accused of having murdered the man for the sake of his wife, in turn beheads himself. When the woman, afraid of the scandal that is bound to follow, prepares to kill herself too, the goddess takes pity and comes to her aid. The woman has only to rejoin the heads to the bodies and the goddess will bring them back to life—except that in her confusion she has mixed up the heads. The story ends with the question: who is now the real husband, the one with the husband's head or the one with his body?

The answer given in the *Kathasaritasagara* is: since the head represents the man, the person with the husband's head is the husband.

Mann brings his relentless logic to bear upon this solution. If the head is the determining limb, then the body should change to fit the head. At the end of Mann's version, the bodies have changed again and adjusted themselves to the heads so perfectly that the men are physically exactly as they were at the beginning. We are back to square one; the problem remains unsolved.

As I said, the story initially interested me for the scope it gave for the use of masks and music. Western theatre has developed a contrast between the *face* and the *mask*—the real inner person and the exterior one presents, or wishes to present, to the world outside. But in traditional Indian theatre, the mask is only the face "writ large"; since a character represents not a complex psychological entity but an ethical archetype, the mask merely presents in enlarged detail its essential moral nature. (This is why characters in *Hayavadana* have no real names. The heroine is called Padmini after one of the six types into which Vatsyayana classified all women. Her husband is Devadatta, a formal mode of addressing a stranger. His friend is Kapila, simply "the dark one.") Music—usually percussion—then further distances the action, placing it in the realm of the mythical and the elemental.

The decision to use masks led me to question the theme itself in greater depth. All theatrical performances in India begin with worship of Ganesha, the god who ensures successful completion of any endeavor. According to mythology, Ganesha was beheaded by Shiva, his father, who had failed to recognize his own son (another aggressive father!). The damage was repaired by substituting an elephant's head, since the original head could not be found. Ganesha is often represented onstage by a young boy wearing the elephant mask, who then is worshipped as the incarnation of the god himself.

Ganesha's mask then says nothing about his nature. It is a mask, pure and simple. Right at the start of the play, my theory about masks was getting subverted. But the elephant head also questioned the basic assumption behind the original riddle: that the head represents the thinking part of the person, the intellect.

It seemed unfair, however, to challenge the thesis of the riddle by using a god. God, after all, is beyond human logic, indeed beyond human comprehension itself. The dialectic had to grow out of grosser ground, and I sensed a third being hovering in the spaces between the divine and the human, a horse-headed man. The play *Hayavadana*, meaning "the one with a horse's head," is named after this character. The story of this horse-headed man, who wants to shed the horse's head and become human, provides the outer panel—as in a mural—within which the tale of the two friends is framed. Hayavadana, too, goes to the same Goddess Kali and wins a boon from her that he should become complete. Logic takes over. The head is the person: Hayavadana becomes a complete horse. The central logic of the tale remains intact, while its basic premise is denied. [. . .]

Naga-Mandala is based on two oral tales I heard from A.K. Ramanujan. These tales are narrated by women—normally the older women in the family—while children are being fed in the evenings in the kitchen or being put to bed. The other adults present on these occasions are also women. Therefore these tales, though directed at the children, often serve as a parallel system of communication among the women in the family.

They also express a distinctly woman's understanding of the reality around her, a lived counterpoint to the patriarchal structures of classical texts and institutions. The position of Rani in the story of *Naga-Mandala*, for instance, can be seen as a metaphor for the situation of a young girl in the bosom of a joint family where she sees her husband only in two unconnected roles—as a stranger during the day and as lover at night. Inevitably, the pattern of relationships she is forced to weave from these disjointed encounters must be something of a fiction. The empty house Rani is locked in could be the family she is married into.

Many of these tales also talk about the nature of tales. The story of the flames comments on the paradoxical nature of oral tales in general: they have an existence of their own, independent of the teller and yet live only when they are passed on from the possessor of the tale to the listener. Seen thus, the status of a tale becomes akin to that of a daughter, for traditionally a daughter too is not meant to be kept at home too long but has to be passed on. This identity adds poignant and ironic undertones to the relationship of the teller to the tales.

It needs to be stressed here that these tales are not left-overs from the past. In the words of Ramanujan, "Even in a large modern city like Madras, Bombay or Calcutta, even in western-style nuclear families with their well-planned 2.2 children, folklore . . . is only a suburb away, a cousin or a grandmother away."

The basic concern of the Indian theater in the post-independence period has been to try to define its "Indianness." The distressing fact is that most of these experiments have been carried out by enthusiastic amateurs or part-timers, who have been unable to devote themselves entirely to theatre. I see myself as a playwright but make a living in film and television. There is a high elasticity of substitution between the different performing media in India; the participants—as well as the audiences—get tossed about.

The question therefore of what lies in store for the Indian theatre should be rephrased to include other media as well—radio, cinema, audio cassettes, television and video. Their futures are inextricably intertwined and in this shifting landscape, the next electronic gadget could easily turn a mass medium into a traditional art form.

Perhaps quite unrealistically, I dream of the day when a similar ripple will reestablish theatre—flesh-and-blood actors enacting a well-written text to a gathering of people who have come to witness the performance—where it belongs, at the centre of the daily life of the people.

NABANEETA DEV SEN

b. 1938

(Bengali)

Nabaneeta Dev Sen was born into a distinguished family of poets. Her mother, Radharani Datta, and her father, Narendra Dev, together published the first anthology of modern Bengali poetry. Rabindranath Tagore was a family friend. In a memoir piece, Dev Sen writes of how when she was three days old an envelope arrived. It was addressed to her with the words inside, "Since you are too young to reject my gift, I give you this name." It came from Tagore. Her passionate poetry probes the inner life of the heart and evokes in startlingly direct fashion the trials and tribulations of a woman's life. She writes copiously—poetry, plays, novels, short stories, essays. Her first book was a volume of poems, Pratham Pratyay *(1959). Her volume of essays,* Nati Nabaneeta, *appeared in 1983. A much-traveled and deeply cosmopolitan writer, she speaks of her struggles with her poet mother over what language to write in. Dev Sen's words reveal a fissure at the heart of twentieth-century Indian writing. In the essay "The Wind Beneath My Wings" we read about Radharani, Dev's mother:*

> *She [Radharani Datta] was against my writing in a regional language. "Write in English," she insisted, "let the whole world read you." She was not happy with the little bit of regional success that I had. National and international readership was her idea of success. And this was long before the Seths and the Roys, even before the midnight's child. I did not follow her advice. I had a moral and political aversion in those days*

against Indians writing in English. I continued to write in my mother tongue, and it continued to inhibit my speech, standing over me like my own mother.

For Dev Sen, writing as a woman is something that is instinctive and does not need to be justified: "I do not have to write as a woman because no matter how I write my pen remains in the hand of a woman." At the same time she guards her right to change her mind, as when she allows the imagination its free flow.

A writer who is marvelously at home in several genres, Dev Sen thinks of poetry as her first love, her refuge. In her startling poem "Alphabets," language becomes a bird she is able to cage, but then it flies off, leaving her wordless. The erotic mingles with the sharpness of desire as the poet sets words into a luminous order. Her important works include poems, the novel Bama-bhodini (1986) and the novella Sheet Sahasik Hemantolok (Defying Winter, 1988). In 1992, she received the Mahadevi Verma Award.

"In Poetry"

Stay alive
be in full bloom
be the inevitable passport photo
stay awake in every line
like an unquenchable thirst
yes, you, my pain,
the pain that tears my heart apart
be in full bloom
do not hide from me
as long as I breathe in poetry.

"Alphabets"

When night falls
I search for him
I bring him home
I look him in the eye

And I cage
Language

When day breaks
Once again the world
Wraps around my eyes
And off he flies
Taking each word
That alphabet bird

"Combustion"

As powerful
As the volcano range
Is this range of alphabets
Touch it
And you'll burn to ashes
Instantly

"The Year's First Poem"

Pretending
as if nothing at all has happened,
picking up the heart
from the sand, dusting it clean
pushing it back inside my blouse
secretly, the year's first poem gets written.

Will you kiss me now?
I followed every instruction
of my brain.

"Broken Home"

Once again you glow, on the brink of love
Once again you're dazzling in heartbreak
Is it for the sake of poetry, then,
Once again you're hunting for pain?

Do you break your home just for poetry,
Time and time again?

From *My Life, My Work*

Sometimes I wonder why I write. There was a time when I wrote because I could not pass a single day without scribbling something on a piece of paper. And today? It has been nearly a month that I have not written a poem. And I do not feel different. But there was a time when I felt immensely unhappy if I had written nothing in the whole of the 24 long hours. There was an inner pressure that forced me to write. Words were important. Putting myself into words was a part of forming myself. *How do I know who I am until I have written myself and read myself on a piece of paper in front of me? There I was, me, Nabaneeta, taking shape, on a piece of paper.* It was extremely important that I wrote every day. Maybe what I write today will be thrown into the wastebasket tomorrow, yet a whole day without a single line was a sad day. A barren day. It had nothing to do with earning; writing poems did not fetch money. It had to do with your own self-image, *it had to do with who you were*.

There was a period in my life when suddenly the whole world had set like the sun, the colour of the universe had changed for me. At a moment like that it was the poetry of Tagore's songs that held my hand in the dark, distant land where I had no support, and it was my pen that became a walking stick and kept my feet strongly upon the ground.

I had to write each and every day. The children were small, the job was new, there were too many new responsibilities. Yet writing every day was a must. It reminded me who I was. I know now that writing is what binds me to this planet.

Yet, now I have taken it for granted that there will be some days when I shall not write at all, and others when I shall write like mad, day and night, relentlessly.

That is where the writer fights for her existence. Magically. Yes, it is the magic of creativity that protects her. Creativity itself, I do believe, is an expression of divine grace. And the expression of divine anger is through the endless interviews that kill your time. The other day I was asked by a radio interviewer did I write as a woman, or as a person? The question set me thinking. The answer is not simple. Do I write as a person, just anyone, or as a woman, me? I suppose I write just as Nabaneeta, the person. Not as Everywoman. Besides, one does not always function as a gendered individual. But the gendered experience of life colours our vision. But no matter what is written by me, it is always a woman looking at life, it is always a woman interpreting life, it is always a woman reflecting life. I do not *have to write as a* woman because no matter *how* I write my pen remains in the hand of a woman. I know this can be challenged and maybe ten years from now I shall say something very different from today. I believe in growing, changing and developing. There is no question of floor-crossing in creative life. I jealously guard my freedom to change my views.

Exile and immigration is something that has always occupied my mind. Living away from home for a very long period, during a crucial formative period of my life, when my life was taking shape, made me identify with those in exile. Exile and immigration keeps coming back in my novels. In six novels I have dealt with immigration, partition, and displacement (*Swabhumi, Prabase daiber bashe, Anyadweep, Pari, Ural, Deshantar*). The locations are varied: Canada, USA, France, England, and Czechoslovakia, a country that no longer exists; the people belong mainly to India and Bangladesh, also to Puerto Rico.

I have also tried to write about the trauma that families of HIV AIDS patients face, about the problems of acceptance and adjustment, in two of my novels (*Maya roye gelo, Ural*). I have, unfortunately, experienced the trauma that a family goes through when a member fights a terminal disease.

My novel, *Albatross*, published last year, where I have once again experimented with form and theme, is about an obsessed relationship, a mild psychological thriller. The newest novel, published in October, is about ageing, disease and love (*Ekti iti-bachak prem kahini*). A romance about senior citizens. And a children's adventure novel has come out recently as well.

I have experimented with literary form in my non-fictional prose as well. For example, after writing a book of literary criticism using classical critical jargon (*Ishwarer Pratidwandwi*) which was exceedingly well received in India and Bangladesh, I changed my style, and wrote serious critical articles which read like personal essays (*Shabda parhey tapur tupur*). These are transgressive but not quite subversive. Subversion is what I do with the Puranic texts, with the epic tales, with the *Ramayana* and the *Mahabharata*.

I write essays and novels. But it was in the looking glass of poetry that I saw my face for the first time. Poetry was my first confidence. When I was seven—two poems and a prose piece came out in the school magazine *Sadhana*. The Bengali poem, called *Chini O Noon*—Sugar and Salt—was a bit like Khawna's maxims; the subject of the English poem was a frog; and the prose piece was a description of a *kaalbaishakhi*—a Norwester storm. Though I began as a bilingual writer, writing poetry and prose, Bangla and English at the same time, it was Bengali poetry that stuck to me. As I told you just now, my grown up attempt at prose came much later. Poetry has always been my primary confidence. Have I cut down on poetry because I'm more into prose? Has my vision changed from the poetic to the prosaic?

I wonder.

A single kid in a large house, each afternoon I pottered around the house discovering the world alone. There was a picture of Jesus Christ on the Cross that hung next to my parents' bed—the beautiful face, sad eyes looking up into the empty sky, blood trickling from his palms and feet, the crown of thorns, drops of blood upon his brow, and the smile upon his lips . . . enchanted me. How can he bear it? Why is he smiling? The nails used to hurt me—they hurt me even now when I remember those days.

And there were these letters INRE written below the cross, what did they mean? I decided those letters must be a *mantra*. Some *mantra* that meant peace. I do not know where the picture is today, but when I was asked to write something on my poetic process I do not know from where this painting floated up to me, as if it was the vision of poetry. I cannot explain it in words, it is just a feeling deep within me. Those bleeding palms, those smiling lips, those praying eyes . . .

I used to climb upon my bed and examine the calendar hanging on the wall with great attention. Next to the dates were graphics of the phases of the moon, and tiny little icons representing festivals like *Doljatra, Jhulan, Durga Puja*, or *Bhratri Dwitiya*. Then there were the *tithis*—the lunar calendar—for *Akshay Tritiya, Bhoot Chaturdashi, Nil Shasthi* etc. They were all very mysterious but there were three special words in the calendar that attracted me infinitely. Secret words, which were like poetry to my ear—they showed me pictures, they offered me music, they took me on far, far-away journeys. Of my 3 favorite, secret and beautifully musical mystery-words "*Fateha-doaz-daham*" was one. "*Fateha*"—the sharp high tympanic clang of the brass plate, the *Kansar*, accompanied by "*dwaz daham*" dwazz dahammm . . . dwazz dahammm . . . the deep low rumbling, echoing beat of the *dhak*, the drum. I could hear the percussion in the words clearly. My second secret word was "*Id-uz-zoha*"—it carried me across a wide river bridge into the darkness of the night on a long-distance train. As the train crossed the bridge, it sang in tune: "*id—ooh-zzoha*" "*id—ooh-zzoha*" "*id-ooh-zzoha*" into my ear. Similarly, "*Id-ul-fitr*" activated a spinning wheel on the moon. Have any of you ever heard the old woman on the moon spinning her *charkha?* If you haven't, then here it is, listen to this.—"*idull . . . fitrr*" "*idull . . . fitrr*" "*idull . . . fitrr*"? Can you see her now? Listen carefully, *Idull fitrr . . . ?*

To me those three musical words had remained a beautiful mystery till my teenaged daughter, Piccolo (my eldest, Antara), cracked it one day— "You know Ma why that happens? Because you don't know the meaning of the secret words. If you knew what the words meant they would lose their mystery and their lyrical quality too. They would have been just as mundane as *Ekadoshi, Purnima.*"

That's it! Precisely because I didn't know the meaning of those words, they had been transformed into pure harmony, into simple sounds, to be absorbed solely by my senses. They were not confined by comprehensible definitions, and came across as pure resonance, as abstract expressions. That's exactly what they were. Music.

Mysterious, rhythmic words enticed me right from my childhood. On my way back from school one afternoon, I heard a poem on the radio ringing out of someone's window—"*Kuala lampur . . . Kuala lampur . . . elaam koto door . . . elaam koto door.*" Instantly, the phrase slipped into my brain. I haven't been able to get rid of it since. Apart from the alliteration, and the metrical charm, the words contained something more precious— distance and uncertainty, and of course the mystery of the unknown. I didn't have a clue as to the geographical location of Kualalampur then. This lack of information added to its romantic call. If I recite "*Boho-ro rompur*" "*Boho-ro rompur*," it's the same rhythm but the effect is not the same! It's a familiar place-name! To this day, I don't know the complete poem, but the mystery continues.

Of course, being unaware of the full poem is not always a drawback. A friend once pointed out to me the extraordinary pathos in "*Ki phul jhorilo bipul andhokaare*" that begins and ends with this one line. *What flower was it that dropped in the darkness deep?* As the poem progresses, too many words follow, and the magical impact is lost. We had agreed that in this composition by Rabindranath, the single sentence would have been enough.

One day my friend Amiyo and I discovered a really amusing poem in our French class. It was called "The Window"—"Fenêtre fenêtre fenêtre fenêtre / Fenêtre fenêtre fenêtre fenêtre"—it ran on for four lines. We were in splits. But later on, as I thought about it the poem didn't seem funny at all. This repeated yearning for a window, a window, started to haunt me. And haunts me still.

One significant lucky break for me was getting great poets for my teachers. Buddhadeva Bose, Sudhindranath Datta, Naresh Guha, Alokeranjan Dasgupta, were teaching us European, English and Bengali literature. Akademi award winning poets, all of them. Wasn't that a special advantage to have poets as mentors, apart from having poets for parents?

I was lucky enough to closely observe two souls dedicated to the literary world, who believed that staying alive and poetry were indistinguishable. One was my father, Narendra Dev, the other was my teacher, Buddhadev Bose. They belonged to different eras, they were as different in nature as they were in appearance, but they were identical in one detail. They were helpless outside the world of literature. Both contributed very little to the daily domestic affairs in their respective homes—from morning till night they were confined to either their writing tables, or to literary discussions in the living room with other writers and younger poets. This singular devotion to poetry made them infinitely energetic, indifferent towards worldly possessions, and with eternal faith in human goodness. As for me, just being close to my father and Buddhadev Bose was good enough. Just by watching them read and write all day I knew writing was fun. It could fill all of life and wipe out a great deal of the rest of the world, or, rather, replace it.

And both had married two extraordinary women of enormous self-confidence that grows from intelligence and a disciplined thought process. Both were creative writers as well as practical home-management experts, Radharani, my mother, and Protibha, our mashima . . . Only because they took upon themselves complete household responsibilities, including the finances, could the husbands freely indulge in the arts. Watching these two women, writers both, I knew for a woman the story was different.

Baba had introduced me to the technicalities of writing poetry. Metres and rhyme schemes. *Uttam meel, adham meel, madhyam meel. Poyar, Tripodi, Mondakranta, counting matra.* Puns and alliteration. Similes, metaphors. He was the hands-on coach for the young contributors of *Paathshala,* the first teenage literary magazine in India that he had established and edited. He would teach them how to write a poem. And I learned a lot simply by observing those creative writing classes. *Ma* taught me personally how to write sonnets. Her favourite form was the fourteen-line, fourteen-syllable rhyming verse—stick to *ab ba, ab ba,* and the rest as you please. "Poetry should be compact. Most of it should be implied. Do not state things, do not explain, just suggest," *Ma* used to say. "A poem is not a speech, it's a personal expression."

Sometimes, when a greenhorn editor of an obscure magazine tells me, "Okay, if you don't have prose, why not send a poem-*shoem* or whatever?," it drives me to tears. Do they not know that it is forbidden to say "a poem-*shoem* or whatever"? That Saraswati is incensed by such thoughtless remarks? Do they not know what it takes to create one decent poem?

Language is a wild stallion. Breaking the animal and training him to leap through fiery hoops to the rhythm of music, is poetry. How can it ever be an easy task?

Poetry is like war. A war with oneself. Finally, only when there is victory and peace, poetry follows. As poetry nestles deep in the soul, it is akin to profound wisdom. But even wisdom is sometimes rolled up and tossed at us by life. But poetry? Never, ever. It is the test of one's skills with the weapons hauled down from the *Shomi* tree. Poetry has to be earned.

Whenever I have to choose between poetry and life, I decide in favour of life, knowing full well that life was most treacherous, whereas poetry would offer, as ever, the final refuge. It will never let me down. Every time I was flooded over, and drowning, poetry pulled me up onto dry land. I survived.

There were, however, countless changes within.

One who has grown up alone does not fear solitude. In fact I thoroughly enjoyed my solitude, alone, in the winter of 1989 at Colorado Springs, snowbound in a house all by myself. But I do know that some day age will catch up, faculties will fail and the crowded living room will be deserted. Loneliness in advanced years does not scare me. There is only one fear—that poetry may abandon me. That would be a crippling blow, a dreadful loneliness. Poetry has been my *kabach-kundal*—my charmed amulet, my magic armour. Poetry is my *Bijon Jibon Bihari* in the true sense—the one who roams the solitary corners of my existence. Every word written is a lifelong quest for that ultimate poem.

Will I be able to write the poem? The lines that will live on after me?

ADIL JUSSAWALLA
b. 1940
(English)

Adil Jussawalla was born into a Parsi family in the city of Bombay. In an essay he writes of his mother tongue, Parsi Gujarati, which he searched out after his long years in England, where he had gone as an architecture student and decided to stay on. In his essay "Being There: Aspects of an Indian Crisis," he writes, "When, in 1970, after many years abroad, I returned to my native land, I had a native language but no literature in it to return to." And so it is English he chooses, a language inevitably marked by the conflicts he experienced in the racialized world of Britain. But back in a postcolonial India, English, the language of his poetry, seemed discrepant from the landscape in ways that deeply troubled him. Still, it provided him with a supple instrument to craft a self in words. Jussawalla's passionate, ironic book Missing Person *(1976) was influential with generations of Indian poets, and in it he gives voice to the fragmented life of a protagonist who effectively has nowhere to go but within, and is effectively forced to piece together a self from the shards of several civilizations, none of which would want to claim him whole. Indeed, it is possible to see a kinship with Aimé Césaire and read this long title poem as Jussawalla's own* Cahier d'un retour au pays natal. *The growing political consciousness of the speaker and the sense of the painful absurdity of a life lived in a foreign land emerge in this book. In the poem "Missing Person" we read, "You're polluting our sounds. You're so rude. / 'Get back to your language' they say."*

Jussawalla has written film scripts for BBC TV, and he wrote his own syn-

dicated column after his return to India. He has edited a groundbreaking anthology, New Writing from India *(1974)*, and was one of the founders of the Bombay poetry collective Clearing House, which included the poets Arvind Krishna Mehrotra and Arun Kolatkar among its members. Decades after Missing Person *Jussawalla published a third book of poems*, Trying to Say Goodbye *(2011)*. *More recently he published a collection of essays*, Maps for a Mortal Moon *(2014)*, *and a gathering of his poems, fiction, and nonfiction*, I Dreamt a Horse Fell from the Sky *(2015)*.

"Being There: Aspects of an Indian Crisis"

One never knows when the blow may fall, says Graham Greene's sad narrator in *The Third Man* and of course he is right. Since History is full of nasty surprises, the writer, like everyone else, will do no more than fall flat on his face several times in his life if he's lucky, or get censored or killed if he's not.

A historical date makes its mark suddenly, a hole in a once-clean target, and stays with us till we die. August 15, 1947 is one such date in India. So also is June 25, 1975, when the Emergency was declared.

Suddenness is history's trapdoor, through which we fall—armchair critics along with our armchairs, bombed civilians, those dispossessed of their homelands, those sifting through garbage for food, those dragged out of their homes at midnight, our cups, saucers, pets, everything through that same trapdoor—to certain oblivion—unless there is someone who doesn't flinch from seeing what happened and sets it down.

The resilience of individual writers has helped them survive the worst shocks of history, and there's nothing so bad about the situation in India that will silence its writers permanently. But if Indians who write in English don't normally consider it important to produce novels of social history or write poetry that fully confronts the social and political realities of their time—despite their real admiration for such work from other countries—there must be a reason—perhaps several reasons—and I think it's important to examine them. Some of us, certainly, are going through a crisis which is making us question the validity of our work and our usefulness as agents of social change. Now, more than ever before, we are unsure of ourselves as witnesses. Far from helping to change the course of history, we are finding ourselves its bullied victims. It's as though History had become the Englishman in Victor Anant's novel *The Revolving Man*, telling the writer, as the Englishman tells the novel's protagonist, "Spin, you Hindu bastard. Spin!" And the bastard goes on spinning.

The expectation the Indian writer has had of himself since Independence has been the expectation of writers in some Commonwealth countries, not all, and some of the phrases I use, like "agent of social change," may sound absurdly inappropriate to, say, an Australian or Canadian writer. But I believe that no Indian writer can avoid taking a moral stand on the many social evils in his country, especially when, in view of the obvious poverty and distress there, it's a social privilege to be able to write, or travel abroad and pontificate, as I am doing.

So, when I speak of the crisis some Indian writers are going through, I imply that it's as much a moral crisis as an artistic one. It is intimately connected with what we thought we would write shortly after Independence—as also with our reader's expectations of what we *should* write—and what we find ourselves writing or not writing now. So the writers I have in mind are those who have experienced the two disturbances of jailbreak and re-imprisonment: the exhilaration of being free to write as we chose, of being able to overturn British norms of language and literature (and even decency) and the oppression, forty years later, of finding ourselves strapped, rather like forks choked with spaghetti. Our ends may appear to be dipped in blood—the prescribed blood of others that is meant to baptize the "real" writers of this century—but in fact it's the usual ketchup. We just haven't dared enough.

I could have chosen a less cosy simile, but it seems an appropriate one to apply to those of us who have chosen to stay on in "the soiled and cluttered kitchens of the mind"—to lift a phrase from an old poem of mine—with our gaze turned away from the great public events on the sub-continent—events that are affecting at least as many million lives as the last global war did.

Why do Indian novels and verses have so little to say about those events? Why don't we do more than we *have*? What's the problem?

The problems of Indians who write in English are boring to themselves and to others and I suspect they've activated many unsuccessfully stifled yawns at ACLALS conferences too. But since the problems, like the

English language itself, refuse to go away, we return to them again and again. Indian writers have done so obsessively. And it is characteristic of our approach to our problems that we blame the English language for a lot of them. In fact, our attitude to English is one of the major aspects of the crisis I referred to earlier.

So, in a poem, R. Parthasarathy writes of his "tongue in English chains" and of speaking "a tired language." Meena Alexander, in an essay, speaks of being "exiled by a dead script." Arvind Krishna Mehrotra, in another essay, shows the language to be honeycombed with traps, any of which the unwary writer may sink into. Keki Daruwalla sees the language he uses as an exasperating mistress. And English language and literature are subjects of attack in my poem Missing Person, in which the colonizer himself joins in the attack, asking his creature to get back to his (own) language.

Getting back to one's language, returning to one's native land, are familiar refrains in colonial and post-colonial writing and every writer haunted by them has had to lay the ghosts in his own way. Speaking for myself, when, in 1970, after many years abroad, I returned to my native land, I had a native language but no literature in it to return to—there are no poets and novelists in the Parsi Gujarati I speak, though it is freely used in adapted versions of foreign plays; it's very much a spoken dialect, full of literary potential, but regrettably unexplored. So I've remained as English-language writer, affected by works in English produced in whatever country the language is spoken and written, and by works translated into English. Oddly enough, I didn't realise how precarious that made my position until three years ago and it was the Hindi novelist Nirmal Verma who helped me see it.

Having spent many years of his life in Prague, Verma was very much the cosmopolitan author on an extended return ticket until he went back to India in 1968. In an essay, *Returning to One's Country*, he speaks of the anguish of being home and not being home, of being "a native stranger who has come back—an alien Indian who is suspect everywhere, most of all to himself."

When I met him three years ago, he held the Nirala Chair for Literature in Bhopal—a city in India's Hindi-speaking belt—and he offended me a little by saying that I couldn't possibly have any idea about any kind of young Hindi writer who came to him with his work and what his problems were. I replied with some heat that I didn't see why that writer should be any different from young writers in Bombay and why his problems should be so very different either. Verma came back with great vehemence. "They are different because they write and talk only in *Hindi*," he said. "They don't know a word of *English!*"

Since then I've thought a lot about the hypothetical young writer in Bhopal and am appalled by what he must think of me. Not having access to a vast body of international literature—Hindi being poor in translations from other literatures—he can't but resent my privilege. Or he may choose to ignore me, taking the narrow view that the experience of any literature outside Hindi is not worth having. We would have two different views of history and we would not be able to argue which was more falsifying—my "Eng. Lit" view or his. But I hope we'd share at least one thing—an anxiety not to falsify, to witness authentically, to truthsay, because we are aware of what falsified history did in Germany and is doing in Soviet Russia and South Africa. We'd share the hope that the only way to be a responsible writer was to be true to oneself and what one saw; that we were responsible to those who came after us—to bear witness to what the official lie or the censor or Time was always trying to wipe out. If we agreed on that, then we might find our strategies within two languages—whether we were writing poetry or prose—not very different. We might find both our languages—his Hindi, my English—in their currently accepted forms in daily commerce—wholly inadequate to fill out the poetic and fictional worlds of our witnessing. We would then have to chip away at the language, or pummel it, or pare away at its outer shell to get at its kernel and draw out its life-giving essence. We would have to make it new, create new forms with it, make it nourishing.

That this has been the ambition of some novelists writing in England during the last fifteen years, is clear from works like Angus Wilson's *As If by Magic,* Anthony Burgess' *Earthly Powers,* Rushdie's *Midnight's Children* and Naipaul's *Guerrillas* and *A Bend in the River*—their writers very much historical witnesses.

I'm glad to know that one critic thinks that because of works like these, it's no longer necessary to be defensive about the English novel, as was the fashion in the sixties, and I'm glad that writers from Commonwealth countries other than England are contributing so much to its importance. However, our Commonwealth brothers don't seem to be in any hurry to get easily assimilated nor do some of their critics want them to be. So Rushdie, in order to stress that he hasn't written an "English" novel, will link it to oral storytelling in India, and a sympathetic critic will emphasize its dilatory Scheherezadian element. (I haven't read Amitav Ghosh's *Circle of Reason*, but he has said in an interview that he has based the three parts of his novel on the musical raga.)

Of other Indian novelists, it's been said that Mulk Raj Anand "has Indianised literary and political models derived from the West, and Westernised traditional values," that both in *Kanthapura* and in *The Serpent and the Rope*, Raja Rao has tried to tell "a breathless, endless tale in the manner of the Mahabharata" and that R. K. Narayan uses the dialectics of maya in *The Guru*.

Yes, we're not too pleased to be fitted into any of Eng. Lit's formal categories, and try hard to reject its formative influence.

In an interview published in 1978, I said that "if you break away from that structure (of Eng. Lit) completely, if you attempt to completely smash this structure of English culture or Eng. Lit, a very fundamental personal disintegration takes place too. I have not found the alternatives. I can only suggest that by smashing this structure, you go through a process of terrible disintegration. What follows I'm not sure."

Nine years after the interview I'm more certain that while *Missing Person* is about such disintegration, my own personal disintegration has neither been very fundamental nor terrible. I have not changed. And "Change" was the cry we rallied around at Independence. Change was what we thought would come over us when we overthrew the British norms of language and literature I spoke about earlier. But they have proved tougher than we thought; some of us have become the new colonials, and our expectation of ourselves has been false.

I hope it's clear to you now that this is a crisis of identity. We have so far touched on two causes for it and they have both to do with distrust. I mentioned Nirmal Verma's distrust of himself as an observer when he returned to India, but it's a familiar enough malaise among writers who have never left India as well. And then there is a distrust of the English language and English literature. But what if you begin to distrust your whole being, distrust your modernity and everything that's made you modern? Can you write anything at all then, when it was the very force of modernism that compelled you to write a certain kind of literature in the first place?

In a justly celebrated paper, the Kannada novelist U. R. Ananthamurthy deals with precisely these questions. He describes an Indian writers' conference that was disturbed almost literally by a stone. The writers, gathered in a North Indian city, were discussing very much what we are in Singapore: "Why is the Western mode of thought and writing the model for us? Why are we unoriginal in our treatment of form and content in the novel, drama and poetry? While Indian dance and music are uniquely Indian, why does contemporary Indian literature take its bearings from the literature of the West? Are we a nation of mimics, victims of English education, which has conditioned the faculties of our perception so much that we fail to respond freshly to the immediate situation in India?"

A painter who was present then told a story which impressed Ananthamurthy deeply. He said that during his wanderings through villages in the North, he came across a hut in which he saw a stone. It was decorated with red powder and flowers, which meant it was an object of worship. He asked the owner of the hut—a peasant—if the stone could be brought outside the hut since he wanted to photograph it. The stone was brought outside and the photograph taken. The painter then realised that he might have polluted the stone by shifting its position, and apologised to the peasant. The peasant said it didn't matter. He'd just fetch another stone and anoint it with the powder. So, the painter said, any piece of stone on which the peasant put the powder became God for him. The objective and subjective were one in such a person. He belonged to the illiterate Indian mass—seventy per cent of the population. Western education had alienated those at the seminar from him and those like him. If they didn't understand the structure and mode of his thinking, they couldn't become true Indian writers.

The painter's argument shook Ananthamurthy, as I said, and though he was later nagged by a doubt that "the authentic Indian peasant ... was also an imported cult figure of Western radicals against their materialist civilisation," his self-doubt, common to "educated Indian writers of (his) generation," nagged him more. The peasant continued to bother him.

The poor peasant, the trapped young writer in Bhopal, the contracted tribal breaking stones on a city street—they aren't figments of an Indian writer's imagination but indelibly part of his consciousness. Blanking them out can only be momentary. He doesn't have to go far in India to see them or people like them. So Nirmal Verma, on returning to his native land, steps out of the brief embrace of a cinema hall and is appalled at the obscenity he is subjected to—a commercial which shows "smooth-faced healthy children being fed cornflakes by their smiling mother"—nothing he'd get too worked up about if he were in London—but in India he can't reconcile the children he sees on screen with the children outside it—"wilted faces under merciless sun." It's the context which makes the commercial obscene; there's a wide gap between the streets and the screen—just as there is a wide gap between me and the peasant, the young writer and the tribal.

Development used to mean bridging the gap, of creating a more modern, more just society and until a few years ago very few of our nation-builders doubted that the way to bring such a society about was by spreading literacy, education and benefits of science throughout the country. The die-hard capitalist and the Naxalite differed in their methods but their goal was the same—to create a modern developed state, totally free of India's crippling anachronisms.

Now the word "development" itself has begun to stink and a few anxious people in the Third World are seriously beginning to question whether some of the old ways were that anachronistic after all.

In India, for example, millions of lives have been marginalised by the construction of dams, hydro-electric projects and the hydro-politics behind them. The marginalisation of the Indian writer—whether writing in the Indian languages or English—is indeed petty when compared to the reach of that marginalisation, which is ferocious and devastating. But when the tribal sees his land gone does he simply take to the bottle and slink away? Yes, he does, but he also sings. He speaks out:

> Which company came to my land, to a "Karkhana?"
> It awakened its name in the rivers and the ponds calling itself the
>   D.V.C
> It throws earth, dug by a machine, into the river.
> It has cut the mountain and made a bridge. The water runs beneath.
> Roads are coming; they are giving us electricity, having opened the
>   "Karkhana."
> All the praja question them. They ask to what this name belongs.
> When evening falls they give paper notes as pay. Where will I keep
>   these paper notes?
> They melt away in the water.

> In every house there is a well which gives water to grow brinjal and
>   cabbage. Every
> House is bounded by walls which makes it look like a palace.
> This Santal tongue of ours has been destroyed in the district. *You
>   came and made this*
> Bloody burning ghat, calling yourself the D.V.C.

The song is by an unknown Santhal from West Bengal and it appears in an essay by an Indian scientist who argues, as the blurb of the essay says, "that the crisis of survival—from survival of the poor to the survival of the human race—is not a result of a failure of the modern project of development, of modernisation, of science and technology, but a consequence of their very success."

In the essay itself he states that "the tragedy of modernisation in the Third World is doubly violent. It has sprung not only from the violence of the West through colonialism and science but also from the modernist impulse of our elites, internationalised without a clue to its doubts or its genealogy." If this is correct, then it has serious repercussions for the modernist impulse in literature, and is the greatest threat to the modern writer's identity. Such a truth, if it is the truth, can pierce his heart, the heart of language and nail his tongue to his palate permanently. Its scope has room for Ananthamurthy's self-doubt and mine but also puts us in our place. Where did we modern Indian writers think we were going when we so little questioned our modernity?

Well, as another poet said, "I learn by going where I have to go," and I have to come to Singapore fully knowing that I've travelled this far, not on the wings of a modernist impulse—though without that impulse I wouldn't have gone this far—but on those of a modern aircraft. Nor, despite my doubts about development, have I come here to argue that I'd have preferred to travel by bullock cart because I suddenly prefer the good old ways. I don't. But the scientist's words help me see that I'm part of an elite—an international elite with many Third World writers in it—that has too easily taken its modernizing role for granted. Caught up in the convention of a conference to make ourselves heard, we may or may not listen to one another. But we're fairly certain who won't listen to us back home. Who are we writing for there?

Edwin Thumboo has said in an interview that the historical perspective is important to Singaporeans because, owing to the rapid modernization of the city, they are in danger of losing their historical hinterland. That is also true of those who live in Bombay as I do. But it's possible that the historical perspective may not come in the form in which Thumboo and I expect it. It may not come in the shape of a grand novel or poetic epic. It may come—as it already has—in a series of speak-outs—like the song of the Santhal and, in English, the poems of Dilip Chitre, Keki Daruwalla, Kamala Das, Nissim Ezekiel, Jayanta Mahapatra, Arvind Krishna Mehrotra and Gieve Patel, which deal with historical events like the Bangladesh War, the Emergency or the Bhopal disaster, or with local and family history.

Speaking out, *saying* it, is how India's bhakti poets set about their work, trying to change social consciousness, singing to the lower castes that God was in their hearts and not in Brahminic temples. Now, when it's essential to get back our sense of the sacredness of things—of land, river, tree, even the peasant's stone—it may be that these poets will help us, showing us that a linear view of history and development—even literary development—was not modern at all but against life itself and contained the seeds of its own destruction.

I implied in my opening remarks that the word "witness" is not very satisfactory when applied to writers. But there's one in which it applies perfectly—and that is, of "being there." It was Whitman's position in an open society, as it is also the position of those writers who live in oppressive regimes, in states of special fear or on the margins of history.

That sense of "being there," in works of fiction and poetry, is never finally dependent on where the writer is physically situated. The Sunderbans of *Midnight's Children* are no less real for the writer's never having visited them. (I consider the chapter on them to be one of the richest in the book.) That sense is finally dependent on the quality of the writer's imagination and the strength of his talent.

"Literature is not in the business of copyrighting certain themes for certain groups," says Rushdie. "And as for risk: the real risks of any artist are taken in the work, in pushing the work to the limits of what is possible, in the attempt to increase the sum of what is possible to think. Books become good when they go to this edge and risk falling over it—when they endanger the artist by reason of what he has, or has not, artistically dared."

In his Nobel lecture, Milosz speaks of the poet's double role. "He is the one who flies above the earth and looks at it *from above*, but at the same time sees it in every detail." The near and the far. And though he says "distance is sometimes impossible," and soaring above earth's good and evil seems "a moral treason," yet, in a precarious balance of opposites, a certain equilibrium can be achieved thanks to a distance introduced by the flow of time. "To see and to describe" may also mean to reconstruct an imagination. A distance achieved with thanks to the mystery of time must not change events, landscapes, human figures into a tangle of shadows growing paler and paler. On the contrary, it can show them in full light, so that every event, every date becomes expressive and persists as an eternal reminder of human depravity and human greatness. Those who are alive receive a mandate from those who are silent forever. They can fulfil their duties only by trying to reconstruct precisely things as they were and by wresting the past from fictions and legends.

There are a score of sub-Rushdies in the making of India, I was told by a young writer just before I left Bombay. There may well be half a dozen sub-Miloszs too. If their solutions to the problems of distance and authenticity are as inspiring, it may be a hopeful sign. But it will take a lot of time and, considering what needs to be done in India, I am perilously close to agreeing with Milosz that "all art proves to be nothing compared to action"; I too readily accept his anguish.

At the same time as Milosz says those words as someone "who wrote a certain number of poems out of the contradictions engendered by an earth polluted by the crime of genocide," he also confesses, as a pained historical witness, that he "would have preferred to have been able to resolve the contradiction while leaving the poems unwritten."

adil jussawalla

AMBAI (C. S. LAKSHMI)
b. 1944
(Tamil)

C. S. Lakshmi, who writes under the nom de plume *Ambai, was born in Coimbatore. Her love of the Tamil language was nourished by both her grandmother and mother, a singer and musician. As an adult, Lakshmi moved to the north of India, first to Delhi for her doctoral work and then to Bombay where she has lived now for several decades. Her works were first published in small literary magazines that allowed a tightly lyrical and experimental writing to emerge. Ambai, who crafts a highly charged prose, bordering at times on prose poetry, thinks of herself as a feminist but not in any simple-minded fashion. In her work, even as the constraints of the social world are acknowledged, there is an equal and opposite thrust toward a fluid identity, a quicksilver self that can never be trapped, whether within walls of mortar and brick or the given script of language. Focusing much of her attention on the complexity of women's lives, she has written of the kinship of writing to music and the intrinsic freedom of the creator. In a talk prepared for an awards ceremony (she was honored by the Tamil Literary Garden in Toronto in 2009), she evokes the "bodiless space" in which she used to float and the way in which both the "I" and its truth are constantly altering. Here she writes, "A Zen monk once dwelled in a cave for many years. On his return, the king summoned him to the royal court. [. . .] The monk took out the flute tucked at his waist and blew a short musical note and left. The truth of literary life is also similarly as simple and as complex." In a story called "Squirrel," the unnamed narrator enters the ancient, dusty ar-*

chives and suddenly glimpses countless lives, women from a past impossible to reach: "Isn't it possible that some relationships should extend from dreams into reality, and others be the spillover from reality to dream?" Ambai's creative writing exists side by side with her scholarly work. In Bombay she continues, with her foundation, SPARROW (Sound and Picture Archives for Research on Women), to document the work of women artists. She has written short stories, novels, plays, and scholarly works. Her important works include Kaatil Oru Maan (In a Forest a Deer, 2000) and A Purple Sea (1992).

From "Squirrel"

Long verandahs of spacious buildings which were once the offices of the British government. The verandahs are enclosed by meshed windows with angled tops. At every ten feet, there are ornamental arches above. As one walks along, passing under the arches of that shadowy verandah where the sun does not enter, one experiences a sense of anticipation, that at the end of the darkness, there will be a library. Impossible to say why exactly, but one feels that expectation the moment one sets foot within the verandah. A quickening of the breath. A watering of the mouth. And often enough, it is there at the end, a library in truth. Yellowed. Stretched out in iron shelves.

One occasion. It was the time of year when it darkens early. The sun had only just set. As soon as I set foot in the verandah, there was a face as if suspended in space, floating in front of me. It was as if, starting from a pair of owl-like eyes, the flesh of the cheeks and neck had all slithered down like a waterfall. I was startled. I went cold. Then a few teeth appeared in a smile which pushed aside the wrinkled folds of skin.

"Were you frightened, madam?"

The light was switched on. A long verandah took shape. Endless archways. A sensation as if I was entering a cave. At the end of it, a soft red light shone behind a steel door, chequered all over with steel wires. Above and below the door, a reddish smoke spread. It seemed like a shadowy door leading to a different world. I imagined that the instant the door opened, I would see Urvashi dancing to the sound of her own anklet bells.

(Whatever narrow passage I entered, to me it became a verandah. I began to think that at the end of every path, there were only old books, lying on their backs, their tongues hanging out. If you picked one up, you'd find a dog-eared fold on the cover. Next to that a scratch. Heavy. Painful. Sometimes the spine of the book was broken by its own weight. If you touched it there, you heard a sudden snap. Each book that was stroked and awakened to life was a very Ahalya. But which epic was there that recorded its history?)

The phantom door stood in front of me as material reality. He opened it. There was a small garden path. At the end of that a heavy wooden door stood open.

"They've all gone. I waited for you to come. Here is the book you asked for."

There was a sudden gust of wind. The pages rustled, beating against each other. When I put my hand on the cover, pressing it down, the trembling of the leaves passed into me. The old man was no longer beside me. Except for the light in the front part of the building, all the others had been turned off. Open iron shelving reached up to the high ceilings. Inside, there were two upper levels, with iron-sheeted floors, reached by an iron staircase. I was alone, my hand resting on the book. In the corner, by the door, the rustling of the pages set off by the wind now joined into a thud-thudding sound. It was then that it appeared before me. It sat upon a pile of books which had just been mended with paste. It threw me a brief glance and began to lick the paste with great enjoyment.

"Don't do that," I said. "That's *Chintamani*, the women's journal that Balammal ran. That faded picture at the back, that's she in a nine-yard sari."

(My relationship with her has only just begun. We have not yet conversed with each other. I don't as yet know everything about her, only that she was not all that fond of Vai Mu Ko.)

The squirrel listened. It took a quick look at Balammal and went away. The wind, the rustling of the pages and the throbbing under my fingers continued.

All this had happened so often, both in dream and in reality, that I could no longer separate one from the other. Neither did it seem all that important to do so. It was a fact that the pages crumbled and fell to pieces beneath my fingers. A fact that the crumbling bits stuck to my fingers. A fact that the apsaras who first advertised Kesavardini hair oil crumbled away with

ambai (c. s. lakshmi)

those pieces. But this happened many times, both in dreams and reality. That's why I didn't try to separate the two. When I was sure I was dreaming, the electric fan would suddenly stop and I would find myself bathed in sweat. Certain that it was real, I would raise a book in order to smell it, and be awakened by the raindrops splashing on to my face through the open window. I didn't worry about it. Isn't it possible that some relationships should extend from dreams into reality, and others be the spillover from reality to dream?

A heavy dictionary, yellowing with age, lay upon a sloping desk by the window. When the wind blew, its huge pages would move. If I bent down, the pages touched my face. Moving, as if to stroke me, the pages would roll from "B" to "J." And then the wind would stop. I would put it back to "B." One page alone would reach up to touch me affectionately on the cheek and then return to its place, leaving behind a faint smell.

I always move from one end of the open shelves to the other touching the books. Establishing a relationship. I touch the dust as if I were caressing a naked child. I share a relationship with all of you, did you know? It was my fingers that smoothed the crease running through the centre of the letter which Mary Carpenter wrote in the nineteenth century, asking to set up a women's teacher training college. It was I who blew off the rust-coloured dust which had spread over the "Rani Victoria Kummi" published in *Viveka Chintamani*. When a speck of that dust flew up against my lip, I flicked out my tongue and swallowed it. And so an older generation descended into my stomach. Perhaps if some Yasoda had looked into my mouth, she would have seen a Victoria kummi.

It seems that as soon as this library was set up, Krishna appeared in his chariot and preached his sermon of non-attachment there, giving as example the way water rolls off the lotus leaf. Nothing that the library contained touched anyone who was working here. Their only interest was in each one's knee-high stainless-steel tiffin carrier. On the third floor, the Buckingham Carnatic Mill workers went on strike in May 1921. But downstairs the concerns were different.

"Ei, have you brought meat today? It smells good."

"Yes, di. I cooked minced meat this morning. We don't eat meat for the whole month of Purattaasi, and I have been feeling quite weak. My husband himself ground all the spices for me. But it's not yet time to eat.

It's only twelve yet. Let's sit under the trees today. We'll take the water pot with us."

"We could buy some betel leaf."

"Watch out. Sir is coming."

"Well, girls? Chatting about food are you? My wife says I must only eat fruit. She says I've got a paunch. I should have been lucky enough to be born a woman, to bear a couple of children and then bloat out and wear a chokingly tight choli."

"Sir, it's true you've actually got a bit of a paunch. Maybe that's why she says that."

"I shall have to be born a woman in my next birth. Then my flesh can hang around my waist, like Elizabeth's."

"Why this, sir? Why do you drag me into all this? There is no malice in me, sir. That's why I'm not as thin as a stick."

"Are you going out to buy betel leaf? Get me half a dozen fruit."

"Jackfruit, do you mean, sir?"

"Who said that? People come to work in this place half dead with hunger. Doesn't like my paunch, she says. Why can't she show me even a spoonful of ghee? What's lost if some onion tossed in butter is spread on a bit of bread for me? Don't I toil hard enough through the day? Now, you lot . . ."

"What have we done, sir?"

"Get on with your work, girls. Five lakhs of books are waiting to be catalogued. That's enough about minced meat and husbands who grind spices."

Laughter.

Kk . . . kwik.

It came and sat upon the Factory Act. Once again it screeched.

"Look here, you are an eater of nuts. What business do you have here? Aren't there enough trees outside? What's there for you in this paste? Go and climb a tree. Go up. Come down. What sort of bad habit is this?"

All of a sudden it spread out its four legs on the book and lay prone on its stomach. A ray of sunlight, refracted through a hole in the window mesh, struck it softly on the head. It closed its eyes.

I did not touch it. I have no faith in miracles. Even if I did, I would not put it to the test. I am not used to conversing with fairy princes.

ambai (c. s. lakshmi)

The third floor was a somewhat neglected place. The man who catalogued Telugu books in one corner was given to muttering to himself every now and then. All the rest of the books were either torn, or just about to come apart, or had been pasted together in an effort to postpone death, and were waiting to be catalogued. The floor was of iron sheeting with a pattern of holes. Through these, you could see through to the ground floor. On one occasion, the book of chants used several years ago at the Madurai Meenakshi temple to exorcise evil spirits had slipped from my hand and fallen all the way down and onto the librarian's head.

And he had once climbed the ceiling-high open iron shelves in order to fulfill my wish, even forgetting his paunch.

"I can't reach to the top, sir, please look and tell me what there is up there."

When he reached up there, he struck at the topmost stack of books with his hand. The dust rose in waves. When I craned my neck to look at him as he stood there, his legs spread apart and planted firmly on the shelves facing each other, his head immersed in clouds of dust, one hand pressed against his chest to prevent an imminent sneeze, he seemed like the good, obedient genie who appears and demands work at the merest rub of the magical lamp.

"What's up there, sir?"

"Dust . . . dust . . ."

"No sir, what books?"

"I'll look, madam. There are lots of good books written, though, without my having to climb up like this for them. This is all rubbish, madam, rubbish."

"If you want, I'll climb up, sir."

"No. no, madam. This is my duty." He sneezed about ten times. "These are all just women's books, madam. Do you want them?"

"Throw them down, sir."

They fell with a thud. First, *Penmadhi Bodhini*, then *Jagan Mohini*. Several others followed. The notion of falling became closely linked in my mind with these books. It became an everyday occurrence to me to imagine them tearing their way through the roof and splitting their sides. For one who did not believe in miracles, I continued to experience a number of such illusions. When I touched the spine of an old mended nineteenth century book, an ecstatic tremor rose from the soles of my feet and passed through me, like an orgasm. When Anna Sattianadhan lay upon her deathbed, asking her husband to pray for her, there were only I and the squirrel on the third floor to share her grief. The evangelist who rode horseback to propagate Christianity broke through the meshed windows of this same third floor. When a Bengali girl set fire to herself after leaving a note for her father, telling him he must not sell his only house in order to meet her marriage expenses, the flames chased through this very place, like snakes. The flames spread throughout the third floor and disappeared, having revealed their form only to the squirrel and me. The Telugu cataloguer was not there that day.

What the third floor contained was not just books, but a whole generation, throbbing with life. Respectable older women in nine-yard saris, with shoes upon their feet and rackets in hand, played badminton with white women. Many preached untiringly to younger women how best they could please their husbands. They took great pains to explain the dharma that women should follow, addressing their readers as "my girl," and putting on compassionate faces. Nallathangal chased her son even when he pleaded with her to let him go; pushed him into a well and jumped in after him. When a Brahmin stubbornly refused to do the last rites upon a girl who was an unshaven widow, her knee-length hair was removed from her very corpse. Devadasis dedicated to temples sang, "I cannot bear the arrows of Kama," as they danced to the point of exhaustion. Gandhi addressed women spinning at their charkas. Uma Rani of *Tygabhumi* rang out, "I am no slave." In the women's pages, "Kasini" wrote about new styles in bangles. The cover-girl of *Ananda Vikatan* swept along, swinging her arms while her husband carried her shopping bag. Taamaraikanni Ammal proclaimed, "We will sacrifice our lives for Tamil." Her real name—a Sanskrit one—was Jalajakshi. Ramamrutham Ammal confronted Rajaji head on when he wrote that Gandhi would not come unless he was paid money.

All, all these women were present there. And so was I. Sometimes they were weightless, as if made of smoke; at other times full of mass, heavy. The day the widow's head was shaven, a heaviness pressed upon my heart. Razor-blades appeared everywhere. Each lock of hair fell away with a loud sound. Each lock of hair rubbed abrasively against my cheek. I came to life only when the squirrel tapped its tail twice and raised the dust. It was leaning against the issue of *Kalki* which had Ammu Swaminathan on the cover. Apparently it had finished eating up the paste.

I looked downward through the holes in the floor. The librarian's head was eased back against the chair. On the desk, a file inscribed, Subject: STRING. This was his favourite file. Three years ago it had been a shining violet in colour; now it was fading and dog-eared. The file began with a letter requesting some string so that the old magazines could be sorted out and tied according to their months and years. Back came the answer that it was not customary to supply string to libraries and demanding a full explanation for breaking this rule. Following upon this were other letters. If the magazines were not separated according to their months, they became chaotic and useless. Useless to whom? To researchers. Which researchers? Were they from Tamilnadu or elsewhere? And so it went on. One day the librarian pulled out a ball of string from his trouser pocket. After this he wrote a letter asking to be reimbursed for the cost of a ball of string, which set off another series of letters. Every day the file would appear on his table. The money had still not been paid.

The squirrel screeched. Keech keech. My only link with reality. At the same time my companion in the world of illusions.

Yes, I know. It is late. The paste is finished. But I haven't the mind to leave these women. There seems to be a magical string that links us, I hear them speak. As Shanmuga Vadivu strikes the first note of the octave upon her vina, the sound floods into my ears. K.B. Sundarambal sings, "Seeking the bright lotus, seeing it, the bee sings its sweet song . . . utterly lost." And Vasavambal, accompanying her on the harmonium, joins in, with "utterly lost." On the Marina beach, Vai Mu Ko hoists the flag of Independence. The women who oppose the imposition of Hindi go to prison, their babes in their arms.

Look, this is another world. That paste should have made you aware of at least a taste of it. A world which we share, you and I.

"Are you coming down, madam?" He was smiling as he looked up and called out.

"In a minute."

He came up.

"We've been sent the Rule."

"What Rule?"

"It's very expensive to mend and repair all this. Not many people read them either. Perhaps one or two like you. How can the government afford to spend money on the staff and paste and so on? They are going to burn the lot."

"Burn what?"

"Why, all these old unwanted books."

Not a single thought rose in me. Except for one, at the edges of my mind. So the file on string has finally been closed. Only its burial is left now.

"Come, madam."

I came to the iron stairs and then turned to look. The evening sun and the mercury lamp combined to spread an extraordinary light on the yellowing books, like the first flood of fire that spreads over a funeral pyre. Then he put out the light.

Darkness mingled with the dim red light, turning it into deep crimson, like magical flames. The squirrel lay prostrate in front of the window, its four legs spread out, in an attitude of surrender.

As I climbed down the stairs, a small wave of thought hit me: the window faces north.

PAUL ZACHARIA

b. 1945

(Malayalam)

Paul Zacharia was born into a Catholic family in the small town of Urulik-kunnam, Kerala. His elegant short stories and novels, composed in his mother tongue, Malayalam, have brought him great literary renown as well as mired him in public controversy. In his writing Zacharia, a master stylist, reveals his iconoclastic roots by striking out at received doctrine. As a result he has endured attacks from Hindu fundamentalist groups and radical Marxists, as well as the Christian hierarchy of Kerala. In the short story "A Nazrani Youth and Goulisastram," the central character comes to believe in the power of "goulisastram," a curious mode of augury that relies on the movement and small noises made by house lizards. The lizards hide behind cupboards and the framed portraits of political leaders like John F. Kennedy. Zacharia writes of his protagonist that he believed equally in Goulisastram, Marxism, the theology of Saint Augustine, socialism, and the multiplication table. His short story "Kannadi Kanmolavum" ("Till You See the Looking Glass") caused a furor when it was published in a literary magazine in 1997. A Catholic bishop condemned the story, likening it to a second crucifixion of Christ. The tale evokes the interior consciousness of Jesus of Nazareth, a man besieged by his own image in a barber's mirror. Zacharia points out that he was inspired by Luis Bunuel's surreal movie Milky Way *(1969). In this 1997 interview in Rediff with Venu Menon, Zacharia clarified his task as a fiction writer. "As a fiction writer my job is not to replicate the Biblical Christ. [. . .] As a writer I have to figure out ways in which*

I can approach this 2,000-year-old man who has been covered over by all kinds of fancy adjectives and overstatements. [. . .] Jesus puts his head in Mariam's lap and finds peace there. Why do you find a sexual connotation. [. . .] I wanted to show a Christ like you and me who happened to sweat and who happened to wear dirty clothes." In "Annamateacher: A Memoir," the writer's lyrical gifts, his profound ability to depict the human condition, come to the fore as he tells of the life and death of an unmarried schoolteacher. Zacharia's works have been widely translated and some have been turned into movies. Other important works include Salaam America: Kathakal *(1998)*, Bhaskara Pattelar and Other Stories *(1994), and* Praise the Lord and What's New Pilate? *(2002)*.

From "Sinning in Mysore"

At the everlasting age of sixteen, like green-horn Adam into the Garden of Eden, I was released into the bustling alleys of Mysore city. And I, rascal of a dreamer, was dumb enough to imagine that I had become a freeman at last in the sprawling and anonymous city. For, Mysore was so far, far away from my tiny village in the spice-hills of Kerala where intoxicating Sin flowered and fruited lovingly everywhere along with pepper, ginger and papaya. It rippled down the rocky streams. And God patrolled us relentlessly and inexorably. For all I knew, God partook of our sins and laughed in secret from the dark caverns of the rubber plantations, exulting shamelessly in his double-facedness.

Mysore in those days had the eternal odour of horse-dung and urine, of jasmine and masala dosa and of coffee and cow-dung cake whose smoke rose in blue whirls like wraiths melting in the sun. And as I discovered to my utter horror, God stalked every nook and cranny of Mysooru Nagara, round the clock, as a thundercloud of unknowing and a chastising mystery. He sat upon the summit of Chamundi Hills, disguised as the far-away row of lights burning in the cold night, filling us with an unspeakable longing for the black sky as we lay in our hostel beds looking out the window through the white and mesmerizing veil of the mosquito net. [. . .]

Up the hill. Past the Fountain Circle. Past the black mountain of the

Church. Past its grotto where Mother Mary stands open-armed, speaking ghostly words of wisdom. Down shabby Ashoka Road with its row of Marwadi pawn-shops to Nehru Circle. Go round the Circle to the right and take Irwin road till you turn left on Sayyaji Rao Road. Down you go till you see the two kings, Krishnaraja Wodeyar and Chamaraja Wodeyar, their bulging crowns and flowing gowns splattered with the white shrapnel of bird-shit, looking over the city from marble balconies, immune, frozen like autistic warriors wrapped in amnesia. We never enquired whether Krishnaraja and Chamaraja were good kings or bad. We were just happy that they stood there as reliable landmarks. The great Palace of the Wodeyars was a few thousand feet away, its towers and domes soaring behind the high walls like a magic mountain. We did not ever gather sufficient courage to seek to enter the Palace grounds. Once in a while we would furtively go up to the southern gate pretending to worship at the temple there, but essentially to peek at the sex-sculptures that decorated its walls. It took a lot of staring and screwing up of eyes to decipher the precise nature of the erotic activities of the figures on the granite panels placed high up on the wall, but we always managed to get an erection or two. Our giggles and exchanges of lewd looks must have alerted the pujaris and worshippers to our profane intentions, but no one took our pornographic pursuits seriously enough to evict us.

In the horizon loomed Chamundi Hills, rocky, near-barren and blue-grey. The temple and the palace on its summit looked, from afar, like a white patch shorn off a passing cloud. We knew the hill-top also held a huge granite holy bull whose robust and smooth balls always received our admiring attention, and a big, techni-colour rakshasa with unsheathed sword in hand, his mouth gaping, bloody and toothy. It was hard to say whether the demon was smiling or screaming. If memory serves me right he was about to eat a baby. Chamundi Hills was one of the targets of our periodic cycling assaults on Mysore. We would huff and puff and push our way up its hair-pin curves, gaping at tourists, wondering at girls and checking out all the usual sights. Then we would let speed swallow us as we raced downhill. In the evening we would tell loud and chattering stories about who fell down and how and who cheated in the bet on pedalling all the way to the top without getting down and pushing.

A time came when I decided to explore the Hill in my own way. By then I had taken to wandering the city all by myself like a secret agent smelling out unchartered territory. Though the acknowledged object of my quests was Sin and I was an inveterate coward, my searches took me into sad and forsaken places, scummy and dangerous city backyards, lonely alley-ways that breathed down your shoulders and made your steps tremble and shake, crowded places where evil walked neck to neck with you, exuding strange smells. I also found sweet places under park trees, benches on the side-walk that hugged you, theatres that kissed you, roads that caressed you and restaurants that bathed you in indescribable desire. I was a specialist in getting lost, panicking and retreating. I was ridiculed, stared at, chased, shouted at, threatened, humiliated, thrown out. I walked into snares that no ordinary damn-fool would walk into. I was the Best Ready-made Schizo in Mysore city.

I was not planning to climb the Hill by the regular road. At one end the Hill gradually sloped down till it flowed into the land. It fascinated me that Chamundi Hill had this secret pact with the soil and that I could, if I wished, touch the Hill at the spot where it grew out of the earth. It thrilled me that the Hill had a beginning and an end and I could connect with that. One late afternoon, keeping the general direction of the hill-end in view, I started walking towards it. Soon I was out of familiar streets and sights and moving farther away into the limbo where village and city met and merged and lost worlds emerged. Then the clusters of huts too vanished and the dusty cart-road straggled for a while, finally leaving me in the middle of wide fields where only the hardiest crops grew in the dry and shallow soil. A few goats and buffaloes wandered around biting at leaves. I looked back and was astonished to see that I had left the city far behind and lights were beginning to glow in it. The sun was sinking and an overwhelming twilight was falling over the land. I understood I had misjudged the distance to the Hill because I could see that it was still a long way off, beyond a lengthy slope covered with bushes. The goats and buffaloes were gone. Suddenly I realised I was all alone, that the Hill was beyond my reach, that I was a stranger under a sun setting over a strange land, that the Hill had stood there for tens of thousands of years and it had no use for me. I felt the evening grow dark all of a sudden. I didn't seem to know the direction I had to take to get back to the city. I stood under a vast sky, with a mountain turning dark before my eyes, listening to a silence that was overpowering, the far-away lights of the city making my loneliness all the more terrifying. I started walking back, looking to the city lights as my guide. It had become cold and I thought I was about to start shivering. At that moment I knew I was being followed. I knew somebody or something was close behind me and getting closer. I jumped round in panic to see who or what it was. There was nothing; only the fields rolling away into the twilight and the Hill covering itself with a sheet of night. I started walking again. This time I had no doubt that I was not alone. There was something close on my heels. It was a most powerful sensation. When I moved, it moved, when I stood still, it stood still. I was sure that when I listened, it watched me listening, and it saw the fear washing over me. I was afraid to move, yet I knew I must move—run. Each time I turned in terror to look back I nearly jumped out of my skin anticipating what I might see. But there was nothing. Absolutely nothing. The Hill stood still. The night was beginning to sweep over the land. I knew I was being stalked and that I was constantly in the stalker's line of sight. I looked at the city lights for support, but they were blinking in another world. In the dim light cast by the black sky I screamed once and ran for my life. In a way I knew I was running away from nothing. But I could feel the stalker, like a heat-seeking missile, keeping up its invisible pressure behind me. I kept sobbing and running. Bushes scratched me and stones bit into my feet. I ran breathlessly through the tide of darkness swiftly rolling in, and slowly the stalker melted away. But with remembered terror I continued to run till I reached the first cluster of huts. I walked through the village quietly like any other stranger meekly passing by. I marveled that none knew that I had just been lured into a phantom world a few thousand feet away from the circles of light of their lamps.

Was it Devil? God? Or was the Hill evicting an intruder through a whiff of its self-hood? Were the fields laying an illusion-trap for a stranger? Was the sky deluding me with a fantasm of anonymous forces? Was the twilight mounting an instant drama in fear? Or was it a random burst of electromagnetic energy that had lost its way and was trying to cling to me like a motherless kitten? I will never know. I like to think it was a part of me that hovered there, lost and afraid, alien and lonely, slinking after my retreating steps. It must have been as terrified as me. Maybe it still wanders out there, alone, all alone. I rule out Devil and God from this event because it would have been very silly of them to waste high-value time chasing me out of Chamundi Hill's evening world. Both are, by profession and by compulsion, hidden persuaders, operating from secret chips in our brain. I think, in general, they had helped my schizophrenia along so that each could manipulate a separate me and have fun watching me trying to be saint and sinner at the same time. When I ran screaming, God might have been an interested bystander and Devil busy in the city lanes—I don't think *he* cares much for greenery.

I wonder what it was that made me fall in love with both boys and girls in Mysore. It was pure love, head over heels, which would transfer itself to another after a while. It was silent love. I never managed to convey my tender sentiments to my lovers. I just allowed myself to be haunted by them and they themselves never knew it. There was my junior hostel-mate, J, a sixteen-something plump boy from South Canara's arecanut groves in half-pants and checked shirt, hardly handsome or pretty but very self-possessed and warm. I used to wrap myself around him and look after his every need. I must have even fantasised Sin but it was unthinkable in real terms, considering the pureness of my love. I taught him cycling and accompanied him on his first solos like a mother. He was a shaky rider, always on the verge of falling off. One day on Irwin road he was riding ahead of me and a bus squeezed him to the road's edge. He lost balance but didn't fall because he and the cycle were leaning on the bus! As soon as the bus passed he fell onto the road and when I picked him up in my hands I overflowed with tenderness. Perhaps I wanted to kiss him then, I don't remember. I was in love with most of the girls too. I think some liked me as a strange toy. When they allowed me to get close I would backtrack, projecting them as mystery creatures from a magical world. Once, my classmate, one of the stars of the college, asked me to go to her house in the evening to help her with English—a language where I had exhibited some talent except in talking—hinting that she would be alone. I crawled the half kilometer from my hostel to NR Mohalla where she lived, like a python who had swallowed too huge a meal, stopping and staring at the cacti hedge, meditating at a wayside pond, climbing the sloping road to the Mohalla as if it was Golgotha. Then, having crept up to her house, I stood hiding myself in the shadows on the opposite side, watched her with pounding heart for a while and returned, empty, defeated, consoled only by the softly rising moon and the music that came floating beneath the just-risen stars. I still hadn't been sanctioned chappals and pants and I was a barefoot lover in a dhoti.

RK Narayan was living in Mysore then. UR Ananthamurthy had, I think, just started teaching there. Prof. CD Narasimhaiah was the uncrowned king of English and Indo-Anglian studies. A galaxy of Kannada writers and thinkers resided in Mysore. Sardar KM Panikker, the historian, was our vice-chancellor. Oblivious to all this, I lived out my close encounters with the Other city. I lived blithely, hand-to-mouth, alternating between diarrheas and constipations, between fevers and falls from the cycle, pawning one day my precious cycle and another day my precious watch, following women on the streets to Restaurants at the End of the Universe and bitter finishes. I learned to confess in English so that I needn't confess to Malayali priests in unambiguous Malayalam and instead pass up a garbled and undecipherable list of sins in English to French and Tamil priests. I certainly must have mixed up nomenclature and categories, for, one well-meaning retreat preacher who heard my confession in English became so overcome by my Sin Agenda that he kept following up on the state of my soul for months afterwards. I had begun to buy my first English books from the grimy second-hand shops and pavement-sellers, was discovering the marvels of Economics as retold by Kewal Krishna Dewett and, more than anything else, immersed, in selling over my soul, lock, stock and barrel, to "Macbeth," "Midsummer Night's Dream," Tagore's "Reminiscences," Keats, Shelley, Tennyson, Wordsworth, Coleridge, Milton and a million-dollar textbook called "An Anthology of Contemporary English Verse" edited by (May God Shower Everlasting Bliss on Her) Margaret J. O'Donnell.

It was only when I had finished my degree in Mysore and started post-graduation in Bangalore and my Kannadiga fellow-students treated me with a certain respect, that I discovered that for the past three years I had been enjoying the singular privilege of studying under *the* Gopalakrishna Adiga, great pioneer of the modernist movement in Kannada poetry. It shows the state of abysmal *maya* in which I spent my years in Mysore. I am amazed at my daftness and sometimes wonder whether I might not be equally daft today about many things even as I experience them. To me Gopalakrishna Adiga was, all those years, just Adiga Sir whose every word I captured, chewed, swallowed, and regurgitated. So much so he would ask to see my notebook to refresh his memory on something he discussed a week back. He would also admonish me that I must think beyond what he taught, and not be just a copyist. Little did he know that he was dealing with a cunning cannibal of sorts—that I was a ruthless alien waiting to be born as soon as sufficient life-soup had been sucked in. For, I was not only a guaranteed schizophrenic but also an overfed, greedy bookworm. Nearly all my reading was in Malayalam and I had gnawed into almost everything that was to be had in local libraries around my village, good, bad and ugly. Now, all my instincts were gathered and poised for the next change-over, fueled by nostalgia, emboldened by freedom, powered by awakening adulthood, fired by sexuality and instigated by the city. All my reading and experiencing were now on their toes on the spring-board of chance. And Gopalakrishna Adiga threw the door wide open and let me in to a world whose existence I never had suspected. He was not doing it specially for me. He was, like any great teacher, giving his students everything he had. And there were only four of us majoring in English Literature, two beautiful Coorgi girls who were essentially beating time (one of whom had invited me for the aborted homework), a boy called Victor and myself. I was just learning to speak English, though on the writing of it I had some claims. Victor was an earnest and bright student but I had an edge over him as a diehard bookworm. It was upon this motley group that Adiga bestowed his magic as teacher and—now that I know what he was—as poet. He made me step through the looking glass of imagination and see literature in reverse—as a process. He showed me the bits and parts that made creation work. With great ease he went behind the work and brought into view the blueprint of aesthetics and technique. Everything I had read now stood before me in a different light. I slowly realised that literature was not only about reading yourself into an ecstasy, that it had a premeditated form, purpose and plan, that it was possible to create literature if you tried. In my interior tours with Adiga Sir, I became both Macbeth and Lady Macbeth, sat with Keats near the wine-press, breathed the west wind with Shelley, laughed with Gulliver at the Liliputs, climbed to precipices with Wordsworth.

> "In the sun that is young once only,
> Time let me play and be
> Golden in the mercy of his means,
> And green and golden I was huntsman and herdsman, the calves
> Sang to my horn, the foxes on the hills barked clear and cold,
> And the sabbath rang slowly
> In the pebbles of the holy streams."

Once Adiga Sir had taken me indoors of Eliot, Auden and Dylan Thomas, the alien-seed in me was ready to pounce.

In my third year, I left college hostel and moved, adult and free, into the annexe of Carlton Hotel, a Victorian establishment run by Mr. Mysorewala, a Parsi gentleman with polished manners and, if my memory is not wrong, unpolished greed. The annexe was an outhouse of sorts with a few dark and dingy rooms where students and such-like lower phenomena stayed as lodgers. We ate at the main table in the Hotel with the regular guests which involved learning western table manners and making conversation in English with those guests who would ask us a kind question or two. The boy from Urulikunnam was now learning to breathe in another, rarified air. I fell in love with almost every white woman guest of the Hotel, most of whom were in their fifties. That we were a lower form of life was evident from the fact that we had, with the help of the attendant Hassan, established peep-holes into most bedrooms of the Hotel, from the roof-top and from other vantage points. Therefore, other things being equal, any love-making and female undressing that took place in the Hotel had at least a dozen breathless viewers. My room was at one end of the outhouse, with a small, mesh-wired window opening on to a dirty veranda and staircase, beyond which was a side-lane. The staircase led to a Marwadi residence and I was laved with music levitating down the whole day, Radio Ceylon and Binaca Geethmala embroidering my unrest and sorrows with the greatest melodies of our times. A beggar woman and her child took shelter on the veranda at night and left behind disquieting odours. Sometimes for days both were ill. At other times dogs took their siesta there.

The door to the veranda was permanently locked and it was inconceivable for me that I should enter the world on the other side, seemingly a million miles away. However the door had a wooden board which could be shaken loose from the veranda. A young, precocious boy from the Marwadi house upstairs would sometimes remove the board and squeeze in through the gap. He was a master of tantalising, excruciatingly oblique sexual stimuli, played out with great innocence. I practiced yoga, read and re-read Dale Carnegie, took postal courses in self-improvement and hypnotism and pored over Quiller-Couch and Fowler, trying to fight my way into the English language. For days I had been trying to translate "Preludes" into Malayalam for no other reason than that Eliot haunted me like one of my phantom lovers. I was, therefore, working face to face with the bewitching clockwork of his craft and the bookworm's hoard of Malayalam words were being put to the test. One day, moving away from the translation, I tried to write something of my own. I wrote it in English and abandoned it after a few sentences. Another day I ran into it again, completed it in Malayalam and found, to my great surprise, that it had a beginning, a middle and an end. It was a story about my home, my stream, my farm and my childhood. Adiga Sir had let loose the alien and he was now ready to swap bodies, invade minds and travel time's secret places. I drank Eliot's blood and grew. I ate Dylan Thomas's flesh and flourished. I devoured them all. I was a full-grown cannibal. And I had learned how to mix memory and desire to make seducers out of words.

Mysore remains a great and calm city. It has become bitterly crowded, but seems to retain its sanity. I go back there once in a while and walk my old trails. The obscure landmarks of my tramping paths are gone. I can't even recognize my favourite theatres. But I was immensely happy to find in its old place the little magazine-vend on Sayyaji Rao Road where I had bought the Republic Day issue of *Mathrubhumi Weekly* carrying my first story. Mysore was also the favourite city of my elder brother Joseph. It was he who brought me to Mysore and he died there. Many things have died with him. But I return to Mysore because, as I said, perhaps a part of me waits for me there. God, I am sure, still stalks sinners in Mysore. But all His old lairs must be gone. About the jukeboxes, I am certain. So where does He dispense music from? Does He still burn brightly from Chamundi's summit? Does He still waylay sex-maniacs in the form of hard-hearted women? Does He still suffer schizophrenics to fall in love without gender-compulsions? He gave me a long rope in Mysore and may He continue to be lenient to all sinners there as He was to me. May Mysore flourish and grow ever more sensuous!

K. SATCHIDANANDAN
b. 1946

(Malayalam)

K. Satchidanandan was born in Pullut, a small Kerala village. A prolific poet, he grew up close to the natural world and its rhythms of everyday life. He also learned firsthand the pain of insanity, witnessing its ravages in his own grandmother. Satchidanandan read copiously: traditional Malayalam literature, the Bible, the Dhammapadda, and the Communist Manifesto. *He speaks of his great admiration for Latin American poets including Pablo Neruda and Nicanor Parra. In a memoir piece "About Poetry, About Life," he writes, "I also share Neruda's concept of impure poetry, poetry that bears the dust of distances and smells of lilies and urine, a poetry that is often created out of words salvaged from the wreck of languages and nations." As a young man he was a close friend of Ayyappa Paniker, and like his mentor was deeply involved in the Modernist turn in Malayalam literature. This required a renunciation of oratory and figures drawn from myth. Instead, the poets use the sharp, surreal details of everyday life and the sometimes miraculous forms of the natural world. Satchidanandan published the little magazine* Jwala *and was closely allied with the journal* Keralakavita. *When he moved to Delhi, he edited the journal* Indian Literature. *He was also a translator into Malayalam of many world poets including Neruda, Louis Aragon, Leopold Senghor, and Bertolt Brecht. As a poet who came to adulthood in a time of tumult, Satchidanandan absorbed what he calls "a new political alertness" concerning questions of caste and human rights. In addition to numerous books of poetry, he has composed plays, memoirs, essays, and scholarly writings. His important works of po-*

etry include Atmagita *(The Song of the Self, 1974),* Satchidanandante Kavithakal *(Satchidanandan's Collected Poems, 1962–82, 1983), and* Vikku *(Stammer, 2002).*

"Gandhi and Poetry"

One day a lean poem
reached Gandhi's ashram
to have a glimpse of the man.
Gandhi spinning away
his thread towards Rama
took no notice of the poem
waiting at his door
ashamed as he was no bhajan.

The poem cleared his throat
and Gandhi looked at him sideways
through those glasses
that had seen Hell.
"Have you ever spun thread?" he asked,
"Ever pulled a scavenger's cart?
Ever stood the smoke
of an early morning kitchen?
Have you ever starved?"

The poem said: "I was born
in the woods, in a hunter's mouth.
A fisherman brought me up in his hamlet.
Yet, I know no work, I only sing.
First I sang in the courts:
then I was plump and handsome;
but I am on the streets now,
half-starved."

"That's better," Gandhi said
with a sly smile, "but you must
give up this habit

k. satchidanandan

of speaking in Sanskrit at times.
Go to the fields, listen to
the peasants' speech."

The poem turned into a grain
and lay waiting in the fields
for the tiller to come
and upturn the virgin soil
moist with the new rain.

"Stammer"

Stammer is no handicap.
Is a mode of speech.

Stammer is the silence that falls
between the word and its meaning,
just as lameness is the
silence that falls between
the word and the deed.

Did stammer precede language
Or succeed it?
Is it only a dialect or
a language itself?
These questions make
the linguists stammer.

Each time we stammer
we are offering a sacrifice
to the God of meanings.

When a whole people stammer
stammer becomes their mother-tongue:
just as it is with us now.

God too must have stammered
when He created man.

That is why every word of man
carries different meanings.
That is why everything he utters
from his prayers to his commands
stammers,
like poetry.

"Burnt Poems"

I am a half-burnt poem.
Yes, you guessed right,
a girl's love poem.

Girls' love poems have
Seldom escaped fire:
father's fire, brother's fire,
even mother's, an heirloom.

Only some girls half-escape:
those half-charred ones
we call Sylvia Plath,
Anna Akhmatova
or Kamala Das.

Some girls, to escape fire
hide their desire
under the veil of piety:
thus is born a Mira,
an Andal, a Mahadevi Akka.

Every nun is a burnt
love-poem, addressed to
the ever-young Jesus.

Rarely, very rarely,
One girl learns to
laugh at the world
with that tender affection

only women are capable of.
Then the world names her
Wislawa Szymborska.

Of course, Sappho:
she was saved only as
her love poems were
addressed to women.

"About Poetry, About Life"

I cannot tell from where poetry came to me; I had hardly any poet-predecessors. Whenever I think about it, I hear the diverse strains of the incessant rains of my village in Kerala and recall, too, the luminous lines of the Malayalam Ramayana I had read as a schoolboy, where the poet prays to the Goddess of the Word to keep bringing the apt words to his mind without a pause like the endless waves of the sea. My mother taught me to talk to cats and crows and trees; from my pious father I learnt to communicate with gods and spirits. My insane grandmother taught me to create a parallel world in order to escape the vile ordinariness of the tiringly humdrum everyday world; the dead taught me to be one with the soil; the wind taught me to move and shake without ever being seen and the rain trained my voice in a thousand modulations. With such teachers, perhaps it was impossible for me not to be a poet, of sorts. I have looked at my genesis with detachment in an early poem "Granny": "My grandmother was insane / As her madness ripened into death / My uncle, a miser, kept her in our storeroom / Covered in straw / My grandmother dried up, burst / Her seeds flew out of the windows / The sun came and the rain / one seedling grew up into a tree / Whose lusts bore me / How can I help writing poems / About monkeys with teeth of gold?" It was not only my grandma who was insane; there were three in the family, all women. That explains the celebration of madness and the suspicion of sanity in many of my poems.

Our village was beautiful though I was unaware of its charms as long as I lived there. It had paddy fields that would fill with water during floods and with blue flowers after harvest in August; hills with named and nameless creepers and flowers; backwaters on which little open boats plied with men and merchandise; little peaceful temples, mosques and churches, which bred genuine gods and not devils as they sometimes seem to do now. The northern part of our village, Pulloot, was dominated by communists and the south by Congressmen. My primary and upper primary schools were in the north, which meant I was a tiny communist there, but at home all went with the Congress. Even our gods whose pictures adorned the pooja room seemed to belong to either of these parties, though a little more violent than the party men were, for they never wore garlands of skulls, carried swords and spears nor had several heads like the gods. Still, the Goya-figures the family worshipped seemed to go well with those post-Gandhian times. That was also my second lesson in surrealism, the first having been the three-month-long fever that nearly killed me when I was four and gave me Dali-like nightmares that crowded my early poetry.

I was born in a middle-class home, and by the time I was born it was a unitary family, with my parents who had not been educated beyond high school, and a sister and a brother who were elder to me. My father did odd jobs, farming on our family land—where we helped, too—working in a lawyer's office, helping people prepare legal documents for land transactions. Earlier he was in the police force from which he had voluntarily retired. Two of my sisters had died in accidents before I was born; I have written a poem addressed to one of them who appeared before me one night, put her soft betel-leaf hand on my palm and invited me to her enchanting land, slightly above the earth but below heaven. My mother taught me to respect all religions, and I accompanied my friend Abdul Khader to *chandanakkudam*, the festival in the mosque, with the same enthusiasm with which I attended *thalappoli*, the temple festival, and enjoyed the *pathiri* made at his home by his sister Khadeeja. My brother used to write poetry, though he ended up as an engineer, and by the time we needed higher education, the family, now larger with my sister's children, had been rendered even poorer by the inevitable land reform that took away a good part of our land, which had been with the tenants. But scholarships helped us pursue studies in college. My divorced sister had now married V.T. Nandakumar, a fiction writer, adding one more writer to the family already struggling with two aspirants. My friends in the Malayalam-medium schools in the village were mostly from very poor families: I have remembered them in a poem on my classmates, Kunjimuhammed, Vasu and Janaki, none of whom went to college. Some of my teachers, especially in the high school at Kodungallur (the little temple town, earlier Muziris, a port that brought Greeks, Romans and Arabs to Kerala) that I reached after crossing a river and walking miles, encouraged me to write. Raghavanmaster, my Malayalam teacher, would send me to every poetry competition and I seldom disappointed him. I cannot forget Sankaran, a mad man, said to have been a Malayalam *munshi*, who introduced me to Kumaran Asan's great poetry, which he would sing and interpret every morning to an eager crowd in the village square. I would reach school late, but this was better education. My first poems were published in the manuscript journal of the village library and the high school magazines.

Christ College, a well-run Carmelite institution where I did my graduation in biology, had a well-stocked library. My early readings had already been done in the village library that bears the name of Kumaran Asan. That is where I read not only the great Malayalam fiction writers and poets, but translations of Tagore, Bankim, Saratchandra, Tarasankar, Manik Banerjee, Bimal Mitra, Yashpal, Jainendrakumar, Tolstoy, Dostoevsky, Hugo, Zola, Maupassant, Flaubert, Thomas Mann and several others. The Malayalam weeklies of the time serialized at least one novel each in translation, especially from Bengali or Hindi. But it was in Christ College that I began reading in English somewhat systematically, guided by the librarian, John Master, who was a Latin scholar. I read the Holy Bible with great attention and that had a lasting impact on my vision and imagination; many of its books were great literature besides being moving human documents. I especially liked the *Book of Job*, *Revelation*—that was my third lesson in surrealism—and the *Psalms*, especially of David. Perhaps only the Mahabharata, which I read later in Kunjikkuttan Thampuran's Malayalam translation, had a similar impact on me. Buddha's *Dhammapada*, which I read when I was nineteen, also had a great impact on my ethical imagination. *The Communist Manifesto* was another book that awakened my moral sensibility. At Christ College I also read the complete works of Shakespeare, spending a whole vacation on it and making notes, and the collected works of Wordsworth, Shelley, Keats and Byron and translated some of their poems, including Shelley's "To a Skylark," "The Cloud" and "Ode to the Westwind," Keats's "Ode to a Nightingale" and many short lyrics of Byron. Translation, however, was not new to me: I had translated a lot of Omar Khayyam's *rubayis* while in high school from the Fitzgerald version. (I translated all the sonnets of Shakespeare much later, for a volume of Shakespeare translations edited by Ayyappa Paniker.) Looking back, I feel they were a part of my training as a poet.

Maharaja's College in Ernakulam, where I did my post graduation in English, played an even greater role in my evolution as a writer. My reading grew more intense and focused. I also read a lot of theory including the Marxist classics. I got my real taste of modern literature as Yeats, T.S. Eliot, James Joyce and Samuel Beckett were part of the syllabus and I was burning midnight electricity on Sartre, Camus, Kafka, Baudelaire, Rilke and the Black poets. My poems and critical articles had begun to appear in Malayalam magazines by now, and I had a small circle of eccentric admirers. That, however, did not ensure my victory in the college elections—I was an independent candidate supported by the Students' Federation who always lost to a local party, the Democratic Front. My good friends included the late T.K. Ramachandran, who grew into a leftist intellectual, N.S. Madhavan, now a major fiction writer in Malayalam, P.V. Krishnan Nair, who later became secretary of the Kerala Sahitya Akademi, Sankaranarayanan (Nambu as we called him), who is now with the *Deccan Herald* in Bangalore, besides others. This was the time when I met Ayyappa Paniker, the pioneer of New Poetry in Malayalam, and a fine scholar who was to play a major role in my life. He sent me to various festivals of poetry and made me translate several poets from across the world for the poetry journal he edited, *Kerala Kavita*, which also published my first important poems. Later, he encouraged me to come to Delhi to take up the editorship of *Indian Literature* at the Sahitya Akademi. Maharajas College had some excellent teachers of literature and provided me the kind of ambience I was looking for, with heated discussions on literature and politics, sharing of books and creative confusions. I was an angst-ridden existentialist and at the same time a half-baked Marxist, besides being attracted to the radical humanist ideas of M.N. Roy, introduced to me by the senior intellectual and poet M. Govindan. There was a little circle of active Royists at that time around the town of Trichur. I occasionally joined their discussions. My roommate C.T. Sukumaran (who later joined the IAS and was murdered by the mafia) also joined me at times.

I began to take my poetry seriously in the mid-1960s when Malayalam poetry was undergoing a sweeping transformation in terms of theme, mood and form. The new poets, tired of the excesses of the Romantics and the shallowness of the Progressives, were striving to create a novel poetic idiom that would capture the conflicts and complexities of contemporary life in its totality. They had learnt their lessons from three sources: the specific—oral as well as written—traditions of Malayalam poetry; the larger—classical as well as modern—traditions of Indian poetry; and the avant-garde practices of modern European poetry. New rhythms, metaphors, images, word patterns and structures of feeling and thought and radical deployment of archetypes, myths and legends from diverse cultures together transformed the landscape of poetry in my language as in many others at that time. The change had its impact on my poetic practice, giving it new directions and dimensions. We rallied round *Kerala Kavita*, and the release of each quarterly issue became an occasion for discussions on poetry as well as readings, some of them directed by theatre and film directors like Kavalam Narayana Paniker and G. Aravindan. In the 1970s I published a little magazine, *Jwala*, with my friend P. K. A. Raheem, a great supporter of the new movements. It carried the latest in Western thought and writing—Allen Ginsberg, John Cage, Limericks, Concrete Poetry, Argentine microtales including Borges. A new fraternity based on modern sensibility was evolving in Kerala that included modern painters, sculptors, film-makers and playwrights besides writers. I wrote a series of articles on modern painting as well as other art forms and also took to painting for a brief while when I had lost my faith in language and suffered a crisis of faith and consequent depression. My first collection of poems, *Anchusooryan*, had been published in 1971 and a book on modern poetry, *Kurukshetram*, one year before it; many short collections followed, almost one every two years. That was also the time of the Film Society movement and we organized one in Irinjalakuda, the town where I was teaching, holding many retrospectives of film-makers from Eisenstein and Bergman to Godard and Tarkovsky. Later, I added many more to my favourites, from Kurasowa and Jansco to Kieslowsky, Parajinov and Angelopoulos. I had never thought of becoming a critic, but there were few to interpret the emerging modern sensibility and I was constrained to play that role, writing books or articles on new poetry, new fiction and modern painting. My academic research in post-structuralist poetics and critical endeavours cannot be said to have helped my poetry, but they did improve my understanding of the complex linguistic processes involved in creative writing and the essentially anonymous and polyphonic nature of all writing. Consequently, I became less possessive about my own writing.

In the second half of the 1970s, a new political alertness revitalized this modern poetry; it was now ready to take on larger social issues and historical situations and interrogate the status quo. The new poetry got the eyes of history and the impetus came chiefly from the New Left (Maoist) movement that attracted several young idealists in Kerala as it did in Bengal and Andhra Pradesh. I can now see that its politics were problematic, but it did generate a lot of creative energy that transformed our poetry, fiction, theatre and cinema. There was a reorganization of the earlier high modernist fraternity. Some poets were changed completely, giving birth to what Yeats would call "a terrible beauty," while some got partially transformed and were sympathetic. Even senior poets like Ayyappa Paniker, N.N. Kakkad and Attoor Ravivarma wrote poems fired by the new social awakening with tribals and landless peasants at its core, and there were poets like K.G. Sankara Pillai and Kadammanitta Ramakrishnan who were in the forefront of the new cultural ferment. We were all active in *Janakeeya Samskarika Vedi*, the Forum for People's Culture that upheld avant-garde practices. Journals like *Prasakti* and *Prerana* gave a new impetus to the movement. Street and proscenium theatres flowered with new plays and adaptations. Translations (most of them mine) of Latin American poets like Pablo Neruda and César Vallejo, Black poets like Senghor and David Diop, and European poets like Paul Éluard, Louis Aragon and Bertolt Brecht provided new models. The campuses became vibrant with poetry readings and campus plays. This was the time that I also adapted some plays of W.B. Yeats, Lady Gregory and Bertolt Brecht. My play on Gandhi's last days was written later on the request of the Secular Artists' Forum that I had also helped found along with other artists and writers at a time when communalism was beginning to malign even Kerala's body politic. I had by this time also become a regular invitee to the literary events at Bharat Bhavan, Bhopal, thanks to Ashok Vajpeyi, the cultural visionary. These readings and workshops acquainted me with a lot of major Indian writers, especially poets, including the likes of Navkant Barua, Neelmoni Phookan, Subhash Mukhopadhyay, Sunil Gangopadhyay, Kunwar Narayan, Kedarnath Singh, Sitakant Mahapatra, Ramakanta Rath, Jayanta Mahapatra, Dilip Chitre, Arun Kolatkar, Namdeo Dhasal, Sitanshu Yashaschandra, and Ali Sardar Jaffri, besides poets from abroad like Derek

Walcott, Tomas Tranströmer and Philippe Jaccottet, though I did meet a lot of other poets—from Kim Chi-hai and Tasos Denegris to Mahmoud Darwish, David Diop and Bei Dao—during my readings outside India.

The '70s movement ended tragically, producing several young martyrs who were killed by the police or committed suicide out of disillusionment. I escaped their fate only because I had always kept a critical distance from the political formation and its closed ideological stance, and managed to honestly articulate even this moment of retreat, isolation and fragmentation in my poetry. I also used this interval for introspection and fresh theoretical enquiries and launched the journal *Uttharam* (For an Answer). (Later, I edited a third journal, *Pacchakkutira* [The Green Horse], for arts, creative writing, translation and social and literary theory.) There were also new social movements centred round human rights, consumer rights, issues of environment and tribals', dalits' and women's emancipation which gave hope. I could see a new politics of "microstruggles" or "transversal struggles"—as Michel Foucault calls them—emerging in Kerala, which shared their ethical concerns with the '70's movement. It was around this time that Ayyappa Paniker prompted me to move to Delhi and take up the editorship of *Indian Literature* at the Sahitya Akademi.

Leaving my job in the college and my role in the cultural scene of my state was not at all easy, but the adventurer in me got the better of the sober soul, and to the surprise and even the chagrin of many, I decided to take the plunge. Frankly, I do not regret the decision when I compare what I lost with what Delhi gave me: fresh exposures to art forms, a deeper interest in Indian literature that led to many fresh explorations, some of which are collected in my three books in English on the subject, the advantage of distance from my native state that helped me look at it at times nostalgically and at times critically, the many poems on Kerala and in Malayalam, a large circle of writer-friends across the country and abroad, the new directions I could give to the Akademi's journal as its editor and later, as its executive head, to its activities, travels in three continents that often inspired a lot of my poems and also won my poetry a lot of friends and translators abroad. My readings across the globe have helped reaffirm my faith in the power of poetry to speak to people across nations, languages and communities. It is the shared mother tongue of human beings that survived the Babel. No wonder it has survived Plato's Republic, Hitler's

Auschwitz and Stalin's Gulag, and still whispers its uneasy truths into the human ear trained over centuries to capture the most nuanced of voices.

Poetry as I conceive it is no mere combinatorial game. It rises up from the ocean of the unsayable to name the nameless and to give a voice to the voiceless. It is no mere reproduction of established values and recognized truths. It is, as Italo Calvino says, an eye that sees beyond the colour spectrum of everyday politics and an ear that goes beyond the frequencies of sociology. "It upturns the virgin soil, advances on the blank page," to use Nieanor Parra's famous phrase. The truths it discovers may not often be of immediate use, but it will gradually become part of social consciousness. I also share Neruda's concept of impure poetry, poetry that bears the dust of distances and smells of lilies and urine, a poetry that is often created out of words salvaged from the wreck of languages and nations. Poetry differs from prose not by following a metre or rhythm. The difference lies in its power to dissolve paradoxes and its way of imagining things into being and connecting words and memories; rhyme and rhythm may, of course, help to evoke an atmosphere. Its attraction is in what lies beyond the dictionary; it recovers words and experiences exiled from memory. Lorca used to speak of *duende*, a common term in AndaLusia popular discourse: that sudden vision of godhead in Arabic music and dance that makes the audience cry, *Allah, Allah*. It is the intangible mystery Goethe found in Paganini's art, the divine persuasion that the gypsy dancer La Malena felt in Bach's music played by Brailovsky. The search for it a solitary trip without maps, Poetry too has those moments of revelation, when, like a whirlwind, it subverts all logic and pulls down all preconceived projects. Every poet worth his or her salt must have felt the thrill and the terror of such moments of epiphany, at least in the best moments of their inspiration.

I have often been asked what the central themes of my poetry are. It is difficult to reduce poetry to themes as any poem works at many levels. As Umberto Eco says in a recent interview, works are more intelligent than their authors, they may contain possibilities that the author might never have known or imagined. But Rizio Raj, the writer-friend who edited my collected works, has divided my work into three parts: *Akam*, poems of love, domesticity and interiority; *Puram*, poems of social concern; and *Mozhi*, poems where language itself becomes the main theme. If pushed to respond, I would say justice, freedom, love, nature, language and death are the central concerns of my poetry as perhaps of all poetry. And the chief elements that helped shape me as a poet have perhaps been the traditions of poetry, local, national as well as global; experience; observation—of nature and of human beings; travel; interaction with other arts like music, painting and cinema; reading and translation, all turning into the fibres of my imagination. And I have been open-minded when it comes to forms, having employed several verbal registers in Malayalam, from street talk to the language of legal documents and a diversity of metrical and non-metrical devices, folk, classical and modern.

The responsiveness of the 70s is still alive in my poetry though I have distanced myself from all dogma. My commitment is largely ethical to values like justice, equality, freedom, love, respect for all forms of life. These have become all the more significant in a world governed by the values of the market and increasingly and violently being colonized by the forces of globalization. While I have continuously raised the issues of women's emancipation, the rights of the marginalized, ecological harmony and a world without wars, and kept responding to the tragic turns of social events, from the Emergency to the rise of communalism in our society, I have not ceased asking the deeper existential questions, of being, freedom, instinct, nature, relationships, death. I find no contradiction between the sacred and the secular; I can be spiritual without being religious. This is something I have learnt from our Saint and Sufi poets and reformers like Kabir and Gandhi who battled against hierarchies of every kind, challenged power in its diverse manifestations and interrogated the superfluous externals of practised religion. A poet does not need any religion other than poetry itself. I fear only the suffocating silence of a world where the soul has ceased to speak and man cannot decipher the language of leaves and waterfalls. I hope not to survive to see that day when the universe is deprived of its sacredness and evil prevails unquestioned.

ARVIND KRISHNA MEHROTRA

b. 1947

(English)

Arvind Krishna Mehrotra was born in Lahore in what is now Pakistan in *1947, the year of Partition. His family migrated to India, and he grew up in Allahabad. His mother tongue is Hindi, but like several of the poets in this anthology, English became his chosen medium of writing. One of the circle of Bombay poets, Mehrotra's work draws on the spare imagistic language he prized in the writing of twentieth-century American poets such as Ezra Pound. There are powerful cosmopolitan currents that run through his writing and feed into his work both as a poet and as an acclaimed translator. He has translated the Gāthāsaptaśatī poems compiled in the second century* CE *by King Hala and more recently the fierce, witty poems of the medieval mystic Kabir. When he was a student at Allahabad University, Mehrotra, together with a friend, started a small literary magazine,* damn you/a magazine of the arts, *modeled on a magazine they had read about in a copy of the* Village Voice. *It was in this little magazine that his earliest poems were published. In a memoir piece, "Partial Recall," Mehrotra speaks of typing away on an old Royal typewriter that was a gift to his parents from his maternal grandfather. Bought secondhand from an Englishman who was selling his effects prior to leaving the country, it was a portable model that had the weight of a saddle quern and came in a high black case. He was a close friend of Arun Kolatkar and edited his poems and literary notebooks. Mehrotra's own poems with their tight form and reliance on edgy images evoke landscapes of the soul, sometimes border-*

ing on the mystical. There is a fine precision to his language, and the objects he evokes are frequently charged with bristling emotion. He has published four books of poetry, two volumes of translations, and a history of Indian writing in English. His poetry includes Nine Enclosures *(1976)*, Distance in Statute Miles *(1982)*, Middle Earth *(1984)*, The Transfiguring Places *(1998)*, and Collected Poems, 1969–2014 *(2014)*.

"Engraving of a Bison on Stone"

The land resists
Because it cannot be
Tempted, or broken
In a chamber. It records,
By carefully shuffling the leaves,
The passage of each storm, rain,
And drought. The land yields
In places, deliberately,
Having learnt warfare from the armies
It fed. The land is of one
Piece and hasn't forgotten
Old miracles: the engraving of a bison
On stone, for instance. The land
Turns up like an unexpected
Visitor and gives refuge, it cannot be
Locked or put away. The land
Cannot sign its name, it cannot die
Because it cannot be buried,
It understands the language,
It speaks in dialect.

"Distance in Statute Miles"

On maps it always takes
The same position: away from the coastline,

arvind krishna mehrotra

Two inches below
The mountain range. But the man
Who is turning the page doesn't know
That it is flat as a blade, more
Vulnerable than a child, inaccessible
By road or air. It is in front of me.
I can see the towers
From my window, I call out
And it responds to its name,
It is easily frightened.
This is a winter afternoon and the sun
Makes unequal rectangles
Of light in each courtyard, by evening
The birds will again be visible.
Far from us, near the river
Which was once leased out to fishermen,
A small East German tractor is sending up smoke.

"Where Will the Next One Come From"

The next one will come from the air
It will be an overripe pumpkin
It will be the missing shoe

The next one will climb down
From the tree
When I'm asleep

The next one I will have to sow
For the next one I will have
To walk in the rain

The next one I shall not write
It will rise like bread
It will be the curse coming home

"Inscription"

Last night a line appeared,
Unbidden, unsigned:
It had eight memorable
Syllables. *I'll keep you,*

I said, falling asleep.
It's gone now,
And I write this to requite it,
And to mark its passage.

SALMAN RUSHDIE
b. 1947
(English)

Salman Rushdie was born in Bombay to a prosperous Muslim family. He was educated there and in England. His superb talent burst onto the world scene with the publication of Midnight's Children *(1981), a novel that broke the old wood and shot Indian English writing free of conventional Anglophone style with its old colonial echoes and seemingly seamless language. In his pulsating syntax and fragmented sentences, Rushdie gives us a bizarre yet curiously apt narrator, Saleem Sinai, born at the stroke of midnight, August 15, 1947, the very moment at which India attained independence from the British Raj. The narrator's body is filled with loud voices, mimicking the nature of the new republic, a raucous, ancient civilization bubbling with new life, torn apart at the seams. The brilliant novel allowed for a radically new way of conceiving of Indian writing on the world stage. In the title essay of his nonfiction book* Imaginary Homelands *(1992), Rushdie speaks of the past, of the writer looking back at the world he has lost, and how that world must be remade in memory. He offers us a powerful image for the narrative technique he perfected with Saleem Sinai's narration: "It may be that when the Indian writer who writes from outside India tries to reflect that world, he is obliged to deal in broken mirrors, some of whose fragments have been irretrievably lost. [. . .] But there is a paradox here. The broken mirror may actually be as valuable as the one which is supposedly unflawed." Rushdie's brand of magical realism allows him to examine the complications of a divided subcontinent as well as the difficulties of a diasporic existence. In* Satanic Verses *(1988), we see the fraught lives of new immigrants, colored people in Britain, some able to see themselves as Black British, others alienated from their roots and adrift in a world they cannot accustom themselves to.*

That novel includes a character, Salman the Scribe, who inscribes words of the Koran, changing them as he sees fit. In certain Muslim communities the novel was viewed as a blasphemous critique of Islam, and an infamous fatwah was issued by Ayatollah Ruhollah Khomeini. The book was banned in several countries including India, and Rushdie had to go underground for fear of his life. In Joseph Anton: A Memoir *(2012), he gives us a taste of the terrible hardship of those days. Currently living and writing in the United States, Rushdie continues with his writing and his work on behalf of writers and free speech. In addition to his numerous novels, he has published several books of nonfiction. Rushdie has also been involved with the filming of his most celebrated novel,* Midnight's Children, *writing the script himself and producing the voiceover. A prolific writer, his other important works include the novels* Shame *(1983),* The Moor's Last Sigh *(1995),* The Ground Beneath Her Feet *(1999),* Shalimar, the Clown *(2005), and, inspired by Scheherazade's storytelling, the fierce, surreal* Two Years, Eight Months and Twenty-Eight Nights *(2015). In 1981,* Midnight's Children *won the Booker Prize for Literature, and in 1993 by public vote the novel was awarded the Best of the Bookers, to mark the twenty-fifth anniversary of the prize. His novel* The Golden House, *drawing on the turbulence of recent American politics, was published in 2017.*

"Imaginary Homelands"

An old photograph in a cheap frame hangs on a wall of the room where I work. It's a picture, dating from 1946, of a house into which, at the time of its taking, I had not yet been born. The house is rather peculiar—a three-storeyed gabled affair with tiled roofs and round towers in two corners, each wearing a pointy tile hat. "The past is a foreign country," goes the famous opening sentence of L.P. Hartley's novel *The Go-Between*, "they do things differently there." But the photograph tells me to invert this idea: it reminds me that it's my present that is foreign, and that the past is home, albeit a lost home in a lost city in the mists of lost time.

A few years ago I revisited Bombay, which is my lost city, after an absence of something like half my life. Shortly after arriving, acting on an impulse, I opened the telephone directory and looked for my father's name. And, amazingly, there it was: his name, our old address, the unchanged telephone number, as if we had never gone away to the unmentionable country across the border. It was an eerie discovery. I felt as if I were being claimed, or informed that the facts of my faraway life were illusions: that this continuity was the reality. Then I went to visit the house in the photograph and stood outside it, neither daring nor wishing to announce myself to its new owners. (I didn't want to see how they'd ruined the interior.) I was overwhelmed. The photograph had naturally been taken in black and white; and my memory, feeding on such images as this, had begun to see my childhood in the same way, monochromatically. The colours of my history had seeped out of my mind's eye; now my other two eyes were assaulted by colours, by the vividness of the red tiles, the yellow-edged green of cactus-leaves, the brilliance of bougainvillaea creeper. It is probably not too romantic to say that that was when my novel *Midnight's Children* was really born: when I realized how much I wanted to restore the past to myself, not in the faded greys of old family-album snapshots, but whole, in CinemaScope and glorious Technicolor.

Bombay is a city built by foreigners upon reclaimed land; I, who had been away so long that I almost qualified for the title, was gripped by the conviction that I, too, had a city and a history to reclaim.

It may be that writers in my position, exiles or emigrants or expatriates, are haunted by some sense of loss, some urge to reclaim, to look back, even at the risk of being mutated into pillars of salt. But if we do look back, we must also do so in the knowledge—which gives rise to profound uncertainties—that our physical alienation from India almost inevitably means that we will not be capable of reclaiming precisely the thing that was lost: that we will, in short, create fictions, not actual cities or villages, but invisible ones, imaginary homelands, Indias of the mind.

Writing my book in North London, looking out through my window on to a city scene totally unlike the ones I was imagining on to paper, I was constantly plagued by this problem, until I felt obliged to face it in the text, to make clear that (in spite of my original and, I suppose, somewhat Proustian ambition to unlock the gates of lost time so that the past reappeared as it actually had been, unaffected by the distortions of memory) what I was actually doing was a novel of memory and about memory, so that my India was just that: "my" India, a version and no more than one version of all the hundreds of millions of possible versions. I tried to make it as imaginatively true as I could, but imaginative truth is simultaneously honourable and suspect, and I knew that my India may only have been one to which I (who am no longer what I was, and who by quitting Bombay never became what perhaps I was meant to be) was, let us say, willing to admit I belonged.

This is why I made my narrator, Saleem, suspect in his narration: his mistakes are the mistakes of a fallible memory compounded by quirks of character and of circumstance, and his vision is fragmentary. It may be that when the Indian writer who writes from outside India tries to reflect that world, he is obliged to deal in broken mirrors, some of whose fragments have been irretrievably lost.

But there is a paradox here. The broken mirror may actually be as valuable as the one which is supposedly unflawed. Let me again try and explain this from my own experience. Before beginning *Midnight's Children*, I spent many months trying simply to recall as much of the Bombay of the 1950s and 1960s as I could; and not only Bombay—Kashmir, too, and Delhi and Aligarh which, in my book, I've moved to Agra to heighten a certain joke about the Taj Mahal. I was genuinely amazed by how much came back to me. I found myself remembering what clothes people had worn on certain days, and school scenes, and whole passages of Bombay dialogue verbatim, or so it seemed; I even remembered advertisements, film-posters, the neon Jeep sign on Marine Drive, toothpaste ads for Binaca and for Kolynos, and a footbridge over the local railway line which bore, on one side, the legend "Esso puts a tiger in your tank" and, on the other, the curiously contradictory admonition: "Drive like Hell and you will get there." Old songs came back to me from nowhere: a street entertainer's version of "Good Night Ladies," and, from the film *Mr 420* (a very appropriate source for my narrator to have used), the hit number "Mera Joota Hai Japani,"[1] which could almost be Saleem's theme song.

1. *Mera joota hai Japani*
   Yé patloon Inglistani
   Sar pé lal topi Rusi—
   Phir bhi dil hai Hindustani

—which translates roughly as:

O, my shoes are Japanese,
These trousers English, if you please,
On my head, red Russian hat—
My heart's Indian for all that.

I knew that I had tapped a rich seam: but the point I want to make is that of course I'm not gifted with total recall, and it was precisely the partial nature of these memories, their fragmentation, that made them so evocative for me. The shards of memory acquired greater status, greater resonance because they were *remains;* fragmentation made trivial things seem like symbols, and the mundane acquired numinous qualities. The broken pots of antiquity, from which the past can sometimes, but always provisionally, be reconstructed, are exciting to discover, even if they are pieces of the most quotidian objects.

It may be argued that the past is a country from which we have all emigrated, that its loss is part of our common humanity. Which seems to me self-evidently true; but I suggest the writer who is out-of-country, even out-of-language may experience this loss in an intensified form. It is made more concrete for him by the physical fact of discontinuity, of his present being in a different place from his past, of his being "elsewhere." This may enable him to speak properly and concretely on a subject of universal significance and appeal.

But let me go further. The broken glass is not merely a mirror of nostalgia. It is also, I believe, a useful tool with which to work in the present.

John Fowles begins *Daniel Martin* with the words: "Whole sight: or all the rest is desolation." But human beings do not perceive things whole; we are not gods but wounded creatures, cracked lenses, capable only of fractured perceptions. Partial beings, in all the senses of that phrase. Meaning is a shaky edifice we build out of scraps, dogmas, childhood injuries, newspaper articles, chance remarks, old films, small victories, people hated, people loved; perhaps it is because our sense of what is the case is constructed from such inadequate materials that we defend it so fiercely, even to the death. The Fowles position seems to me a way of succumbing to the guru-illusion. Writers are no longer sages, dispensing the wisdom of the centuries. And those of us who have been forced by cultural displacement to accept the provisional nature of all truths, all certainties, have perhaps had modernism forced upon us. We can't lay claim to Olympus, and are thus released to describe our worlds in the way in which all of us, whether writers or not, perceive it from day to day.

In *Midnight's Children,* my narrator Saleem uses, at one point, the metaphor of a cinema screen to discuss this business of perception: "Suppose yourself in a large cinema, sitting at first in the back row, and gradually moving up, . . . until your nose is almost pressed against the screen. Gradually the stars' faces dissolve into dancing grain; tiny details assume grotesque proportions; . . . it becomes clear that the illusion itself is reality." The movement towards the cinema screen is a metaphor for the narrative's movement through time towards the present, and the book itself, as it nears contemporary events, quite deliberately loses deep perspective, becomes more "partial." I wasn't trying to write about (for instance) the Emergency in the same way as I wrote about events half a century earlier. I felt it would be dishonest to pretend, when writing about the day before yesterday, that it was possible to see the whole picture. I showed certain blobs and slabs of the scene.

I once took part in a conference on modern writing at New College, Oxford. Various novelists, myself included, were talking earnestly of such matters as the need for new ways of describing the world. Then the playwright Howard Brenton suggested that this might be a somewhat limited aim: does literature seek to do no more than to describe? Flustered, all the novelists at once began talking about politics.

Let me apply Brenton's question to the specific case of Indian writers, in England, writing about India. Can they do no more than describe, from a distance, the world that they have left? Or does the distance open any other doors?

These are of course political questions, and must be answered at least partly in political terms. I must say first of all that description is itself a political act. The black American writer Richard Wright once wrote that black and white Americans were engaged in a war over the nature of reality. Their descriptions were incompatible. So it is clear that redescribing a world is the necessary first step towards changing it. And particularly at times when the state takes reality into its own hands, and sets about distorting it, altering the past to fit its present needs, that the making of the alternative realities of art, including the novel of memory, becomes politicized. "The struggle of man against power," Milan Kundera has written, "is the struggle of memory against forgetting." Writers and politicians are natural rivals. Both groups try to make the world in their own images; they fight for the same territory. And the novel is one way of denying the official, politicians' version of truth.

The "State truth" about the war in Bangladesh, for instance, is that no atrocities were committed by the Pakistani Army in what was then the East Wing. This version is sanctified by many people who would describe themselves as intellectuals. And the official version of the Emergency in India was well expressed by Mrs Gandhi in a recent BBC interview. She said that there were some people around who claimed that bad things had happened during the Emergency, forced sterilizations, things like that: but, she stated, this was all false. Nothing of this type had ever occurred. The interviewer, Robert Kee, did not probe this statement at all. Instead he told Mrs Gandhi and the Panorama audience that she had proved, many times over, her right to be called a democrat.

So literature can, and perhaps must, give the lie to official facts. But is this a proper function of those of us who write from outside India? Or are we just dilettantes in such affairs, because we are not involved in their day-to-day unfolding, because by speaking out we take no risks, because our personal safety is not threatened? What right do we have to speak at all?

My answer is very simple. Literature is self-validating. That is to say, a book is not justified by its author's worthiness to write it, but by the quality of what has been written. There are terrible books that arise directly out of experience, and extraordinary imaginative feats dealing with themes which the author has been obliged to approach from the outside.

Literature is not in the business of copyrighting certain themes for certain groups. And as for risk: the real risks of any artist are taken in the work, in pushing the work to the limits of what is possible, in the attempt to increase the sum of what it is possible to think. Books become good when they go to this edge and risk falling over it—when they endanger the artist by reason of what he has, or has not, *artistically* dared.

So if I am to speak for Indian writers in England I would say this, paraphrasing G.V. Desani's H. Hatterr: the migrations of the fifties and sixties happened. "We are. We are here." And we are not willing to be excluded from any part of our heritage; which heritage includes both a Bradford-born Indian kid's right to be treated as a full member of British society, and also the right of any member of this post-diaspora community to draw on its roots for its art, just as all the world's community of displaced writers has always done. (I'm thinking, for instance, of Grass's Danzig-become-Gdansk, of Joyce's abandoned Dublin, of Isaac Bashevis Singer and Maxine Hong Kingston and Milan Kundera and many others. It's a long list.)

Let me override at once the faintly defensive note that has crept into these last few remarks. The Indian writer, looking back at India, does so through guilt-tinted spectacles. (I am, of course, once more, talking about myself.) I am speaking now of those of us who emigrated . . . and I suspect that there are times when the move seems wrong to us all, when we seem, to ourselves, post-lapsarian men and women. We are Hindus who have crossed the black water; we are Muslims who eat pork. And as a result—as my use of the Christian notion of the Fall indicates—we are now partly of the West. Our identity is at once plural and partial. Sometimes we feel that we straddle two cultures; at other times, that we fall between two stools. But however ambiguous and shifting this ground may be, it is not an infertile territory for a writer to occupy. If literature is in part the business of finding new angles at which to enter reality, then once again our distance, our long geographical perspective, may provide us with such angles. Or it may be that that is what we must think in order to do our work.

Midnight's Children enters its subject from the point of view of a secular man. I am a member of that generation of Indians who were sold the secular ideal. One of the things I liked, and still like, about India is that it is based on a non-sectarian philosophy. I was not raised in a narrowly Muslim environment; I do not consider Hindu culture to be either alien from me or more important than the Islamic heritage. I believe this has something to do with the nature of Bombay, a metropolis in which the multiplicity of commingled faiths and cultures creates a remarkably secular ambience. Saleem Sinai makes use, eclectically, of whatever elements from whatever sources he chooses. It may have been easier for his author to do this from outside modern India than inside it.

I want to make one last point about the description of India that *Midnight's Children* attempts. It is a point about pessimism. The book has been criticised in India for its allegedly despairing tone. And the despair of the writer-from-outside may indeed look a little easy, a little pat. But I do not see the book as despairing or nihilistic. The point of view of the narrator is not entirely that of the author. What I tried to do was to set up a tension in the text, a paradoxical opposition between the form and content of the narrative. The story of Saleem does indeed lead him to despair. But the story is told in a manner designed to echo, as closely as my abilities allowed, the Indian talent for non-stop self-regeneration. This is why the narrative constantly throws up new stories, why it "teems." The form—

multitudinous, hinting at the infinite possibilities of the country—is the optimistic counterweight to Saleem's personal tragedy. I do not think that a book written in such a manner can really be called a despairing work.

England's Indian writers are, of course, by no means all the same type of animal. Some of us, for instance, are Pakistani. Others Bangladeshi. Others West, or East, or even South African. And V.S. Naipaul, by now, is something else entirely. This word "Indian" is getting to be a pretty scattered concept. Indian writers in England include political exiles, first-generation migrants, affluent expatriates whose residence here is frequently temporary, naturalized Britons, and people born here who may never have laid eyes on the subcontinent. Clearly, nothing that I say can apply across all these categories. But one of the interesting things about this diverse community is that, as far as Indo-British fiction is concerned, its existence changes the ball game, because that fiction is in future going to come as much from addresses in London, Birmingham and Yorkshire as from Delhi or Bombay.

One of the changes has to do with attitudes towards the use of English. Many have referred to the argument about the appropriateness of this language to Indian themes. And I hope all of us share the view that we can't simply use the language in the way the British did; that it needs remaking for our own purposes. Those of us who do use English do so in spite of our ambiguity towards it, or perhaps because of that, perhaps because we can find in that linguistic struggle a reflection of other struggles taking place in the real world, struggles between the cultures within ourselves and the influences at work upon our societies. To conquer English may be to complete the process of making ourselves free.

But the British Indian writer simply does not have the option of rejecting English, anyway. His children, her children, will grow up speaking it, probably as a first language; and in the forging of a British Indian identity the English language is of central importance. It must, in spite of everything, be embraced. (The word "translation" comes, etymologically, from the Latin for "bearing across." Having been borne across the world, we are translated men. It is normally supposed that something always gets lost in translation: I cling, obstinately, to the notion that something can also be gained.)

To be an Indian writer in this society is to face, every day, problems of definition. What does it mean to be "Indian" outside India? How can culture be preserved without becoming ossified? How should we discuss the need for change within ourselves and our community without seeming to play into the hands of our racial enemies? What are the consequences, both spiritual and practical, of refusing to make any concessions to Western ideas and practices? What are the consequences of embracing those ideas and practices and turning away from the ones that came here with us? These questions are all a single, existential question: How are we to live in the world?

I do not propose to offer, prescriptively, any answers to these questions; only to state that these are some of the issues with which each of us will have to come to terms.

To turn my eyes outwards now, and to say a little about the relationship between the Indian writer and the majority white culture in whose midst he lives, and with which his work will sooner or later have to deal:

In common with many Bombay-raised middle-class children of my generation, I grew up with an intimate knowledge of, and even sense of friendship with, a certain kind of England: a dream-England composed of Test Matches at Lord's presided over by the voice of John Arlott, at which Freddie Trueman bowled unceasingly and without success at Polly Umrigar; of Enid Blyton and Billy Bunter, in which we were even prepared to smile indulgently at portraits such as "Hurree Jamset Ram Singh," "the dusky nabob of Bhanipur." I wanted to come to England. I couldn't wait. And to be fair, England has done all right by me; but I find it a little difficult to be properly grateful. I can't escape the view that my relatively easy ride is not the result of the dream-England's famous sense of tolerance and fair play, but of my social class, my freak fair skin and my "English" English accent. Take away any of these, and the story would have been very different. Because of course the dream-England is no more than a dream.

Sadly, it's a dream from which too many white Britons refuse to awake. Recently, on a live radio programme, a professional humorist asked me, in all seriousness, why I objected to being called a wog. He said he had always thought it a rather charming word, a term of endearment. "I was at the zoo the other day," he revealed, "and a zoo keeper told me that the wogs were best with the animals; they stuck their fingers in their ears and wiggled them about and the animals felt at home." The ghost of Hurree Jamset Ram Singh walks among us still.

As Richard Wright found long ago in America, black and white descriptions of society are no longer compatible. Fantasy, or the mingling of fantasy and naturalism, is one way of dealing with these problems. It offers a way of echoing in the form of our work the issues faced by all of us: how to build a new, "modern" world out of an old, legend-haunted civilization, an old culture which we have brought into the heart of a newer one. But whatever technical solutions we may find, Indian writers in these islands, like others who have migrated to the north from the south, are capable of writing from a kind of double perspective: because they, we, are at one and the same time insiders and outsiders in this society. This stereoscopic vision is perhaps what we can offer in place of "whole sight."

There is one last idea that I should like to explore, even though it may, on first hearing, seem to contradict much of what I've so far said. It is this: of all the many elephant traps lying ahead of us, the largest and most dangerous pitfall would be the adoption of a ghetto mentality. To forget that there is a world beyond the community to which we belong, to confine ourselves within narrowly defined cultural frontiers, would be, I believe, to go voluntarily into that form of internal exile which in South Africa is called the "homeland." We must guard against creating, for the most virtuous of reasons, British-Indian literary equivalents of Bophuthatswana or the Transkei.

This raises immediately the question of whom one is writing "for." My own, short answer is that I have never had a reader in mind. I have ideas, people, events, shapes, and I write "for" those things, and hope that the completed work will be of interest to others. But which others? In the case of *Midnight's Children* I certainly felt that if its subcontinental readers had rejected the work, I should have thought it a failure, no matter what the reaction in the West. So I would say that I write "for" people who feel part of the things I write "about": but also for everyone else whom I can reach. In this I am of the same opinion as the black American writer Ralph Ellison, who, in his collection of essays *Shadow and Act,* says that he finds something precious in being black in America at this time; but that he is also reaching for more than that. "I was taken very early," he writes, "with a passion to link together all I loved within the Negro community and all those things I felt in the world which lay beyond."

Art is a passion of the mind. And the imagination works best when it is most free. Western writers have felt free to be eclectic in their selection of theme, setting, form; Western visual artists have, in this century, been happily raiding the visual storehouses of Africa, Asia, the Philippines. I am sure that we must grant ourselves an equal freedom.

Let me suggest that Indian writers in England have access to a second tradition, however, quite apart from their own racial history. It is the cultural and political history of the phenomenon of migration, displacement, life in a minority group. We can quite legitimately claim as our ancestors the Huguenots, the Irish, the Jews; the past to which we belong is an English past, the history of immigrant Britain. Swift, Conrad, Marx are as much our literary forebears as Tagore or Ram Mohan Roy. America, a nation of immigrants, has created great literature out of the phenomenon of cultural transplantation, out of examining the ways in which people cope with a new world: it may be that by discovering what we have in common with those who preceded us into this country, we can begin to do the same.

I stress this is only one of many possible strategies. But we are inescapably international writers at a time when the novel has never been a more international form (a writer like Borges speaks of the influence of Robert Louis Stevenson on his work; Heinrich Böll acknowledges the influence of Irish literature; cross-pollination is everywhere); and it is perhaps one of the more pleasant freedoms of the literary migrant to be able to choose his parents. My own—selected half-consciously, half-not—include Gogol, Cervantes, Kafka, Melville, Machado de Assis: a polyglot family tree, against which I measure myself, and to which I would be honoured to belong.

There's a beautiful image in Saul Bellow's latest novel, *The Dean's December*. The central character, the Dean, Corde, hears a dog barking wildly somewhere. He imagines that the barking is the dog's protest against the limits of dog experience: "For God's sake," the dog is saying, "open the universe a little more!" And because Bellow is, of course, not really talking about dogs, or not only about dogs, I have the feeling that the dog's rage, and its desire, is also mine, ours, everyone's. "For God's sake, open the universe a little more!"

AGHA SHAHID ALI

1949–2001

(English)

Agha Shahid Ali was born in Delhi to a Kashmiri Muslim family. After his early years in India, he came to the United States as a graduate student. His poetry, composed in English, is marked by a filigreed texture, deeply influenced by Urdu and Persian poetry. Kashmir, his homeland, becomes a central, tragic zone, sometimes bodied forth as the lost Beloved of Sufi writing. Splintered geographies, often brilliantly colored, are pieced together even as memory struggles for precisely what history cannot afford—a paradise on earth. Ali was influential in American poetry, popularizing the ghazal, *a poetic form drawn from Urdu and Persian using multiple rhyming couplets, any of which, while contributing to the effect of the whole, is capable of standing apart. Often the ghazal has an erotic or mystical meaning that might flow into or indeed stand in counterpoint to the last line of the very last couplet, which embeds the author's name, the "I" who has voiced the ghazal. The elegiac power of Ali's poetry, while persistent throughout, rises to a particular intensity in his last book,* Rooms Are Never Finished *(2002). It opens with a moving elegy for his mother entitled "Lenox Hill," the name of the hospital where she died of brain cancer, the disease that was to claim Ali himself: "How her breathing drowns out the universe / as she sleeps in Amherst. Windows open on Kashmir: [. . .] / O Destroyer, let her return there, if just to die." His work creates a shimmering dissonance, one place tearing open to reveal another, the whole held together in the intricacy of form. Often, even as the voice reaches into the pain of history, the poem addresses an intimate Other, a fellow poet or friend living or dead. Ali has translated poems from the Urdu of Faiz Ahmed Faiz, which he published as* The Rebel's Silhouette *(1995). Influences on Ali's work include Faiz himself, Emily Dickinson, and James Merrill, as well as poets such as Constantine Cavafy and Gabriel Garcia Lorca. In Ali's work there is a poignant and tender connection with the writing of other gay men, ghosts who haunt the poet and allow him to enter into an invisible community. Ali's important works include* The Half-Inch Himalayas *(1987),* The Country Without a Post Office *(1997), and the posthumously published collected poems,* The Veiled Suite *(2009).*

From "In Search of Evanescence"

"It was a year of brilliant water."
—THOMAS DE QUINCEY

I

Students of mist
climbing the stairs like dust
washing history off the shelves
will never know this house never
that professors here in glass sneakers
used window squares for crosswords
moving the weather from sky to sky
under their arms new editions of water

while mirrors left lying on coffee tables
tore the glare from the windows
and glued vanishing rainbows
to the walls the ceilings

will never know the sun's quick reprints

2

It was a year of brilliant water
in Pennsylvania that final summer
seven years ago, the sun's quick reprints

in my attaché case: those students
of mist have drenched me with dew, I'm driving
away from that widow's house, my eyes open

to dream of drowning. But even
when I pass—in Ohio—the one exit
to Calcutta, I don't know I've begun

mapping America, the city limits
of Evanescence now everywhere. It
was a year of brilliant water, Phil,

such a cadence of dead seas at each turn:
so much refused to breathe in those painted
reflections, trapped there in ripples of hills:

a woman climbed the steps to Acoma,
vanished into the sky. In the ghost towns
of Arizona, there were charcoal tribes

with desert voices, among their faces
always the last speaker of a language.
And there was always thirst: a train taking me

from Bisbee, that copper landscape with bones,
into a twilight with no water, Phil,
I never told you where I'd been these years,

swearing fidelity to anyone.
Now there's only regret: I didn't send you
my routes of Evanescence. You never wrote.

3

When on Route 80 in Ohio
I came across an exit
to Calcutta

the temptation to write a poem
led me past the exit
so I could say

India always exists
off the turnpikes
of America

so I could say
I did take the exit
and crossed Howrah

and even mention the Ganges
as it continued its sobbing
under the bridge

so when I paid my toll
I saw trains rush by
one after one

on their roofs old passengers
each ready to surrender
his bones for tickets

so that I heard
the sun's percussion
on tamarind leaves

heard the empty cans of children
filling only with the shadows
of leaves

that behind the unloading trucks
were the voices of vendors
bargaining over women

so when the trees
let down their tresses
the monsoon oiled and braided them

and when the wind again parted them
this was the temptation
to end the poem this way:

The warm rains have left
many dead on the pavements

The signs to Route 80
all have disappeared

And now by the road is a river
polished silver by cars

The cars are urns
carrying ashes to the sea

                        4

Someone wants me to live   A language will die with me

                    (once
spoken by proud tribesmen
in the canyons east
of the Catalinas   or much farther north

in the Superstition Mountains)   It will die with me

(Someone wants me to live)

It has the richest consonants   exact
for any cluster of sorrows

that haunts the survivors of Dispersal   that country
which has no map

but it has histories   most
of them forgotten
scraps of folklore   (once

agha shahid ali

in mountains   there were silver cities
with flags   on every rooftop
on each flag a prayer   read

by the wind   a passer-by forgiven all
when the wind became his shirt)

Someone wants me to live
so he can learn

those prayers
that language   he is asking me
questions

He wants me to live

and as I speak he is freezing
my words   he will melt them
years later

to listen   and listen
to the water   of my voice

when he is the last
speaker of his language

5

From the Faraway Nearby—
of Georgia O'Keeffe—these words—
Black Iris—Dark Iris—Abstraction, Blue—
her hands—around—a skull—

"The plains—the wonderful—
great big sky—makes me—
want to breathe—so deep—
that I'll break—"

From her Train—at Night—in the Desert—
I its only—passenger—

I see—as they pass by—her red hills—
black petals—landscapes with skulls—

"There is—so much—of it—
I want to get outside—of it all—
I would—if I could—
even if it killed me—"

6

"I have no house, only a shadow."
—MALCOLM LOWRY

In Pennsylvania seven years ago,
it was a year of brilliant water,
a resonance of oceans at each turn.

It's again that summer, Phil, and the end
of that summer again: you are driving
toward the Atlantic, drowning in my

brilliant dream of water. I too am leaving,
the sun's reprints mine. There are red hills
at the end of my drive through three thousand

miles of Abstraction, Blue—the Blue that will
always be here after all destruction
is finished. "Phil was afraid of being

forgotten." But it's again a year of water,
and in a house always brilliant with lights
I'm saying to a stranger what I should

have said to you: "I have no house only
a shadow but whenever you are in need
of a shadow my shadow is yours."

agha shahid ali

NAMDEO DHASAL

1949–2014

(Marathi)

Namdeo Dhasal was born into an Untouchable family in the village of Pur-Kanersar outside Bombay. He recalls how as a child he swam with friends in the village well. The children were stoned by the guard, who feared that Untouchable children would pollute the well. Poetry came to him early. In an autobiographical essay, "Namdeo on Namdeo," he writes, "For what makes one speak or write are the themes that create an excruciating turmoil inside you, heighten your sensitivity and leave you tenderly troubled. This is the sort of inner disturbance from which my poems come." His imagination was molded by the violence he experienced, both in his childhood village and in the metropolis of Bombay where his parents took him as a young child. There he earned a living as a taxi driver, living and working in the red-light district, involved in the life of gangsters, prostitutes, and drug dealers, an infernal underworld he dubbed "do number ki duniya"—number two world—a netherworld cut from seeming normalcy, a twilight zone that he called the true source of his inspiration. His volume of poetry Golpitha *(1972), the name of a notorious red-light district, brought him early acclaim. Fellow poets and critics admired his surreal imagery, coruscating language, and the ways in which the argot of the place was woven into literary Marathi, creating a rhythmic, strophic line of great aural power. For Dhasal, his dark muse, a female prostitute, enticed him into the stench and nausea of the netherland to which he was bound. In "Namdeo on Namdeo" the poet says, "Even* Golpitha *was an attempt to inter-*

pret myself. What is poetry but autobiography anyway? Even political poetry is autobiographical. Take the examples of Mayakovsky and Neruda." Dhasal was one of the founding members of the Dalit Panthers, an organization modeled on the Black Panthers that advocated violent resistance against an unjust caste system. Ever the activist, he launched the Tiraskrut Nari Sanghatana (Association of Loathed Women) for the empowerment of sex workers. But it was poetry that gave him a true anchorage in the world. He is reported to have said to his friend Dilip Chitre that poetry saved him and if he had not been a poet, he would have been the keeper of a brothel or a gangster. The songs and poetry he heard as a child, poems of the mystical bhakti movement, inspired him to go in search of poetic redemption. In his poem "Mandakini Patil: A Young Prostitute, My Intended Collage," the abecedary is used to great effect, highlighting the surreal process of forging a poetic language out of a fixed script. The emptiness of mere words is set by the side of sensual reality, the dark and vital realm of flesh. For many years, side by side with his poetry and Dalit activism, Dhasal wrote political columns for Marathi newspapers. In addition to Golpitha, Dhasal's important works include volumes of poetry such as Khel *(1983)* and Mee Marale Sooryacha Rathache Ghode Saat *(I Slew the Seven Horses of the Sun, 2005),* as well as two novels. In 2004, he received the Sahitya Akademi Lifetime Achievement Award.

"Approaching the Organized Harem of the Octopus"

We are approaching the organized harem of the octopus
I am the seal bearing the image of the bull dated March '65
My properties are Mohenjodaro
I am the one who drew the head on the lion pillar
My ornamental daily weather
Radiates from the feet
From hand-to-hand I release my catacombs
Go scatter curds milk butter in the courtyard
Organised harems of the octopus are approaching us

Frightening grotesque people eating
Starvation underlined in decimals
In the womb of 1970

Menstruating broad
The capable hand in bed holds a partisan inferno
Bhang in the intestines
Those who are wearing gum-boots may raise their hands
Organised harems of the octopus are approaching us
After she conceives the female eats up the male
1234567890 are all numbers on the trees
We have to absorb the slowness of a day in our own momentum
Place a weathered face in the flesh market
Pluck it out of the flesh market
There is a four and a zero before us
The zero can generate four scattering away in four dimensions

If a zero is placed after four it becomes forty
If a zero is placed under four it gets a strong foundation
Four-zero accompany us when we say "*Inquilaab Zindabaad!*"
We plant "*the Banner of Blood*"
Those who were gloomy while frisking four and zero
Remained forever the slaves of slaves
After she conceives the female eats up the male
Go scatter curds milk butter in the courtyard
Organised harems of the octopus are approaching us.

"Mandakini Patil: A Young Prostitute, My Intended Collage"

On a barren blue canvas
Her clothes ripped off, her thigh blasted open,
A sixteen-year-old girl surrendering herself to pain.
And a pig: its snout full of blood.

The face that seems attractive is not really a face:
Behind it lies the bitter reality of a skull, the ordinary truth.
When someone's flesh is ripped out
To what terminal do the parts of the skeleton lead you?
In the backyard of love, all you find is fruits of fear and disgust.

An infinite and sovereign nothingness stalks us all.
People whom we regard as our own are mere heaps of dust or
   smoke.
Alif is for anar
Be is for bandar
Pe is for pankha
Te is for talwar
Te is for tattoo
Se is for samar

So is the worship of the geographic contours of man
And the romance of arse-fucking

Manda
Your mind is neither of ash nor marble
I feel your hair, your clothes, your nails, your breasts

as though they were my own: they reveal to me, within myself
colonies of the dead; hunchbacks left to die in the streets;
Sandwiches; streets; milk of a she-dog that's just given birth to her
   litter;
They do not let me reach up to you; up to your lips; up to your
   eyes.
Until now, you and I were unrelated to each other.
And there were no calls to each other burrowing holes in us.
This period is as long as ten miles; as close as ten seconds;
And in its aria
You: Me: Seeds: A splinter of glass nibbling us;
And a thousand states of being.
Never before had I seen a face so devoid of light
As was yours; and of a thousand other females like you.
Flashing out from so many countries, and so many cages;
And bearing so many different names.
Now I've developed a taste for a withered tree; as well as its
   dried-up bark.

"The Day She Was Gone"

The day she was gone,
I painted my face black.
I slapped the savage schizophrenic wind hard in its face.
I picked up small pieces of my life
And stood naked in front of a cracked mirror.
I allowed me to wreak vengeance upon myself.
I stared condescendingly at the Sun and said, "You screwball!"
I showered choice curses upon all artists who paint dreams;
I walked from the East towards the West;
I picked stones I found on the way and hurled them at myself.
How boisterously flows this water in its fit of laughter
Through mountains and gorges.
What ocean is it seeking to meet?
Or will it seep
Into the soil at sea-level?
Did even I belong to myself
On the day she was gone?
I could not even embrace her dead body
And cry my heart out.
The day she was gone,
I painted my face black.

namdeo dhasal

MEENA ALEXANDER

b. 1951

(English)

Meena Alexander was born in Allahabad and brought up in her grandparental home in Kerala. As a child she was able to roam freely in the paddy fields and orchards. She left India with her mother to join her father, who was posted to Khartoum, Sudan. On that first ocean voyage, an event that was to mark her deeply, the child turned five. Alexander's earliest poems were composed both in English and French and published in Arabic translation in Sudan. She writes of how her mother tongue, Malayalam, as well as French and Arabic, braided together in her imagination. In a book of essays, Poetics of Dislocation, *she writes, "Can one find a home in language? I feel so. At least, that is what I have tried to do. [. . .] The English I use bends and flows to many other languages. For me it is the language of Donne and Wordsworth as well as a postcolonial tongue and it exerts an intimate violence, even as I use it, make it mine." In a long poem, "Illiterate Heart," the speaker evokes the shock of being forced to learn a script, construed by the child as a prison house. There is a longing instead for the syllables to remain as voice and rhythmic speech. The poets Jayanta Mahapatra and Kamala Das were important influences in Alexander's years as a young writer in India. Alexander's book* Raw Silk *(2004) includes a cycle of poems entitled "Letters to Gandhi," composed after a visit to the relief camps in Gujarat for the survivors of the ethnic violence. Questions of dislocation, metamorphosis, and self-identity recur in her poems, and much of her work is stitched through with elements of urban life, evoking*

New York City where she has lived for many years. Even as the present anchors her, place in her poems becomes a palimpsest that in its many layers reveals what no longer exists, what appears only in the imagination—an elsewhere and with it a past that has disappeared. As with other diasporic writers, we find the poet searching time and again for a space to call home. In her poems she evokes the shelter that the act of writing provides. In addition to poetry, Alexander has published essays, two novels, and a memoir, Fault Lines *(1993). In 2003 a new edition of the memoir appeared with an addition, "Book of Childhood," based on memories that were previously lost. Her volumes of poetry include* Illiterate Heart *(2002),* Birthplace with Buried Stones *(2013), and* Atmospheric Embroidery *(2018).*

From "Illiterate Heart"

11

How did I come to this script?
Amma taught me from the Reading Made Easy
books, Steps 1 & 2 pointed out Tom and Bess
little English children
sweet vowels of flesh they mouthed to perfection:
aa ee ii oo uu a (apple) b (bat) c (cat) d (dat)
Dat? I could not get, so keen the rhymes made me,
sense overthrown.

Those children wore starched knickerbockers
or sailor suits and caps,
waved Union Jacks,
tilted at sugar beets.

O white as milk
their winding sheets!

I imagined them dead all winter
packed into icicles,
tiny and red, frail homunculus each one
sucking on alphabets.

Amma took great care with the books,
wrapped them in newsprint lest something
should spill, set them on the rosewood sill.
When wild doves perched they shook
droplets from quicksilver wings
onto fading covers.

The books sat between Gandhi's *Experiments
with Truth* and a minute crown of thorns
a visiting bishop brought.

He told us that the people of Jerusalem
spoke many tongues including Arabic, Persian,
Syriac as in our liturgy, Aramaic too.

Donkeys dragged weights through tiny streets.
Like our buffaloes, he laughed.
I had to perform my *Jana Gana Mana* for him
and Wordsworth's daffodil poem—
the latter I turned into a rural terror,
my version of the chartered streets.

III

What beats in my heart? Who can tell?
I cannot tease my writing hand around
that burnt hole of sense, figure out the
quickstep of syllables.

On pages where I read the words of Gandhi
and Marx, saw the light of the Gospels,
the script started to quiver and flick.

Letters grew fins and tails.
Swords sprang from the hips of consonants,
vowels grew ribbed and sharp.
Pages bound into leather
turned the color of ink.

My body flew apart:
wrist, throat, elbow, thigh,
knee where a mole rose,
bony scapula, blunt-cut hair,

then utter stillness as a white sheet
dropped on nostrils and neck.

Black milk of childhood drunk
and drunk again!

I longed to be like Tom and Bess
dead flat on paper.

IV

At noon I burrowed through
Malayalam sounds,
slashes of sense, a floating trail.

Nights I raced into the garden.
Smoke on my tongue, wet earth
from twisted roots of banyan
and arbor-tristis.

What burnt in the mirror
of the great house
became a fierce condiment.
A métier almost:

aa I ii u uu au um aha ka kh
ga gha nga cha chha ja ja nja
njana (my sole self), *njaman* (knowledge)
nunni (gratitude) *ammechi, appechan,*
veliappechan (grandfather).

Uproar of sense, harsh tutelage:
aana (elephant), *amma* (tortoise)
ambjuan (lotus).

A child mouthing words
to flee family.

I will never enter that house, I swore,
I'll never be locked in a cage of script.

And the lotus rose, quietly, quietly,
I committed that to memory,
later added: *ce lieu me plaît
dominé de flambeaux.*

v

In dreams I was a child babbling
at the gate splitting into two,
three to make herself safe.

Grown women combing black hair
in moonlight by the railroad track,
stuck forever at the accidental edge.

O the body in parts,
bruised buttress of heaven!
she cries,

a child in a village church
clambering into embroidered vestments
to sing at midnight a high sweet tune.

Or older now
musing in sunlight
combing a few white strands of hair.

To be able to fail.
To set oneself up
so that failure is also possible.

Yes,
that too
however it is grasped.

The movement towards self-definition.
A woman walking the streets,
a woman combing her hair.

Can this make music in your head?
Can you whistle hot tunes
to educate the barbarians?

"Crossroad"

In memory of Mahasweta Devi 1926–2016

I

So there I was, almost at the crossroad
Stuck in a sudden storm of bikers, men in leather, engines snarling.
Flags spurt skywards.

I froze at the metal barricade, the seam of sense unpicked,
Brown body splayed.
In the aftermath of light, what proof is there of love—

Buoyancy of the soul hard to mark
Apart from the body
Its tenuous equilibrium unpicked,

Wave after wave of arrival
Etching questions in encircling air
As if life depended on such flammable notations.

II

You come, sari with blue border blowing,
Just as I saw you first, head bare.
A sudden turn on asphalt, you reach out your arms

As if in a palash grove and call to me—
Come over here!
Sometimes the bleeding petals bring down a house

Bring down a Republic.
Children are bought and sold for money—
Ghee to burn her. Teen taka. Ten rupees. Ek taka one rupee.

Cloth to cover her with.
Camphor for the burning. Bhang to make her drowsy.
Turmeric. Chandan.

You halt at the crossroad, hair thrummed by a savage wind
(Later I try to follow marks of feet, touch cold cotton
That lashed your flesh in place).

III

I hear your voice—
Brood, and it will come, a seizure of sense, a reckoning:
Write with chalk, sticks of lead, anything to hand

Use a bone, a safety pin, a nail, write on paper or stone
Let the poem smolder in memory.
In the desolation of time write

How one inked the bubble with a woman's name
Way at the top of the paper ballot, saw her own hand quiver.
This was in the school with empty metal desks, near Fort Tryon
    Park.

One set her nipple to her infant's lips
Felt her heart sprout wings, flit over the barbed wire
Of the Immigration Detention Center.

One whimpered in her sleep—Mother, I know I am a tree,
I trail my roots behind me, the man with bad hair will axe me
    down.
One daubed her face with white paint, crawled

Into a cage outside the museum, hung a sign round
Her own neck—*We are barbarians come to live amongst you,*
Some of us speak this language.

IV

Hoarse already, you whisper—
Come closer to me.
You who were born in the Gangetic plains

A year after mid-century
Consider the fragility of the horizon,
The arc of stars into which your father raised you.

When you fall, as surely you will one day
Try to swim forward into blackness
Arms pointing to where you imagine the vault of heaven to be

As Draupadi did, a great-throated cry
She made in the forest,
Only the birds could save her, they picked up her cries.

Think of Antigone, who anointed her brother's corpse with dirt
To keep away the wild dogs,
She too made bird sounds, guttural cries.

Go to Standing Rock, where people mass outside their tents
In splintering cold, to guard the quiet springs of water.
There the palash blooms,

Tree used for timber, resin, dye,
Tinting the nails of the love god.
On its leaves names swarm—

Anna Mae Aquash, Balbir Singh Sodhi, Eric Garner, Freddie Grey,
Julia de Burgos, countless more.
Thrust from earth's core

From the shadow of musk deer,
The green throat of the humming bird,
In the honeycomb of light, they step forward to be counted.

meena alexander

GITHA HARIHARAN
b. 1954
(English)

Githa Hariharan was born in Coimbatore and grew up in Bombay and Manila. She currently lives and works in Delhi. Her fiction, composed in English, often links the everyday life of a modern Indian woman to earlier ways of being, lives lived out in the traditional households of Brahmin south India, a past that the female protagonist needs to relinquish and then return to in memory, even as she seeks out her own freedom to live and love. Hariharan's imagination is powerfully linked to the political world and the struggle for social justice. In a court case in 1995, she fought the Hindu Minority and Guardianship Act, which would have prevented her as a married woman from being an equal guardian to her two young sons. Indeed, the rights of women are central to her concern with civil liberties in a country that has time and again pitched toward sectarian violence. In her novel Fugitive Histories *(2009), a young scriptwriter, Sara (who has a Muslim father and a Hindu mother), travels to Ahmedabad, the scene of a pogrom against Muslims, to collect material for her film script. But the young woman's life is invaded by memories: some from her own past, others from the traumatized children of the refugee precinct. In the novel, even as Sara enters the "dark smoky pit of the story," she wonders about her own rights in the matter. She hears a voice ask, "Can your voice ever be theirs? Who are you to speak for them?" And Sara's mother, Mala, in the struggle to reinvent herself after her husband's death, is forced to confront the old world of religious and caste divisions. As she mourns his death, Mala recovers her artist husband's sketchbooks with stark images that evoke a zone words cannot reach.*

The preoccupation with storytelling as a way to make sense of life was there from the start in Hariharan's work. In the finely chiseled first novel The Thousand Faces of Night *(1992), the stories are passed down from the grandmother to the granddaughter. In* When Dreams Travel *(1999), based on a retelling of the Arabian 1,001 Nights, the novelist writes of her fascination with the story within the story and her desire to reinvent Scheherazade, who was able to battle against death with the power of her words: "We too share Scheherazade's situation—but only in the 'real life' of dreams, of imagination, of possibility. I say 'real life,' because without a belief in the possibility of reason containing violence, what business do we have to continue living?" Other works include* The Ghosts of Vasu Master *(1994) and* In Times of Siege *(2003). In 1993, she was awarded the Commonwealth Writers Prize.*

"A Note on Writing *When Dreams Travel*"

I have always been fascinated by Scheherazade. Going by the evidence, this is a fascination shared by many others over the centuries.

In fact, the entire frame story of the Arabian Nights is irresistible. There is a man who rules, as so many have done and as so many do. And like many powerful men, this man, Sultan Shahriyar, is vulnerable, and his vulnerability makes him madly cruel. Shahriyar has decided that the only way to cope with the fear of betrayal—in his case, by his wife—is to bed a woman, then kill her before she can be unfaithful to him. The sultan's fear is specific, and so is his strategy to contain it. But the situation that results asks a universal question. What do you do when a ruler, or an official, or someone in a position of power and responsibility, uses force to extract obedience? When he sheds blood to keep his authority from being challenged? It's the response offered to this question that makes the story so perfect. In this battle with violently oppressive power—the worst kind of power—the weapons are made of words. And the most important soldier on the battlefield is a young woman.

Scheherazade undertook the most unique mission ever undertaken by either a subject or a storyteller—saving her life, and that of her fellow-citizens, through her body of stories. At the heart of the Scheherazade story, a story that has travelled in so many different forms to different parts of the world, is this oddity that needs to be explained in some way or the other. In this story of a subject bringing a ruler to his senses, a story of a storyteller reconciling her audience to the difficulties of continuing with normal life despite fear of betrayal, it is not a man, the sultan's venerable wazir for instance, who performs the difficult task. It's a woman.

Though Shahriyar's tactics are somewhat extreme, his situation—the man of power who has become a despotic enemy of the people—is not really unfamiliar to us. It's Scheherazade's position that is trickier to describe, though her story as a speaking fighter, an activist who talks the tyrant into putting reason before force, has had such a strong resonance for people through the ages. We too share Scheherazade's situation—but only in the "real life" of dreams, of imagination, of possibility. I say "real life," because without a belief in the possibility of reason containing violence, what business do we have to continue living? It would be impossible to live with the prospect of being ruled, of being subjected by this or that oppressive authority, if we could not see the possibility of a rescue mission.

To me, the most interesting fact of the Scheherazade story is not just that it is a storyteller who undertakes such a rescue mission, but a woman storyteller. My suspicion is that this explains much of the fascination with the figure of Scheherazade—and much of the need to explain her, tame her, and in reaction to this domestication, re-appropriate her into a feminist icon.

Whether you are reading Borges or a bowdlerized children's book, or seeing the "exotic" harem-world of Scheherazade in famous European paintings or a B-grade Hollywood film on the Arabian Nights, you come face to face with a reconstruction of Scheherazade. And the way in which she is reconstructed—how she looks, what her weapons are, says a great deal about whoever is doing the imaginative remembering.

Scheherazade told stories for a thousand and one nights. But what happened during the days that came before the nights? Did she have a team behind the scenes supporting her, helping her prepare for the night's assignment? When did she have her children? And what kind of a life did she make for herself from the thousand and second day onward? These were just a few of the questions that teased me as I wrote a story called "A

Night with Scheherazade." The questions grew in number and complexity once the story was done. Maybe that's why "A Night with Scheherazade" changed, over time, into "The Morning After," the last chapter of my novel *When Dreams Travel*. (Over the first several drafts, the novel was called *Dreaming with Scheherazade*.)

The novel began, at an obvious level, with the mother of all storytellers, Scheherazade. Or Shahrzad, a more meaningful name to me since it indicated clearly that she was "born of the city." But the real entry point into the novel came as the next step. I saw, in the darkness surrounding Shahrzad, a silent accomplice, her sister Dunyazad. Dunyazad occupied a part of the stage that was almost unlit. It is always this mysterious, unknown corner of a story that sets the writer going. I was not sure that my voice could be grafted on to Shahrzad's. I needed a more silent space to fill up, a relatively voiceless woman to be made articulate. Dunyazad, "born of the world," seemed ideal as a vehicle for my traveling story. Dunyazad's position as the unheard younger sister, the yearning, questioning follower, allowed me to step into the story as a writer.

Once I have a beginning that holds me, I do a lot of groundwork—planning, reading, making detailed notes. Then I take the plunge. I put aside what I have read or written, and begin work on what I think of as the skeleton of the book. This, I think, is the hardest part, and you feel as lonely as you might in a wilderness you have to find your way out of. Once I have the skeleton, I go back to reading and making notes. For *When Dreams Travel*, I read a great deal that did not necessarily get used in any direct way in the final manuscript. I read about Baghdad, about Islamic queens, about the concept of the harem, about the Mughals and their buildings, even about maritime links between India and the Middle East. Sometimes it is difficult to stop reading; there is so much you want to hint at in the background of your invented landscape. But I do put away my notes once I go back to my skeleton-manuscript. This is when I begin adding bits of flesh here and there, shaping it as I go along.

My novel *When Dreams Travel* begins at the point when the frame story of The Arabian Nights ends. But to talk of beginnings and endings is to oversimplify the structure of the Nights and the subtle relationships it has with its children and grandchildren, work such as mine. What attracted me in particular about the Arabian Nights? Its inclusive nature, what Borges calls its labyrinthine quality. I love the story within a story format. It allows you to take a theme, in this case power and sexuality, and construct a series of Chinese boxes. You open one box to find another and another and another till your narrative has penetrated to the smallest box, the kernel of the matter. The Arabian Nights also has all kinds of stories—the fabulous, the moral, the bawdy and the childlike. The challenge was to take parts of the framework story as a starting point without losing my way in the extravagance of design or language you find in the Arabian Nights. I wanted my novel to acknowledge the Arabian Nights as an ancestor, not as a model. All the stories in *When Dreams Travel* are my inventions and they have very real links with contemporary lives. Finally, what I wanted to do was create modern myths to help examine power struggles, but with the Arabian Nights as my point of departure.

It was clear to me that the "modern myths" I wanted to construct had to be composite entities. So I could start off with one woman's voice, say Shahrzad's voice, but to understand what she was saying and who she was, I had to have an entire cluster of voices. I had to imagine and write stories that would help an entire army of women speak.

All through *When Dreams Travel* I was fascinated by the different sorts of storytelling voices that make up such an army—including the storytelling voice that is threatened into temporary or permanent silence. There's the Shahrzad sort of storyteller, a "martyr" who talks to save her life. Then there's the other sort of martyred storyteller, the kind who has to actually fall silent to stay alive. In our time of fatwas, not just the ayatollah's fatwa but our own day-to-day fatwas in different parts of the world, this kind of figure is very much part of the storytelling landscape. So I made up a character, a poet called Satyasama—a teller of composite "truths in the sky." (Her name is made up of the Sanskrit *satya* or truth and the Arabic *sama* or sky.) Satyasama is only a "woman poet" and she lives on the margins of society; yet she is perceived as a threat. Exploring this reality could be one way of understanding the tremendous power of story-making, storytelling, as well as listening to stories.

I also wanted the ending of *When Dreams Travel* to be provocative, a direct challenge from that old warhorse Shahrzad. So I have her say, "I fought for myself, and yes, for you as well. And you—what will you do when your turn comes?" The ending had to indicate that the story has to continue, Shahrzad has to live, and the story—and the retold story—will never quite finish. Someone else will come along, pick it up and continue.

VIJAY SESHADRI

b. 1954

(English)

Vijay Seshadri was born in Bangalore and raised in the United States where he arrived at the age of five with his parents. He grew up in Columbus, Ohio, and the feeling of "strangeness" that he speaks of, something he felt as a boy, often permeates his poetry, transmuted into a fascination with the metaphysical. The knotty puzzlement of things, and how we inhere in the world with all its oddities, enters into his writing. Voices sometimes distinctly oddball open up and bear witness to how what is seen and felt by the perceiving self becomes the fabric of the world. In an essay "The Nature of the Chemical Bond" that is in large part about his growing up in the Midwest, Seshadri writes, "We were doubly strange: strange because Indians are strange even in India, having been exiled from time and history by an overdeveloped supersaturated civilization, and strange also because no one remotely resembling us had ever before lived where we lived." Seshadri has acknowledged the importance of Robert Frost and Elizabeth Bishop to his writing, and he speaks of how the poet must often try to deal with a history he has not chosen.

In his poems we are often invited to follow the speaker in his quirky, idiosyncratic wanderings, sometimes on foot, sometimes in a vehicle, and oftentimes in the inner space of a room. A poet for whom both the concrete particular and the horizon of the impalpable take on cardinal importance, Seshadri sharpens his long lines, at times reminiscent of prose lines, charged through with a powerful interior rhythm driving the quest for what cannot be fully named. In "The Long

Meadow," Yudhishthira of the great Indian epic The Mahabharata *appears as an unnamed hero accompanied by his faithful dog, and with the dog he fades into a Brooklyn meadow. In Seshadri's poetry the very ordinariness of things allows the voice to ask the unanswerable question about the meaning of life. In the long poem titled "Personal Essay" we read, "The world is huge and unbearable to think about, and maybe it should be, / maybe it should be the endlessly receding horizon that it is, / which we run after. Who knows?" Seshadri's volumes of poetry include* The Wild Kingdom *(1996),* The Long Meadow *(2004), and* 3 Sections *(2013). In 2014, he was awarded the Pulitzer Prize for poetry.*

"My First Fairy Tale"

I

My first exposure, or the first exposure I can remember, to the pleasures of narrative happened when I was a little over two years old, in Bangalore, in the second half of the nineteen-fifties. My father was in America, studying. My mother and I were living with my grandfather and his family in a house in the neighborhood known as Malleswaram. My grandmother had just died—the second- or third-earliest memory I have (the sequence of events is lost to me) is of making my way through a forest of adult legs to look into the room where she had been laid out on the floor, according to Indian custom, and was surrounded by her children, who sat in a semi-circle and wailed and wept. My mother insists that I can't remember this, that I was too young, but I do, and remember many other things, too; the trauma of those weeks must have induced the birth of my consciousness. I remember the house was large, with mango and pomegranate trees and coconut palms in the garden and flowering bushes—hibiscus, I would guess—dotting the borders; with verandahs, broad teak doors (I didn't, of course, know then that they were teak), broad windows open to the subtropical breezes, and cool marble floors, which left a smooth sensation of stone on the soles of my bare feet. It had a long driveway leading from the imposing iron gates in the wall that separated us from the street to the port-cochere at the main entrance. Sometimes a car, probably a Citroen but maybe an Indian-made Ambassador, would be parked there, its driver idling near it.

My grandfather was entitled to the car and driver because of his position in the administration of the state of Mysore, of which Bangalore was the largest and most important city. He was the chief engineer of the state, and had reached a position eminent enough that it made the subsequent and rapid decline of his fortunes in the next decade even more unaccountable and shocking. His narrative is the one that dominates my mother's side of the family, and it had a tragic arc, given shape by the elements that often define tragedy—hubris (he was caste-proud, proud of his intellect, and indifferent, or seemed indifferent, to the vulnerabilities of others); fate (which took form in my grandmother's untimely death, in his diabetes, which he was too self-indulgent to control properly, and in the terrible, self-destructive rebellion of some of his children), and a series of incalculable, unforeseeable, and disastrous coincidences. It was anything but a fairy tale, and not just because it didn't have a happy ending. Unlike a fairy tale, it had no conclusion. Its morals were forever withheld; its meaning could never be resolved; nothing came full circle but, instead, trailed off into the enigmatic and incomprehensible. I sometimes think nothing is more important to my mother than finding a way of telling her father's story that will force it to resolve. She tells it over and over again, to herself, to us, to whomever will listen, re-creating in helpless, frustrated, Balzacian detail, in order to find an escape hatch of narrative conclusiveness and thereby free herself, the early triumphs, the pride they engendered, the recklessness of the self-love, and the horrifying fall, which she avoided witnessing by moving to North America with my father after he received his degree and won a post-doctoral fellowship in Canada. About that fall, for no reason I can see, since she was blameless and couldn't have imagined what would come, she feels unassuageable guilt.

Indians have a talent for grief. I remember a lot of crying going on in that house after my grandmother's death, weeks and weeks of it. Her many children would get together in little groups and talk and weep and weep again, or go off singly to weep in corners, on staircases, near the well in the garden. My babysitters were my teenage aunts, but because of their grief they were lax in watching over me. The house had a large interior courtyard, along one side of which, near the entryway to the kitchen, there was a brazier of coals, over which, among other things, coffee beans were roasted in a round-bottomed pan. I must have been left to myself one day, and I decided it would be fun to run and jump back and forth over the brazier, which had been left burning and unattended. On one jump, I tripped and the coals scattered over my bare legs, giving me extensive third-degree burns. (I had the scars for a long time and I assumed that the discoloration of the skin on my legs was permanent, but looking just now, while writing this, at my legs, I find that, finally, no trace of the scars remains and the discoloration is entirely gone.)

I don't remember pain—the human body supposedly suppresses the memory of pain—but I do remember that I suddenly became the center of attention. I was carried up by the ubiquitous grief, both an object on which it could focus and a distraction from it, and put in the bed my grandmother and grandfather once occupied (my grandfather wouldn't sleep in it anymore), a big four-poster in the biggest bedroom of the house. The doctor came, dressed my burns, and confined me to the bed for weeks. It was there, in a blistering South Indian April, while recuperating under the mosquito netting, that I first heard the story of the birth of Rama, incarnation of the divine principle, embodiment of kingly and husbandly virtue, slayer of the demon Ravana. The three wives of Darsaratha, king of Ayodhya, are barren. The king performs a sacrifice to petition the gods for an heir to his throne. Out of the sacrificial fire a divine messenger appears with a silver chalice full of *paisa*, an ambrosial liquid pudding, which Indians consume to this day, and which is made in our household of milk, sugar, cardamom, saffron, and either vermicelli, poppy seed, or tapioca. The king gives half the *paisa* to his first wife, Kausalya. She will be the mother of Rama, avatar of Vishnu. To his second wife, Sumitra, he gives half of what is left of the *paisa*. To his third wife, Kaikeyi, he gives half of what remains (notice here the delicate hierarchical arithmetic at the heart of the domestic order of Indian kings), who will give birth to Rama's brother Bharata. He bestows what little is left over on Sumitra, who because of this extra portion will give birth to twins—Lakshmana, Rama's shadow, and Shatrunga, bane of Rama's enemies.

2

Do children like fairy tales? And, if children do like fairy tales, why do they like them? The answer to the first question has been deemed obvious by modern and contemporary culture (even though it doesn't follow that because fairy tales often have children as main characters they were told and subsequently written down for children). Yes, children like fairy tales (though I have known at least one child who couldn't stand fairy tales; his favorite bedtime story was about Hans and Peter, two boys in socialist Denmark who build a clubhouse out of odds and ends and invite their parents over for tea). And, moreover, as Bruno Bettelheim has told us, fairy tales have an important cultural function. They're therapeutic; they allow children to process the dark materials of experience. Fairy tales are useful, for both children and society, which contains the answer to the second question. Children like fairy tales because they are an aid to cognition, they help them order the world around them. But is this actually the case? These assertions and explanations aren't self-evident, and seen a certain way they look suspiciously reductive. Could we possibly know what a child likes and why, or what the intensity of his or her approval is? How, for example, would I have responded at the age of two to a Nathalie Sarraute novel? Or what sort of stories was I telling myself? It's hard to say.

But I know that I liked the story of Rama's birth not because of its fairy-tale qualities—the magical potion, the number three, etc.—or because it was an illumination of, or an antidote to, the grief floating around me but because of the *paisa*. I've been told that the entire Ramayana was recited to me while I was recuperating under the mosquito netting in the house in Malleswaram, but the *paisa* episode is the only one I can remember from that time, and it is still the only one in that vast and various epic which has resonance for me, and that was because of the *paisa* itself. *Paisa* was a dessert I loved throughout my childhood, and food is something a two-year-old understands. I can make a case, in fact, at least to myself, that all the fairy tales I liked—the ones I encountered in the English-language school run by Anglican nuns, where I was enrolled at three; in the elementary school in Ottawa, to which I was transferred at the age of five; in the grade school I went to in Ohio—had something to do with eating. The wolf eats or gets eaten; the idiot girl (hasn't she figured it out yet?) eats the apple poisoned on one side; the birds eat the breadcrumb trail; the abandoned boy and girl eat the gingerbread house and will soon, if they don't watch out, be nicely cooked themselves; Goldilocks eats the porridge (a delicious word that made my mouth water when I was a kid). I dislike Hans Christian Andersen's stories almost as much for the fact that his characters rarely eat in them, and certainly never with gusto, as I do for the punitive and hideous Calvinism that secretly infects each sentence.

I was a good eater as a child, and had a capacity for taking things as they came. I didn't have a trace of sentimentality about my grandmother's death (older and more vulnerable to human beings, I did grieve for my grandfather twelve years later, though I had hardly known him). I was puzzled at my mother's behavior, but not overly. Big things were happening around me in those weeks of death, grief, and burns, and I had snapped to attention. It would be years before events made impressions on me as vivid as the events of those weeks did. Also, and this has stayed with me, I developed out of the different elements I was suddenly aware of an excessively precocious maturity about narrative, about stories and storytelling. I've read my share of fantasy fiction, but I have always taken greater pleasure in realism. I read Balzac all the time, and it would be nice to think that such a taste was vouchsafed to me in Bangalore when I was two. I enjoyed the story of Rama's birth. But I like to think that even then I knew it was just a story, while all the other things happening around and to me were anything but.

AMITAV GHOSH
b. 1956
(English)

Amitav Ghosh was born in Kolkata and grew up in India as well as Bangladesh and Sri Lanka. The catastrophes of the world hover at the edges of his writing. Migration, displacement, and the sometimes subtle violence of colonialism are key themes in his writing. He has written in sensitive detail about a childhood experience of seeing refugees in the family garden in Dacca, strangers hovering in a garden and being fed, something the child could not understand. Ghosh was trained as an anthropologist, and his novels bear the richness and complex burden of historical lives. His nonfiction book In An Antique Land *(1992) braids together two narratives—that of the speaker, the "I" persona, modeled on Ghosh himself, living as a graduate student in a small Egyptian village, and another of Abraham Ben Yiju, a Jewish merchant in the twelfth century who traveled to India with his slave, the "slave of MS H6." The narrative is based on fragments from the Geniza manuscripts of Cairo, which the writer had spent time researching.*

His fascination with the Indian Ocean and the opium trade led to the creation of the Ibis Trilogy: Sea of Poppies *(2008),* River of Smoke *(2011), and* Flood of Fire *(2015). In an interview published in 2011 in* Flipkart, *in response to a question about the Indian diaspora and the long history of migrant labor from the subcontinent, Ghosh says, "I have myself traveled a great deal but oddly enough I have become more interested in departures than in arrivals. I wanted to understand what it was like for deeply rooted people from India's heartland to travel across the seas (which they thought of as the 'Kalapani').*

It took a great deal of courage to undertake such a journey." In his essay 'The Testimony of My Grandfather's Bookcase," Ghosh writes of the nature of his earliest travel, through the pages of the books he found as a child. In addition to the Ibis Trilogy, he has published six other novels, including the elegiac, lyrical Shadow Lines *(1988), and books of essays, several based on his life as a world traveler. In 2016, he published* The Great Derangement: Climate Change and the Unthinkable, *where he addresses the crucial need for writers and artists to face up to the terrible reality of climate change.*

From "The Testimony of My Grandfather's Bookcase"

As a child I spent my holidays in my grandfather's house in Calcutta and it was there that I began to read. My grandfather's house was a chaotic and noisy place, populated by a large number of uncles, aunts, cousins and dependents, some of them bizarre, some merely eccentric, but almost all excitable in the extreme. Yet I learned much more about reading in this house than I ever did in school.

The walls of my grandfather's house were lined with rows of books, neatly stacked in glass-fronted bookcases. The bookcases were prominently displayed in a large hall that served, amongst innumerable other functions, also those of playground, sitting-room and hallway. The bookcases towered above us, looking down, eavesdropping on every conversation, keeping track of family gossip, glowering upon quarreling children. Very rarely were the bookcases stirred out of their silent vigil: I was perhaps the only person in the house who raided them regularly, and I was in Calcutta for no more than a couple of months every year. When the bookcases were disturbed in my absence, it was usually not for their contents but because some special occasion required their cleaning. If the impending event happened to concern a weighty matter, like a delicate marital negotiation, the bookcases got a very thorough scrubbing indeed. And well they deserved it, for at such times they were important props in the little plays that were enacted in their presence. They let the visitor know that this was a house in which books were valued; in other words that we were cultivated people. This is always important in Calcutta, for Calcutta is a bookish city.

Were we indeed cultivated people? I wonder. On the whole I don't think so. In my memory my grandfather's house is always full—of aunts, uncles, cousins. I am astonished sometimes when I think of how many people it housed, fed, entertained, educated. But my uncles were busy, practical, and on the whole successful professionals, with little time to spend on books.

Only one of my uncles was a real reader. He was a shy and rather retiring man; not the kind of person who takes it upon himself to educate his siblings or improve his relatives' taste. The books in the bookcases were almost all his. He was too quiet a man to carry much weight in family matters, and his views never counted for much when the elders sought each other's council. Yet despite the fullness of the house and the fierce competition for space, it was taken for granted that his bookcases would occupy the place of honor in the hall. Eventually, tiring of his noisy relatives, my book-loving uncle decided to move to a house of his own in a distant and uncharacteristically quiet part of the city. But oddly enough the bookcases stayed; by this time the family was so attached to them that they were less dispensable than my uncle.

In the years that followed, the house passed into the hands of a branch of the family that was definitely very far from bookish. Yet their attachment to the bookcases seemed to increase inversely to their love of reading. I had been engaged in a secret pillaging of the bookcases for a very long time. Under the new regime my depredations came to a sudden halt; at the slightest squeak of an hinge, hordes of cousins would materialize suddenly around my ankles, snapping dire threats.

It served no purpose to tell them that the books were being consumed by maggots and mildew; that books rotted when they were not read. Arguments such as these interested them not at all: as far as they were concerned the bookcases and their contents were a species of property and were subject to the same laws.

This attitude made me impatient, even contemptuous at the time. Books were meant to be read, I thought, by people who valued and understood them: I felt not the slightest remorse for my long years of thievery. It seemed to me a terrible waste, an injustice that nonreaders should succeed in appropriating my uncle's library. Today I am not so sure. Perhaps those cousins were teaching me a lesson that was important on its own terms: they were teaching me respect, they were teaching me to value the printed word. Would anyone who had not learned these lessons be foolhardy enough to imagine that a living could be made from words? I doubt it.

In another way they were also teaching me what a book is, a proper book that is, not just printed paper gathered between covers. However much I may have chafed against the regime that stood between me and the bookcases, I have not forgotten those lessons. For me, to this day, a book, a proper book, is and always will be the kind of book that was on those bookshelves.

And what exactly was this kind of book?

Although no one had ever articulated any guidelines about them, so far as I know, there were in fact some fairly strict rules about the books that were allowed onto those shelves. Textbooks and schoolbooks were never allowed; nor were books of a technical or professional nature—nothing to do with engineering, or medicine or law, or indeed any of the callings that afforded my uncles their livings. In fact the great majority of the books were of a single kind; they were novels. There was some poetry too but novels were definitely the mainstay. There were a few works of anthropology and psychology; books that had in some way filtered into the literary consciousness of the time: *The Golden Bough* for example, as well as the *Collected Works of Sigmund Freud*, Marx and Engels' *Manifesto*, Havelock Ellis and Malinowski on sexual behavior and so on.

But without a doubt it was the novel that weighed most heavily on the floors of my grandfather's house. To this day I am unable to place a textbook or a computer manual upon a bookshelf without a twinge of embarrassment. [. . .]

About a quarter of the novels in my uncle's bookcases were in Bengali —a representative selection of the mainstream tradition of Bengali literature. Prominent among these were the works of Bankim Chandra, Sarat Chandra, Tagore, Bibhuti Bhushan, Bonophul & Syed Mustafa Ali. The rest were in English. But of these only a small proportion consisted of books that had been originally written in English. The others were translations from a number of other languages, most of them European: Russian had pride of place, followed by French, Italian, German and Danish. The great masterpieces of the 19th century were dutifully represented: the novels of Dostoevsky, Tolstoy and Turgenev, of Victor Hugo, Flaubert, Stendhal, Maupassant and others. But these were the dustiest books of all, placed on shelves that were lofty but remote.

The books that were prominently displayed were an oddly disparate lot—or so they seem today. Some of those titles can still be seen on bookshelves everywhere: Joyce, Faulkner and so on. But many others have long since been forgotten. Marie Corelli and Grazia Deledda for instance, names that are so little known today, even in Italy, that they have become a kind of secret incantation for me, a password that allows entry into the brotherhood of remembered bookcases. Knut Hamsun, too, was once a part of this incantation, but unlike the others his reputation has since had an immense revival—and with good reason.

Other names from those shelves have become, in this age of resurgent capitalism, symbols of a certain kind of embarrassment or unease—the social realists for example. But on my uncle's shelves they stood tall and proud, Russians and Americans alike: Maxim Gorky, Mikhail Sholokov, John Steinbeck, Upton Sinclair. There were many others too, whose places next to each other seem hard to account for at first glance: Sienkiewicz (of *Quo Vadis*), Maurice Maeterlinck, Bergson. Recently, looking through the mildewed remnants of those shelves I came upon what must have been the last addition to that collection. It was Ivo Andric's *Bridge on the Drina*, published in the sixties.

For a long time I was at a loss to account for my uncle's odd assortment of books. I knew their eclecticism couldn't really be ascribed to personal idiosyncrasies of taste. My uncle was a keen reader but he was not, I suspect, the kind of person who allows his own taste to steer him through libraries and bookshops. On the contrary he was a reader of the kind whose taste is guided largely by prevalent opinion. This uncle, I might add, was a writer himself, in a modest way. He wrote plays in an epic vein with characters borrowed from the Sanskrit classics. He never left India and indeed rarely ventured out of his home state of West Bengal.

The principles that guided my uncle's taste would have been much clearer to me had I ever had an interest in trivia. To the quiz-show adept the link between Grazia Deledda, Gorky, Hamsun, Sholokov, Sienkiewicz and Andric will be clear at once: it is the Nobel Prize for Literature.

Writing about the Calcutta of the twenties and thirties Nirad Chaudhuri writes: "To be up to date about literary fashions was a greater craze among us than to be up to date in clothes is with society women, and this desire became keener with the introduction of the Nobel Prize for literature. Not to be able to show at least one book by a Nobel Laureate was regarded almost as being illiterate."

But of course the Nobel Prize was itself both symptom and catalyst of a wider condition: the emergence of a notion of a universal "literature," a form of artistic expression that embodies differences in place and culture, emotion and aspiration, but in such a way as to render them communicable. This idea may well have had its birth in Europe but I suspect it met with a much more enthusiastic reception outside. I spent a couple of years studying in England in the late seventies and early eighties. I don't remember ever having come across a bookshelf like my uncle's: one that had been largely formed by this vision of literature, by a deliberate search for books from a wide array of other countries.

I have however come across many such elsewhere, most memorably in Burma, in the house of the late Mya Than Tint—widely regarded as one of the most important Burmese writers of the 20th century.

Mya Than Tint was an amazing man. He spent more than a decade as a political prisoner. For part of that time he was incarcerated in the British-founded penal colony of Cocos Island, an infamous outcrop of rock where prisoners had to forage to survive. On his release he began to publish sketches and stories that won him a wide readership and great popular esteem in Burma. These wonderfully warm and vivid pieces have recently been translated into English and published under the title *Tales of Everyday People*.

I met Mya Than Tint in 1995, at his home in Rangoon. The first thing he said to me was, "I've seen your name somewhere." I was taken aback. Such is the ferocity of Burma's censorship regime that it seemed hardly possible that he could have come across my books or articles in Rangoon.

"Wait a minute," Mya Than Tint said. He went to his study, fetched a tattered old copy of *Granta* and pointed to my name on the contents page.

"Where did you get it?" I asked, openmouthed. He explained, smiling, that he had kept his library going by befriending the ragpickers and paper-traders who pick through the rubbish discarded by diplomats.

Looking through Mya Than Tint's bookshelves, I soon discovered that this determined refusal to be beaten into parochialism had its genesis in a bookcase that was startlingly similar to my uncle's. Knut Hamsun, Maxim Gorky, Sholokov, all those once familiar names came echoing back to me, from Calcutta, as we sat talking in that bright, cool room in Rangoon.

amitav ghosh

I also once had occasion to meet the Indonesian novelist Pramoedya Ananta Toer, another writer of astonishing fortitude and courage. Of the same generation as Mya Than Tint, Pramoedya has lived through similar experiences of imprisonment and persecution. Unlike Mya Than Tint, Pramoedya works in a language that has only recently become a vehicle of literary expression, Bahasa Indonesia. Pramoedya is thus widely thought of as the founding figure in a national literary tradition.

At some point I asked what his principal literary influences were. I do not know what I had expected to hear but it was not the answer I got. I should not have been surprised however; the names were familiar ones—Maxim Gorky and John Steinbeck.

Over the last few years, unbeknownst to itself the world has caught up with Mya Than Tint and Pramoedya Ananta Toer. Today the habits of reading that they and others like them pioneered are mandatory among readers everywhere. Wherever I go today, the names that I see on serious bookshelves are always the same: Garcia Marquez, Vargas Llosa, Nadine Gordimer, Michael Ondaatje, Marguerite Yourcenar, Gunter Grass, Salman Rushdie. That this is ever more true is self-evident: literary currents are now instantly transmitted around the world and instantly absorbed, like everything else. To mention this is to cite a jaded commonplace.

But the truth is that fiction has been thoroughly international for more than a century. In India, Burma, Egypt, Indonesia and elsewhere this has long been self-evident. Yet curiously this truth has nowhere been more stoutly denied than in Europe, where the novel has its deepest roots: indeed it could be said that this denial is the condition that made the European novel possible.

The novel as a form has been vigorously international from the start: we know that Spanish, English, French and Russian novelists have read each other's work avidly since the eighteenth century. And yet, the paradox of the novel as a form is that it is founded upon a myth of parochiality, in the exact sense of a parish—a place named and charted, a definite location. A novel, in other words, must always be set somewhere: it must have its setting, and within the evolution of the narrative this setting must, classically, play a part almost as important as those of the characters themselves. Location is thus intrinsic to a novel: we are at a loss to imagine its absence no matter whether that place be Mrs. Gaskell's Cranford or

Joyce's Dublin. A poem can create its setting and atmosphere out of verbal texture alone: not so a novel.

We carry these assumptions with us in much the same way that we assume the presence of actors and lights in a play. They are both so commonplace and so deeply rooted that they pre-empt us from reflecting on how very strange they actually are. Consider that the conceptions of location that made the novel possible came into being at exactly the time when the world was beginning to experience the greatest dislocation it has ever known. When we read Middlemarch or Madame Bovary we have not the faintest inkling that the lives depicted in them are made possible by global empires (consider the contrast with that seminal work of Portuguese literature, Camõe's *Lusiads*). Consider that when we read Hawthorne we have to look very carefully between the lines to see that the New England ports he writes about are sustained by a far-flung network of trade. Consider that nowhere are the literary conventions of location more powerful than in the literature of the United States: itself the product of several epic dislocations.

How sharply this contrasts with traditions of fiction that predate the novel! It is true, for example, that the city of Baghdad provides a notional location for the One Thousand and One Nights. But the Baghdad of Scheherazade is more a talisman, an incantation, than a setting. The stories could happen anywhere so long as our minds have room for an enchanted city.

Or think of that amazing collection of stories known as the *Panchatantra* or *Five Chapters*. These stories too have no settings to speak of, except the notion of a forest. Yet the *Panchatantra* is reckoned by some to be second only to the Bible in the extent of its global diffusion. Compiled in India early in the first millennium, it passed into Arabic through a sixth century Persian translation, engendering some of the best known of middle eastern fables, including parts of the Thousand and One Nights. The stories were handed on to the Slavic languages through Greek, then from Hebrew to Latin, a version in the latter appearing in 1270. Through Latin they passed into German and Italian. From the Italian version came the famous Elizabethan rendition of Sir Henry North, *The Morall Philosophy of Doni* (1570). These stories left their mark on collections as different as those of La Fontaine and the Grimm brothers, and today they are inseparably part of a global heritage.

Equally, the stories called the Jatakas, originally compiled in India, came to be diffused throughout southern and eastern Asia and even further with the spread of Buddhism. The story, both in its epic form as well as its shorter version, was vital in the creation of the remarkable cultural authority that India enjoyed in the Asia of the middle ages: not until the advent of Hollywood was narrative again to play so important a part in the diffusion of a civilization.

Everywhere these stories went they were freely and fluently adapted to local circumstances. Indeed in a sense the whole point the stories was their translatability—the dispensable and inessential nature of their locations. What held them together and gave them their appeal was not where they happened but how—the narrative in other words. Or, to take another example, consider that European narrative tradition that was perhaps the immediate precursor of the novel: the story of Tristan and Isolde. By the late middle ages this Celtic narrative, which appears to have had its origins in Cornwall and Brittany, had been translated and adapted into several major European languages. Everywhere it went the story of Tristan and Isolde was immediately adapted to new locations and new settings. The questions of its origins and its original locations are at best matters of pedantic interest.

In these ways of storytelling, it is the story that gives places their meaning. That is why Homer leaps at us from signs on the New York turnpike, from exits marked Ithaca and Troy; that is why the Ayodhya of the Ramayana lends its name equally to a street in Banaras and a town in Thailand.

This style of fictional narrative is not extinct: far from it. It lives very vividly in the spirit that animates popular cinema in India and many other places. In a Hindi film, as in a kung-fu movie, the details that constitute the setting are profoundly unimportant, incidental almost. In Hindi films, the setting of a single song can take us through a number of changes of costume, each in a different location. These films, I need hardly point out, command huge audiences on several continents and may well be the most widely circulated cultural artifacts the world has ever known. When Indonesian streets and villages suddenly empty at four in the afternoon, it is not because of Maxim Gorky or John Steinbeck: it is because of the timing of a daily broadcast of a Hindi film.

Such is the continued vitality of this style of narrative that it eventually succeeded in weaning my uncle from his bookcases. Toward the end of his life my bookloving uncle abandoned all his old friends, Gorky and Sholokov and Hamsun, and became a complete devotee of Bombay films. He would see dozens of Hindi films: sometimes we went together, on lazy afternoons. On the way home he would stop to buy fan magazines. Through much of his life he'd been a forbidding, distant man, an intellectual in the classic, Western sense: in his last years he was utterly transformed, warm, loving, thoughtful. His brothers and sisters scarcely recognized him.

Once, when we were watching a film together, he whispered in my ear that the star, then Bombay's reigning female deity, had recently contracted a severe infestation of lice.

"How do you know?," I asked.

"I read an interview with her hairdresser," he said. "In *Stardust*."

This was the man who'd handed me a copy of *And Quiet Flows the Don* when I was not quite twelve.

My uncle's journey is evidence that matters are not yet decided between different ways of telling stories: that if Literature, led by a flagship called the Novel, has declared victory, the other side, if there is one, has not necessarily conceded defeat. But what exactly is at stake here? What is being contested? Or to narrow the question: what is the difference between the ways in which place and location are thought of by novelists and storytellers of other kinds? The contrast is best seen, I think, where it is most apparent: that is in situations outside Europe and the Americas, where the novel is a relatively recent import. As an example, I would like to examine for a moment, a novel from my own part of the world—Bengal. This novel is called *Rajmohan's Wife* and it was written in the early 1860s by the writer Bankim Chandra Chatterjee.

Bankim Chandra Chatterjee was a man of many parts. He was a civil servant, a scholar, a novelist and a talented polemicist. He was also very widely read, in English as well as Bengali and Sanskrit. In a sense his was the bookcase that was the ancestor of my uncle's.

Bankim played no small part in the extraordinary efflorescence of Bengali literature in the second half of the 19th century. He wrote several major novels in Bengali, all of which were quickly translated into other

Indian languages. He was perhaps the first truly "Indian" writer of modern times in the sense that his literary influence extended throughout the subcontinent. Nirad Chaudhuri describes him as "the creator of Bengali fiction and . . . the greatest novelist in the Bengali language." Bankim is also widely regarded as one of the intellectual progenitors of Indian nationalism.

Bankim Chandra was nothing if not a pioneer and he self-consciously set himself the task of bringing the Bengali novel into being by attacking what he called "the Sanskrit School." It is hard today, looking back from a point of time when the novel sails as Literature's flagship, to imagine what it meant to champion such a form in nineteenth-century India. The traditions of fiction that Bankim was seeking to displace were powerful enough to awe its critics into silence. They still are: what modern writer, for example, could ever hope to achieve the success of the *Panchatantra*? It required true courage to seek to replace this style of narrative with a form so artificial and arbitrary as the novel: the endeavour must have seemed hopeless at the time. Nor did the so-called Sanskrit School lack for defendants. Bankim, and many others who took on the task of domesticating the novel, were immediately derided as monkey-like imitators of the West.

Bankim responded by calling for a full-scale insurrection. Imitation, he wrote, was the law of progress; no civilization was self-contained or self-generated, none could advance without borrowing. He wrote: "Those who are familiar with the present writers in Bengali, will readily admit that they all, good and bad alike, may be classed under two heads, the Sanskrit and the English schools. The former represents Sanskrit scholarship and the ancient literature of the country; the latter is the fruit of Western knowledge and ideas. By far the greater number of Bengali writers belong to the Sanskrit school; but by far the greater number of good writers belong to the other . . . It may be said that there is not at the present day anything like an indigenous school of writers, owing nothing either to Sanskrit writers or to those of Europe."

How poignantly ironic this passage seems a hundred years later, after generations of expatriate Indians, working mainly in England, have striven so hard to unlearn the lessons taught by Bankim and his successors in India. So successfully were novelistic conventions domesticated in the late nineteenth and early twentieth centuries that many Indian readers now think of them as somehow local, homegrown, comforting in their naturalistic simplicity, while the work of such writers as G.V. Desani, Zulfikar Ghose, Salman Rushdie, Adam Zameenzad, Shashi Tharoor and others appears, by the same token, stylized and experimental.

RAGHAVAN ATHOLI

b. 1957

(Malayalam)

Raghavan Atholi, poet and sculptor, was born to an Untouchable family in the Kerala village of Atholi—the place that, in traditional south Indian fashion, he uses as his last name. He is renowned both for his sculptures, which have been exhibited all over the country, and for his poetry, which he has performed at numerous literary festivals and cultural gatherings. Whether in sculpture, using the red soil of his native land, or in poems, using voice and words, Atholi sees his task as setting free the buried voice of the Dalit people. His first book of poetry, Kandathi *(1996), evokes the name of his own mother, the word in Malayalam meaning woman who works in the field, or peasant woman. The poet Ayyappa Paniker, well known for his courageous support of the writing of minority groups, wrote a preface to the book, publishing it in the series* Keralakavitha. *Paniker's preface, titled "Aesthetic of Blackness," heralded a new poetic voice in the language. The phrase alludes to the powerfully local strain in Atholi's poetry that taps into the pain of being Outcaste, as well as to its profoundly universalist appeal. "There is only one poetry," Atholi writes, "for the entire universe. I can only be part of that." In the same interview, the poet makes an overt connection with the African American experience. He speaks of hearing Mahalia Jackson's gospel songs: "'Black' is a powerful symbol that overcomes even the national boundaries of the possibility of the word 'Dalit.' My heart pulsates when I hear Jackson sing. Blackness is a representational term that unifies oppressed people the world over. That's why it occupies so much space in my poetry." In a poem titled "Thanichirippaval" ("She Sits Alone"), he addresses a muse figure: "Black woman / Become poetry / Sting my body." His works include the volumes of poetry* Mozhimattan *(1996) and* Mounashilakalude Prayanayakkurippukal *(1999), as well as the novel* Choraparisham *(2007).*

"The Poet with a Forest Fire Inside"

PRADEEPAN PAMPIRIKUNNU: *Kandathi* is your first published collection of poems. Could you tell us a little about the circumstances of its publication?

RAGHAVAN ATHOLI: I have always wanted to record the caste-related experiences and survival of the subordinated castes. Such a record would also be the record of my own life. I had been asking the Kerala government publication department since 1986 to publish the book. But they didn't do anything until 1996, after Geethanandan and I approached Ayyappa Paniker for a preface to the collection. Paniker not only wrote the preface, but also got it published in the signature series, *Keralakavitha*.

PP: Could you talk a little about the poetic language used in *Kandathi*?

RA: For some years before I wrote the poems in *Kandathi*, I had been experimenting with rhythms and trying to bring some of that into my poetry. The aim was to create an intense beat that lies between prose and poetry; an effort to become the rhythm of my people —a rhythm that also provides the energy for their hard work. It is not a rhythm to sit still and reflect upon. Poetry, for me, is not the worship of beauty either.

PP: There's also a certain note of lament in your poetry. Is that part of this rhythm?

RA: Poetry is both lament and uproar. In my case, it is also a process of identifying with subordinated people all over the world; an awareness of our oneness. That is how the thread of nationalism develops in this poetry—as a universal brotherhood of communities, including black people.

PP: It is generally accepted that emotions welling up from real life are characteristic of dalit poetry and that your poetry is emotional. What is the basis for the emotionalism in your poetry?

RA: So far, no one has ever asked me about poetry, let alone about the nature of its emotion. Well, no one actually thought that we had a life to speak of! I feel that in any given period, someone is entrusted to give expression to the form and feeling of the time. The sorrows and problems that have been left unspoken for centuries, the people who've been denied a voice to talk about them—it is for them that I lament, that I scream. The souls of our ancestors come back through art forms like *theyyam*. They shriek, they cry. Inside me I have the lament of our ancestors as well as the sorrows of our contemporaries. When I write, they sit beside me, and I forget myself and my surroundings. Poetry, for me, is neither complaint nor salvation. It is a historical commitment.

PP: Do you think there is a difference between this emotion and the sentimentality of the romantics?

RA: The emotion in my poetry is a living heritage. It is not based on either completely spiritual or completely material emotions. It is based on emotions that have been formed entirely by social humiliation, experiences of caste, poverty. Yes, they are entirely different from the sentimentality of the Malayalam romantics.

PP: Do you consider folk songs the foundation for subaltern poetry? Have you tried to purposely bring the beauty, rhythms and patterns of these songs and their music into your poetry?

RA: My writing comes through my unconscious mind, thus providing a passage for generations. I'm only an agent, a cause. The rhythms are already there, as in the songs that my mother sings. That is why I gave my first collection her name—Kandathi. "All the leisure literature of the landlords does not add up to a single exhalation from my mother," I once said.

PP: Are you critical of the Malayalam poetic tradition?

RA: There is only one poetry—for the entire universe. I can only be part of that. The current context has some specific demands and that is what creates dalit poetry. I have no objection to a poetic tradition. But I insist on knowing how it was produced: the present tradition was created by copying and taking over my ancestors' songs and words. The task today is to re-possess those words. Remember, in the whole body of Sangam literature, only one brahmin is found.

PP: But Malayalam poetry follows the lineage of Sanskrit literature and not that of Sangam literature—don't you agree?

RA: Even before the Sangam period, there were rhythms—of the one who cut wood, the one who harvested the paddy fields, the one who pound the paddy. These are not upper-caste or upper-class rhythms. Aristocratic experiences have been sneaked into these rhythms and songs. What I feel is that we have to re-capture these primordial rhythms. My tradition is that of the original, primordial man.

PP: Is it possible to divide Malayalam poetry into upper caste and untouchable (*savarna* and *avarna*)?

RA: Of course! But even in this division, a brotherhood has to be possible between them. One tradition cannot or should not stifle the other. The contemporary tradition of Malayalam poetry is one of a people with no experience. Which upper-caste person has the experience of cultivating paddy fields? How many children have they lost to poverty and hunger? Do the upper-caste people have such experiences? No. What we call "dalit" is not the experience of one person, but of a whole humanity.

In other words, there is no need to name poetry as "dalit poetry" or "Malayalam poetry." It is the upper caste that names it in this way. The names they give represent their experiential realm. We have no authority. We have to develop an authority as a people, become a significant political force. We have to recognize our own voices, our own languages, mark our songs and art. This will be a process of marking another kind of nationalism.

PP: Is caste the principal force in your poetry? If you did not belong to this caste, would you be writing poetry?

RA: When I write, there is no caste in me. Poetry is my mother tongue. My people are my language. What I do is establish them in my poetry. I don't know if that constitutes caste. Kandathi, Chathan, Aritheyi are all in my poems because they are the ones who form my poetic consciousness.

Their centrality in my experiences is of course due to our shared caste. What I have seen is their lives and their troubles. Whatever I write, I come back to them. When I write, I'm not concerned whether this constitutes dalitness. I am concerned whether this constitutes poetry.

PP: What are your thoughts when your poetry is marked out as dalit poetry?

RA: I don't think I write dalit poetry. I am a dalit and I write universal poetry.

PP: Could you explain that a little?

RA: I don't think my poetry is to be confined to Kerala or even India. It is for everyone around the world. That is what I mean by universal poetry.

PP: But such an idea of the universal runs the risk of silencing the regional and the national, surely?

RA: No. What I mean by nationalism is a shared identity of oppressed communities. Oppressed groups all around the world constitute a "nation." It is from this point of view I envision my poetry as universal.

PP: Sharan Kumar Limbale has said: "What is important to me is not the word, but the pain and sorrow that it represents." Do you see language as important in your poetry?

RA: The dalit has a mother tongue. But he cannot talk to the larger society in it—there is no space for his language there. So he has to use written Malayalam. Dalits are people who were denied the freedom of movement by day. So they spoke in a different language. Panan, parayan, mannan—all of them have their own language. We have not been able to bring any of that into poetry. Not just poetry—the possibilities embedded in those languages have not been explored by Malayalam. There is a whole continent of lost words there.

PP: Then who do you write for in Malayalam?

RA: The poetry that I write is for the whole world. I do try to use the language of my clan when possible. My novel *Choraparisham* is an attempt to use the language of our caste. I don't have the authority to tell you to read or listen to my poetry. I believe that I have a share in all the beauty and narration in this world—I am part of a people who have produced that world. I will use everything that my society has created as an instrument for the progress of my community.

PP: Do you see a weakness in the new poetry in Malayalam?

RA: New poetry has not succeeded in bringing today's society and times into poetry or poetry into today's times. They think poetry is a solitary experience. Not for me. As I write, an entire community comes surging in . . .

PP: Kandan, Kandathi, Eyilandi, Arippandi, Kariyathan, Vellayyi—you have used several names from oppressed communities as titles for your poems. What was your intention here?

RA: There are multitudes of books and not one of them has people from my community. I believe that there is a need to inscribe them. I believe that to be my assignment as a poet. All I am doing is to verbalize the inner agitation of a people who have been silenced for so long.

PP: The communists in Kerala have upheld poetry as social resistance. They have also seen themselves as representing oppressed people. But they have never considered you as a communist poet. The progressive literary movement has also not given much attention to your work. Why do you think this is?

RA: I have written a poem titled "Brahmunism." It deals with the casteist underpinnings of communism. In India, this has been formed by an alliance between brahmins and communists. They see those of us who raise the issue of caste as enemies. They have been blind to caste and to people like us who have been forced to live the oppressions of caste.

PP: In the poem "Thanichirippaval" (Alone She Sits) you wrote:

> Black woman
> Become poetry, and
> Sting my body.

Ayyappa Paniker called his preface to your book "the aesthetics of blackness." What do you understand as the aesthetics of blackness?

RA: "Black" is a powerful symbol that overcomes even the national boundaries of the possibility of the word "dalit." My heart pulsates when I hear Jackson sing. Blackness is a representational term that unifies oppressed people the world over. That's why it occupies so much space in my poetry.

PP: What is your appraisal of the poet Raghavan Atholi?

RA: I don't think I am a poet yet. On the primordial grasslands of my people, there is poetry. I might yet become a poet when I get there. That will be my true poetry.

JEET THAYIL
b. 1959
(English)

Jeet Thayil was born in Mamalasserie, Kerala, and brought up in Hong Kong, Bombay, and New York. A poet and novelist, he writes libretti, works with performance materials, and has edited anthologies of poetry. As a musician and songwriter, he is part of the contemporary music project Sridhar/Thayil. Thayil's poetry is marked by a tight, concise form through which he works the richly braided histories that have marked his life. In the poem "Malayalam's Ghazal," which like all his poetry is written in English, the speaker plays with a form drawn from Urdu and Persian to evoke the mellifluous lines of Malayalam, Thayil's mother tongue, a southern Indian language he would be incapable of writing in, since all he has are "scraps." In the essay "One Language Separated by the Sea" Thayil writes about the audience of the Indian-English poet, which exists both everywhere and nowhere since such a writer has no specific region out of which his language springs: "Where a Malayalam poet has a distinct readership, English language poets do not. They are known only to themselves. This has led to crises of identity." The novel Narcopolis *(2012), which brought him critical acclaim, is written in sentences of varying lengths, often hypnotic in their power. Set in the opium dens of Bombay, it depicts the life of those caught in the dark seams of urban existence. Christians, Muslims, and Hindus all mingle in the pages, all drawn to a twilight zone where names and places slip away and the reader is plunged into a nowhere zone that seems truly hallucinatory. The erotic is caught in the noose of despair, and the "I" can only discover itself in an opium haze, twin sister to the imagination. The novel* Narcopolis *shifts locations, and part of it is set in China where the narrator imagines a metamorphic self, gigantic, poisoning the urban landscapes with cities turned into "repositories of waste and poison [. . .] at the center of it all was a character who was neither man nor woman, a charismatic autodidact who changed identity at will. Was it a kind of imagined autobiography?"* Thayil's other works include the volumes of poetry These Errors Are Correct *(2008)* and English *(2009)*.

"The Heroin Sestina"

What was the point of it? The stoned
life, the chased, snorted, shot life. Some low
comedy with a cast of strangers. Time
squashed flat. The 1001 names of heroin
chewed like language. Nothing now to know
or remember but the dirty taste

of it, and the names: snuff, Death, a little taste,
H—pronounce it etch—, sugar, brownstone,
scag, the SHIT, ghoda gaadi, #4 china, You-Know,
garad, god, the gear, junk, monkey blow,
the law, the habit, material, cheez, heroin.
The point? It was the wasted time,

which comes back lovely sometimes,
a ghost sense say, say that hard ache taste
back in your throat, the warm heroin
drip, the hit, the rush, the whack, the stone.
You want it now, the way it lays you low,
flattens everything you know

to a thin white line. I'm saying, I know
the pull of it: the skull rings time
so beautiful, so low
you barely hear it. Itch this blind toad taste.
When you said, "I mean it, we live like stones,"
you broke something in me only heroin

could fix. The thick sweet amaze of heroin,
helpless its love, its knowl-
edge of the infinite. Why push the stone
back up the hill? Why not leave it with the time-
keep, asleep at the bar? Try a little taste
of something sweet that a sweet child will adore, low

in the hips where the aches all go. Allow
me in this one time and I'll give you heroin,
just a taste
to replace the useless stuff you know.
Some say it comes back, the time,
to punish you with the time you killed, leave you stone

sober, unknowing, the happiness chemical blown
from your taste stem, unable to hear the word *heroin*
without wanting its stone one last time.

"Malayalam's Ghazal"

Listen! Someone's saying a prayer in Malayalam.
He says there's no word for "despair" in Malayalam.

Sometimes at daybreak you sing a Gujarati garba.
At night you open your hair in Malayalam.

To understand symmetry, understand Kerala.
The longest palindrome is there, in *Malayalam*.

When you've been too long in the room of English,
Open your windows to the fresh air of Malayalam.

Visitors are welcome in The School of Lost Tongues.
Someone's endowed a high chair in Malayalam.

I greet you my ancestors, O scholars and linguists.
My father who recites Baudelaire in Malayalam.

jeet thayil

Jeet, such a drama with the scraps you know.
Write a couplet, if you dare, in Malayalam.

"Spiritus Mundi"

I was born in the Christian South
of a subcontinent mad for religion.
Warriors and zealots tried to rule it.
A minor disciple carried his doubt
like a torch to temple and shrine.
I longed for vision and couldn't tell it.

The cities I grew up in were landlocked.
One, a capital, buff with architecture,
the other lost for months in monsoon.
One was old, one poor; both were hot.
The heat vapourized thought and order,
drained the will, obliterated reason.

I settled, 20 and morose, in a town
built by a patricidal emperor
whose fratricidal son imprisoned him,
for eight years, with a view of the tomb
he built for his wife, to remember her.
I was over conscious of my rhyme,

and of the houses, three, inside my head.
In the streets, death, in saffron or green,
rode a cycle rickshaw slung
with megaphones. On the kitchen step
a chili plant grew dusty in the wind.
In that climate nothing survived the sun

or a pickaxe, not even a stone dome
that withstood 400 years of voices
raised in prayer and argument. The train
pulled in each day at an empty platform

where a tea stall that served passers-
by became a famous fire shrine.

I made a change: I travelled west
in time to see a century end
and begin. I don't recall the summer
of 2001. Did it exist?
There would have been sun and rain.
I was there, I don't remember

a time before autumn of that year.
Now 45, my hair gone sparse,
I'm a poet of small buildings:
the brownstone, the townhouse, the cold water
walkup, the tenement of two or three floors.
I cherish the short ones still standing.

I recognize each cornice and sill,
the sky's familiar cast, the window
I spend my day walking to and from,
as if I were a baffled Moghul in his cell.
I call the days by their Hindu
names and myself by my Christian one.

The Atlantic's stately breakers mine
the shore for kelp, mussels, bits of glass.
They move in measured iambs, tidy
as the towns that rise from sign to neon sign.
Night rubs its feet. A mouse deer starts across
the grass. The sky drains to a distant eddy.

Badshah, I say to no one there.
I hear a koel in the call of a barn owl.
All things combine and recombine,
the sky streams in ribbons of color.
I'm my father and my son grown old.
Everything that lives, lives on.

ARUNDHATI ROY

b. 1961

(English)

Arundhati Roy was born in the hilly region of Shillong. After spending her first two years there, she grew up in Kerala, in her maternal home. Her mother, Mary Roy, was an activist for women's rights; her estranged father was a tea planter. The setting of Kerala and in particular of the Syrian Christian family in Central Travancore is central to Roy's novel The God of Small Things *(1997). The lush landscape and the complicated family rituals enthrall the narrator, a woman who needs to break free from the ancient rituals and burdens of the past. Love with an Untouchable man becomes part of the weave of this novel. Female sexuality, even as it seeks its own freedom, necessarily breaks down other barriers, including the centuries-old caste system that the Syrian Christians, in spite of not being Hindu, have traditionally espoused. The taut, lyrical language of the book becomes at times its own subject, allowing the characters' entry into a world of story, one where the confusions of desire and the malaise of a crumbling social order are held up to scrutiny. In an interview Roy speaks of her early affinity for language: "I have a clear memory of language swimming towards me. Of my willing it out of the water. Of it being blurred, inaccessible, inchoate [. . .] and of it emerging. Sharply outlined."*

In recent years, Roy has crafted an identity as a passionate activist on local as well as global issues, tackling the oppression of the Kashmiri people; the struggle of the adivasis, *or forest people, in areas where the Indian government is strip mining; and the plight of Maoists involved in armed insurrection against the Indian state. Her book* Walking with the Comrades *(2011) opens* with a quote from Pablo Neruda: "Your blood asks, how were the wealthy / and the law interwoven?" *Elsewhere Roy speaks of her attempt to use a private, lyrical language to speak of common concerns, so she might stand as someone who speaks "from the heart of a crowd." Her advocacy of human rights issues has resulted in much controversy, including death threats to her from the far right. But clearly her voice in recent years has been that of the nonfiction writer. Among her books of essays are* The Algebra of Infinite Justice *(2002) and* Listening to Grasshoppers: Field Notes on Democracy *(2009). In 1998, for her celebrated novel* The God of Small Things, *she was awarded the Booker Prize. In 2017, twenty years after that publication, she published a second novel,* The Ministry of Utmost Happiness.

From "Like Sculpting Smoke: Arundhati Roy on Fame, Writing and India"

KATHY ARLYN SOKOL: You were just honored by the Booker Prize Committee for having written the best book of 1997. What is excellence to you? How do you maintain it? Do you even want to maintain it?

ARUNDHATI ROY: I'm not somebody who puts much stock in prizes. I'm not even sure that there is such a thing as a best book, it's such a subjective thing. That is not what books are about. So, I think we should just leave aside the Booker Prize. It's the roll of the dice, that prize. I said the night I received the prize that if it had been five other judges, it could have been another book selected. Prizes are much more for readers than for writers. When there are so many books being published, these are ways that the publishing world has of underlining things or marking them out or saying "read this one" or "read that one." When I was writing my book I just knew when it was ready, when it was true and that's all that mattered. The process of writing a book is such a lonely and yet wonderful process. And at the end of that process, for the person who was writing, the process of doing it was more important than what eventually came out, though what came out is necessarily bound to that—the process of polishing it, of making it as good as you possibly can. It is such a wonderful privilege to have spent five years doing something which I know is the best that I could possibly have done, whatever anyone else might think of it, it is a blessing and a privilege. The fact that I finished it is something that I am eternally grateful for. For me, the biggest achievement in all of this is that I actually finished it. Excellence is again something that is perceived by someone else, whereas for you, it is only completeness, isn't it? It's only what you think of as "now it's finished" and that satisfaction.

KAS: Does being recognized by others give you some sort of validity of this process?

AR: No, after all, a story is the simplest way of presenting a complex world. That's why I am a writer, because I can't simplify it any further. If I could I would be a politician. I would have slogans, I would have a manifesto. I don't. Or I would be an architect or whatever. It's a very internal process trying to make sense of the world to yourself, and when you do that and that eventually becomes something which makes sense to others, too, there is a satisfaction in it. But the fact is that whether it made sense to three people or to three million people, it would have been the same book. I thought my book would be read—if it were really successful—by 3,000 people or 8,000 people. The fact that you can kind of tunnel through the world in this way is wonderful, but also very frightening. [. . .]

KAS: From having been a baker, selling cakes on the beaches of Goa, to having written screenplays, you said that you finally found something that was closest to not having a profession. Do you feel that the word is so close to you, is so much a part of you that it doesn't require work for it to come forth from inside you?

AR: I did say that language is the skin on my thought. It clothes my thought. Sometimes I wonder if I had a pre-verbal thought, you know. But, of course, it requires work. My book is not something that I sat down and reeled off. It's like sculpting smoke. Smoke comes out but then, of course, it is given form and shape and structure. It took me five years to write and it is not a long book. For me, not having a profession has nothing to do with not working. It just means doing whatever you do professionally but not just growing in one direction. That's all. It means that one works at whatever one does, at everything as opposed to just doing one thing.

KAS: With this computer-aided technology and the way that the word is transforming, what do you see as the evolution of language in the future?

AR: I wrote my book on a computer and I don't think that I could have written it this way without a computer, because technically it's like laying a soundtrack. My computer was my memory and I was laying echoes and rhythms, you know? If I had to go through thousands of pieces of paper and insert . . . theoretically I could have done it, but practically it would have been a less successful attempt. Because in the computer the minute I thought of it, I could summon it up, where I wanted to put what. Whereas if you're writing by hand, it's a more tedious process and a lot of your intentions can fall by the wayside. So, in this endeavor, it was much more important than I imagined it would be just because of the way the book is structured.

KAS: How do you see the evolution of language itself?

AR: Just a few years ago you had these establishment writers who were accepted as the "big dudes" of literature and they would write books and everyone would go crazy over them. I think that process is going to become much more democratic, because writing is something that so many people are doing. There are so many books and writings from other places now rather than from just what has been perceived to be the center of the universe, Europe and America. People from other places are going to start telling their stories. That's what I mean by fame is democratic, there are more and more people like me who are going to be first-time writers who have a story to tell and who are heard. So in a way, the stories are going to become more diverse. But then I think also there is going to be a kind of standardization because of this huge global culture that is happening. So the generation after me in India is going to be very different; the children are going to be people who have been brought up on the same things as other children all over the world, on MTV and all of this. It's going to be very sad, but there is nothing that you can do about it.

KAS: You really think there's nothing you can do?

AR: Yeah, there is nothing you can do about it because you have to let people make their choices. In a country like India, it's not just terrible that there's MTV. It also becomes the questioning of a lot of things which are unacceptable in our traditions, anyway. Someone like me spends a lot of energy fighting to get away from traditional lifestyle, as a woman in a little place. So, I can't just embrace my history and tradition unquestioningly. I don't accept that. I think it's much easier for men to do than for women, because they don't pay the same price. So, on one hand, I enjoy the idea of it being shaken up. I do. And I believe that ultimately, when you have a very strong tradition, it's not that easy for people to just get up and abandon a civilization that is this old. They are going to take things from other cultures, but also from their own. When I was an architect I knew that there was no sort of ultimate divine committee that decided what is an ugly building and what is a good building. Of course, your own sense of aesthetics is completely and deeply entrenched in you, but you have to be able to understand that this man likes his pink house. And you are nobody to tell him it's ugly. So, I suppose it's like being supportive of free speech. You have to be able to accept that people are not just going to say what you want them to say; or like what you want them to like.

KAS: In your book you wrote, "Men without curiosity, without doubt. They looked at the world and never wondered how it worked. They knew. They worked it." In your book you break many taboos. Did breaking the taboos in the book serve as a way of somehow reorganizing this control over our lives?

AR: I think that writers are always two people. I'm one person who lives my life and the other part of me watches me live my life, you know, and that part is the writer who is sort of detached from everything and watches. It doesn't make you live your own life less passionately, but yet there's a part of you that is sitting on the ceiling fan and watching it and smiling or whatever. In everything I do or have ever done in my life, I feel anger towards authority, and I'm even frightened of ever having a child because I don't want authority over that small person. It's very confusing for me and anyone who is involved with me. Because it's just this permanent questioning of every little thing, every sentence . . . I mean, it becomes a wall which is quite tiring sometimes. I suppose often these emotions are awakened in you through whatever you have been through in your childhood and nothing that happens to you as an adult ever quells those questions or those fears or that anger. It will always be there. And yet, I know, that if you were to speak to anybody who knows me they will say, "Oh, she's so calm." And the fact is that I am very calm, but that is only in my day-to-day interaction, but I am not at all calm about major issues or major questions, you know. And that's not a sort of shouting kind of anger that I have, but a very cold anger.

KAS: Your constant questioning of authority is very similar to believing that much of what we think, see or believe is filtered through society's eyes.

AR: I don't know. I don't feel like that. I feel the opposite of that. Because as a child I was not wanted or accepted or not needed by anybody in the place I grew up. I never saw things through their eyes at all. Sometimes I wonder why I see things the way I do, because it's completely the opposite of the way people are conditioned to see things here, especially women. For instance, I sometimes think I am perhaps the only woman in India, maybe the only woman in the world, who never thought about getting married or wanting children. The fact that I am married has nothing to do with wanting to be. That's why one has this constant questioning of everything. You almost get tired of never having a place to stand, never having the ability to just say, "Yeah, this is how it should be." It's all the time saying, "Why this?" and "What does it mean?" and "What should I do?" There is no place to rest. That's the way it is for me. [. . .]

KAS: I wonder what aspects of India you think you represent to the international community?

AR: I will tell you one thing about the West. I always say that you know that someone doesn't know anything about India the minute you see them striving to understand it. Because those of us who live here have ceased to try. It doesn't matter. You don't understand it any more or less than you understand anything else, but you just live in it and get on with it. And this is also true in people's literature who come from here—this kind of all-purpose, multi-talented Indian. You want somebody to hook on to who represents India, but the fact is that I don't represent India and nobody represents India and nobody can claim to. I am me. I am not interested in flags and nations. I am not even interested in being the first Indian citizen on a Monday night to have won the Booker Prize. I keep saying I am the first aerobics instructor to have won the Booker Prize. The reason this book has done what it has done is not because it's Indian, but because it's universal. What does it matter if an Indian or an Estonian or Albanian wrote it? Only journalists and pundits and critics are interested in these tags; readers are interested in reading. They are not going to read it because it's Indian or it's Albanian. In fact, if you see what happens to books that try and trade on this kind of exotic, ethnic thing, they are just sort of on the margins; they never become mainstream because they are too precious. Of course my book is Indian, because that is the world I know. It doesn't compromise on its sense of detail, and that detail is Indian, but that is just coincidental. The characters are human and anybody recognizes them.

KAS: But there is this big debate in India itself on what is Indian literature . . .

AR: Exactly, and it's so puerile. And they'll say, "Oh, you're selling India to the West" or "You're not selling India to the West" or "Is this authentic?" And I say, what do you mean by these words? "Oh, but she uses Elvis Presley so that's not really Indian." But what is really Indian? That you sit and chant Vedas in some temple? How do you define Indian? People do strive to inhabit the definition that India has been given by the West. That does happen. But it's complete nonsense. I keep saying just replace authenticity with honesty.

KAS: But do people read your book in India?

AR: It's incredible what has happened in India because it has just broken through all these barriers of who reads books. A literary book in India usually does not sell. They usually have print runs of

2,000, 3,000 copies for a normal writer. A big writer, even writers like Rushdie, would sell say 12,000 copies a year. And he's the biggest Indian writer. And my book has sold, I think, more than any book ever in India. So people are reading it and people get very angry here. If your book doesn't transcend national borders, if it doesn't get published anywhere else, then you are a failure, but if it does then you are attacked for it. So there's always debate about what I have done, and not showing India in the proper light and all of that stuff. But there's also this negative definition that the West has of India, thinking it is full of poverty—and they only want to hear about poverty and the caste system. But should we not address it because you don't want to define yourself negatively to the West? You just have to be true to yourself and forget about what others say.

KAS: Balzac called fiction the secret history of nations. Do you think that you in a way are writing something that is true, that this is history, this is not just fiction?

AR: I would agree with that. The stories you tell, the fiction you write, is a way of seeing the world and there are many, many ways of doing this, which is why I hate getting into debates about literary theory. First of all, I am not an academic and secondly, I don't have any rules—the only rule I have is that there are no rules. So, it's important that the secret history is written by many people, so that there are conflicting ways of looking at the same thing.

KAS: You said that you would probably never write another book unless there was another book inside you to write. Is the writing a process to unleash the inner self?

AR: I don't know. I am a bit suspicious of this kind of personal therapeutic approach to writing. I think it is fine, but then you just have to understand that it is therapy, and literature is something else. Literature is about art and craft and not just about your feelings and your coming out of yourself. No one cares about you except you, whether you come out of yourself or help yourself or don't help yourself is entirely your business. But literature is about art, about creating something. I've always said that amongst great writers there are selfish writers and generous writers; selfish writers leave you with the memory of their brilliance whereas generous writers leave you with the memory of the world that they have evoked. And to me, writing must be an act of generosity, not an act of self-indulgence or therapy. I'm not going to burden the world with what it did for me or didn't do for me.

KAS: Literature, you once said, is not divided according to language but according to stories, and as a writer you govern language. What is this governing of language?

AR: The context in which I said that was a program on which I appeared with Salman Rushdie. He said in the introduction to his book of the best Indian writers that the only good writing coming out of India was in English and that the writing in regional languages was not worth anything. And a lot of people including me were very upset with that. This is again that claim to represent India and no one language can claim to represent it, no one person, no one culture, no one caste, no one religion, because everything is true about India. I tried to explain to him that there are so many writers in regional languages who are closer to him in many ways than I am. So, you divide literature according to the ways in which you tell stories, not according to the language you use. Then there is this big colonial debate about writing in English. They ask me "Why do you write in English?" And they say, "But your writing is not like any American or British writers." And I reply, "Naturally I am not American or British. Don't make the mistake of assuming that because I use English, my thoughts are British." I govern language; the language is mine to express my thought in. As a writer, it is my medium. You use that medium to do what you want it to do. [. . .]

KAS: Do you think that there is something about your formative years that prepared you for this position in life? Where is your grounding now?

AR: Everything that happens to you, even when it seems dark and terrible when it's happening to you, you can learn from. And I think I have learned from everything that has happened to me. And I continue to learn from everything that happens to me. If I had not been who I was and I had not been through the experiences I have been through, I would have been killed off. I would not have known how to handle it. I would have thought, "It is all so wonderful and it's so sweet and everybody loves me and I'm so famous." But I know what the whole thing is about. I have seen the other side too much to be able to just accept this joyfully. That's the greatest piece of good fortune that I have had. Just two years before this happened to me I was totally on the other side of the fence, because of a huge debate I had about a film called *Bandit Queen*, and I wrote this series of articles called "The Great Indian Rape Trick." And all the beautiful people denounced me. The invective and the things that they said about me in the press were terrible. So, this is almost ridiculous. It just makes me laugh because it confirms my opinion of them. When I was going through it, it was traumatic. It was a complete and direct attack on my self-esteem and it was very hard to take at the time.

KAS: What happened with the lawsuit pending against you? You are being castigated for having written about an upper caste woman who has an affair with an untouchable.

AR: The two guys who have filed this case are just not representative of what is happening in this country with the book. Much as I would like to portray myself as a writer who is being hunted down, I am not. The lawsuit is a terrible pain to have to deal with, but I am quite sure that it has been brought to harass me. I will handle it by myself because the courts are not as regressive as people think they are. I am sure that the case will be thrown out. But the courts take so long and it will go on and on. When you live in India you know that India lives in several centuries simultaneously and they are all at war with each other in a sense. There is nothing you can do that is of any importance that will not end up in some kind of trouble or controversy. And this is the fallout of literature. It has created so much debate in Kerala. Some condemn me, some praise me, but that's what literature is all about. It's not about winning the Booker Prize and wearing nice clothes and feeling famous. Literature is about touching people's lives. It is absurd in a way, but absurdity also suggests surprise and this reaction doesn't surprise me. People get angrier with the same book when it wins the Booker Prize. It's as if the text changes the bigger the book becomes. Those who filed the case against me also happen to be lawyers, and they want some publicity. It's so easy. Just put a finger on *The God of Small Things* and you're in the *New York Times*.

KAS: What is the god of small things? One critic wrote that social propriety is the novel's victor. The deity of love and happiness loses out in the end. Is social propriety the god of small things?

AR: That's perhaps exactly the opposite of what I think. But a lot of people have this simplistic reading where they say, "Oh, anybody who breaks the love law suffers, so what you're saying actually is that you shouldn't break the laws." That kind of simplistic reading of crime and punishment is nonsense. The god of small things is the inversion of what god means; it's the god of loss. Take the way the novel is structured. The structure ambushes the story in that it begins at the end and it ends in the middle. And it tells you that, of course, the consequences of what happened were terrible, but the fact that they happened at all were wonderful. That's what I mean when I say that the novel belongs to everybody. I don't really want to legislate what people should make of it because it's their book to think what they want. But certainly it's not what I would have hoped that somebody would draw from it. [. . .]

KAS: You said that the writer is like a child . . .

AR: You move between worlds that are perceived to be real and worlds that are supposed to be imaginary without acknowledging the boundaries. That's why I guess madness lurks so close by. It's just being curious, isn't it? Curious and non-judgmental; being able to experience something without clamping down on it. I really don't want to make any claims for writers as a group. I am speaking for myself. I don't think most writers are like that. I think most are just the opposite—very old and tired people.

KAS: It took you almost five years to write this book, sitting in front of your computer every day. So, there seems to be a balance between being a disciplined human being and maintaining this open, child's perspective.

AR: As I said, it's like sculpting smoke. First you have to generate it and then you have to sculpt it because I don't believe in this "I wrote my book in one week" kind of approach. Something that lives with you over the years is something important; it is something that stands the test of your growing. It isn't that I didn't change in five years. It's just that it still worked for me. I am manically disciplined when I work, in that sense, because it is something that you are giving and you don't want to give a half-hearted offering. If you are doing it, do it properly.

AMIT CHAUDHURI

b. 1962

(English)

Amit Chaudhuri was born in Bombay and raised there and in Calcutta. He went to England for his university studies. The details of everyday life are rendered in his fiction, which probes the complexities of inner lives bound to a changing world. In the novel A Strange and Sublime Address, *the young narrator notices a poor relative in search of a job who arrives with "a white layer of prickly heat powder around his neck." The man is startled to realize that the child facing him hopes to become a writer in English, rather than in their mother tongue, Bengali. "English? And what will you write when you grow up?" the man asks. Memories, dreams, reflections abound in Chaudhuri's writing, and his finest work has the clarity of language that allows one to dwell on the individual sentences, each crafted with care, achieving the luminous quality one commonly associates with lyric poetry. In the autobiographical essay "Interlude," he writes of how as a student in England he started to write poetry.*

In nonfiction that often springs from the details of his own life as a writer, Chaudhuri broods long and hard on the meaning of a cosmopolitan, transnational life, and what it might mean to make a shelter through words. Instead of seeing Rushdie's prodigious work Midnight's Children *as the beginning of a whole new mode of Indian writing, Chaudhuri traces the roots of new Indian writing in English to a language and sensibility rooted in an older network of vernacular languages that have all bodied forth their own modernities. In his introduction to* Clearing a Space, *Chaudhuri argues against the overly simple binaries of colonial vs. postcolonial: "What we're witnessing," he writes, "is not the rise of internationalism, but its interruption and eclipse, and its replacement by a new mythology of travel, displacement, movement, and settlement, with, paradoxically, its new anxious awareness of the 'other,' the foreign and the native." In addition to his writing, Chaudhuri is also a classically trained vocalist. He performs lyrics with his band, experimenting with different musical traditions. His works include the novels* Freedom Song *(1998),* The Immortals *(2009), and* Odysseus Abroad *(2015), and the volume of essays* Clearing a Space: Reflections on India, Literature and Culture *(2008).*

From "Interlude"

In 1984, my parents moved to a small, appealing flat in St Cyril Road, Bandra. My father had retired from his corporate position—as the head of a company—the previous year: the year I'd gone to England as an undergraduate. At the time of retirement, we moved out of the 4,000-square-foot four-bedroom flat on the twenty-fifth storey of Maker Towers "B" on Cuffe Parade, and briefly occupied the company guest flat at "Brighton" in Nepean Sea Road, overlooking the sea (I had lived, from when I was about nine years old, in buildings that had an unobstructed view of the sea). From there we moved to the first flat my father actually owned in Bombay, a two-bedroom apartment in a building in Worli called "Sea Glimpse," whose lift had a sign saying, "Use Lift at Your Own Risk." The sea, from here, was a blur. But buildings in Bombay have their own biographies and destinies, and are named, at birth, with presumably the same mixture of wishful thinking and superstition as our children are. [. . .]

Suddenly, one day, I heard the flat in Worli had been sold and the one in St Cyril Road purchased, the exchange of money and the simultaneous relinquishing and exchange of properties taking place almost overnight. The Worli flat had been sold to a family called Ambo for thirteen lakhs; the new flat in the Eden of St Cyril Road had been bought for fifteen. The difference had been made up with my mother going to Calcutta to sell some of her gold jewellery. The remaining one lakh my father had borrowed from the HDFC. The jewellery had been sold for two reasons; although my father had been a Finance Director, then a Managing Director, of a multinational company, his income had had a huge tax imposed upon it—seventy-five per cent—and a stringent ceiling—it could rise no higher than ten thousand rupees—under Indira Gandhi, and the ceiling and the tax would substantially remain unchanged until a long time later, when the country entered (too late for my father) the era of "liberalisation." The other reason, of course, was that my parents came from East Bengal; they had no ancestral property, no hinterland, no inheritance, to fall back on; they had started their lives from scratch after 1947.

"Yes, it's happened," said my mother on the phone to me, recounting how Mr Ambo, in the end, had paid my father ten thousand less than thirteen lakhs, how he'd been distressed because his own father was unwell, and pleaded that my father accept the twelve lakh ninety thousand, which he did. I have never seen Mr Ambo and never will, but his name is enough for me to feel the proximity of his presence; I see him, and his family, enter the new flat, with the blurred view of the sea from the balcony, close the door behind them, and then I don't have to think about them again. There had been a moment of panic, my mother told me—it was all interesting in hindsight—when my parents realised they had given Mr Ambo the key to the flat before they had taken the money from him. She was now speaking to me from the flat in Bandra, where she would be ensconced for a few years to come.

I arrived at the flat, I think, in the summer of '84. It was after midnight; most flights from London to Bombay landed in the small hours of the morning. The door was opened by a man I didn't recognise; a corridor led to the phone at the end, and on the left were three rooms—the sitting room; my room; and my parents'. The kitchen and the guest room, which had been converted into the dining room, were on my right. At 2 AM, awake with what felt like a heightened caffeine-induced awareness, but what was the deceitful alertness of jet lag, I couldn't have taken in these details. I sat in my parents' room, excited, surrounded by bags and silence, and talked in a way it is possible to at such moments, when the rest of the world is asleep. Later, I went to my room to lie down, like an interloper who's been put in his place.

I should have slept the next morning till ten, but was woken up by half past six or seven. There was an eerie chorus about me, disorienting and frightening, urgent enough not to be confused with the final moments of a nightmare; it was birdcall. For more than fifteen years I'd lived in tall buildings; I had forgotten how violent this sound could be, how it could drown out everything else. [. . .]

I must have been lonely in that old life; sometimes I was conscious of that loneliness, and sometimes I mistook it for a sort of unease. But I can find no other explanation for my welcoming of St Cyril Road into my life. It wasn't that the flat was the first one my father properly owned in Bombay. It was the discovery of a community—made up, predominantly, of Goan Christians—and of the lanes and by-lanes in which that community existed. What I had missed in my childhood, without knowing it, was community; we had camped—our nuclear family; my father, my mother, and myself—in company apartments; I had surveyed, from windows and balconies, the expanse of the city, and, through binoculars, the windows and balconies of other multi-storeyed buildings. I had not suspected the need, in myself, for physical contact, the need to be close to ground-level, within earshot of my surroundings, to be taken out of myself, randomly, into the lives of others.

Like a shadow moving first in one direction, then another, itinerants came and went. The lane changed with seasons; there was a gulmohur tree facing our verandah, which shed its blossoms during the monsoons, and, by summer, was again orange with flowers. I found these little changes marvellous.

The birds that had woken me the first morning after my arrival became a part of our daytime lives, as we did theirs; their excrement hardened into green scabs, every day, on the balcony's bannister. In the mornings, they fought upon the air conditioners, and I could hear their claws scraping against metal. Each morning, their twenty-minute bout started afresh. Opening the bathroom window, I could see the air conditioner protruding outward; occasionally, a pigeon or crow set up home on it, and would fight off intruders. If I saw a pigeon alighting on the verandah with a twig in its beak, I knew a home was in the making somewhere, either on the branches of the jackfruit tree that stood next to our balcony with a kind of awareness, or on one of the air conditioners, our compulsory accomplices in middle-class comfort.

Our building itself stood in the place of a cottage that had once belonged to a Christian family. I had heard the family lived in the ground-floor apartment, but I had never seen them. Perhaps they rented the flat out, or had paying guests; because employees of Air India came and went from it at odd times of the day, including a beautiful girl, infrequently glimpsed from my verandah, who was supposed to be an air hostess. And there were other cottages and houses in the lane, I'd noticed, that seemed to be going in the direction that the house that had once stood here had gone, towards disappearance and non-existence.

This was the place I returned to in the summer, and for the short break in the winter. The rest of the year I lived in England. It was my ambition to be a poet; the ambition had taken me to England.

I was doing nothing much in London; I hardly had any friends. I hardly attended lectures at University College. But I was writing poems; these poems were like little closed rooms, like the rooms I lived in in England; they were closed to everything but literary influence. No door or window was left open to let in the real world, or to admit the self that lived in that world; in the closed room of the poem, I tried on yet another literary voice, or a style I had recently found interesting. I speak of this in architectural terms because that is what would strike me most when I returned to Bombay, to St Cyril Road, for my holidays: the continual proximity of the outside world; a window left open; the way the outside—manifested as noise, as light—both withheld itself and became a part of the interior life.

I wrote a poem in 1985, while living in the studio apartment on Warren Street. It was called "St Cyril Road, Bombay," and I must have written it between avoiding lectures, looking despondently out of the window, and eating lunch at half past three. From where, at the time, St Cyril Road came back to me, I don't know; here, though, is the poem.

> Every city has its minority, with its ironical, tiny village
> fortressed against the barbarians, the giant ransacks and the pillage
> of the larger faith. In England, for instance, the "Asians" cling to
>   their ways
> as they never do in their own land. On the other hand, the English-
>   man strays
> from his time-worn English beliefs. Go to an "Asian" street
> in London, and you will find a ritual of life that refuses to compete
> with the unschooled world outside. In Bombay, it's the Christian
>   minority that clings

like ivy to its own branches of faith. The Christian boy with the
    guitar sings
more sincerely than the Hindu boy. And in St Cyril Road, you're
    familiar
with cottages hung with flora, and fainting, drooping bougain-
    villaea,
where the noon is a charged battery, and evening's a visionary
    gloom
in which insects make secret noises, and men inside their single
    rooms
sing quaint Portuguese love songs—here, you forget, at last, to
    remember
that the rest of Bombay has drifted away, truant, and dismembered
from the old Bombay. There, rootless, garish, and widely cosmo-
    politan,
where every executive is an executive, and every other man a
    Caliban
in two-toned shoes, and each building a brooding tyrant that
    towers
over streets ogling with fat lights . . . Give me the bougainvillaea
    flowers
and a room where I can hear birds arguing. I won't live in a pillar
    of stone,
as ants and spiders live in the cracks of walls, searching for food
    alone
in the sun-forgotten darkness. That's why I've come to St Cyril
    Road
to lose myself among the Christians, and feel Bombay like a huge
    load
off my long-suffering chest. Woken up at six o' clock in the
    morning,
by half-wit birds who are excited in the knowledge that day is
    dawning
on the sleeping lane—that's what I want. The new day enters my
    head
like a new fragrance. I rise, dignified, like Lazarus from the dead.

"I like the parody of Yeats," said a friend after reading it. "Yeats?" I said disbelievingly; I hadn't been thinking of Yeats. "Yes, silly," she said, smiling, and pointed out my own lines to me: "where the noon is a charged battery, and evening's a visionary gloom / in which insects make secret noises, and men inside their single rooms / sing quaint Portuguese love songs . . ." I saw now that, unknowingly, I'd tried to transform St Cyril Road into Innisfree; to trace a similar journey of desire. "There midnight's all a glimmer, and noon a purple glow / And evening full of the linnet's wings," Yeats had said. I replaced the linnet's wings with the nocturnal sound of crickets I'd heard each day after sunset.

The view from the room I lived in on Warren Street was very different from St Cyril Road. There was a restaurant opposite, Tandoor Mahal; it was one of the three or four Indian restaurants, all of which seemed fairly successful, English people hunched inside them mornings and afternoons, except this one. It looked like the family of the man who owned it—a balding Sylheti Muslim in a suit with a round face and compassionate eyes—were in and out of the restaurant all day; but almost no one else. I can remember seeing the two daughters, who would have been in their early teens, and the energetic little boy, their younger brother, many, many times, but never a single customer.

I was not quite sure if this was England, or somewhere else; I was never sure how to characterise or categorise this place. It certainly did not approximate any idea of England I previously might have had. Next to the restaurant was another three-storeyed house, like the one I lived in, in whose attic lived a tall Englishman who I presumed was a painter. I thought this because he often went about carrying large canvases. A friend came to see him frequently; a shorter stockier man who had moustaches, whom I used to call "Lal" because he resembled a man of the same name who used to be a director in the company my father had retired from. There was a graceful bonhomie in their meetings, which mainly took place on the pavement before the black door to the house, near a parking meter, and it was always interesting to note, in passing, the angularity of the taller man juxtaposed with, and almost reaching toward, the settled centre of gravity of the stockier companion. The tall man seemed in danger of being blown away by a wind. Lal, the stocky man, sometimes had a dog with him. There was a strange loneliness, or aloneness, about them; they seemed impervious to the passers-by making their way towards the Warren Street tube on the right.

What was I doing here? It was a question I often asked myself. I had come to England to become, eventually, a famous poet. The ambition left me lonely. I hardly went to college or attended lectures. Instead, I sleepwalked through that area around Fitzroy Square, Grafton Street, and Tottenham Court Road, stepping in and out of newsagents', surreptitiously visiting grocers' and cornershops, while I waited to become famous. Knowing my attachment to Larkin, my mother bought me his new book of selected prose, *Required Writing*, for my twenty-second birthday. There were two interviews in it. Larkin was a reluctant interviewee; he was always politely admonishing the interviewer for his stupidity. When asked by Robert Phillips of the *Paris Review*, "Was it your intention, then, to be a novelist only?" because of Larkin's two early novels, Larkin said, in his unfriendly but interesting way, "I wanted to 'be a novelist' in a way I never wanted to 'be a poet,' yes," as if "wanting to be" was a necessary but misleading part of a writer's life. As for myself, I wanted to "be" a poet; I had never thought of "being" a novelist. It was towards this end that I'd come to England; and sent out my poems to the National Poetry Competition, as advertised in the *Poetry Review*, a pound the entry fee for each poem submitted.

   Those first years of living in London made me acutely aware of light, and space, and weather, and how they influence ways of life. And it was partly this, I suppose, that made me see St Cyril Road in a new way, that made me, in Warren Street, write the poem, and allowed, for the first time, a "real" place, a real locality, to enter my writing. At that time, I didn't know anything unusual had happened. I was pleased enough with the poem; but I was pleased with almost every poem I wrote. Later, that poem would become my first publication in England; it would appear in the *London Review of Books*, its long lines clustered at the bottom of a page, in 1987.

   By the time the poem was published, we were already thinking of leaving St Cyril Road. The flat that had been bought with such excitement three years ago—the small three-bedroom flat with its perspective of the lane—was up for sale. On long walks down St Cyril and St Leo road, my parents had discussed the matter with me, and we had come to the same conclusion. For a variety of reasons, my father was under financial pressure; and the debt of one lakh rupees from HDFC had still not been quite resolved. We would move to Calcutta; my father had bought a flat there in a government-erected block in 1975. My father, at that point of time, could not afford, we decided, the luxury of two flats in two cities; and his plan, anyway, had always been to retire to Calcutta.

I didn't mind the idea of moving to Calcutta; I encouraged it. All my life, I'd been vociferous about my dislike of, my impatience with, Bombay, and the fact that Calcutta was my spiritual home. And the money, once the flat was sold, would be a comfortable investment for my father. In the meanwhile, I continued to explore the area, and the explorations continued to result in poems. In 1986, when I took a year's break between graduating from University College, London, and leaving for Oxford, I wrote "The Bandra Medical Store":

When I first moved here, I had no idea whatsoever
where the Bandra Medical Store really was. But someone

in the house was ill. So I ventured out, let my legs
meander to a chosen path, articulate their own distances.

I guess my going out for medicine, even the illness, were just
excuses for me to make that uninsisting journey

to a place I hadn't seen. Two roads followed each other
like long absences. The air smelled of something not there.
    Branches

purled and knitted shadows. There was a field, with a little land-
    slide
of rubble, and a little craggy outline of stone.

I drifted past heliotropic rubbish-heaps, elderly
white houses. An aircraft hummed overhead. And did

the houses look like rows of slender barley from the pilot's
window, row pursuing row, held in a milieu of

whiteness, unswayed by a clean, flowing wind?
Then the plane donned a thick cloud. All it left was a cargo

of loaded silence. I supposed that I must be lost.
It grew evening. Trees fluttered in the dusk-sough

like winged, palaeolithic moths eddying towards
the closing eye of the sun. I asked someone, "Do you know

where the Bandra Medical Store is?" The directions
he gave me were motionless gestures scrawled on

a darkening fresco. I stepped forward, intentionally
trampled a crisp leaf, which then made the only

intelligible comment of the evening. But I took care
not to squash a warrior-ant that scuttled before me.

He was so dignified, so black. Had I been smaller, I'd have
ridden him back home, or off into the sunset.

I sent this and four other poems to Alan Ross, and he wrote back to me in two weeks, a note with a few scribbled comments on the poems, saying he would keep it and another one for publication. The poems would appear in the *London Magazine* during my first term in Oxford, in October 1987. But the lane itself was changing; the cottages were being torn down; six-or seven-storeyed buildings, like the one we lived in, were coming up in their place.

At around this time, when I was writing these poems, I also began to write a novel. I went to one of the small Gujarati-run shops on Turner Road and bought a lined notebook, such as shopkeepers and accountants use; its hardboard cover bore the legend "Jagruti Register." I wrote a few lines every day; and, on certain days, I wrote nothing at all. I wrote without anxiety, and tried to allow the petit-bourgeois life of my uncle's family in Calcutta into the excitement of the written word. I tried to solve, as I wrote, the paradox of why this life, so different from the world I'd grown up in on Malabar Hill and in Cuffe Parade, had been a joy to me; the same paradox that made the location of my father's post-retirement life a joy.

Film stars came to see the flat (who but film stars, businessmen, and companies can afford Bombay real estate prices?). I was told that Naseeruddin Shah was looking to move from his two-bedroom flat to a three-bedroom one; and, one morning, I saw him in our sitting room with his mother-in-law, Dina Pathak, who, right away, seemed to know her own mind, and his. I struggled not to look too hard at him, because he had recently won a prize at an international festival. He was shy, if stocky and muscular after his workouts for *Jalwa*, and sent a momentary smile in my direction. Then he went about peeping into our rooms.

A property takes time to sell in Bombay, for the same reason it takes time to buy one. And so the final transaction—and my parents' departure to Calcutta, and the flat itself—remained in abeyance. "White" money was scarce; my father wanted payment in "white." Helen came to see the flat, Helen, who had danced for us so many times, settled into matrimony and middle age, wearing a salwar kameez. She was an utterly charming woman; she had deliberately exchanged her sensual aura for an air of ordinariness; and yet she had a style of interaction that was seductive in its openness and warmth. She loved the flat and the lane; she had the thrilled air of a convert that I'd had when I first moved here. "I *must* have the flat, Mr Chaudhuri," she said to my father irresistibly, and I could almost visualise her living in it.

By the time I returned home from Oxford in the summer of 1988, I had a first draft. An extract—chapter seven in the finished book—had appeared in a national periodical; publishers had written to me, enquiring after the novel. As potential buyers wandered through the flat, I found, going through the pages of the notebook, that, to my alarm, I would have to excise the first two or three chapters, for which, now, there seemed no need, and rewrite the beginning and several other chapters. As I began to cut out and jettison what I had once thought were necessary links and co-ordinates, I noticed a form taking shape, a form that absorbed and pleased me. And then I fell ill, probably with the strain: my condition was diagnosed as hepatitis. I couldn't fathom how I'd got it; I never drank anything but boiled water.

Nine days in the Special Wing of Nanavati Hospital, on the drip; then back to the flat in St Cyril Road. I missed Michaelmas term in the new academic year in Oxford. "Oh, hepatitis!" said the hushed voice of the accommodation officer at Holywell Manor, wondering if she might catch it from a long-distance call. "Yes, *do* take your time."

That Christmas, as in my poem, the young men came to the lane, guitar in hand, singing carols. I had finished revising the novel, after a horrible, protracted period, and then typed it on my father's Olympia typewriter. The typescript, after my excisions, came to 87 pages. I sent this to the agent who'd been in touch with me after the publication of the extract. At first, she was worried by the size of the manuscript; later, she said she'd send it to William Heinemann. Recovered from hepatitis, back to health and normalcy and the routine disappointments they bring, I returned to England in January 1989, after it had lately snowed around London. I got a phone call which informed me that William Heinemann were "excited" about the manuscript. I was still to become familiar with the language publishers use.

The flat was sold—not to Helen, but to a Punjabi businessman called Chandok. He could pay the entire amount in "white." Two months ago, when I went to Bombay, I walked into the building on St Cyril Road and saw that Chandok's name is still there on the nameplate. I have no idea what this small investigation was meant to confirm.

My agent, after a considerable silence, called me one evening to say, "Amit, I have two pieces of bad news for you. The first is that Heinemann have turned down your book." "What's the other one?" I asked. "I've stopped being an agent." She was getting married.

I then went to another agent, Imogen Parker, who too had expressed enthusiasm for my work. She was one of the most determined and plain-speaking, and most intelligent, people I met in the business; like Helen, she was a survivor, and had an odd, sparkling beauty. "Don't worry," she told me (she would herself marry and leave the agency in a couple of years), "your book will be published."

SUDEEP SEN
b. 1964
(English)

Sudeep Sen was born in Delhi into a literary Bengali family. In a 2010 interview published in World Literature Today *he speaks of growing up in a "trilingual situation—I spoke Bengali at home, Hindi on the streets and English at school, not by design but by circumstance. So, this wonderful tripartite situation was such that I could slip in and out of several mother tongues and languages." Sen's poetry is marked by the sharp facets of color and sense that burst onto the page, strung together with a delicate armory of syntax through which desire and its aftermath pour through the textures of the poem. His work as a photographer stands side by side with his writing, and in each there is a subtle architecture that undergirds bursts of image and light. His earliest collection of poetry, a limited edition chapbook,* Leaning Against the Lamp-Post *(1983), was published with help from his grandfather. Sen, who is fascinated by the materiality of writing, evokes the messy process of cyclostyle through which the pages were duplicated, and each edition hand sewn by the local printer, himself a poet. In "Photons, Graphite, Blood," we see the detailed material grounds of writing in the midst of a power outage in Delhi and the way a fly hovers over the paper choosing a very special spot to land on the manuscript. There is something both surreal and magical in the process of creation: "I also saw—lines that I had not written—imprinted in my own script, planted on the page." In "Postcards," the speaker finds in the perpetual unhousedness of the poet a fit ground for the emergence of the poem, a built thing with its own skeleton of syntax and line-breaks. Sen was invited in 2013 by Derek Walcott to give a lecture and read his poetry at the Nobel Laureate week in St. Lucia. Sen's books include* Distracted Geographies *(2003) and* Fractals: New & Selected Poems/Translations (1980–2015).

"Photons, Graphite, Blood"

There is a lamp—blue and white enamelled—that hangs straight down from my room's heaven-white concrete. The electric noose balances the bulb's epi-centre directly above my desk. Conical curvature of the shade's inner wall contracts every electron in sight. It is well made and hardy and cheap.

I had picked it up at a random flea-market sale. It lay innocuously next to a stack of old seventies blues records and a box containing pins, clips, angles, lead, string, bandages, and pieces of magnet. Curiously, this lamp-shade beckoned to be rescued from this *potpourri* of discards. Something about its shape had attracted me—its mathematical precision, its nonchalance, its latent heat, and its misplaced future.

A few weeks later it found a place of pride in my studio. It became my invisible body, a talkative metaphor making up for all the uncomfortably annoying silence in this space. It took over my space, colonised it, and then started writing my pieces for me.

It had been dark for many days. I didn't know whether I had lost my sight, or it was one of those infamous marathon Delhi power-cuts, or whether the act was waiting for a curtain call before the next show. There was no show, or if there was, it was a show for an audience that failed to show up.

I got used to this darkness. I even started liking it. There is something wonderfully warm and safe about the dark. It allows you to hide, it allows you to rant, it allows you to weep, and it allows you to die unnoticed and emerge as another person—if you are lucky—without anyone else realising that an intense metamorphosis has taken place.

Another night—I had returned from the outside to the dark safety of my small space. There was a glow, a light that I had always imagined but failed to see, or perhaps always seen but failed to notice. But it was the next act, the unwritten stanza that altered the entire narrative.

A pool of light lay splashed on my desk. Its circular cast shimmering thoughtfully on the page where my poem was arrested in mid-flight. At its edges, the circumference began to fade, inaccurately. Even the power of pulse-wattage showed its fragility when one of many flies buzzing on this sweaty night sat on the metal shade. Then everything changed.

There was another power-outage, a major one, but that was normal in the country's capital at this time of the year. However, this lampshade remained magically lit in full flight. Its rays billowed out as if it had caught the right trade winds on an unnamed sea. There were no generators or invertors to assist this "load-shedding"—I can safely assure you of that. It was as if my blue and white conical companion had mysteriously extracted all the electricity in visual sight, condensed it into the tiniest invisible atomic space, and then like escaping blood let it ooze out gently, as it would after an accidental pin-prick.

The blood spread, surreptitiously approaching the lone fly that had by now flown from the lampshade's edge onto the tabletop. It sensed war, flexing its winged muscles; it prepared to take the right stance, so there would be minimal bloodshed.

The light's heat and intensity made the fly forget its natural act of flight. It started moving, centipede-like, towards the approaching lava. The blood-trickle changed tracks, carefully avoiding an unwanted spill, not smudging my metaphors or the neatly constructed lines. The fly chose to use the moment of enjambment at the end of stanza three as its vantage point. The blood-stream, sensing a birth of a new metaphor, stopped in its tracks, allowed itself to gather into a bulbous expanding sphere of crimson, and then, using the overhead light's strength, gathered speed, training its path between line-spaces, dextrously dodging images that protested its progress.

I had used hand-written italics as my script. The trail my HB pencil left calculated the latitudes and longitudes of the paper-space very carefully, unknown even to me. Amid the dark doldrums of this *papier-mâché* seascape, the unscripted theatre seamlessly enacted itself.

Suddenly my eyes distractedly went to the last unfinished line. There I saw a dead fly, totally frozen amid the glass-ruins of a burst electric bulb, splattered with blood, and the shattered lead's shimmering graphite. I also saw lines that I had not written imprinted in my own script, planted on the page. The poem was suddenly alive, screaming, weeping, nervous, calm.

I looked up and saw a new bulb. A red bulb had replaced the vanished one in the lampshade. The shade's colour had altered dramatically to a rusty metallic—almost like stale blood. The pool of light had permanently frozen on the page. And there was also a poem—an unannounced gift of hidden light.

"Postcards"

For decades, I have received postcards with an annoying sense of regularity. They have appeared from all possible places—from a burnt-out garage-warehouse where a Beat-poet friend and I once shared an echoey studio-space; from the hop-stained boiler-room of an English pub's brewery; from subterranean "larger-than-life" "sewer-pipe-dwellers," who every-so-often would surface to leave bits of text for the groundlings. I got one postcard *even* from god, but most of them came from hell. The last pile gave me the most comfort, understandably. But amid all that, I had to carry a perennial burden, an unwanted guilt, for not having replied to any one of them.

Choicelessly, I have preserved these postcards with a sense of undisclosed fervour. It is quite unlike the one that grips you when one numismatically collects copper-nickel disc-change, or mint-condition serrated-quadrilaterals in search of philately. And all this comes with their inherent quest for value and nationality, their insistent obsession for identity and status—"permanent resident," "resident alien," or the "other." Residence and permanence have little meaning for me, only the postcards with their unexpected origins, their marginality, their addresslessness, provide safety to my kind.

On the obverse six-by-four papier-mâché space of laminated gloss, my created cast of characters variously enact themselves—Milo, Yacoub, Madelaine; Anna, Alexandra, Zoe; my lost brother Jake and many others.

Their postures pose truths and [un]truths that ultimately make sense, even if to only a few.

Cards arrive from the remotest corners of the planet—from a half-restored 15th century mansion, "Gartincaber" in Doune, lost in the Scottish wilds; from a moss-ridden ancestral house, "Chandradham" in Bankura, soaked in rural Bengal as its age-brittle bricks try hard to keep the concrete and lineage cemented; from an invisible deck-hand on an abandoned rust-ridden ship run aground Bombay's Bandra shores, a cinema-set "Gold-mist" balcony in the frame without Basu-da's presence—all these and much more, constructed by fate, reason, and madness.

Madness is the only space I can inhabit, the only space left for me that makes complete sense. I am not allowed to do anything else—my hands have long been severed by the executioner, my bank-account robbed clean by my employers, and my blood caught in a corpuscle-thickening dance that unwinds itself in deliberate movements—slow and artful.

And all along my alter-ego constructs buildings of fantastical proportions —made of titanium, gossamer, and glass—their skeletons held together by enjambments and line-breaks that defy even geometry and gravity. I trapeze along—sketch with the likes of Wright, Kahn and Le Corbusier. I find it astonishing that I remain unelectrocuted, having balanced my laser-linear space on the death-torque steel of high-tension wires. I spin ferociously heading towards the fountainhead, where the topography of the atlas shrugged off its dead weight and epi-centre. I wanted to be an architect, and a mapmaker.

Every morning I wake up with the peculiar and unmistakable "brass-and-wood" sound of the postman sliding insidious parcels through the letter-box—epistles, epigrams, epigraphs; lyrics, lust, latex; cantos, cantilevers, cadavers—all scored in perfect pantoums and set in arranged arias in a lattice-looped typeface.

But I am not awake, I mean *really* awake. The diurnal time distrusts me— weighing me under the albatross-noose of a day-job, the persistent fetid tones of telephone calls, the distressing iambs of food-shopping, dish-washing, and keeping the mortgage-till in order. The day passes, unremarkably. Then it is evening and soon night-time. Now I am awake, certainly much more fully.

I go through the morning rituals—gurgle my throat with the black-ink of chilled stout, wash my mouth with vodka laced with more vodka, followed by a smooth stream of single malt—and slowly, very slowly, I reach a plateau, deftly suspended in gentle equilibrium.

My mind, now, perfectly poised to kill any distracted gerund in sight or snap up any misplaced metaphor loitering around. Nothing can stop me, not even the fangs of the contorted walrus-toothed Everyman—that desultory Smirnoff copywriter—who rewrote the very definition of "spirit-level" itself. Heaney would be happy. So would Joseph, Walcott, Neruda, and Paz; as well as the entire distilling tribe.

An invisible song erupts. I see myself in an old church. A swan-graced cellist with the electric beauty of pale youth swims in to steady the waves. Her angelic brows dip, as the long lamentation of her deep-oaked cello breathes, resuscitating the congregated air with secret notes, notes that strangely escaped from my hidden postcards. I hoarded them all these years not knowing their implications or their desires. Now they bloom, magical, and perfectly intoned.

I run to the temple. There is no faith left in the apse—only the memory of slender fingers stroking the cello, *Chandipath*'s baritone invoking the myth of Durga's verse, and images of italicised scribbles.

It is morning again—time to retire. I put my night-gods to sleep. Another postcard threatens to arrive through the door's letter-vent. I am grateful for such meagre company.

But all of a sudden—I am apyretic, apyrous, and aqua-cool—I am not at all my own self. It is merely the beginning. I can scent a bloodstained epistle on its way.

ARUNDHATHI SUBRAMANIAM
b. 1967
(English)

Arundhathi Subramaniam was born in Bombay and raised and educated in that most cosmopolitan of Indian cities. Intimately involved in the cultural life of the city, she worked for several years at the National Centre for Performing Arts where she led a discussion group on the connection between different art forms. She was active in the Poetry Circle, a place for the otherwise isolated English-language poets to gather and share work. She is a follower of the mystic and spiritual leader Sadghuru, and she travels frequently away from Bombay to spend time at his ashram and yoga center in Coimbatore. Arundhathi Subramaniam's first book, On Cleaning Bookshelves *(2001), reveals the seemingly opposed elements that make up her life. Her poems evoke the fraught realities of daily existence as well as the spiritual worlds for which the speaker searches. Her fierce, nervy poetry has marked her as an important figure in a new generation of English-language poets who, while living and working in India, are quite unapologetic about their use of English, which they consider quite their own, an utterly Indian idiom. Still, as her poem "To the Welsh Critic Who Doesn't Find Me Identifiably Indian" reveals, there is something bitter in the postcolonial pill, some ingredient that would uncover the speaker as the exotic Other, tearing apart the identity she crafts for herself. In the poem "Where I Live" her lyric line works into the immediate present with all its splintering elements— "City of septic magenta hair-clips / of garrulous sewers and tight-lipped taps"—then moves to an inwardness that, though it is the site of conflict, becomes the source of a possible transcendence. In "Winter, Delhi, 1997," an intimate poem of family, the voice seeks out the self, "eighth grandchild, peripheral, half-forgotten," and discovers something akin to comfort: "My credentials never in question / my tertiary nook in a gnarled family tree / non-negotiable." Arundhathi Subramaniam has written a prose book about the life and work of the visionary mystic,* Sadhguru: More Than a Life *(2010), as well as a book on the Buddha. Her other volumes of poetry are* Where I Live *(2005) and* Where I Live: New and Selected Poems *(2009).*

"To the Welsh Critic Who Doesn't Find Me Identifiably Indian"

You believe you know me,
wide-eyed Eng Lit type
from a sun-scalded colony
reading my Keats—or is it yours—
while my country detonates
on your television screen.

You imagine you've cracked
my deepest fantasy—
oh, to be in an Edwardian vicarage,
living out my dharma
with every sip of dandelion tea
and dreams of the weekend jumble sale . . .

You may have a point.
I know nothing about silly mid-offs,
I stammer through my Tamil,
and I long for a nirvana
that is hermetic,
odor-free,
bottled in Switzerland,
money back guaranteed.

This business about language,
how much of it is mine,

how much yours,
how much from the mind,
how much from the gut,
how much is too little,
how much is too much,
how much from the salon,
how much from the slum,
how I say verisimilitude,
how I say Brihadaranyaka,
how I say vaazhapazham—
it's all yours to measure,
the pathology of my breath,
the halitosis of my gender,
my homogenized plosives
about as rustic
as a mouth-freshened global village.

Arbiter of identity,
remake me as you will.
Write me a new alphabet of danger,
a new patois to match
the Chola bronze of my skin.
Teach me how to come of age
in a literature you have bark-scratched
into scripture.

Smear my consonants
with cow-dung and turmeric and godhuli.
Pity me, sweating,
Rancid, on the other side of the counter.
Stamp my papers,
lease me a new anxiety,
grant me a visa
to the country of my birth.
Teach me how to belong,
the way you do,
on every page of world history.

arundhathi subramaniam

"First Draft"

It's just old fashioned, they say,
to use pen and paper for first drafts

but I still need
the early shiver of ink
in a white February wind

the blue slope and curve
of letter
bursting into stream

the smudge of blind alley
the retraced step, the groove
of old caravan routes, the slow thaw

of glacier, the chasm that cannot be forded
by image.

And I need reprieve, perhaps a whole season,
before I arrive at that first inevitable chill

when a page I dreamt piecemeal
in some many-voiced moon-shadowed thicket

flickers back at me
in Everyman's handwriting

filaments of smell and sight
cleanly amputated—
Times New Roman, font size fourteen.

S. SUKIRTHARANI
b. 1973
(Tamil)

S. Sukirtharani was born into an impoverished Dalit family in a small village in Tamil Nadu. In a memoir piece she writes of how her only reading materials were her schoolbooks, many of which she had to beg or borrow from others. There were a few poems included in the textbooks, and she was able to read these over and over. In an autobiographical piece prefatory to her poems in the anthology No Alphabet in Sight: New Dalit Writing from South India *(2011), she writes, "I feel there is a natural connection between poetry and my heart." Here we learn that in early adulthood she encountered feminist texts, and these allowed her to instill her poems with intense questions of embodiment and personal identity. Sukirtharani is part of a new generation of women poets in Tamil, including writers such as Salma and Kutti Revathi, each writing about growing up as a girl child, about body, sexuality, the strictures of family. There is a lyrical tenderness to Sukirtharani's writing, a way of attending to difficult, daily realities through the emotive power of images. Natural forms, grass and leaves, rocks and trees, take on great importance and are often enfolded into the image of the female body, which is revealed as part of a natural world that nourishes it, a world whose language human beings have not yet learned to hear. In an untitled poem, the first line of which reads, "When they skinned the carcass / of a dead cow," we listen to the voice of a young girl in an Outcaste family forced to face up to the grief she feels at being so marginalized. She must gather up bits of leftover rice tossed out by well-to-do families, even as her father is forced to wear a drum around his neck and beat it to warn passersby of his Untouchable status. The poem ends with a clear resolution— the child determined to be truthful. If anyone asks she will respond, "Yes, I am a pariah girl." Sukirtharani has made a documentary film,* She Writes *(2005), and has been active in political issues, including protests against the violence faced by the Tamil minority in Sri Lanka. Her works of poetry include* Kaipidithu En Kanavukel *(2002) and* Iruvaimirukam *(*Night Beast, *2004).*

"Night Beast"

Like a young woman's
love-sickness,
darkness had begun
to engulf the world.

After shutting the door,
I sat alone
in the yellow light of candles.

It was then that its
daily, unwelcome visit
came to pass.

Even as I was watching,
it pulled me out
and brought forth
another version of myself.

Before I was startled,
I had finished reading
the book that bore
the imprint of intimacy.

The light beams of my eyes
were fixed on the loose clothes
of the man asleep
in the front room.

Along with the wine
that filled the cup and overflowing,
my body drowned
and floated to the top.

While I was absorbed
in pleasuring myself, uttering
obscene phrases in a low moan,
hearing the rustle of birds' wings
the night beast fled,
returning me to myself.

"Gigantic Trees"

Gifted with the cycle
of seasons, my body
ripens and gathers into a heap—
like a mushroom.

Secret organs are carefully woven
onto its front and back.
The smoky aroma of clarified lust
rises from the skin that crawls
with gooseflesh all over.

My body is etched with
lukewarm cheeks, plump
around the yielding waist,
and cowries of desire, arranged
like an upturned triangle.

Arriving now in a misty haze,
a street artiste performing without make-up,
you untie the knots in the front of my bodice,
savouring the breasts that nourished you once;
now you are ashamed even to utter their name.

I brandish the fork of my breasts
as a lethal weapon in combat.
From this day on, you must
serenade aloud from below
those firm, unyielding breasts
which hold aloft the pennant
of this territory under my reign.

It is ages now
since breasts morphed
into gigantic trees.

"Untitled Poem—2"

When they skinned the carcass
of a dead cow,
I would chase the crows away.

After eating
the communal food
I collected after waiting
for a long time
outside every home,
I'd brag that it was
a hot meal I ate.

Encountering my father
on the street
with a funereal drum
slung around his neck,
I'd pass him quickly,
averting my face.

Unable to state
my father's vocation
and his annual income
in the classroom,

I'd fall victim
to the teacher's cane.

Sitting friendless
in the back row,
I'd cry secret tears.

But now,
should anyone happen to ask,
I tell them readily:
Yes, I am a pariah girl.

"Pariah God"

You say
the heat that sears our side
is a pariah sun.

You say
the beak that steals
the worm-ridden grain spread out to sun
is a pariah crow.

You say
the mouth that snatches
food along with your wrist
is a pariah dog.

When the land is tilled
and sweat is sown
you say
it is pariah labour.

If this is how everything is named
what is the name of that pariah god
who walks the earth blood-thirsty?

s. sukirtharani

Acknowledgments

This has been quite a journey and education. A gathering of spirits, of words, of flesh and blood even, a space where so many are gathered. There has been much reading and sifting and sorting, shuffling of pages and texts till finally precariously the shape clarifies and it is done.

This house of words, this mansion of many rooms, would not have been possible without diverse voices and words and hands. I think of Edward Hirsch, poet and friend, who, in a conversation over coffee, started me on this project. Without his support and wise counsel this book would not have come to pass. I think of my agent, Priya Doraswamy, who supported me through thick and thin and guided me with a steady hand when I got entangled in the seemingly endless undergrowth of rights and permissions. I think of my editor, Jaya Chatterjee, who has always believed in this anthology of Indian writers from our various languages, writers who in ways both overt and elliptical have seen fit to reflect on their own acts of meaning making. I think of Susie Tibor, permissions agent, to whom I entrusted the hardest sources and who helped me through with unfailing clarity and warmth.

And clearly this work could not have been dreamed of in the first place without the fine work of the writers gathered here. So many friends, fine writers old and new, generously gave me permission to use their work and expressed their support. And there are so many others, wonderful writers whose works we could not use. The roots of this book lie in the soil of many subcontinental languages: my gratitude to the translators and editors to whom I reached out who freely granted permissions. And thanks are due to the numerous publishers spread over several continents who have allowed us to reprint these writings.

I thank those who gave me advice as this project took shape especially—Arvind Krishna Mehrotra, Amitav Ghosh, K. Satchidanandan, P. P. Raveendran, Susie Tharu, Githa Hariharan, Ritu Menon, Tahira Naqvi, David Lelyveld, C. M. Naim. While some people are clearly identified in the credits, I want to acknowledge family members as well as friends of the writers and translators who generously gave their help—Professor K. N. Chaudhari, Prithvi Chaudhuri, Satarupa Chaudhuri (for Nirad C. Chaudhuri); Neil Gross (for David Rubin, translator of Premchand); Amitananda Das, Aparna Das, Ratna Lahiri, Clinton Seely (for Jibanananda Das); Daniel Simon, Susan Raja Rao (for Raja Rao); Ashok Vajpeyi, Om Thanvi, and the Vatsal Nidhi Nyas (for Agyeya); Svati Joshi (for Umashankar Joshi); Ayesha Jalal, Jeffrey Hasan (for Saadat Hasan Manto); Gayatri Spivak, Naveen Kishore (for Mahasweta Devi); Krishna Ramanujan, Krittika Ramanujan (for A. K. Ramanujan); P. P. Raveendran, Meena Ayyappa Paniker, Sreeparvati Ayyappa Paniker (for K. Ayyappa Paniker); Priya Doraswamy, Anuradha Ananthamurthy, Esther Ananthamurthy (for U. R. Ananthamurthy); Devindra Kohli, Madhav Das Nalapat, Jaisurya Das (for Kamala Das); Antara Dev Sen, Nandana Dev Sen (for Nabaneeta Dev Sen); Mark Holmström (for Lakshmi Holmström, translator of Ambai). Lakshmi, who, even when she was grievously ill, took the time and effort to sign the permission form. To our sorrow she passed away before this book was completed. P. P. Raveendran kindly translated Ayyappa Paniker's "Why Write?" for this anthology, and N. Kalyan Raman thoughtfully provided fresh versions of his translations of poems by Sukirtharani.

Perhaps mortality is the undersong of any act of writing, but how much more so for an anthology that stretches back into a previous century. In the course of making this book together two great writers of the Indian subcontinent left us—U. R. Ananthamurthy and Mahasweta Devi. They have bequeathed us their vital, glowing words. Before his death, Ananthamurthy, who was a friend and mentor, sent me an essay. I am grateful to his daughter Anuradha for connecting me to her mother, Esther Ananthamurthy, who after her husband's death kindly granted us permission to use the piece. The inimitable Mahasweta Devi passed away earlier this year and her publisher, Naveen Kishore, kindly sent me an interview he had done with her.

My thanks to what has for many years been my home institution, the City University of New York, a cosmopolitan space filled with immigrants, that, like the city itself, often seems to stand at the crossroads of the world. My thanks to Hunter College of the City University of New York for a grant in aid that helped with the cost of multiple permissions. The Ph.D. program in English at CUNY Graduate Center made space in our quarters on the fourth floor of 365 Fifth Avenue, setting up an extra filing cabinet for me, in what was the Xerox room, so I could house these accumulated materials. At the Graduate Center I have had the good fortune to work with gifted research assistants, doctoral students, who one by one over the course of several years helped me research, sort, type, and check the materials: Erin Glass, Karen Lepri, Mahendran Thiruvarangan, Sara Deniz Akant, Susan Kalaz, and Genevieve Bettendorf. I thank Genevieve, who took on the particular burden of checking the complicated edited text. My thanks to Margaret Hogan, who copyedited the work with care, and to Mary Pasti and all at Yale University Press for bringing this book into the light of day.

My gratitude to my friends Gauri Viswanathan, Kimiko Hahn, and Andrea Belag who over cups of coffee or glasses of wine supported me in what seemed at times a foolhardy task. My thanks to Adam Lelyveld and Svati Lelyveld, who already in childhood had learned to put up with a mother who hid away from time to time, scribbling lines of poetry. Adults now, they were able to look on, offering me support without querying overmuch what I was up to. My love and thanks to my husband, David Lelyveld, who dipped into his knowledge of subcontinental matters, connecting me with thoughts and ideas that had never crossed my mind. In our conversations on our morning walks through Fort Tryon Park with its great trees and flowering bushes, he helped ease the difficulty this project with its multiple translated languages, rights, and crossings sometimes inspired in me.

During the years of making this anthology much has been lived through and many things have come to pass. In closing I think of the lines in Kalidasa's *Meghadutam*, a work I love: "Resting awhile on that mountain / in whose bowers the brides of foresters sport / and lightened by your waters' outpouring / you'll speedily cross the road beyond."

Credits

I am grateful to those listed below for permission to reprint the materials included in this anthology.

Agyeya (Sachchidananda Vatsayan). "The Signs," "Words and Truth," "Three Words to Make a Poem," "The Revolving Rock XVI," and "The Revolving Rock XXV." In *Signs and Silence*, translated by the author and Leonard E. Nathan, 121–25, 146, 151. Intercultural Research Institute Translation Series 1. Delhi: Simant Publications India, 1976. Reprinted by permission of Vatsal Nidhi Trust.

Alexander, Meena. Excerpt from "Illiterate Heart." In *Illiterate Heart*, 63–68. Evanston, Ill.: TriQuarterly Books / Northwestern University Press, 2002. Copyright © 2002 by Meena Alexander. Published 2002 by TriQuarterly Books / Northwestern University Press. All rights reserved. "Crossroad." In *Atmospheric Embroidery*. Evanston, Ill.: TriQuarterly Books / Northwestern University Press, 2018. Copyright © 2018 by Meena Alexander. Published 2018. All rights reserved.

Ali, Agha Shahid. Excerpt from "In Search of Evanescence." In *A Nostalgic's Map of America*, 38–48. New York: Norton, 1991. Copyright © 1991 Agha Shahid Ali. Used by permission of W. W. Norton and Company, Inc.

Ambai (C. S. Lakshmi). Excerpt from "Squirrel." In *A Purple Sea: Stories by Ambai*, translated by Lakshmi Holmström, 81–92. Chennai: Manas, 1992. Reprinted by permission of C. S. Lakshmi (author) and Lakshmi Holmström (translator).

Ananthamurthy, U. R. Excerpt from "Five Decades of My Writing." In *Indian Literature* 51, no. 5 (2007): 112–35. Reprinted by permission of Esther Ananthamurthy, Estate of U. R. Ananthamurthy.

Antherjanam, Lalithambika. "Childhood Memories." Reproduced from Lalithambika Antherjanam, "Balyasmriti" ("Childhood Memories"). In *Cast Me Out If You*

Will: Stories and Memoir, translated by Gita Krishnankutty, 134–42. Kolkata: Stree, 1998. Copyright © 1997 compilation, introduction, notes, and translation by Gita Krishnankutty. Reprinted by permission of the publisher.

Atholi, Raghavan. "The Poet with a Forest Fire Inside." Raghavan Atholi in conversation with Pradeepan Pampirikunnu, translated by Jayasree Kalathil. In *No Alphabet in Sight: New Dalit Writing from South India, Dossier I: Tamil and Malayalam*, edited and introduced by Susie Tharu and K. Satyanarayana, 340–45. Delhi: Penguin Books, 2011. Reprinted by permission of Raghavan Atholi and Jayasree Kalathil.

Basheer, Vaikom Muhammad. Excerpt from "Pattumma's Goat." In *Me Grandad 'Ad an Elephant!* Edinburgh: Edinburgh University Press, 1980. Reprinted by permission of Edinburgh University Press. https://edinburghuniversitypress.com.

Chaudhuri, Amit. Excerpt from "Interlude." In *Dublin Review* 42, no. 14 (2004), http://thedublinreview.com/article/interlude/. Reprinted by permission of the author.

Chaudhuri, Nirad C. Selections from "My Birthplace," "The English Scene," and "The Englishman in the Flesh." In *The Autobiography of an Unknown Indian*, 13–21, 108–15. Berkeley: University of California Press, 1968. Copyright © 1951, by Nirad C. Chaudhuri. Reprinted by permission of Prithvi N. Chaudhuri, Estate of Nirad Chaudhuri.

Chugtai, Ismat. "We People." In *My Friend, My Enemy*, translated by Tahira Naqvi, 101–10. New Delhi: Kali for Women, 2001. Reproduced with permission from Women Unlimited. Originally published by Kali for Women, 2001; reprinted by Women Unlimited (an associate of Kali for Women), 2015.

Daruwalla, Keki. "The Decolonised Muse (A Personal Statement)." Presented as a talk, Internationale Literaturtage '88, Erlangen, West Germany, 1998. Reprinted by permission of the author. http://www.poetryinternationalweb.net/pi/site/cou_article/item/2693/The-Decolonised-Muse/en.

Das, Jibanananda. "The Professor," "Name Me a Word," "Poetry," and "The Windy Night." In *Selected Poems*, translated by Chidananda Das Gupta, 3, 11, 37, 57–58. New Delhi: Penguin Books India, 2006. Copyright © Amitananda Das. English translation copyright © Chidananda Das Gupta (late). Reprinted by permission of Amitananda Das, Estate of Jibanananda Das, and Aparna Sen, Anuradha Lahiri, Estate of Chidananda Das Gupta.

Das, Kamala. Excerpts from *My Story*, 8–10, 149–51. New Delhi: Harper Collins, 2009. Reprinted by permission of the publisher. "The Old Playhouse" and "An Introduction." In *Selected Poems of Kamala Das*, edited by Devindra Kohli, 5–7, 69. Delhi: Penguin India, 2014. Reprinted by permission of the publisher.

Desai, Anita. "On Being an Indian Writer Today." In *Wasafiri* 24, no. 3 (2009): 27–28. Reprinted by permission of the author. A version of the essay appeared in *The Telegraph*, Kolkata, in 2007.

Devi, Mahasweta. "So Many Words, So Many Sounds." Mahasweta Devi in conversation with publisher and photographer Naveen Kishore, at her home in Calcutta, on September 10, 2002. Reproduced in Mahasweta Devi, *Romtha*, translated by Pinaki Bhattacharya, vii–xxi. Calcutta: Seagull Books, 2004. Courtesy Seagull Books.

Dev Sen, Nabaneeta. "In Poetry," "Alphabets," "Combustion," "The Year's First Poem," "Broken Home," and an excerpt from *My Life, My Work* (presented on August 12, 2004, at Sahitya Akademi, New Delhi). In *Make Up Your Mind: 25 Poems About Choice*, translated by Nandana Sen, 17, 29, 33, 11, 47, Bloomington, Ind.: iUniverse, 2013. Reprinted by permission of the author Nabaneeta Dev Sen and the translator Nandana Dev Sen. Translations were revised for this edition.

Dhasal, Namdeo. "Approaching the Organized Harem of the Octopus," "Mandakini Patil: A Young Prostitute, My Intended Collage," and "The Day She Was Gone" were first published by Navayana Publishing Pvt Ltd., New Delhi, in *Namdeo Dhasal: Poet of the Underworld, Poems 1972–2006*, translated from the Marathi by Dilip Chitre, 50–51, 56–60, 131. Chennai: Navayana, 2007. Reprinted by permission of the publisher.

Ezekiel, Nissim. "Background, Casually" and "Poet, Lover, Birdwatcher." In *Collected Poems*, 135, 179–81. New Delhi: Oxford University Press, 1989. Reproduced with permission of Oxford University Press India. Copyright © Oxford University Press 1989.

Ghosh, Amitav. Excerpt from "The Testimony of My Grandfather's Bookcase." *Kunapipi: A Journal of Postcolonial Writing* 19, no. 3 (1998): 1–9. Copyright © 1998 by Amitav Ghosh, used by permission of the Wylie Agency LLC.

Hariharan, Githa. "A Note on Writing *When Dreams Travel*." Copyright © 2016 by Githa Hariharan. Printed by permission of Georges Borchardt, Inc., on behalf of the author.

Hyder, Qurratulain. "Beyond the Stars." First published as "Beyond the Stars: A Dialogue with Qurratulain Hyder" by Sukrita Paul Kumar, *India International Centre Quarterly* 16, nos. 3–4 (Monsoon 1989–Winter 1989): 79–86. Reprinted by permission of Sukrita Paul Kumar and the India International Center Quarterly.

Joshi, Umashankar. "My Four-Sided Field" and Acceptance Speech for the 1968 Bharatiya Jnanpith Award. In *Journal of South Asian Literature* 9, no. 1 (1973): 25–27, 76. Excerpt from "The World of Birds." In *Saptapadi and Other Poems*, translated by Sudarshan V. Desai, 94–106. Suverna: Sadar Estate, 2005. Reprinted by permission of Svati Joshi, Estate of Umashankar Joshi.

Jussawalla, Adil. "Being There: Aspects of an Indian Crisis." Presented at the 7th ACLALS Conference, Singapore, June 1986. Published in Adil Jussawalla, *Maps for a Mortal Moon: Essays and Entertainments*, edited by Jerry Pinto, 255–66.

Delhi: Aleph Book Company, 2014. This excerpt is reprinted by permission of Aleph Book Company.

Karnad, Girish. Excerpt from "Author's Introduction." In *Three Plays: Naga-Mandala, Hayavadana, Tughalq*, 1–18. Delhi: Oxford University Press, 1995. Reprinted by permission of the author.

Kolatkar, Arun. "From an Undated Sheet" and excerpt from "Making Love to a Poem." In *Collected Poems in English*, edited by Arvind Krishna Mehrotra, 344, 345–51. Northumberland, U.K.: Bloodaxe Books, 2010. Reproduced with permission of Bloodaxe Books on behalf of the Estate of Arun Kolatkar. www.bloodaxebooks.com.

Mahapatra, Jayanta. Excerpt from an Autobiographical Essay. In Mark Zadronzy, *Contemporary Authors: Autobiography Series*, 9:137–50. Detroit: Gale, 1988. "Grandfather," in *Selected Poems*, 67–68. Delhi: Oxford University Press, 1987; first published in *The Sewanee Review*, Sewanee, USA. "The Abandoned British Cemetery at Balasore," in *The False Start*, 70–71. Bombay: Clearing House, 1980; first published in *Critical Quarterly*, Manchester, UK. "Hunger," first published in *A Rain of Rites*, 44. Athens: University of Georgia Press, 1976. All copyrights held by Jayanta Mahapatra. Reprinted by permission of the author.

Manto, Saadat Hasan. "First Letter to Uncle Sam." In "Letters to Uncle Sam," the First Letter, published in *Bitter Fruit: The Very Best of Manto*, translated and edited by Khalid Hasan, 610–15. Delhi: Penguin India, 2008, by permission of Jeffrey Hasan / Estate of Khalid Hasan.

Mehrotra, Arvind Krishna. "Engraving of a Bison on Stone," "Distance in Statute Miles," "Where Will the Next One Come From," and "Inscription." In *Collected Poems, 1969–2014*, 101, 102, 108, 150. Delhi: Penguin India, 2014. Reprinted by permission of the author.

Naidu, Sarojini. "To Arthur Symons (July 31, 1896)," "From a Letter to Edmund Gosse (October 6, 1896)," "To Rabindranath Tagore (November 16, 1912)," "To Rabindranath Tagore (undated, probably December 1913)." In *Sarojini Naidu: Selected Letters, 1890s to 1940s*, edited by Makarand Paranjape, 24–27, 27–30, 82–83, published originally by Kali for Women (India), 1996. Reprinted by permission of the publisher.

Narayan, R. K. Excerpts from *My Days: A Memoir*, 60–64, 97–103, by R. K. Narayan. Copyright © 1973, 1974 by R. K. Narayan. Reprinted by permission of Harper-Collins Publishers.

Paniker, K. Ayyappa. "Why Write?" Translated by P. P. Raveendran for this volume. Malayalam original published in *Ayyappa Panikarude Lekhanangal, 1990–2005*, 270–77. Kottayam: DC Books, 2005. Printed by permission of P. P. Raveendran and Kumari Meena Ayyappa Paniker for Sreeparvathy Ayyappa Paniker, Estate of K. Ayyappa Paniker. "Upon My Walls" and "Epitaph." In *Selected Poems of Ayyappa Paniker*, 56, 9. Trivandrum: Modern Book Center, 1985. Excerpt from "Passage to America." In *Journal of South Asian Literature* 15, no. 2 (1980): 141–46. Reprinted by permission of Kumari Meena Ayyappa Paniker for Sreeparvathy Ayyappa Paniker, Estate of K. Ayyappa Paniker.

Premchand (Dhanpat Rai). "Two Autobiographical Sketches." In *The World of Premchand: Selected Stories of Premchand*, translated by David Rubin, 204–11. Bloomington: Indiana University Press, 1969. Copyright © Premchand, 1908–1936, © Sons of Premchand, 1969. English Translation: copyright © David Rubin, 1969. Reprinted by permission of Neil Gross, Executor, Estate of David Rubin.

Pritam, Amrita. "To Waris Shah." Translated by Kiron Bajaj and Carlo Coppola, *Mahfil: A Quarterly of South Asian Literature*, Amrita Pritam Issue, 5, no. 3 (1968–69): 27–28. Reprinted by permission of Carlo Coppola. Excerpt from *The Revenue Stamp*, by Amrita Pritam (pp. 11–17, "My Sixteenth Year," "A Shadow"), translated by Krishna Gorowara. With permission from Vikas Publishing House Pvt. Ltd., India.

Ramanujan, A. K. "Elements of Composition" and "Saturdays." In *The Collected Poems of A. K. Ramanujan*, 121–23, 150–52. Delhi: Oxford University Press, 1995. Excerpt from "Is There an Indian Way of Thinking? An Informal Essay." In *The Collected Essays of A. K. Ramanujan*, edited by Vinay Dharwadker, 34–37. Delhi: Oxford University Press, 1999. Courtesy of the Estate of A. K. Ramanujan.

Rao, Raja. "Entering the Literary World." In *World Literature Today* 62, no. 4 (1988): 536–38. Authorized revised version copyright © 1988 by the Board of Regents of the University of Oklahoma. Reprinted by permission of *World Literature Today* and by permission of Susan Raja Rao, Estate of Raja Rao.

Roy, Arundhati. Excerpt from "Like Sculpting Smoke: Arundhati Roy on Fame, Writing and India." By Kathy Arlyn Sokol. Originally published in *Kyoto Journal* 38 (1998): 66–73. Reprinted by permission of the *Kyoto Journal*.

Rushdie, Salman. "Imaginary Homelands." In *Imaginary Homelands: Essays and Criticism, 1981–1991*, 9–21. Copyright © 1982 by Salman Rushdie. Used by permission of Viking Books, an imprint of Penguin Publishing Group, a division of Penguin Random House LLC. Copyright © 1981, 1982, 1983, 1984, 1985, 1986, 1987, 1988, 1989, 1990, 1991 by Salman Rushdie, used by permission of the Wylie Agency LLC.

Sahgal, Nayantara. "Rejecting Extinction." A talk delivered at the University of Rajasthan, Jaipur, September 20, 2007. Copyright © Nayantara Sahgal, printed with permission of the author.

Satchidanandan, K. "Gandhi and Poetry," "Stammer," and "About Poetry, About Life." In *While I Write: New and Selected Poems*, 28–29, 71–72, ix–xix. New Delhi: HarperCollins, 2011. "Burnt Poems." In *The Missing Rib: Collected Poems, 1973–2015*, 197–98. Mumbai: Poetrywalla, 2016. Reprinted by permission of the author.

Sen, Sudeep. "Photons, Graphite, Blood" and "Postcards." In *Ero Text: Desire, Disease, Delusion, Dream, Downpour*, 56–60, 130–35. Mumbai: Random House, 2016. Reprinted by permission of the author. These two pieces first appeared in *Ero Text: Desire, Disease, Delusion, Dream, Downpour* (Vintage: Penguin Random House, 2016) and *Fractals: New & Selected Poems / Translations 1980–2015* (India: Gallerie, 2015 / USA: Wings Press, 2016).

Seshadri, Vijay. "My First Fairy Tale." In *Brothers and Beasts: An Anthology of Men on Fairy Tales*, edited by Kate Bernheimer, 147–51. Detroit: Wayne State University Press, 2007. Reprinted by permission of the author.

Subramaniam, Arundhathi. "To the Welsh Critic Who Doesn't Find Me Identifiably Indian" and "First Draft." In *Where I Live: New and Selected Poems*, 16–18, 46. Northumberland, UK: Bloodaxe Books, 2009. Reprinted by permission of the author.

Sukirtharani, S. "Night Beast," "Gigantic Trees," and "Untitled Poem—2." Translated from Tamil by N. Kalyan Raman. "Pariah God." Translated by Meena Kandasamy. In *No Alphabet in Sight: New Dalit Writing from South India, Dossier I: Tamil and Malayalam*, edited and introduced by Susie Tharu and K. Satyanarayana, 314–15, 315–16, 317–18, 313–14. New York: Penguin Books, 2011. Reprinted by permission of the author (Sukirtharani, a humble human being who can write poems) and the translators; translations from the Tamil by N. Kalyan Raman revised especially for this volume.

Tagore, Rabindranath. "Letter 80 (May 8, 1893)." In *The Essential Tagore*, edited by Fakrul Alam and Radha Chakravarty, 73, 76–77. Cambridge, Mass.: The Belknap Press of Harvard University Press. Copyright © 2011 by the President and Fellows of Harvard College. Excerpt from *Boyhood Days* by Rabindranath Tagore, translated into English by Radha Chakravarty; published by Hesperus Press Ltd., 2011. Reprinted by permission of the publishers. "Sickbed 21" and "Recovery 4." In *Final Poems*, selected and translated by Wendy Barker and Saranindrath Tagore. English translation copyright © 2001 by Wendy Barker and Saranindrath Tagore. Reprinted with the permission of George Braziller, Inc., New York, www.georgebraziller.com. All rights reserved.

Thayil, Jeet. "The Heroin Sestina," "Malayalam's Ghazal," and "Spiritus Mundi." In *60 Indian Poets*, edited by Jeet Thayil, 229–31. New Delhi: Penguin Books, 2008. Reprinted by permission of the author.

Verma, Nirmal. "Returning to One's Country." In *India and Europe: Selected Essays*, edited by Alok Bhalla, 63–68. Shimla: India Institute of Advanced Study, 2000. Reprinted by permission of the Indian Institute of Advanced Study, Shimla. First published by IIAS.

Zacharia, Paul. Excerpt from "Sinning in Mysore." Sent by the author. Printed by permission of the author. Original version, "Remembering Mysore," in *The Hindu* (Chennai, India), September 21, 2003.